The Great Pacific Victory

FROM THE SOLOMONS TO TOKYO

GILBERT CANT

With maps and battle diagrams

The John Day Company • New York

To
MY MOTHER

Contents

Maps and Battle Diagrams

1. Where Were We?

THE WHOLE Allied world breathed easier on February 11, 1943.
For then it was that the United States Navy announced: "Japanese forces on Guadalcanal Island have ceased all organized
resistance."

Some thoughtless ones, after the delayed and costly victory
at Guadalcanal, talked as though the road to Tokyo now lay
wide open, inviting Allied armies to their goal. But all those
in the armed services who had had anything to do with fighting this remote and little understood war had few illusions as
to what lay ahead. No doubt they all under-estimated the time
it would take to reach Tokyo, but they did not under-estimate
the difficulties of supply, the miserable conditions of tropical
warfare, or—most important of all—the dogged tenacity with
which the Japanese would resist each new Allied advance.

What were the positions from which the Japanese had to be
eradicated, as of February 11, 1943?

Working clockwise around the map of the enemy's holdings,
we find that he had advanced bases not only in his own Kuril
Islands, a northeasterly extension of the "home islands," but
also in the Aleutians: at Attu and Kiska. (Agattu, occupied
with the two others in the summer of 1942, had been abandoned.) At Attu and Kiska, the Japanese did not constitute
an active threat to Alaska or to Canada and the United States;
but from these two bases they were able to maintain aerial and
submarine patrols and if they had shown skill and resourcefulness in developing the islands they could have become a
considerable latent threat to North America proper. So long
as they were entrenched there, any dreams of an American
advance through the Aleutians, the fog factory of the Pacific,
toward the Kurils and Hokkaido were impossible of fulfillment.

From the Kuril-Aleutian chains south to Micronesia, there

is a great emptiness of ocean, with no flyspeck island to sully its flawless surface until Marcus is reached, in about 25° North Latitude, and 1,150 statute miles southeast of Tokyo. Next is Wake, also a valuable base for reconnaissance planes, and perhaps a staging point for submarines. For all its sentimental value, Wake had little military importance.

Vastly more important, and seemingly inaccessible to American arms in February, 1943, were Japan's heaven-sent stepping stones: the Izu, Bonin, Volcano and Marianas groups (including Guam), lying west of Marcus and Wake. They led directly, like the upright of an inverted letter T, to the Caroline Islands which sprawled across 2,000 miles of ocean from within fighter plane range of the Philippines to within fighter plane range of the Marshall Islands. The Marshalls, and the next occupied group to the south, the Gilbert Islands, represented the Japanese front line in Micronesia. The main positions in the Marshalls were well prepared for both offense and defense. So was Tarawa, the principal atoll in the Gilberts.

East and south of these was a little archipelagic no man's land: Howland and Baker, under the American flag, had not been developed for military purposes when war came to the Pacific, so they had been abandoned to the sea birds. The Japanese did not take advantage of the owners' absence. Thus, except for the enemy infiltration into the Aleutians, the International Date Line formed the oceanic front between the Japanese and Americans as far south as the Equator and for about 350 miles farther, to the neighborhood of the Ellice Islands. There the Date Line veers away to the southeast; if it followed the 180th Meridian it would cut clean through the Ellice group. The front may be said to have followed the meridian, for the Ellice Islands were not securely held by either side. The few British who had been there in December, 1941, had been withdrawn, and the Japanese had sent patrols through the atolls. But neither could claim them in February, 1943. It was the development of one of these islands, Funafuti, which began the great series of leapfrog operations through the Gilberts and Marshalls to the Marianas.

The Ellice Islands peter out in about 10° South Latitude, and here the front made a right angle turn to the west, following the tenth parallel across 1,200 miles of water to the Sol-

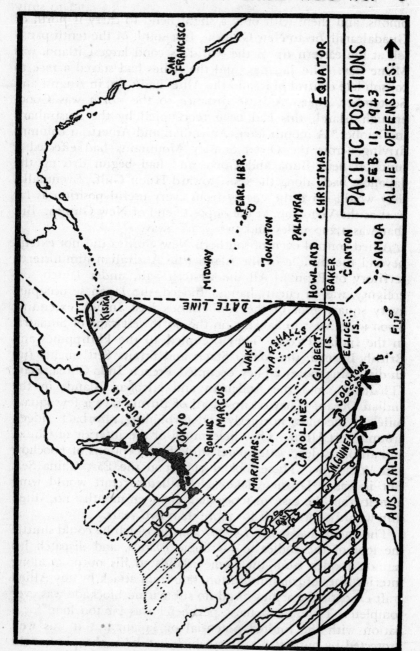

PACIFIC POSITIONS
FEB. 11, 1943
ALLIED OFFENSIVES:

omons, and then, with only a slight bend to carry it north of Guadalcanal, on to New Guinea. Just south of the tenth parallel, at the eastern tip of the world's second largest island, was Milne Bay. The Japanese and the Allies had staged a race to consolidate control of it, and the Allies had won, in August and September, 1942. A little distance to the north was Goodenough Island; this had been reoccupied by the Australians in October. A month later, Australian and American columns driving across the Owen Stanley Mountains had effected a junction near Buna and Gona, and had begun driving the Japanese back along the coast toward Huon Gulf. Eventually, they would drive the enemy from every useful position as far west as the Vogelkop, at the opposite end of New Guinea. But that was 1,200 miles and two years away.

Allied control even of southern New Guinea did not extend beyond the middle of the island (the Australian-administered territory of Papua). All the western half, under Dutch sovereignty, was in enemy hands. Indeed, the Japanese occupied every square foot of the Netherlands East Indies, extending 3,000 miles west to Sabang, on the northwest cape of Sumatra, in the Indian Ocean. They occupied all the Philippines and British Borneo, the Malay States and Straits Settlements (including Singapore). They occupied French Indo-China, Siam (Thailand), and the Andaman and Nicobar Islands in the Indian Ocean. They occupied all of Burma save a few square miles of the most northerly and forbidding razorback ridges, around Fort Hertz. They held much of the interior of China, and all of its deep-water ports with the exceptions of Foochow and Wenchow. These looked out upon the East China Sea. But it was a Japanese lake. No Allied aircraft would wing over it from the east for more than eighteen months; no Allied ship would penetrate it for more than two years.

The enemy had a vast *Lebensraum* in which he could shuttle the loot of the Indies to his home islands, and dispatch his cannon fodder from the home islands to his outposts along interior lines of communication, safe from attack by any Allied craft except submarines. And no submarine blockade was ever complete. True, his defense perimeter was far too long for a nation with the limited potential of Japan, but it was well protected by outpost positions which had been cheaply bought and could be sold dear. His inner fortress (Japan, occupied China north of the Yangtze, Korea and Manchuria) was virtually self sustaining, so that even after all the outworks had been lopped off, it would remain highly defensible, and immensely difficult to assault. The task confronting the United Nations fighting in the Orient was formidable indeed.

How did the weapons with which they would undertake this task compare, in quality and in quantity, with those of the enemy?

It will be most convenient to take them in descending order of range, from heavy bombers down to bayonets. In the first category, the United Nations, represented by the United States, were far ahead of the enemy. In medium bombers, the opponents were about equal. In torpedo bombers the versatile Grumman Avenger was incomparably better than anything the Japanese had until they began to produce substantial numbers of their own new types of torpedo craft, in 1943, and the balance was redressed. In dive-bombers, the United States had a clear advantage.

There has always been controversy as to the relative merits of Japanese and American fighter planes. The prototype of all enemy fighters in the early years of the war was the Mitsubishi S-oo, or Zero. It was light. It was fast. It was highly maneuverable. It could out-climb anything the Allies had in the early days. It packed a powerful punch in two 20-mm. cannon and two machine guns. The first Allied fighter planes to oppose it had not enough speed, not enough climb, maneuverability or enough armament. Their pilots had not had enough training or experience against an opponent of this kind to make an effective showing. They tried to dogfight it, which was the same as fighting the Zero on the Zero's terms. With improved tactics and rapidly improving aircraft, Allied pilots were taking the measure of the Zero in early 1943.

Much of the war against Japan had to be fought over great reaches of ocean, and for this task, a sea-going air force was essential. However, there were all too few carriers in the Allied navies at this time. Four American flat-tops had been sunk since Pearl Harbor: the *Lexington, Yorktown, Wasp* and *Hornet*. The *Ranger* was still in the Atlantic. The *Enterprise* had been continuously on duty in the Pacific since April, 1941; she had taken bomb damage in the Battle of the Eastern Solomons and the Battle of Santa Cruz. Although she was kept in the South Pacific, in reserve, through the Southern Hemisphere summer of 1942-43, she was soon sent back to Pearl Harbor and eventually to the United States. This left only one American combat carrier fit for action, the *Saratoga*. None of the new carriers was yet ready for action: the *Essex*, launched on July 31, 1942, had been commissioned on the last day of the year, but she was still shaking down. The new *Lexington* had been launched (September 26, 1942), as had the *Bunker Hill* (December 7), but neither was ready for commissioning. The new *Yorktown* was not launched until January 21, 1943. The *Saratoga* could not be left to carry the burden alone against the Japanese squadrons. (It now seems clear that even Naval Intelligence did not know how many carriers the Japanese had left at this time, or of what types. But subsequent sinkings show that there must have been several combat carriers, besides escort carriers which were larger and faster than the *Long Island* or other American types then in commission.) To help even things up, the British Admiralty assigned H.M.S. *Victorious* to duty in the Pacific. Operating under Admiral Halsey's South Pacific command, she was teamed with the *Saratoga* in the first months of 1943.

The Japanese appear to have had some advantage also in battleships. Of the heavy units struck at Pearl Harbor, the *Arizona* was gone for ever; the *Oklahoma* would not fight again; the *California* and *West Virginia* were still unready for service. That left eleven pre-war battleships, and of these, four old ones were in the Atlantic. To the seven veterans in the Pacific there had been added some of the new 35,000-ton ships mounting nine 16-inch guns: the *North Carolina*, *Washington* and *South Dakota*. The last-named was under repair following damage in the Battle of Guadalcanal. The *Massachusetts*, blooded at Casablanca, was due to leave for the Pacific. The *Indiana* had just reached the Pacific, and the *Alabama* would arrive shortly.

From the welter of confusion about the enemy's battle line, it is now safe to infer that there were ten battleships and battle cruisers in commission at the beginning of 1943. Some may have been under repair. None was to be risked in battle for many months to come.

There is even more confusion about the enemy's cruisers and destroyers. His squadrons and flotillas have been sunk two or three times over in Allied communiqués. There must be some mistake, for he continued to send cruisers and destroyers into action in substantial numbers, as late as the end of 1944.

It is just as difficult to assay the quality of the enemy's ships as it is to assess their numbers. Some have shown extraordinary tenacity of life after suffering severe damage. Some have revealed expert gunnery, as in the Battle of Savo Island. Some have been well handled, both individually and in squadrons or fleets. But the Japs' performance has been inconsistent. Sometimes they have bull-headedly followed a predetermined plan when quick thinking on their feet would have produced far better results. As the war progressed they showed a tendency to resort to cunning, complex tactics in the hope of pulling off a cheaper victory than they had any right to expect— shopping for bargains in the marts of war. Aside from their peculiar mental processes, this can only reflect certain characteristics in their weapons; their radar, while not to be sneezed at, was not as good or as plentiful as that of the Allied forces; their gunnery, being largely dependent upon radar, suffered accordingly. Their ships were in general fast, maneuverable, well armored and excellently compartmented.

But ships' performance depends to a great extent upon the officers who command them. Among the Japanese, these proved to be most uneven in quality. They were at their best when executing a surprise raid, operating under rigid orders. But in virtually every case where the Japanese had to adapt their plans to changing conditions in the heat of battle, they showed a rigidity of thinking and a lack of enterprise which are incomprehensible to an American or British officer.

Much the same is true of Japanese commanders aground. Of course, they looked good when they were winning. But when the heat was turned on them, their defects became apparent. Their defensive strategy was wooden. Their tactics followed a monotonous pattern. In its early stages, the pattern was not bad. It provided for aggressive infiltration of Allied lines, night attacks on command posts and similar disruption.

The frontal attacks for which it occasionally called were often unintelligently executed, as mad rushes into a withering fire. The next stage was the *banzai* charge, which may be good Shinto, but is not a sound military tactic.

The most conspicuous and effective characteristic of the Japanese fighting man has been his tenacity. Small positions would hold out until every man faced certain death.

No Japanese general officer ever surrendered until his emperor so ordered. Of about 70,000 Japanese disposed of on Leyte, the highest ranking prisoner was an army captain. In most campaigns, especially in the early days, the proportion of Japanese prisoners taken to Japanese killed was about one to a hundred. Up to the end of 1943, only 277 Japanese military prisoners had been taken by the United States. To a great extent, Shinto and modern Japanese "thought control" were responsible for this. Japanese enlisted men, injected with the military virus at the age of eight, had no knowledge of the outside world except what their military leaders wanted them to have. They had been taught that capture by the "white barbarians" meant torture. They had been taught that to die for the emperor, even by suicide *(seppuku* or *hara-kiri)*, meant a glorious apotheosis, whereas to permit oneself to be captured was an unspeakable disgrace, worse than death.

How did Allied (especially American) officers and enlisted men compare with those of the Japanese?

It is easiest to generalize about the enlisted men. Not one in ten had had military training or experience comparable with those of the Japanese who had practiced in Manchuria and China proper. Not one in ten had any active desire to fight the Japanese or any other aggressor. Indeed, the greatest weakness in morale among the American fighting men was that they had no clear conception of why they had to fight. Fearful of a jealous Congress, the War Department sedulously avoided giving United States Army men any indoctrination which bordered on the political. It prohibited discussion groups in which politics might be raised. The result was that when a war correspondent or an itinerant Congressman asked a G.I. what he was fighting for, the answer usually was: "A piece of mom's apple pie." This may have been more laudable than the Japanese soldier's desire to establish the emperor's domination over hundreds of millions of his fellow men, but it did not make the American more effective militarily. In the last analysis, of course, it was an expression of the American's desire to "Get the job over with and get the hell home." The War Department and the Congress must take the blame for having neglected to make clear to the millions of men they drafted that there was an intermediate step, the defeat of the enemy, which had a vital bearing on the question whether they would have any home to get the hell home to.

As a military technician, the American enlisted man had two great advantages over his adversary: he was an individualist, capable of readily adapting himself or his plans to changed circumstances, and he was mechanically adept (from a boyhood in which his spare time had been spent watching work in an automobile or combine repair shop), so that the ponderous weapons of modern war held no terrors for him.

American officers were just as little experienced in the practice of war as the enlisted men, except for those senior officers —by now, nearly all colonels or generals—who had seen service in World War I. A military establishment in peacetime is no place for the development of initiative. The regular army officer who can rise above the pettiness of time-serving and post society is the exception. The war in the Pacific does not appear to have produced an outstanding ground commander in the Army: the fame of such men as General MacArthur and General Krueger was established before Pearl Harbor. In the Marine Corps, General Vandegrift and Lieut. Generals Holland Smith and Roy Geiger have recorded notable achievements, but their rôle is not comparable with that of Army officers of equivalent rank. The Marine Corps, for all the brilliance of its successes, is still an appendage of the Navy, which does much of the Corps' administrative and staff work. The men who have become general officers in the rapidly expanded Marine Corps would have commanded regiments in the older, smaller establishment, and it is no derogation of them to say that in the main they have handled divisions as though they were battalions, and amphibious corps as though they were regiments. The Marine Corps is long on assault tactics, but short on strategy—again, with the few exceptions who only prove the rule.

Of the general officers of whom I have personal knowledge, it can be said that none was sensationally good, but most were fully adequate to their commands. (It happened that among them there was only one of the four who were relieved of command during a campaign.) The outstanding exception was a young brigadier general in the Air Corps, who lacked the confidence and respect of all his subordinates, from colonels to corporals.

Probably the greatest weakness was at the next lower level: regimental and battalion commanders. Most of these officers were too young to have had noteworthy experience in the last war; they were too old to have the elasticity of mind which their company commanders had, or to have the same understanding of their men.

To a great extent, the weaknesses of the Army command were the direct result of rapid expansion. The Army of the United States in 1943-44 was 50 to 75 times as large as the United States Army prior to the passage of the Burke-Wadsworth Act in September, 1940. In the same period, the Japanese army had expanded only two- or threefold. The United States Navy had expanded about tenfold.

Most of the admirals exercising important commands had had more experience than their equivalents in the Army ground forces or air forces. Their record is better in about the same proportion as their experience.

Overshadowing all other personalities in the Pacific (as distinct from the Southwest Pacific) were Admirals Halsey and Nimitz. The former was immensely popular with both officers and men before Pearl Harbor: he enhanced both his popularity and his reputation in the early carrier task force operations—the hit-and-run raids. It is ironic that he should have acquired great renown as a dashing, fighting fleet admiral without ever having met the enemy in a major engagement until the Second Battle of the Philippine Sea, in October, 1944. But Halsey's capabilities were beyond question.

However, the keystone of the entire Pacific war structure was a middle-sized, white-thatched man whose responsibilities were so vast that he could not fulfill them save by spending most of his time at Pearl Harbor, the nerve centre of all communications. His name was Nimitz.

II. CinCPac, CinCPOA

MANY LANGUAGES which would sound strange to the ears of modern Americans have been spoken in the Pacific islands since man first learned to sail the vast reaches of ocean, but it is doubtful that any of these tongues was stranger than the military jargon which has been spread there by Americans in the 1940s. It is an agglutinative speech, and in it the word for chief or head man is CinCPac. It is derived, complete with capital letters amidships, from Commander in Chief, Pacific, the word "fleet" being understood since it is a Navy term. In those idyllic days, now so difficult to recall, when war in the Pacific was a remote and unthinkable thing, CinCPac was the admiral who commanded whatever force of warships might be assigned to the Pacific Fleet by the Chief of Naval Operations in Washington. When war in the Pacific became less remote, and the bulk of the United States Fleet was assigned to that ocean, the title of CinCPac was overshadowed by that of CinCUS (Commander in Chief, United States Fleet), which was held by the same admiral.

But after Pearl Harbor, the very word CinCUS seemed like a bad jest, so it was dropped entirely. With the United States engaged in a worldwide naval war, it was necessary for the Commander in Chief of the Fleet to stay in Washington. There, Admiral Ernest J. King was reduced to flying his four-starred flag in the yacht *Dauntless,* tied up in the Navy Yard at Anacostia. The title of CinCUS having been sunk without trace, King adopted in its stead CominCh.

At this time, no theater or fleet command anywhere among the United Nations was more important or more forbidding than that of Commander in Chief, Pacific Fleet. In an hour, the Japanese had shattered the keep of the fortress upon which the defense of the United States was hinged. For a few weeks after the attack of December 7, 1941, Hawaii would be so weak that if the Japanese returned with an invasion force, they would have an excellent chance of occupying it. Admiral Husband E. Kimmel had been relieved of his command; President Roosevelt and Secretary Knox were discussing the choice of his successor. Knox recalled that a year earlier he had submitted two names to the President for the post (then CinCUS and CinCPac combined): Kimmel and Nimitz. The President then had chosen Kimmel. Now that the President had to make the choice again, he asked Knox for an expression of his preference. Knox replied concisely: "I'll be satisfied with the second name on the list." So Chester William Nimitz was designated as CinCPac.

Nimitz, then serving as chief of the misnamed Bureau of Navigation (now properly called the Bureau of Personnel), had other ideas. He told Secretary Knox that the Pacific command should go to Vice Admiral William S. Pye, who had been commander of the battle force until the Japanese sank most of its battleships, and then had been named successor *ad interim* to Kimmel. The suggestion was typical of Nimitz, one of the most fair-minded of men, and reflects one of the characteristics which have made him such an outstanding success as CinCPac. While the sundowners afloat and the martinets in Army camps had been vociferating their criticisms of Kimmel, Pye and Lieut. General Walter Short, the more judicial Nimitz had calmly and carefully thought out what might have happened if he, and not Kimmel, had been in command of the fleet that fateful December morning. And he had come to the conclusion that diplomatic, political and other considerations being what they were, he might have had the fleet sunk under him, just as had Kimmel and Pye. In other words: "There, but for the grace of God, go I."

Knox felt that a new broom was needed at Pearl Harbor for "a clean sweep down, fore 'n' aft," so Nimitz prepared to leave Washington to take over the crushing responsibilities of what seemed certain to be an unhappy command. He studied in detail the reports coming in from Pearl Harbor: reports of the evaluation of damage done by the Japanese, assessments of the length of time it would take to repair the sunken battleships (three were resting on the bottom, but could be raised; only the *Arizona* and *Oklahoma* appeared to be total losses) and the three which had suffered only superficial damage. He noted the estimated time of arrival in the Pacific of ships now ordered to that ocean from the Atlantic. He studied the progress reports of the fleet which was under construction: 35,000- and 45,000-ton battleships; dozens of 10,000-ton (light) and 13,000-ton (heavy) cruisers; destroyers and small craft in incredible numbers. Nimitz already knew that the United States some day would have the greatest fleet in history; the question was how much of it could be ready in time to be of use to him in holding the positions which he had been ordered to hold. For the defense of the United States, the Alaska-Hawaii-Panama triangle long had been considered an area which must be kept inviolate. Now, Japanese submarines were sinking ships off the Pacific Coast, and occasionally lobbing shells into remote and non-vital spots on the mainland itself. Furthermore, CominCh King had drawn a line from Midway, through Pearl Harbor and Samoa and New Caledonia to Australia, and had told the new CinCPac to hold this line at any cost. For this was not only the United States' war; it was the United Nations' war. And the concept of what the United States Navy would have to do in case of war against Japan had undergone a corresponding enlargement.

It is difficult to see how Nimitz could have been encouraged by what he learned in his last few days in Washington. But he was not of a mercurial temperament, and just as he would have shown little outward emotion upon learning of good news, so he showed little upon analysing the bad news which now poured in upon him.

Nimitz flew from San Diego to Pearl Harbor. There he met Admiral Kimmel and handed him a letter from Knox, in which the Secretary expressed sympathy and regret at the necessity for relieving him. Nimitz added his own expression of professional feeling: "You have my sympathy—it could have happened to me." Then Nimitz set about restoring order amid the physical chaos at Pearl Harbor, and more important, restoring order in the minds of men whose faith had been jarred by Japanese bombs and torpedoes, who had been infected with the jitters (almost as bad in Hawaii as in California or Washington), and who needed urgently to know how they were to transform defeat, which stared them in the face, into victory, which seemed but a mocking mirage.

Nimitz had his admiral's flag (four white stars on a blue ground) hoisted at the Submarine Base on Southeast Loch, Pearl Harbor. He had been commander of the base in the 1920s, and felt at home in its dingy offices. It was the base to which his only son, Lieut. Commander Chester W. Nimitz, Jr., would bring in his submarine from a poaching expedition into the private fishing preserves of the Emperor of Japan. The quarters were stuffy and crowded, and cluttered with officers, both Army and Navy, coming and going in a great hurry to conceal the fact that they did not themselves know whether they were coming or going. And most of them expected to receive new duty, probably exile in some inhospitable spot, when the new broom gave a clean sweep down, fore 'n' aft.

Nimitz called a staff conference on December 31. He told the officers how he had urged the designation of Admiral Pye to succeed Admiral Kimmel, but had been overruled. Then he astonished them all by expressing faith in their ability, and asking them to stay on under him. Self-respect began to return to these men who felt that their countrymen, even their kinsmen, had held them responsible for the most humiliating disaster in the nation's history. In the few minutes that it took Admiral Nimitz to tell his story, these men again became useful officers in the service of the United States Navy. The word spread, the work went faster, and although there were to be many setbacks along the way, the task ahead never again seemed so difficult as it had before Nimitz spoke those few words to the officers assembled in the Sub Base.

As the tide of war ebbed and flowed across the Pacific, it became necessary for the Commander in Chief, Pacific Fleet, to assume jurisdiction over land installations stretching from the shores of the Bering Sea to the storied Society Islands, from Alaska to New Zealand. The Navy is as precise in its language as in its gun calibers: Nimitz's title had to be broadened to cover these growing responsibilities; so he became CinCPOA (Commander in Chief, Pacific Ocean Areas) as well as CinCPac. Amateur geographers have estimated that the Pacific Ocean Areas comprise 64,000,000 square miles; actually, about half of that has been the scene of military operations under Nimitz's direction. Whatever the total area, it is mostly water—perhaps as much as 99 per cent.

But it should not be assumed, because the area is so wet, that it was exclusively a naval command. Great numbers of land-based aircraft, many of them furnished by the Army Air Forces, were needed to defend the myriad islands which dot its surface, and to attack the decreasing number of such islands held by the enemy. For the same purpose, powerful ground forces were required, and many divisions of these were furnished by the Army. In addition, the Navy disposed a sizable army of sea-going infantry and aviators in the United States Marine Corps. Both the Army and the Navy had tens of thousands of men in more or less permanent installations for their supply and medical services, to name but two of a growing number. To them the Wacs and Waves and Lady Leathernecks must be added. For three years, Nimitz commanded all these, wherever they might be in the Pacific.

It would be silly to pretend that these hundreds of thousands of men and women in the armed services constituted, under Nimitz, one big, happy family. Inevitably there were inter-service and intra-service frictions and jealousies. A commander who devoted himself exclusively to the problems of personnel relations might have done a little better than Nimitz did in ironing out these difficulties. But such a commander would have no time left for his principal duty of fighting and winning a war. It is characteristic of Nimitz that he did better than most theater commanders in minimizing rivalry and factionalism within his command without ever losing sight of his main objective, which was a place called Tokyo and not a diploma in social sciences.

The one conclusion that emerges from a study of Nimitz the man and his relationship to his task is that he has no single, remarkable feature of the kind that leads to fatal over-simplification in our judgments of most prominent men. It is almost impossible to caricature Nimitz, either in line or in words. And it is this very absence of the abnormal, which in itself is so unusual among high-ranking commanders, that has made Nimitz one of the least conspicuous and one of the most successful of Allied war leaders. In the last analysis, I believe, it will be found that a gyroscopic sense of balance is the best explanation of Nimitz's ability to discharge his duties with so little criticism and such great success.

Perhaps it was this sense of balance which kept Nimitz out of the limelight during the years which preceded his appointment as chief of the Bureau of Navigation in 1939. Events did not conspire to bring the spotlight on him, and Nimitz did not conspire to influence the course of events in any unconventional manner.

At the end of his high school days in Texas, he was seeking an appointment to the United States Military Academy. His chances were not good. But a Congressman held a competitive examination for appointments to the Naval Academy. Nimitz won—and the Army lost.

But even then it was not all plain sailing. Before the year 1901 was out, Cadet Nimitz had reason to doubt that he was as well suited for a career on the rolling seas as he might have been for one on the rolling hills of his home country. He writes: "My sea-going aspirations were very nearly obliterated by a Sunday excursion on a sailing boat. I got frightfully seasick, and must confess to some chilling of enthusiasm for the sea." He stuck it out. In his last two years, Midshipman Nimitz (5 feet 9½ inches, 150 pounds) stroked the crew. He was good: he had a nice sense of balance and of timing. But he was not a standout.

For his class yearbook ('05), Nimitz wrote: "I have enjoyed every one of my assignments and I believe that it has been so because of my making it a point to become as deeply immersed and as interested in each activity as it was possible for me to become." A fellow Texan adds: "I never knew Chester Nimitz to start anything he didn't finish."

After graduation (as a "passed midshipman") Nimitz served his battleship duty in the *Ohio* and, he says, "had a fine cruise to Manila."

In 1908, Nimitz was assigned to submarines. At this time, as he puts it, "undersea craft were regarded as a cross between a Jules Verne fantasy and a whale." He might have added that some of the elements of a death-trap were included. However, he liked submarine duty, won quick promotion to a full lieutenancy, and was awarded the Silver Life Saving Medal for rescuing an oiler who could not swim. (Only in recent years has the Navy begun to insist that enlisted men, as well as officers, shall be able to swim.) The admiral is still a strong swimmer.

In World War I Nimitz was on the staff of the commander, Atlantic Submarine Fleet. There was little in his record during the long armistice of 1918-39 to suggest that he would be called upon to play his present role. He had a couple of years of battleship and cruiser duty; he commanded Submarine Division 14 and later the Submarine Base at Pearl; he had a year at the Naval War College. Perhaps his most broadening experience during this period was his assignment in 1926-29, to organize a Reserve Officers' Training Corps at the University of California. His extensive contacts with civilians during this time, taken in combination with his naturally pleasant personality, go far to explain why Nimitz today gets along better with civilian officials than any other fleet or theater commander.

There was little opportunity in the early days of the Pacific war for Nimitz to conduct operations which would make the headlines in the newspapers back home. Gradually, the sunken units of the battle fleet were raised from the mud of Pearl Harbor and towed to the United States for reconstruction. Those victories in the battle of salvage were guarded secrets. For months, the only overt military actions which could be presented to the American people as good news were the carrier task force raids on the Gilbert and Marshall Islands, on Wake and Marcus. Although Nimitz was responsible for these operations, he gave all the credit to "Bull" Halsey, then a vice admiral, who commanded the task forces. The newspapermen and the public made a hero of the more flamboyant Halsey, and virtually ignored CinCPac. Nimitz's popularity with newspapermen grew slowly; it grew as the result of his own qualities, and in spite of the qualities of the small staff of public relations officers he maintained in those days.

If Nimitz cared about being beaten by the Army on publicity, he did not show it. His attention was fixed on the main objective. But after Midway, and more particularly after the turn of the tide in the campaign for Guadalcanal, he was able to live more like a human being and less like an automaton working 16 to 18 hours a day, seven days a week. In the fall of 1942 he moved from the overcrowded Sub Base to new and relatively palatial quarters in a three-story bombproof building half a mile away, on the edge of Makalapa crater. There, in a roomy office, he had a few easy chairs, but most of the space facing his desk was taken up by a score of folding canvas chairs. Nimitz did not like the idea of a supreme commander who had contact only with his own kitchen cabinet. So his morning conferences were attended not only by his staff, but by a dozen or more senior officers who would be charged with the execution of the plans decided upon by the staff. By having these officers present—as many as were in port and available—Nimitz gave them the feeling that they had a part, however small, in formulating the plans. After the conference, he would have a short talk with those just returned to base from operations in a combat zone. Thus he kept constantly informed not only of what his staff and his admirals were thinking, but of what the commanding officers of ships, down to destroyers and tenders, were thinking. The practice could not be applied to all, as the fleet grew; but the principle persisted.

Just how informal Nimitz could be was illustrated one day when a Navy enlisted man showed up and asked to see the admiral, on the sole ground that he was a fellow townsman from Texas. The aide was a little surprised, but knew better than to give the man the brush-off, which is what he would have got from the more hoity-toity aides of less important admirals one can recall. The aide was still more surprised when Nimitz welcomed the young man and kept him talking for almost an hour; he was astonished when Nimitz called for the official photographer and posed with the man. Afterwards he explained: "Well, he was here because his shipmates had bet him $20 he couldn't get in to see me, and I had to see that he got the evidence, didn't I?"

Nimitz has been less fussy about posing for pictures than most officers of equivalent rank. When he attended the opening of the Breakers, a recreation centre for enlisted men at Waikiki, he danced with a native hula girl. The photographers were delighted with the opportunity, and Nimitz ordered the picture released to the press—but only after he had received a copy, which he sent air mail to Mrs. Nimitz in Berkeley, California, to make sure that the first she heard about it should be from him. At Midway on an inspection trip, Nimitz had himself photographed with a young gooney (albatross) of which the men had been making a pet. Oscar was decked out in a high hat (an inverted paper cup), secured with ribbons.

Nimitz's lively sense of humor had free play in the latter part of the mornings, toward the end of his talks with officers who in many cases had been far away, observing radio silence, and out of touch with the oddities which help to make service life bearable in wartime. For them, Nimitz always had a new anecdote. He had a few friends on the mainland who knew his weakness and passed the latest yarns on to him. Some of the admiral's stories were excellent; some were smoking-car tales of average quality; some depended simply on bad puns. Nimitz liked the bad puns almost as much as the good ones; they relaxed him, and set him at ease for the pistol practice which he often took at noon. For this rite, a small range had been set up alongside one end of the headquarters building. A red flag was run up to warn passers-by (although the target was backed up against the foot of a 30-foot cliff, so nobody was endangered); a Marine Corps orderly stood behind the admiral with field glasses, calling his shots.

In his sixtieth year, Nimitz weighed 30 pounds more than when he stroked the Naval Academy crew, and he rarely ate lunch. The meal was served at his house; while his chief of staff and medical officer enjoyed it, Nimitz usually stripped to the waist and stretched out in the sunshine on the lawn. In the latter part of 1944, when Vice Admiral Charles H. Mc-Morris was chief of staff, Nimitz usually would have company on the lawn after lunch. There high strategy often was discussed in its broad outlines. After what seemed like a period of idleness, sometimes shared by the war plans officer, Rear Admiral Forrest Sherman, Nimitz's advisers would walk back to the bombproof air-conditioned basement of the Makalapa building, and set subordinates to work on plans which would blossom, months later, into great amphibious moves such as the invasion of the Marianas. By the way, McMorris was one of Kimmel's staff whom Nimitz had kept on Pacific duty in defiance of all superficial criticism. McMorris, as air officer to CinCUS, had said: The Japanese would never attack Pearl Harbor from the air. That was in the week preceding December 7, 1941.

Nimitz took a short walk each morning before breakfast, but by about 4 o'clock he was ready for more exercise. As late as 1943, it was likely to be a set of tennis. Some months before he left Makalapa to set up headquarters on Guam, Nimitz was persuaded by his medical officer, Captain Thomas C. Anderson, that he had reached an age at which he should give up tennis. But he did not give up either his horse-shoe pitching or his long walks. One of his ideas of fun was to ask a new staff member to accompany him on an afternoon hike from Makalapa to Aiea Mountain, and then watch the tenderfoot wilt as the miles added up—all ten of them. However, when Admiral Raymond A. Spruance was in port, and took the guest room in Nimitz's house, CinCPac was hopelessly outclassed. Spruance could walk the legs off his chief.

Nimitz might work either at his house or at his office during the evening. Only about once a week would he accept invitations to dinner in Honolulu. At such occasions his popularity was deserved: he never made long speeches, and he always had just the right story to fit the circumstances.

There is little, then, that is remarkable about this man who has directed such remarkable operations. He has not favored one weapon in the naval arsenal over another. He is not one of the admirals who learned to fly at the age of 50, to be able to sport gold wings above a row of brag rags on the left breast. That makes him, in the over-easy characterization of naval air officers, a "battleship admiral." Every other "battleship admiral" has been criticized sharply, if not savagely, for having allegedly failed to appreciate the greater glories of air power. But not Nimitz. His first offensive planning, at the beginning of 1942, was for the carrier strikes executed by Admiral Halsey against an assortment of flyspeck islands. He relied heavily on carriers to save Hawaii in the Battle of Midway. Admiral Spruance has been assailed for excessive timidity in the later stages of that engagement, and for a similar supposed timidity in the First Battle of the Philippine Sea; somehow, Nimitz has escaped that sort of criticism. In at least one important instance—the invasion of the Marshall Islands—Nimitz took the advice of air officers over that of battleship officers, and over the recommendation of his own superior, CominCh King.

At the end of 1944, Nimitz drew even with MacArthur in

the matter of status: each was promoted, on the same day, to five-star rank (General of the Army and Fleet Admiral). Almost immediately, Nimitz moved his headquarters to Guam. Not until April, 1945, was the command in the Pacific unified in a geographic sense, with MacArthur over all ground forces, and Nimitz over all naval forces.

Through the whole troublous period from the day he established headquarters in the Sub Base at Pearl to the day he moved them to Guam, Nimitz had made not a single open move which could fairly be called playing politics. But it would be naïve to suggest that so shrewd and skillful an operator had not been aware of the powerful forces which swirled around him, or of the almost equally powerful forces which he disposed. The only conclusion is that this man of medium build, with no foibles or conspicuous peculiarities, a most unrewarding subject for the caricaturist, nevertheless combines three qualities which make him great: an unusual sense of order, an extraordinary sense of timing, and a unique sense of balance.

In any language, CinCPac, CinCPOA spells a great man.

III. Up the Slot

THE MIDDLE PHASE of the offensive against the Japanese was launched by mild-mannered non-combatants of the Navy's Medical Corps and not, as it should have been, by fire-breathing assault troops of the Army or Marine Corps. The scene was not one of the great islands or great atolls of the Pacific whose name will be long remembered in the annals of war, but a group known as the Russell Islands, in the southeastern Solomons.

It was almost an accident that they assumed importance, even in the early weeks of 1943. When the original dividing line had been drawn, in 1942, between General MacArthur's Southwest Pacific Command and the Navy's South Pacific Command, it had run along the 160th meridian, East Longitude. That meridian passed through Guadalcanal, so when the South Pacific commander (then Vice Admiral Robert Lee Ghormley) was ordered to occupy Guadalcanal, the line was pushed west to the 159th meridian. By this means, Ghormley's forces were given free rein in the area immediately surrounding their objective. The area included the Russell Islands, only 20 miles at the nearest point from Cape Esperance on Guadalcanal, 60 miles from Henderson Field, the only place on Guadalcanal that mattered militarily when the campaign ended after six months of attritional warfare. The rest of the Solomon Islands lay to the west of the line, in MacArthur's command.

The only way to get at the middle and upper Solomons, which suffered from a heavy infestation of Japanese, was through the lower Solomons; the only forces in position to do the job were those of the South Pacific Command, now under Admiral William F. Halsey. The nearest major objective was Munda, on the southwest tip of New Georgia Island, 190 miles as the Wildcat flew from Henderson Field. Munda was in

MacArthur's area, and the assault would require coordination of the two commands. But a preliminary step had to be taken: to advance the scope of Allied air power.

The range of the Wildcats, Corsairs, Warhawks and Airacobras, then the newest fighter planes in the Allied air forces, was little more than 500 miles. With almost 200 miles to travel to gain the area in which they would have to fight, and an equal distance to cover on the homeward run, the fighters would have only a few minutes of combat time in their gas tanks.

But 60 miles up the Slot (the channel between the parallel chains of the Solomon Islands) from Henderson lay the Russells. It was believed that the enemy garrison there had numbered up to 800 men. The Russells would not have been worth bothering with if it had not been for those 60 miles—120 miles, round trip—that could be saved by fighter planes operating from there. Those 120 miles, equivalent to 20 minutes of combat time, meant to American commanders all the difference between being able to pursue the campaign up the Solomons under an umbrella of friendly aircraft, and being stymied on Guadalcanal.

The expedition was mounted with elaborate care. The toughest assault troops in the armed forces of the United States were picked for the assignment: one battalion of Marine Corps Raiders and one of Army Rangers. The Raiders, who had been encamped on New Caledonia, left Nouméa on February 12, 13 and 14, aboard a group of transports known as the "Unholy Four," which had been in the original Guadalcanal operation. The ships rendezvoused in the Coral Sea and went north under destroyer escort. On the evening of the 16th, off San Cristóbal, they were attacked by Japanese torpedo planes which first dropped parachute flares, and five aircraft were reported shot down. The next morning, the convoy was at Guadalcanal. The Marines were sorted out and re-loaded aboard destroyer-transports (APDs).

In the first hour of February 21, the expeditionary force set out. It had close cover from destroyers, and there was a battleship task force in the background, just in case. Air cover would be supplied from Henderson Field. In over-all direction of the operation was Rear Admiral Richmond Kelly Turner, a man who was undismayed even by his own cumbersome title of ComAmphibForSoPac (Commander, Amphibious Forces, South Pacific). The 3rd Raiders were commanded by Lieut. Colonel Harry B. Liversedge.

Not a shot was fired as the APDs hove to off Pavuvu and Banika at 5 A.M. Higgins boats were loaded from life nets dropped over the ships' sides. In the dark and confusion off Banika, the Medical Corps men were taken directly to the beach and deposited, while the boats bearing the combat troops were formed up offshore. When the Rangers splashed through the coral and up the beaches, the medics waved them on—"Come on in, the land is fine." The Raiders at Pavuvu had no reception committee, friendly or otherwise. There was not a Japanese on any of the islands. They had left, ten days to two weeks earlier, when the evacuation of their key personnel from Guadalcanal was completed and the fight for that "Bloody Island" was abandoned.

The enemy had left the Russells in haste. Food and ammunition had been abandoned; plantation buildings had not been destroyed. In one of them there was a bottle of rum, only half consumed. On the fourth day, a Marine patrol pushing into the scrub on little Bycee Island found a Japanese medical aid station. Its equipment and supplies of drugs were intact. Within a few minutes, in their hatred of everything Japanese, the Marines had smashed all the equipment and trampled the drugs into the ground. When American medical officers heard about it, it was too late. The opportunity for them to learn about the enemy's jungle therapy was gone.

Day after day, men and equipment were poured into the Russells, to build airfields, cantonments and naval advanced bases. It was a week before the enemy reacted. At noon on February 27, when the beaches were cluttered with supplies and the waters were thick with ships and boats discharging cargo, five Japanese planes made a strafing attack. Seven Americans were killed; material damage was slight. But the security of the operation had been compromised. The enemy knew what was going on, and there was no reason why the people of the United States and of the other United Nations should not have been informed. Still the Navy kept silent. In a few days, great swaths had been cut through the coconut groves to make two air strips on Banika. Turner, the man on the spot and responsible for the success of the Solomons operations, recognized that the continued secrecy was silly: "We've cut all those trees down, and the Japs have flown over and can see for themselves." But it was not until May 4 that a Navy communiqué announced the occupation to the American and Allied peoples. By this time, Corsairs (F4U fighter planes) of Marine Corps aviation squadrons were operating from Banika.

The seizure of the Russells had fulfilled its purpose. From Banika's airfields a continuous combat air patrol could be maintained over the Munda area, 130 miles away. If an enemy base such as Buin, on southern Bougainville, was to be bombed in daylight, heavy bombers could take off from Henderson Field, fly up the Slot, rendezvous with fighters from the Russells, and execute their mission with the aid of an aggressive escort. The greatest geographical obstacle to the advance upon New Georgia had been overcome.

But a great artificial obstacle remained—the 159th meridian. The line between the South and Southwest Pacific commands had been moved once, before the Guadalcanal campaign, but it had not been moved far enough. In all reason, it should have been pushed back all the way to the 154th meridian,

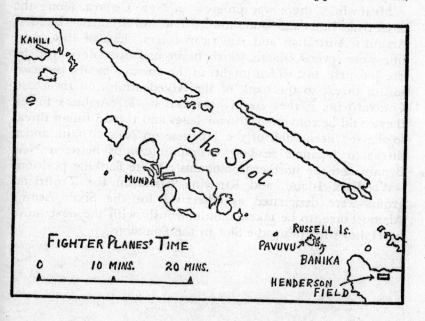

KAHILI

The Slot

MUNDA

FIGHTER PLANES' TIME

0   10 MINS.   20 MINS.

RUSSELL Is.

PAVUVU

BANIKA

HENDERSON FIELD

which runs between the Solomons and the Bismarcks. Then all the Solomons would have been in Admiral Halsey's area, and the Bismarck strongholds of New Britain and New Ireland, which must be tackled from the direction of New Guinea, would have remained in General MacArthur's bailiwick. But there was less reason and more vanity than there should have been in the minds of men responsible for such dispositions.

The result was that Halsey was ordered, early in 1943, to prepare plans for the advance into the central and northern Solomons—plans which his forces would then execute under MacArthur's "strategic direction." Working in the ugly, big French Army building in Nouméa which had recently been taken over as ComSoPac's headquarters, Halsey's staff drew the plans. In April, Halsey packed the plans and flew over to Brisbane to obtain MacArthur's approval. MacArthur and his staff thought that the plans should be altered in some details, principally to enlarge the rôle assigned to Army troops; otherwise they were acceptable. Halsey agreed to the proposed changes; there was little else he could do.

After Halsey's return to Nouméa, the detailed planning went on there and at Turner's headquarters on Guadalcanal.

Meanwhile, there was progress in New Guinea, along the coast from Buna and Gona toward Lae and Salamaua, by MacArthur's Australian and American forces. East of this coastline were several islands which never had been developed by the Japanese, but which might, in the enemy's hands, be made into a threat to the flank of the Allied armies on the coast. Contrariwise, if they could be seized by MacArthur's forces, they could be converted into air bases and turned into a threat to the southern flank of the Japanese on New Britain, and a threat to Japanese sea-borne communications between New Britain and the northern Solomons. These flanking positions —Woodlark Island, and Kiriwina Island in the Trobriand group—were designated as objectives for the Sixth Army's Alamo Force, to be taken simultaneously with the next move by Halsey's forces up the Slot in the Solomons.

IV. The Strange Death of Yamamoto

ONE OF THE MOST remarkable incidents of the Pacific war took place in the Solomon Islands while the invasion of New Georgia was being prepared. On April 17, a top-secret dispatch was delivered to the Commander, Air, Solomons in his headquarters in a gully between Henderson Field and the Lunga River. The message outlined in detail the itinerary then being followed by Admiral Isoroku Yamamoto, Commander in Chief of the Combined Fleet, during an inspection tour of Japanese bases in the South and Southwest Pacific. It stated that he would leave Rabaul the following morning, traveling in a Betty (Mitsubishi '01 twin-engined bomber), with most of his staff in another plane of the same type, and that they would have a close escort of six Zero fighters. The eight-plane flight was due to land at Kahili airdrome at 9:45 A.M., local time. American commanders in the area concerned were directed to exert "maximum effort" to destroy Yamamoto. The message was signed by Frank Knox, Secretary of the Navy.

Although the new airfields on Banika in the Russells were the nearest Allied bases to Kahili, there were no long-range fighters based there, and the assignment fell to a squadron of Army P-38 Lightnings temporarily based at Henderson, commanded by Major John W. Mitchell. Even with belly tanks, these planes had a radius of only about 500 miles; it was 300 miles by the most direct route from Henderson to Kahili, and more than 400 by the circuitous route which the American fliers would have to follow, southwest of the Japanese-held central Solomons, to avoid detection by enemy radar stations. This left such a narrow margin that Yamamoto's flight would have to be attacked close to Kahili. At the suggestion of Major Mitchell and Captain Thomas G. Lanphier, Jr., it was decided to try to intercept the enemy commander at a point 35 miles north-west of Kahili.

Because of a lack of foresight, no effort was made to impose secrecy around Henderson Field, and large numbers of officers and men soon knew what was afoot. Later, this proved to be a great embarrassment to the command.

Eighteen of the squadron's Lightnings were available for the mission, and Mitchell assigned four to operate as an attack group under Lanphier, intending to retain 14 under his own immediate direction for use as a high covering force. It was fully expected that the local Japanese air commander would have a hundred or more of his planes in the air to do honor to the visiting admiral, who had earned the hatred of Americans not only because he held office when the Pearl Harbor attack was planned, but because he had boasted that he would dictate peace in the White House.

One of the four planes in Lanphier's flight blew a tire on the taxiway, and did not get off the ground; another turned back because of a malfunction, and Mitchell assigned another element of two planes to bring up the strength of the attack group, leaving twelve for cover. The flight to Bougainville was made low over the water ("flat-hatting") at about 250 miles an hour, and was uneventful. Five minutes short of the expected rendezvous, the American planes climbed, Lanphier's to 10,000 feet and Mitchell's to 20,000. At 9:33 they passed over the coast of Bougainville.

The success of the mission depended almost entirely on timing—upon Yamamoto's timing. Unfortunately for him, the admiral had a passion for promptness, and American intelligence officers familiar with his habits had assured the Lightning pilots that their quarry would appear at the instant he was due. He was a minute early, by American calculations. At 9:34 the two enemy bombers with their six Zeroes were sighted. The expected cloud of enemy fighter planes from local fields, to provide additional protection, did not materialize.

The lead Zero took on Lanphier, and while he was busy shooting it down the modified bombers carrying Yamamoto and his staff dived to tree-top level. Lanphier followed them and laid a course to intercept the lead plane, at the same time dodging two Zeroes. He was about ten feet above the trees, by his own estimate, when he fired a long burst at right angles across the Betty's line of flight. The right engine and right wing caught fire, and the plane carrying Yamamoto spun into the jungle, crashed and burned. (The Japanese later reported that the admiral was found dead in his seat, his samurai sword still sheathed between his knees.) Lieutenant Rex Barber shot down the second bomber, carrying members of the admiral's staff, in the same fashion after shaking off three Zeroes. The only American loss was the plane piloted by Lieutenant Raymond M. Hine, which was seen losing altitude and trailing smoke after a mêlée with the same Zeroes which had attacked Barber. Hine has not been heard from since.

There was great jubilation at Guadalcanal, and the good news was printed in one of the Air Force news sheets. Then it was realized that if the Japanese knew that the Americans had known that Yamamoto was going to be in that plane, they might be able to trace the source of the information. Apparently the enemy were never certain that the destruction of that particular Betty was anything more than a lucky shot, although they wondered whether there might be something else behind it.

The explanation was really quite simple: American naval intelligence officers had "cracked" the Japanese naval code a year before Yamamoto started on his last flight, and knew his plans from radio intercepts.

v. Halsey's March through New Georgia

THE CAMPAIGN for the New Georgia group began long before any assault troops landed in the islands. It began even before the seizure of the Russells as a stepping stone. The existence of the airfield so cunningly built by the Japanese at Munda had become a menace in the last days of 1942. Aircraft had been sent out regularly from Henderson Field to bomb it, but the forces available were not large enough to do it any crippling damage. A few warships could devastate the target in a few minutes with a greater weight of steel and high explosive than all the bombers then operating from Henderson could carry there in days.

Early in January, Rear Admiral Walden L. Ainsworth set out with a task force of light cruisers and destroyers, to give Munda the first of a series of such shellackings. In the first, dark hours of Tuesday, January 5, the force turned north from the Solomons Sea, past Baniata Point at the western tip of Rendova, and headed straight for Munda. The bombardment force, the *Helena, St. Louis, Honolulu* and *Nashville* (flag), had to operate close to the coral reef known as Munda Bar, in Rendova Strait. The Japanese were asleep. They failed to intercept the force; they failed to answer its fire, and they failed to offer any opposition to the early stages of its withdrawal. About sunrise, a force of Japanese dive-bombers got to Ainsworth's ships ahead of the fighter escort sent out from Guadalcanal to meet them. The *Honolulu* was superficially damaged by near misses. Then the Wildcats from Henderson reached the scene and shot down four of the Japs. Munda had been knocked about, but a dirt runway cannot be put out of action for more than a day or two at a time when the proprietors rush repair crews out immediately to fill in the holes.

This handicap had to be faced. The Japanese were building

a new strip at Vila, a few miles northwest of Munda, on Kolombangara Island. It was believed that Vila and the adjacent Stanmore Plantation area were being used by the Japanese for staging men and supplies into Munda. The latter could not be approached by large vessels, because of its protective reef. The logical way to supply it was by barge, across the narrow southern end of Kula Gulf. On the afternoon of January 23, Ainsworth appeared off Tulagi with his cruisers and picked up a squadron of destroyers under Captain R. L. Briscoe: the *O'Bannon, Nicholas, Radford* and *DeHaven*.

At midnight, off New Georgia, three Japanese planes circled the force and blinked the letter "U": evidently the enemy's recognition signal for the night. They should have known perfectly well that these could not be friendly ships, but no doubt the Japanese had their troubles with recognition and information, too. Gunners aboard the American ships were itching to open fire, but Ainsworth would not let them. Since they did not attack, his decision proved to be as astute as it was unexpected. The security of the force was not compromised, and the Japanese on near-by islands do not appear to have detected it, although the sea was oily smooth and the moon was riding high, a little past full.

The American ships bored into Kula Gulf at high speed, following the New Georgia coast, and turned to make the bombardment run at 2 A.M. Fires soon appeared at Vila. Three Japanese ships seen running out from behind a small island were assigned to the *Helena* and *DeHaven*. Catalina spotting planes overhead reported at least one hit on a supply ship. At the end of 15 minutes, when 200 tons of ammunition had been expended, Ainsworth ordered the force out.

This time the Japanese got on the trail a little faster. Float planes dropped flares ahead of the task force as it steamed past New Georgia. Well before sunrise, bombers and torpedo planes appeared. Ainsworth was credited with a nose for dirty weather: he led the task force in and out of rain squalls which did more than anti-aircraft fire to ward off the Japs. They played a topsy-turvy version of cat and mouse for three hours and then disappeared when four Wildcats from Henderson arrived to cover the ships. The task force was unscathed, and land-based planes which carried on the good work over Vila that afternoon reported that it was unrecognizable.

The persistence of the Japanese was such that in six weeks the job had to be done over again. This time, the American command scheduled a double-header: the new light cruisers *Montpelier* (flag), *Cleveland* and *Denver*, under Rear Admiral Aaron S. Merrill, with a screen of destroyers (the *Conway, Cony* and *Waller*), were to go up the Slot and work over the Kula Gulf targets, while Captain Briscoe was to take his four destroyers (the *Fletcher* replacing the *DeHaven*, which had been sunk in the last days of the campaign for Guadalcanal). The element of surprise was destroyed when the cruiser force encountered two enemy ships emerging from Kula Gulf. Merrill's cruisers opened fire at once, and hit both of the Jap ships,* on their second or third salvoes, before the enemy returned the fire. One blew up and sank almost at once; the second was soon afire and dead in the water. The American force swept past it, and began its bombardment run at the scheduled hour of 1:30 A.M. (March 6), at the same moment as Briscoe's cans opened up on Munda. The routine job done, both forces retired.

From March through June, the South Pacific was the scene of unprecedented activity. Places which had been nothing but miasmic mud-holes during the Guadalcanal campaign were now well-organized bases. Nouméa was by way of becoming a rear area. Even Espíritu Santo, which had been a jungle hell for a year, was made almost habitable for the thousands of American Army, Navy and Marine Corps men deposited there to build a firm foundation for the structure which was to extend through the Solomons. Guadalcanal was cleansed of snipers; the crushed coral roads from Henderson Field to Koli and Lunga were given route numbers, as in the United States. New airfields were built, on better sites than the quaking meadow where the slipshod Japs had laid out Lunga (Henderson). Tulagi was an advanced naval base. The Russell Islands became the headquarters of ComLanCraFlotSoPac—a new and forbidding designation for a new and threatening officer: Commander, Landing Craft Flotillas, South Pacific.

* Said to have been identified later as fast transports carrying aviation personnel.

The man who labored under this titular burden was Rear Admiral George H. Fort, a friendly and forthright officer. In his harbors were occasional LSTs, and regular swarms of LCTs and LCIs. (The abbreviations refer respectively to: landing ship, tanks; landing craft, tanks, and landing craft, infantry.) The conception of these vessels is variously credited to Winston Churchill, the ancient Romans, Louisiana rum-runners, the United States Marine Corps, the Confederate Navy and the Japanese. Undoubtedly, the ideas of all of them were drawn upon. What matters most is that the most vital weapons in the arsenal of amphibious warfare began to come off the shipyard assembly lines in great numbers during the winter of 1942-43. The invasion of Guadalcanal was done entirely from transports, the only bow-ramp craft used being the little Higgins boats. The same was true of the invasion of North Africa and the occupation of the Russell Islands. The next amphibious moves in the Southwest Pacific, the South Pacific and in Europe were to be made with the immeasurable advantage of flat-bottomed, open-bowed craft up to 2,200 tons, which could nose into the beaches and put ashore both men and equipment in a fraction of the time needed by older methods.

The New Georgia show took almost eight months to prepare. The line-up of gold braid was formidable indeed, and was to be more so before victory was achieved. At the outset, General MacArthur was in strategic command; Admiral Halsey had the over-all command of everything in the South Pacific (and was thus answerable both to MacArthur and to his own immediate superior, Admiral Nimitz); Vice Admiral Aubrey W. Fitch was Commander, Air, South Pacific, but simply moved to Guadalcanal and stood by to help while letting Rear Admiral Marc A. Mitscher, as Commander, Air, Solomons, run the show; Rear Admiral Turner was in command of all naval and amphibious forces. When the troops were ashore on New Georgia, command of the attack on Munda would pass to Major General John H. Hester, commanding the 43rd Division.

But there were to be many preliminary moves before that happened. Munda and Vila were bombarded again by cruisers and destroyers in mid-May. The mass of shipping concentrated off Guadalcanal and Tulagi attracted the attention of the Japanese a month later, and on June 16 they sent down a great force of 120 aircraft, including twin-engined bombers, dive-bombers and escorting fighters. No less than 107 are officially listed as having been shot down, for a loss of only six American fighters. The Japanese continued to raid Guadalcanal and the Russells, but with much smaller forces.

The first toehold on New Georgia was to be at Segi, at the southeastern end—as far away from Munda as it was possible to get and still be on the same island. This was needed because there was a Japanese garrison near-by, and another at Viru, between Segi and Munda; also, it was needed because an emergency air strip would further extend the range of the combat air patrols. Segi was selected for three reasons: it had a coconut plantation on a neck of land which could be made into a short, emergency strip in short order; the Australian manager of the plantation had stayed there throughout the Japanese "occupation," thanks to the aid of his native workers; the harbor was marked on old British charts as "foul grounds"—and the Japanese had never bothered to survey it to discover that it was, in fact, navigable for boats of moderate size.

Before daylight on June 20, two companies of the 4th Raider Battalion, loaded in Higgins boats from destroyer transports, nosed between the islets at the entrance to Segi harbor. As they passed, natives on the islets lit fires—a signal to others on the main island that the Americans were coming, as expected. The signal had not been expected by the Marines, who thought at first they had barged into a trap. They went ashore at dawn, in full battle regalia. It turned out that there were no Japanese around. The landing evidently was not detected by the enemy, and the Marines stayed until June 27, two companies of the 103rd Infantry having been landed on June 21 to set up a defensive position.

Meanwhile, the tempo of American air attacks on Japanese positions in the central and northern Solomons had been increased. Mitscher sent out every available plane whenever the weather permitted (which, unfortunately, was not often enough). He had, in theory, 72 heavy bombers: actually, only half of these were usually in the Solomons at one time, the rest being in reserve at Espíritu Santo. He had a squadron of mediums (B-25s), and a total of 165 torpedo planes (adapted to carry bombs or depth charges) and dive-bombers. It was a

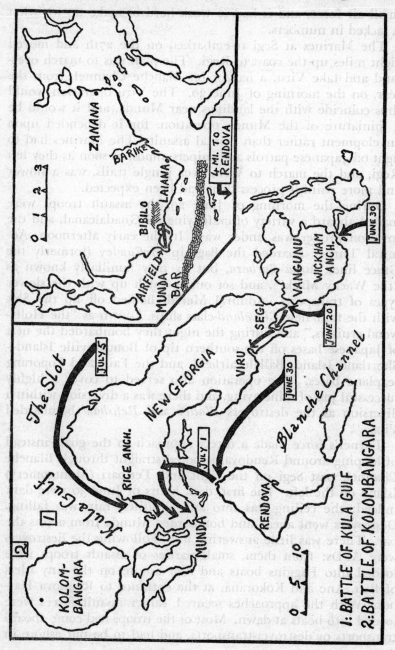

small air force, and it had to work hard to make up for what it lacked in numbers.

The Marines at Segi re-embarked on the 27th and moved eight miles up the coast to Regi. The plan was to march overland and take Viru, a harbor on Blanche Channel, from the rear, on the morning of June 30. The Viru operation would thus coincide with the landings near Munda,. and it would be a miniature of the Munda operation, for it depended upon envelopment rather than frontal assault. The Marines had to fight off Japanese patrols and snipers almost as soon as they left Regi, and the march to Viru, over jungle trails, was a slower and more painful process than had been expected.

During the morning of June 29, the assault troops were loaded aboard a variety of craft lying off Guadalcanal, and the invasion proper was under way. In the early afternoon, Admiral Turner boarded the flagship *McCawley* (formerly the Grace liner *Santa Barbara,* but by now familiarly known as "the Wacky Mack"), and set out to catch up with the slower types of transports. Admiral Merrill hauled off up the Slot with the four new *Cleveland*-class ships, known as "the Hollywood cruisers," and during the night they bombarded the nest of Japanese bases off the southern tip of Bougainville Island— Shortland Island, Ballale airfield, and the Faisi and Poporang seaplane bases. The operation also served to cover a highly successful job of minelaying, and there was a diversion within a diversion as the destroyers *Waller* and *Renshaw* bombarded Vila.

Turner's force made a direct approach to the goal: instead of looping around Rendova, it bored straight through Blanche Channel, past Segi on the right and Tetipari (Montgomery) Island on the left. The first, dark hours of June 30 were dark indeed: the ceiling was zero and a pitiless rain was falling. Destroyers went ahead and bombarded Munda from across the bar. There was little answering fire. Following the destroyers were APDs: from them, small parties of assault troops were loaded into Higgins boats and sent ashore on the tiny islets of Bau, Ane and Kokorana, at the entrance to Rendova Harbor. With the approaches secured, larger assault forces were loaded into boats at dawn. Most of the troops had come aboard transports or destroyer-transports, and had to be put ashore in boats; the slower LSTs and LCTs would come up with heavy equipment when the beachhead was secured. LCIs were used little, if at all, for carrying troops directly to the beach.

The assault troops were elements of the 172nd Infantry Regiment, part of the 43rd Division. They encountered vigorous small-arms and automatic fire going ashore, but the Japanese garrison of Rendova was small: by some estimates, not more than 60 men. Even in this small operation, there were the usual misunderstandings. A team of technicians (non-combat men) was assured that the right-hand sector was secure, and immediately pushed inland with radar equipment to be installed on a hilltop. When their job was half done, the men were told that the area was not secure, and had to return to the beach, pulling heavy equipment through a sea of mud pocked with shell craters. The withdrawal completed, they were told to go ahead—the area was now secure.

The divisional command post, a hospital, supply dumps and anti-aircraft batteries were set up near the beach. Batteries of 155-mm. rifles ("Long Toms") were emplaced near-by and trained on Munda, eight miles away across the strait. The artillery was landed swiftly and expertly, and the batteries were ready for action by mid-afternoon. But the other dispositions were defective, as was to be made clear later.

There had been two air raid alarms during the morning, but no enemy planes had got through the fighter screen. At 3:15 P.M. the transports and their escort began to pull out, the universal sentiment among their men being, "It's too good to be true." It was. At 3:30 the third air alarm came; 25 torpedo planes had been sighted. A torpedo was aimed at the lead destroyer and dropped at a range of less than 200 yards. It bumped and bounced along the side of the ship and then sank without exploding. Another torpedo, set to run too low, passed under the same destroyer.

One of the Japanese pilots picked himself a bigger and softer-looking target than the destroyers. It was the *McCawley*. The torpedo struck her amidships, in the engine rooms, and she was soon dead in the water. A destroyer went alongside and took off the wounded men, along with Admiral Turner and his staff. A second destroyer stayed behind to help shepherd the *McCawley*, which was taken in tow, while the rest of the force went ahead at its modest speed to Guadalcanal. As the *McCawley's* seaworthiness lessened, the rest of her complement was taken off. It was just as well. During the night, two torpedoes ripped into her and she went to the bottom of Blanche Channel. At first the Navy said she had been sunk by an enemy submarine; then it was disclosed that she had been finished off by mistake, by an American PT-boat commanded by an officer famous for his exploits in the Philippines. That officer was Lieut. Commander Robert B. Kelly, one of the heroes of *They Were Expendable,* and as competent and courageous an officer as will be found in the United States Navy. He had been ordered out that night on offensive patrol, and specifically directed to seek out and destroy a damaged Japanese transport which was expected to be leaving the area in tow. He had been informed that there would be no friendly ships in these waters at the time. When the *McCawley* was damaged, and had to loiter in the area, Kelly was not informed of it. Perhaps it was one of the frequent breakdowns in communications and in the distribution of information; perhaps it was unavoidable, because of the need for preserving radio silence. Certainly it was not Kelly's fault.

During the night of June 30-July 1, the 169th and 172nd Regiments of the 43rd Division, and the 145th Regiment (minus its 3rd Battalion) of the 37th Division, began to be ferried across Rendova Strait to Zanana, a beach six miles east of Munda on New Georgia proper. Enemy opposition was negligible; the greatest obstacle to the advance westward was the terrain, a jungle-covered morass, broken only by the Munda Trail. This was a native foot trail, which had to be widened and corduroyed. In this phase, the two regiments of the 43rd, a federalized National Guard division from Maine, Vermont, Rhode Island and Connecticut, were in the line, while the Ohioans of the 145th were in reserve. For the first ten days, progress was maddeningly slow, and comparatively uneventful.

Meanwhile, there was action aplenty all around New Georgia.

The force of Marine Corps Raiders which had pushed into the interior of the island from Regi had fought its way to within sight of Viru Harbor by the afternoon of June 30. The following morning, an all-out attack was launched, and the Japanese garrison was wiped out in a fast-paced, four-hour battle. Some of the enemy troops, rather than surrender, jumped off a cliff. The capture of Viru was a day behind schedule, but no great disadvantage resulted: as soon as the American forces reached the waterfront, and secured the entrances to the harbor, a waiting line of landing craft chugged in from Blanche Channel with a defense unit, Seabees and Supply Corps elements. Viru was to be a staging point for craft supplying the larger forces farther west on the island.

On June 30, the 2nd Battalion of the 103rd Infantry (Lieut. Colonel Lester E. Brown, commanding), had landed near Wickham Anchorage, on Vangunu Island, and after eliminating the small Japanese garrison, estimated at 150 men, had secured another of the approaches to the combat area.

The first large-scale enemy reaction against the beachhead on Rendova took the form of an air attack, launched by about a hundred planes, on July 3. Because the division command post and the hospital were too close to the gun batteries (the enemy's first target), bombs which missed the batteries nevertheless did considerable damage and caused casualties among the surrounding units. After that, the various units were dispersed. Most of the islets enclosing the harbor were used for gun emplacements and as staging points for troops on their way to the New Georgia front; one was used as a hospital, and one as a PT base.

The capture of Munda had been planned as a double envelopment. The second arm was to sweep around from the north, when the first (coming in from Zanana) was well under way, and when the Japanese presumably would have committed their available forces to meet the first threat. The second arm also had a minimum objective: even if it failed to enfold Munda, it should at least result in cutting the supply trail to the airport from the northern shore of New Georgia.

The force selected for this operation, the Northern Landing Group, was a mixture of Army and Marine Corps units: the 3rd Battalion of the 145th Infantry, commanded by Lieut. Colonel George Freer, and the 3rd Battalion of the 148th, commanded by Lieut. Colonel Delbert Schultz; the 1st Marine Raider Battalion, commanded by Lieut. Colonel Samuel B. Griffith, and the headquarters company of the 1st Raider Regiment, the entire group commanded by Colonel Harry B. Liversedge, U.S.M.C. It was to land at Rice Anchorage, only about 13 air miles from Munda, fight its way three miles along the coast to Enogai Inlet and about the same distance to Bairoko Harbor, block the trail from Bairoko to Munda and if possible to advance along it.

As a preliminary to the landing, which was scheduled for about 1:30 A.M., July 5, Rear Admiral Ainsworth took his three veteran cruisers into these familiar waters to knock out enemy shore batteries. The *Honolulu* (flag), *Helena* and *St. Louis* opened up shortly after 12:15 A.M. The Japs had little combustible material on the shore; no fires were visible from the ships, although a Catalina overhead reported a heartwarming blaze, "probably in an ammunition dump." As the cruisers were withdrawing, a Jap float plane dropped a parachute flare over their course, but they were not attacked. Instead, the TBS (short-range radio for "talk between ships") carried the simple message from one of the screening destroyers: "Hurry —come quick." It sounded like a Jap trick, but it was quickly verified as coming from the *Strong,* which had been torpedoed. Two cans stood by to pick up survivors, at the risk of being themselves torpedoed—the *Gwin* and *O'Bannon.* The rest of the task force hauled out of funnel-shaped Kula Gulf at high speed.

At least one Japanese battery south of Rice Anchorage had survived the cruiser bombardment, and had to be attended to by the destroyers which were giving close cover to the APDs and their burden of assault troops. It fell silent, but apparently the Japanese gunners were simply smart enough to lie doggo, for as soon as the warships left, the battery opened up again. There were no Japanese at Rice, and Liversedge's entire force was landed without casualty. At dawn, on the left (west) bank of the Pundakona River, the group formed up, relieved to have the all-night rain let up at last, and pushed off toward the Giza Giza River. This was reached in the afternoon, but was not crossed until morning. In the meantime, a second all-night rain had raised it from an ankle-deep stream to a waist-deep torrent. The vicissitudes of this force were to prove as galling as those of the main landing group near Munda.

As was inevitable in jungle-island warfare, the only clean-cut engagements of the campaign were fought by the Navy. Early in the afternoon of July 5, fourteen hours after its bombardment mission in Kula Gulf, Ainsworth's task force was out in the Coral Sea past Guadalcanal, heading for a rendezvous with a tanker near San Cristóbal. A dispatch from a reconnaissance plane reported that a Japanese task force had reached the Buin-Shortland area off southern Bougainville. It appeared that the Tokyo Express, of accursed memory during the campaign for Guadalcanal, was running again. Ainsworth's force was ordered to omit the refueling, turn 180° and go back to intercept the Japanese if, as seemed likely, they were going into Kula Gulf, either to reinforce Vila or to bombard Liversedge's force strung out along the opposite shore. According to the airmen, the enemy force contained two heavy cruisers, two lights and six destroyers.

If the American cruisers had returned to Kula Gulf by the most direct route, they might have reached there in time to intercept the Japanese force on the way in. As it turned out, it was past midnight when the task force began to cross the mouth of the gulf from Visuvisu Point to Kolombangara, and to search for the enemy.* The Japanese had made better time coming down from the north than the American squadron coming from the south. The Japanese had already entered the gulf, gone to the anchorage for Vila, and unloaded whatever reinforcements they were carrying. (The suggestion that they had entered from the south, through Blackett Strait and the shallow Hathorn Sound, is untenable.) At 1:30 A.M., July 6, they were outward bound: two light cruisers and three destroyers in the van; the two ships identified as heavy cruisers and three more destroyers were about half a mile astern of the lights. Ainsworth's force was on a westerly course, well across the mouth of the gulf, when the enemy was detected with certainty at 1:38.

From the American point of view, the tactical situation was as near perfect as it ever could be, outside of text books. Ains-

* Thanks to the development of modern electronic devices (radar), the word "search" no longer has the same significance as it had in naval campaigns up to and including World War I. Without deviating from its course, a task force can now "search" for an enemy up to or beyond the extreme limit of gun range. With adaptations of radar, the ships' guns can be brought to bear on targets which are invisible to the human eye, even when aided by the most powerful optical instruments.

worth's column was crossing the enemy's T. That is, all the American ships could fire all their guns at once against the leading Japanese ship, and the enemy would be able to reply only with those of his guns mounted forward. The second unit in the enemy column might at first be outranged; as he came within range, he might be blanked by the ship ahead; in any case, only his forward guns would bear.

The *Honolulu* (flag) opened shortly after 1:50, firing in salvoes over the port bow. The *Helena,* next in column, appears for some unexplained reason to have fired her five turrets individually, as fast as each could be loaded. Since modern 6-inch guns can fire at least ten rounds a minute, one or other of the five turrets would be firing every second or so, and the *Helena* appeared to be continuously wreathed in the flame of her own guns. The *Honolulu* and *St. Louis,* on the other hand, were blacked out for a few seconds at a time. It was more difficult for the Japanese to aim at a target, moving 50 feet per second, when it was periodically darkened.

The events of the next few, feverish minutes have been obscured, rather than clarified, by some fanciful accounts of the action. All three of the American cruisers claim to have hit the leading Jap cruiser with one of their first three salvoes; the enemy ship was quickly set ablaze, and fire was shifted to the second cruiser. Again, hits are claimed to have been made on the first or second salvo; on the sixth or seventh salvo, the target blew up.

Neither of these ships is recorded as having fired a shot in its own defense. Not so the destroyers. They charged forward, firing their guns as they advanced, and preparing to launch torpedoes. The American cruisers shifted their fire to as many of the destroyers as they could distinguish. Evidently some torpedoes had already been launched: at 2:08, one struck the *Helena* on the bow, between No. 1 and No. 2 turrets. The *Helena's* bow was sheared off between the two turrets. Virtually every man in No. 1 turret and its handling room must have been killed outright. As the outer plates tore away and the bow became completely detached, most of No. 1 turret fell off into the sea, but the remainder (undoubtedly including the barbette on which the turret was mounted) remained. Its great weight caused the aft end of the detached portion to sink, while the stem, buoyed by watertight compartments such as the chain lockers, rode high out of the water.

The *Helena* fell out of her place in column, and the rest of the task force drove on to the west. But the first five minutes of gunfire had exhausted the available targets. The two Jap heavy units in the second part of the formation are believed to have swung back into the gulf for a while, in an effort to find an opportune moment for slipping out astern of the American task force. But the remaining enemy destroyers were still active. Another torpedo was detected, by its glistening wake, approaching the *St. Louis*. There was no time for the cruiser to turn away. The torpedo struck her amidships, bumped along the side, and fell away—a dud.

Admiral Ainsworth ordered a 180° turn to bring his force to an easterly course, across the mouth of the gulf again, but in the opposite direction. Whether the remaining Japanese ships were now running out of the gulf, and had their T crossed again, or whether they were on a parallel course, is in dispute. By 2:30, the cannonading was resumed. It lasted ten minutes this time, but was less concentrated; when no more targets could be distinguished, Ainsworth ordered the destroyer squadron, under Captain Francis X. McInerney in the *Nicholas*, to search the gulf. At first they found nothing. Then one of them reported over the TBS: "I smell a skunk." He was ordered to close it, and finally to illuminate it with his search-light. The unidentified object fitted the description of no known fighting ship in either of the opposing navies. The flagship asked: "Who is it? Who is it? Acknowledge. Acknowledge." Finally the destroyer answered: "I am sorry to report it is Five Zero."

Five Zero—50—was the number on the *Helena's* bow, all that remained above water of a ship with as proud a record as any in the Navy. At 2:20 she had been struck amidships by two more torpedoes. The forward engine room and fire room were destroyed, scarcely a man in their details escaping, and the ship's back was broken. She began to settle at the point of impact; gradually, the foreshortened forward end (there being no bow) and the stern rose higher and higher, until it seemed that the tops of the two funnels would meet and be telescoped. But a sidewise stress developed, and the cinder guards at the top of the stacks passed each other, the two parts of the remnant of the ship beginning to cross like the blades of a pair of scissors.

Nearly all the men were off before the twisted hulk slid below the surface. There was no explosion. The commanding officer, Captain Charles P. Cecil, who had been the last to leave, so far as he could tell, swam around with other officers, trying to get the men to paddle away from the sinking hulk to avoid the suction. All movement was difficult, for the water was coated with inches of fuel oil, choking, blinding and nauseating the men.

How many enemy ships were sent to the bottom for the loss of the *Helena* may not be known for some time. The consensus is that five ships were sunk and three or four probably sunk, although there is so little conclusive evidence that eight months after the battle, Admiral King, determined to claim nothing of which he was not doubly sure, tallied only two destroyers.

Whatever the precise score, it appeared to have been completed before 3 A.M., and Admiral Ainsworth began to withdraw the bulk of his force, leaving Captain McInerney with the *Nicholas* and *Radford* to pick up the *Helena's* survivors. The commanding officers of the destroyers were respectively Lieut. Commander Andrew J. Hill and Commander William K. Romoser. The *Radford* had found the *Helena's* bow and was gathering up survivors when enemy ships were detected coming out of the gulf. No doubt they were trying to escape, but they would have been glad of a chance to pot a sitting duck like the *Radford,* hove to with its life nets overboard. McInerney ordered Romoser to leave the *Helena's* men for the time being, and the two destroyers dashed off to engage the enemy, who vanished against the shore of Kolombangara. The *Radford* returned to her lifesaving duty, the *Nicholas* standing by to protect her in case further Japanese interference should develop.

It did. This time, of two enemy vessels reported coming out of the gulf, one was a big one. McInerney told Ainsworth over the TBS: "Large ship closing in on us. What shall we do?" The admiral answered: "Engage the enemy. We are returning to aid you." The two surviving cruisers and their two remaining escort destroyers put about, and the *Nicholas* set out to begin the engagement alone. The *Radford* by now had 300 of the *Helena's* men aboard, making her decks slimy with the oil which dripped from them, and unavoidably getting in the way. Romoser again broke off his rescue mission to join the *Nicholas*. At least one of the enemy ships had fired a spread of torpedoes. The American destroyers answered in kind, then illuminated their targets with star shells, and discovered a ship about the size of a cruiser, with a destroyer astern, both afire and incapable of defending themselves. A third enemy ship fled from the scene, and as the two under attack burned to the water, McInerney told Ainsworth: "We have no more targets." The cruisers and the two other destroyers again turned 180° and finally headed for Tulagi. Once more the *Nicholas* and *Radford* returned to the task of picking up the *Helena's* survivors.

The destroyers put three whaleboats over. In the darkest hour before dawn they splashed around the oil-fouled waters, hauling the *Helena's* men inboard, and carrying them over to the mother ships. Just as the eastern sky was beginning to pale, the last Japanese destroyer came nosing out of the gulf again. Both the *Nicholas* and the *Radford* opened on the enemy destroyer with their guns. Before they had done, it was a hulk, burning to the waterline. Then they took the last loads of *Helena* men from their boats.

The destroyers could stay no longer, but their boat crews were willing to stay, and to take their chances on being picked up by a rescue mission later—or caught by the Japanese. Captain Cecil refused to leave his men. Only after the *Nicholas* and *Radford*, overloaded with survivors and filthy with oil, had reluctantly charged off toward Tulagi, Cecil was lifted from the water where he had been clinging to a life raft by a hand line, and taken aboard one of the whaleboats. Almost a hundred men were gathered aboard the three small boats. Between two and three times that number were drifting away to the northwest, with no boats, with only life rafts and life vests and bits of wreckage and the *Helena's* bow to keep them from drowning.

At Tulagi, the 444 survivors picked up by the *Radford* and 313 rescued by the *Nicholas* were transferred to the *Honolulu* and *St. Louis* and were promptly carried back to the receiving hospital at Espíritu Santo.

It was a foregone conclusion that the Japanese would send down another Tokyo Express, and another, so long as they had the ships left to send. In the campaign for Guadalcanal they had shown a fatal tendency to throw good ships after bad. The pattern was beginning to repeat itself in the campaign for New Georgia. Four nights after the Battle of Kula Gulf, the Express made its next recorded run: cruisers and destroyers were caught in the mouth of the gulf before dawn on July 10 and bombed by Liberators, which reported at least two hits with 500-pound bombs. The Japanese undoubtedly accomplished their mission despite this harassment.

By this time, Ainsworth's task force had been filled out to its former numbers by the inclusion of the gallant New Zealand cruiser *Leander,* which had an excellent record in the 1939-41 campaign against Axis commerce raiders. But the *Leander* mounted only a fraction of the *Helena's* firepower: on her 7,270-ton hull were only eight 6-inch guns, as against the *Helena's* fifteen; her secondary battery was eight 4-inchers, as against the *Helena's* eight 5-inchers.

The task force had been slated to have a part in the rescue of the remaining *Helena* survivors from Vella Lavella, but the Tokyo Express started another run and Admiral Turner had to modify his plans. Ainsworth took his task force up the Slot late on July 12. Early on the 13th, well before dawn, it encountered the enemy, again disposed in two groups, each inferior in strength to Ainsworth's force, although probably the two enemy groups combined would both outnumber and outgun the Allied squadron.

This action took place outside the gulf, off the northeast coast of Kolombangara, and should properly be known as the Battle of Kolombangara, although it is often loosely referred to as the Second Battle of Kula Gulf. In the first few, furious minutes, a concentration of fire on the leading Japanese cruiser probably resulted in its sinking. But in those same few minutes, an enemy destroyer launched a spread of torpedoes, one of which hit the *Leander* in the bow. Thus shortened, the Allied battle line had to fight off the second Japanese group. In this phase, the enemy had the advantage, and used it well. His

gunnery was not good enough to impair the fighting efficiency
of the American cruisers, but his torpedo work was. Both the
Honolulu (flag) and *St. Louis* took torpedo hits in the bow.
The *Gwin,* which had so recently won distinction, was raked
by Japanese shells and set afire. She was taken in tow, but as
internal explosions compounded the damage, she had to be
abandoned, and finally sunk by her sister ships. The Allied
cruisers had to fight off a Japanese air attack as they trailed
down the Slot in daylight, capable of only 15 knots.

Again, the extent of the damage inflicted on the enemy is
obscure. However, the price paid in the battles of Kula Gulf
and Kolombangara may not have been excessive. While the
Japanese were not *prevented* from using the Kula Gulf route
to supply and reinforce their garrisons at Vila and Munda,
as an official Navy report erroneously states, they certainly were
discouraged from doing so. Thereafter, enemy traffic into the
gulf for this purpose was on a small scale, and was carried
mainly in barges. There was no other naval action in July.

Meanwhile, the forces on land had been advancing more
slowly than had been expected (the original schedule called
for the capture of Munda on July 11), and new situations arose
which required radical measures.

As Lieut. Colonel Griffith's Marine Raiders slogged through
the muck on the gulf coast of New Georgia from Rice Anchorage toward Bairoko, the men threw away all but the barest
essentials to lighten their burdens in the almost unbearable
heat and humidity. It was only about three-quarters of a mile
from the Giza Giza River to the Tamakau, as the crow flies.
When Griffith mentioned this to one of his men, the latter
replied with the utmost respect: "That may be, colonel, but
we ain't crows." Most of the way the mud was at least knee-
deep; when the force reached the Tamakau, the river had to
be crossed by a single fallen tree, which was used by 1,200 men.

On the morning of July 7, the force reached the south end
of Enogai Inlet and began to work northward along its west
bank toward Enogai Point. So far there had been no Japanese
opposition. The first came at an outpost near the head of the
inlet, when a small Japanese party was dispersed without
American casualties. At Triri (a trail junction), a larger force
of Japanese naval landing troops was encountered. This time,

three Marines were killed. The next morning, a little closer to Enogai, the Japanese were in such strength that one Marine platoon had to be withdrawn under fire. Colonel Liversedge put Companies K and L of the 145th Infantry in defensive positions around Triri, and ordered the Marine Raiders on to Enogai. In this case, cooperation with the natives had not been as close as in other areas. The trails were unknown.

The 1st Raider Battalion reached the vicinity of Enogai Point before the Japanese there were alerted. The enemy garrison comprised part of the 6th Kure Special Landing Group and elements of the Kawasiki Naval Gun Detachment. The Marines used their usual hell-for-leather tactics in taking Enogai, in a two-day action beginning on July 10; about 350 enemy dead are reported to have been counted, while 47 Raiders were killed and 80 wounded. Much equipment was captured. But it was clear that Enogai had no communication with Munda.

The only enemy traffic route was from Bairoko (the next inlet down the coast from Enogai) to Munda. The Japanese had made an excellent harbor for small craft at Bairoko, hiding them under overhanging trees in daytime, and they had started to build a coral road southward to Munda. Fortunately, it was not yet completed. The 3rd Battalion of the 148th Infantry had cut off from the main force at the Giza Giza River on July 6 and spent two days advancing over the most difficult terrain yet encountered, to a point where it stood astride the Bairoko-Munda trail. A Japanese patrol escorting a party of bearers from Munda was ambushed on the 8th; on the 9th, another patrol was ambushed and many of its members killed. On the 10th, a Japanese force of about 500 men struck the trail block, and there was a bloody fight which lasted all night. The enemy left up to 200 dead behind.

The southern front, facing Munda, had bogged down early. Although the officers and men of the 43rd Division had received some training in jungle warfare, it was clear that they had not received enough. In the first days of the advance westward from Zanana, the problem of supply was not solved, and began to appear insoluble.

On July 8, the 169th and 172nd Regiments crossed the Barike River. Major General Hester set up his division command post at Zanana, and elaborate preparations were made for a swift power drive to the west. For two days, the progress was fairly good: a thousand yards a day. Then on July 12 the first major enemy strongpoint was encountered, near the junction of the Munda and Lambeti trails. The nature of this position, and of many others like it, had an important bearing on the campaign for Munda and all later operations.

The Japanese had been at Munda only about 15 months. There was no good harbor near the airfield; there were no wharves where heavy material or equipment could be unloaded, and no roads along which it could be moved to the outer defensive positions. With great ingenuity, skill and patience, the Japanese used the materials at hand. There were only two: logs cut from the trunks of coconut palms, and the native coral sandstone. Foundations were excavated four or five feet deep (about ten feet in the case of a few strongpoints which were to have two stories underground). Nothing but manual labor was used and a few sticks of dynamite to blast rock. Then the walls had been buttressed with coconut logs; these projected a foot or two above ground. Firing slits were obtained by simply cutting some logs a foot short. The roof consisted of a layer of logs, and was supported, in the larger pillboxes, by lally columns of the same material to bear the great weight of lumps of coral sandstone. For camouflage, they threw a few loads of soil on and around the positions, and put sprouting coconuts around. Within two or three months, the rapid growth of vegetation in the rain forest made these positions indistinguishable from a mere hump on the floor of the jungle.

The first major strongpoint of this type encountered in the Munda campaign proved impervious to rifle or machine-gun fire. It was almost impervious to the fire of small mortars; it was too small a target for artillery emplaced across the channel; it was indistinguishable from the air. There were no tanks or tank destroyers available. The 169th Infantry had to be left to contain this strongpoint, while the 172nd resumed the advance on Munda.

On July 13, this regiment reached the coconut plantation at Laiana, a fraction over three miles east of Munda, and established a beachhead there for the landing of further reinforcements and supplies. The first troops to use this more direct route were the 3rd Battalion of the 103rd Infantry, of the 43rd Division. A platoon of six light tanks from a Marine Defense Battalion also was landed, and the division command post was moved up from Zanana to Laiana. After a fairly easy advance of about a thousand yards, the trail led between two enemy strongpoints. The order of battle then was: on the left flank, along the beach, the 3rd Battalion of the 103rd Infantry; in the center, the 172nd Infantry; on the right, the 169th Infantry which had moved up after neutralizing the first strongpoint, farther back.

The tanks were not especially successful; their 37-mm. guns were too small to do more than nick the corners of the coral lumps with which the pillboxes were roofed. Visibility from inside a closed tank is so poor that the tank men wanted infantrymen to walk ahead and direct them. But sometimes, American infantrymen ahead of the tanks found themselves caught in their fire. Telephone communications and command relationships also were unsatisfactory.

In a series of breakouts beginning on July 17, the Japanese drove a wedge between the 172nd and 169th Regiments. Then they made a murderous night attack on the command post of the 169th, which threw the regiment into confusion, and a similar attack, almost as severe, against the division command post at Laiana. The situation was deteriorating so rapidly that a major reorganization of the operation was decided upon. At first, the 169th was withdrawn, and the 145th Infantry (of the 37th Division) was ordered up from reserve to relieve it.

Major General Hester was relieved of command of the 43rd Division, and replaced by Major General John R. Hodge. At the same time, the 43rd was superseded in direction of the campaign by Major General Oscar W. Griswold, who moved his Fourteenth Corps headquarters to Rendova, and decided to commit the full strength of two divisions. Since elements of various units had been detached for operations on the periphery of New Georgia, the order of battle became even more complex: Major General Robert S. Beightler, commanding the 37th, had to get his own 145th Regiment away from the 43rd; both his 145th and 148th Regiments were short one battalion (operating around Bairoko), so he was given the 161st Infantry

(Washington National Guard), detached from the 25th Division, to flesh out his organization.

Major General Beightler set up his division command post near that of Major General Hodge, at Laiana. Four regiments were aligned on a front of only about 1,600 yards: the 103rd, the 172nd, the 161st and the 145th. The total advance in the next five days (to July 25) was only about 300 yards. However, in this time the 161st had reduced the northern strongpoint; the two regiments of the 43rd Division took out the southern strongpoint, and it seemed that at last the way lay open to Munda. Meanwhile, the 148th Regiment had been committed, at the extreme north of the line, beyond the 145th.

The way proved to be only half-open. The 2nd Battalion of the 103rd, on the extreme left flank along the waterfront, broke away on July 25. Company E romped along the beach and the Japs' waterfront wagon trail for 800 yards before discovering that other companies on the right had been stopped; it had Japanese all along its flank, and found itself under heavy enfilading fire. It had to fight its way back, carrying its wounded, on a route which provided no cover.

On the extreme right flank inland, patrols from the 1st and 2nd Battalions of Colonel Stuart A. Baxter's 148th Infantry had a similar experience. They raced ahead of the center, along a saddle leading to Bibilo Hill, which overlooked and almost overhung Munda Point. Japanese trenches along the route were not occupied. Baxter wanted to plunge ahead, but Beightler forbade him to try to take the hill until he could be assured of a supply route.

As it was, Baxter was already so far forward that the Japanese were able to cut behind him, and cut his supply route. It took the 148th two days to fight its way out, and it fought to the rear.

Throughout the month of July, the Japanese positions in the Munda area had been hammered by mortar and howitzer fire from heavy weapons companies and artillery regiments on New Georgia; they had been hammered by corps artillery from Rendova; they had been hammered by naval bombardment on half a dozen occasions; they had been hammered almost daily by heavy bombers, light bombers, dive-bombers, or a combination of them.* By the standards then prevailing in the South Pacific, these strikes constituted a heavy bombing campaign, although the weight dropped never exceeded 190 tons in one day.

The question arises, then, why did it take so long to cover the six miles from Zanana to Munda and seize the strip? Some of the reasons have already been indicated: supply was difficult, and was not as well organized as it should have been; the American mortars were smaller than those of the enemy; there were only a few light tanks available, and these mounted only 37-mm. guns, which were too small to do much good against coral rock or even coconut logs (the fibrous nature of which renders them almost indestructible); much of the equipment used was not as good as that furnished for subsequent campaigns. Communications were bad, and the coordination of the several services engaged was still worse. For example, the PT boats never had enough information about what the air forces were doing, and neither air nor ground forces knew enough about the PTs' plans: the result was that the boats sometimes attacked Allied craft, and were in turn attacked by every kind of Allied aircraft. The great majority of these errors and miscalculations could be laid to inexperience. In the case of the ground troops, the 169th Regiment had to be withdrawn because some of its officers proved unequal to the strain of command in combat.

The most potent reason for the slowness of the advance on Munda became apparent on the last day of July. The night before, the Japanese had been creating a disturbance along the front, but had made no organized attack. At noon, the whole front with five regiments in line began to advance. On the extreme right, the 148th had stiff fighting to dislodge the Japanese from positions on Bibilo Hill which could have been occupied without a shot fired, a few days earlier, if it had not been for the extreme caution about supply lines. On the extreme left, the 2nd Battalion of the 103rd, with Major Ray Dunning acting as commanding officer, broke out of the jungle (shell-torn, but still dense) to the relatively open terrain at

* The heavy bombers (B-24s and a few B-17s) usually carried light bombs of 100 to 500 pounds each; the light bombers (Grumman Avengers) carried the heavy bombs, of 2,000 pounds each. The dive-bombers usually carried 1,000-pounders.

the eastern edge of Lambeti Plantation. The airport was only a mile away.

I had the good fortune to go with Company E of the 2nd Battalion. The advance was virtually undisputed. After their nocturnal noise-making, the Japanese had pulled back. For a distance of half a mile inland, not a tree was intact; every one had been shattered by shellfire or bombing. Except for the foliage which littered the ground, there was no longer any cover left to give the Japanese concealment. It was impossible to walk more than a few yards in any direction without dipping into a shell hole or bomb crater.

But within this area of devastation, most of the Japanese pillboxes seemed to be almost intact. The reason was that there were so many of them. They were, on an average, 50 yards apart in every direction, so arranged that arcs of fire from each one intersected arcs of fire from its neighbors. They were not very large (not as big as the three strongpoints encountered earlier in the advance): most were only 15 to 30 feet long and eight to 12 feet wide. They projected only a foot or two above ground. The result was that only a direct hit by a heavy shell or bomb would knock them out. Many were chambered, so that throwing grenades or bringing a flamethrower to bear through one firing slit would affect the men in only one chamber; those in the other chambers were relatively immune.

The Japanese had been driven from this area because the bombardment had destroyed their installations above ground and all communications. Finally, casualties had become prohibitive, and even with their unrivaled discipline, the Japanese commanders had had difficulty in keeping the shell-shocked survivors together as an effective force.

Throughout the day on August 1 and during the morning of August 2, the American forces met resistance only from scattered pillboxes. Nine out of ten of the positions had been abandoned. Shortly after noon on the 2nd, Company E of the 103rd, with First Lieutenant Edward Moore as its acting commander, was within 150 yards of the airport, at the end of which stood a Zero wrecked by American bombing. While the advance was halted temporarily to permit straightening of the line, a small patrol led by Second Lieutenant Pincus Pesso, with

Pfc. Hiram Fuller and Pvt. Elliot Kilbourne and two war correspondents, went ahead to the airfield. It was reached at 2:15 P.M. But there were still hundreds of Japanese well dug-in around the airfield, and hundreds more with well-emplaced guns on the northwest slopes of Bibilo and Kokengolo hills.

Although the airfield was now within grasp, it was decided to bring an overwhelming superiority of numbers to bear against its defenders. The 27th Infantry (a regular Army regiment), part of the 25th Division, had been landed on New Georgia on August 1 and passed through the regiments then in line. Since the front was being narrowed by the convergence of Bibilo Hill to the beach, the 161st Infantry was pinched out, and joined the 27th. Thus for the first time some order was brought into the order of battle: the 43rd, 37th and 25th Divisions were in the line.

On August 3, the 103rd Infantry reached the beach opposite the middle of the airstrip. The 172nd and both regiments of the 37th were held up on Bibilo, but the two regiments of the 25th got into position for a jump-off on August 4, and made contact with patrols of Colonel Liversedge's Bairoko force. On the 4th, the "Tropic Lightnings" of the 25th flashed through to Kindu, on the western shore of New Georgia. Munda Point and its airfield were now completely surrounded. The next day, General Griswold pulled tight the drawstrings of the sack, the reorganized 1st and 2nd Battalions of the 169th Infantry being first on the airfield. A few Japanese escaped by boat to Arundel Island; a few made off into the jungle and had to be hunted down in the following days. But Munda was taken. Its original garrison of about 5,000 men had stood off a greatly superior force which enjoyed command of the sea and air. In the last days of the campaign, the Japanese had numbered no more than 1,500, and had stood off at least ten times their own number. In all, they held out for 36 days.

Some of the lessons of the New Georgia campaign were appreciated and acted upon. Light tanks were not much better than toys against Jap positions with strong walls and more powerful guns. Medium tanks, which had been considered too heavy for the mud floor of the jungle, could have operated here, because the mud floor was not deep and rested on a foundation of solid sandstone. General Griswold said on

August 3, on his way up to the front: "If there had been a medium tank in the South Pacific two weeks ago, I'd have had it here by now." But there had been none for him to bring in. A lesson which was not sufficiently understood at the time was the necessity for concentrating the preliminary bombardment into a shorter period before the landings, and then making landings and keeping an offensive rolling without giving the enemy a chance to reorganize or effect repairs. Also, the value of the Army's technique of setting up artillery on islets near the main objective was not appreciated by the Navy and the Marine Corps. The price of their skepticism was paid in blood, months later.

The closing stages of the New Georgia campaign were directed by Rear Admiral Theodore S. Wilkinson, who had assisted Rear Admiral Turner in planning the earlier phases, and then relieved him. Similarly, Major General Nathan F. Twining, who had been commander of the Thirteenth Air Force, relieved Rear Admiral Marc Mitscher as ComAirSols. It should be emphasized that both these were previously planned reliefs and involved no reflection on the officers relieved. Both went on to bigger things after leave in the United States.

Halsey's march through New Georgia was in no way characteristic of the man who was ultimately responsible for it. He would have preferred a quick, brisk campaign. Actually, it developed into a slow crawl. But it attained its objective. On August 13, Munda had been made ready by the Seabees and Major Richard M. Baker's Marine fighter squadron was based there. The American air umbrella was extended 135 miles beyond the farthest point it could reach from the Russells.

VI. War in the Williwaws

WAR IN THE Alaska-Aleutians theater had got off to a bad start (from the American point of view) in 1942. It is difficult to say what the greatest handicap had been: the activities of the enemy, the foul climate, the lack of adequate forces and bases, or the inexcusably confused command. Late in 1942, the public was officially assured that the command tangle had been straightened out; actually, it had been made worse. The ground forces stationed in Alaska and the Aleutians constituted the Alaska Defense Command, under Major General Simon Bolivar Buckner. The Army's Eleventh Air Force was placed under Buckner. Administratively, these air and ground forces were answerable to Lieut. General DeWitt's Western Defense Command, in San Francisco. But operationally, they were supposed to be at the disposal of the Commander, North Pacific, who was responsible to Admiral Nimitz at Pearl Harbor. The air, surface and submarine forces of the Navy were, of course, directly under ComNorPac and thus answerable to Nimitz. It must have given the Japanese great comfort to know that their opponents were thus divided; while the division did the enemy no good in the last analysis, it did the American forces immeasurable harm.

The three Aleutian islands occupied by the Japanese in June, 1942, were Kiska, Agattu and Attu. The westernmost, Attu, had been abandoned for a while in the fall of 1942, and its garrison moved over to Kiska. On the face of it, this would have been the time to move into Attu and establish a strong American position there, to outflank the enemy on Kiska. But the American command—or commands—did not have the forces to establish a strong position, and the decision not to take advantage of the Japs' absence probably was wise in the long run. During the winter the enemy moved back into Attu, but withdrew his small forces from Agattu. While the Japanese were redisposing their forces, American forces also were spreading westward along the island chain. Neither side knew much of what the other was doing, because the entire area was blanketed in fog 90 per cent of the time, and lashed by williwaws (gales of near-hurricane force) the rest of the time.

Although the American forces had reduced the distance between themselves and the enemy by occupying Adak and Atka at the end of August, 1942, and building air bases there, the distance was still too great when 1943 opened. In the first, dank days of January, when the long, northern night gave almost complete protection against detection, a major step to the west was taken. A company of Alaska Scouts landed on Amchitka Island, only 75 miles east of Kiska, and reconnoitered it for the engineers who were to follow. These scouts were men especially chosen for their ability to travel light and virtually to live off the land—no mean feat in this barren, treeless area. Commanded by Colonel Lawrence Castner, they were known as "Castner's Cutthroats." On Amchitka they found no enemy throats to cut, and on January 12 they were followed ashore by an air base construction crew. In February the airfield was completed. This engineering feat is to be contrasted with the poor performance of the Japanese, who spent months laboriously hacking short air strips out of the rock on Kiska and Attu, but never got them into condition to fly off more than a few light planes. The Amchitka field could accommodate medium and heavy bombers. In February, the Eleventh Air Force flew nine strikes from it, dropped a thousand tons of bombs through the fog over Kiska, hoped they hit something—and, most remarkable of all, lost no planes.

After that, the aerial campaign was stepped up. In March, the attacks averaged more than one a day; on the 15th, there were six missions. The enemy's reprisal raids were negligible, and the Japanese High Command does not seem to have had any idea, at this time, of extending its operations eastward toward Alaska. But the Japanese are nothing if not tenacious, and they evidently did not consider giving up the two islands they still held.

Rear Admiral Thomas Cassin Kinkaid, who had been assigned to duty as ComNorPac early in 1943, had counted on the

likelihood that the enemy would make some attempt to reinforce his Aleutian garrisons, and sent out a cruiser force to
intercept the expected Japanese convoy. The task force commander was Rear Admiral Charles H. McMorris. He had been
a captain 15 months earlier when, as Admiral Kimmel's war
plans officer, he had miscalculated the chance of a Japanese air
attack on Pearl Harbor. He was still a captain in October, 1942,
when he had command of the *San Francisco* in the highly successful Battle of Cape Esperance. For his first engagement as a
flag officer, he had an ill-assorted force: America's oldest heavy
cruiser, the *Salt Lake City;* one of the oldest and least effective
light cruisers, the ten-gun *Richmond,* in which McMorris flew
his flag; two pre-war destroyers *(Monaghan* and *Dale)* with four
5-inch guns, and two up-to-date destroyers, the *Bailey* and *Coghlan,* also with four guns.

If McMorris could have come upon a lightly escorted Japanese convoy, his force would have been adequate. At dawn on
March 26, 1943, it appeared for a while that this had happened.
Six ships had been detected to the north: three with the high
silhouette and spindle masts of transports and supply ships, and
only three low-slung warships—probably two destroyers and a
light cruiser. For the *Salt Lake City's* ten 8-inch guns, which
already had spilled more Japanese blood into the Pacific than
any other ten guns afloat, such a convoy with such an escort
would be like a raft of sitting ducks. McMorris signaled, "Concentrate on me," and laid a course to the northwest which
would enable him to bring the enemy under the fire of nearly
all his guns,* and leave the enemy cut off from retreat at the
end of the firing run. The thin-skinned Japanese ships turned
away to the north, leaving McMorris to engage in a stern chase.

Then the rest of the Japanese force, hitherto unsuspected,
appeared on the horizon, bearing southward from a position
east of the convoy. There were two heavy cruisers, a light
cruiser and five destroyers. Counting the light cruiser and two
destroyers with the convoy, the Japanese force outnumbered
the American force exactly two to one in each class of ships.
Instead of having the enemy outgunned, McMorris was himself
outgunned; instead of having the enemy trapped, he was him-

---

* The *Salt Lake City* and the destroyers could fire all their guns over either
beam; the ill-designed *Richmond* could fire only seven on either side.

self trapped, cut off from his own bases by the superior force now intervening. There was no sensible alternative for McMorris but to withdraw.

A flag hoist, ordering a turn to the southwest, was almost ready to be run up when, at 8:37, the Nati * leading the Japanese formation opened fire. Eight-inch shells struck the glassy, leaden-hued sea on both sides of the *Richmond*. A straddle on the first salvo was unmistakable warning that while Japanese gunnery may sometimes be laughable, this certainly was not. McMorris held his northwesterly course for a few minutes more: on this heading, the *Salt Lake City* could bring all ten of her 8-inch rifles to bear. At 8:42 she opened, and began walking her salvoes up to the Nati. The *Richmond* also opened fire, although the range of 25,000 yards was too great for her old 6-inchers. The *Salt Lake's* gunners, under the expert direction of Commander James T. Brewer, straddled the Nati on their third salvo and hit her with the fourth. Flames shot out from the base of the enemy flagship's bridge. While the American gunners got more straddles, they got no more hits until the sixteenth salvo, and by this time McMorris had broken out the signal ordering the turn to the southwest. As the flags were hauled in, the American column made its turn, and on the new heading only five of the *Salt Lake's* guns (in her two after turrets) would bear on the pursuing enemy.

It was still only 8:48. The Japanese flagship billowed smoke, but the enemy's damage control was excellent. The American ships' delay in executing their turn had enabled the enemy to close the range to little more than 20,000 yards, and there it held. The Japanese might have been able to close it still more, but each heavy cruiser could fire only four guns dead ahead, and the Japanese admiral appears to have held to a divergent course, so as to be able to fire more of his guns. Observers aboard the *Salt Lake City* speak of salvoes containing ten or 15 shells.

Captain Bertram J. Rodgers did not take the con from the officer of the deck, but stood calmly on the wing of the bridge, observing the fall of the enemy's shells, and coolly calculating how the Japanese would try to correct their range—and, hence,

---

* The name is not italicized when it is used for an unidentified ship of the *Nati* class, rather than for the *Nati* herself. The name is also spelled *Nachi*.

where the next salvo would fall. He was phenomenally successful. Time and again, a salvo ploughed the sea where the *Salt Lake* would have been, if Rodgers had not outguessed the foe and turned away in the nick of time. At 8:56 one of the Japanese light cruisers, which were keeping out of range, on a course almost parallel to the Americans', catapulted a seaplane to observe and report on the fall of shells. Before the aerial spotter could get into position, the *Salt Lake* took her first hit, a glancing blow from a shell which exploded in the water almost under her stern. No damage. At 9:15 the Jap seaplane was within range, and brought under fire by the *Salt Lake's* 5-inch anti-aircraft battery, which sufficed to scare the pilot off to a range where he could do no harm.

At 9:20 the tireless gunners of the American heavy cruiser, who had been bearing the full burden of the battle, were rewarded with a third hit on the Japanese flagship. This one was near her stern, and she slowed down. The enemy seaplane reappeared, and was fired on by both the American cruisers. It flew away smoking, and is believed to have crashed.

At 9:42 the Nati had lost so much way that she was falling out of range, and the Atago passed her. Momentarily, the odds were evened: the light cruisers and destroyers were out of range, and the duel went on, one heavy cruiser against another. But there was no security in this, and McMorris, a bold and quick thinker, decided to try to wring the utmost possible advantage from the enemy's temporary confusion. He ordered a swift turn to the north, in an attempt to get at the Japs' light cruisers. It meant permitting the Atago to close the range, but he was willing to take that chance for the sake of a crack at the enemy's reserve line. Moreover, the maneuver enabled him to get his flagship, the *Richmond,* back into action.

The commander of the leading Japanese light cruiser, finding himself under fire from both the American cruisers, opened the range. One of the American ships got a hit on a Japanese destroyer, which dropped out of the battle line. So far, McMorris's bold counter-offensive was working well.

But at 9:55 the fire on the Nati's stern was out; she gathered speed and cut swiftly in a straight line across the Americans' circling course. Even so, McMorris was still better off for having undertaken his daring maneuver: while he was again outnumbered two to one, the relative positions of the ships were such that all ten of the *Salt Lake's* guns would bear on the enemy. Moreover, the *Richmond* was still within range of the Japanese leading light cruiser. However, the enemy drew the next blood. At 10:10, the *Salt Lake* took her second hit; fortunately, it was above the water line, and did little to impair her fighting power, but it was decided to shield her with smoke, in the hope of gaining some respite.

The laying of smoke served at least to slow down the pace of the battle, and although the Japanese light cruisers tried to swing out on the flanks to get into position for torpedo attacks, they were kept out of range by the *Richmond* and Captain Ralph S. Riggs's destroyers. Under cover of the smoke, also, McMorris was able to turn away to the south, leaving the Japanese heavies dead astern—and leaving him an open escape route.

But at 10:59 the *Salt Lake* was hit on the superstructure; two men were killed and several wounded. Four minutes later she took a far more damaging hit below the waterline; oil tanks were opened, and sea water was let into the fire and engine rooms. Some of the water got into the tanks from which fuel oil was being fed to the boilers. The damage control work in the engine rooms was magnificent: men stood in the icy water to their waists, shutting off valves in damaged lines, calking the leaks to stem the rising flood. At one time they were up to their necks in a foul mess of water and half-frozen, gummy oil, and in one room the engines had to be stopped at 11:25. The *Dale* laid smoke around the limping cruiser. Soon she was running again on all engines.

Then, at 11:40, the captains of the after gun turrets reported that they were almost out of ammunition. Captain Rodgers had an immensely difficult decision to make: either he must run the risk of having his after turrets fall silent and useless in a few minutes, or he must run the risk of opening up the deck hatches (jeopardizing the ship's water-tight integrity), and having powder bags and shells trundled along the open deck from the forward magazines to the after turrets. If the enemy scored a hit during this operation, the jig would be up. Rodgers took the second and more daring choice. The ammunition was transferred. The Japanese gunners missed their chance.

Ironically, the worst misfortune befell the *Salt Lake* only after this hazardous task had been completed. The water which had seeped into her fuel tanks now reached the boilers. The burners were snuffed out, clouds of steam poured from the two funnels, the ship's speed slackened. Minute by minute it fell off, just as the Japanese gunners began to get the range again, and to shake the ship with near misses. At 11:55 Captain Rodgers signaled to McMorris: "My speed zero."

It looked like the end for the *Salt Lake City*, otherwise known as the "Swayback Maru" or the "one-ship fleet," unless the oilers could clear the feed lines.

Captain Riggs had been asking for permission to lead his destroyers in a torpedo attack, and now he had his wish. By all the probabilities, it was a suicide mission. The *Dale* was left to screen the *Salt Lake;* the *Monaghan* led the *Coghlan* and *Bailey* into a hail of Japanese heavy shells. The *Monaghan* was hit by two 8-inch shells from a single salvo before she was within effective torpedo range. She fired her "tin fish" at once. Her speed dropped to 15 knots as the two other cans raced past her; they also fired from extreme range, as the *Monaghan* impudently opened with her 5-inch guns against the armor of the *Atago.* (From their close vantage point, they reported that four of the Nati's five turrets had been knocked askew.)

The Japanese turned in confusion to avoid the torpedoes. The oilers aboard the *Salt Lake City* won their battle on the stroke of noon, and got the burners relighted; steam flowed again to the turbines which drove the propellers, and to the power-operated turrets. From the damaged *Monaghan*, Riggs radioed McMorris: "Enemy retiring westward. Shall I follow them?" McMorris replied in the negative; the suggestion was gallant, but impractical. The *Salt Lake* fired a parting burst from all her guns, and the battle ended.

The Battle of Komandorski was the longest gunnery duel of the war. Throughout its course, it had been a disengaging action by McMorris, yet it had proved to be an American victory: the convoy apparently was turned back. McMorris made good his retirement with his two damaged ships and four whole ones. It is worthy of note that the *Salt Lake City* went back to the Mare Island Navy Yard for repairs, and sailed again on May 12—less than seven weeks after a battle in which she received several damaging hits.

In the meantime, the war in the williwaws had reached its climax. During April, the tempo of the air attacks on Attu and Kiska had been greatly accelerated. The American high command had selected Attu as the island to be invaded first, for three principal reasons: (1), it was more lightly held than Kiska; (2), its capture would outflank Kiska, and isolate it for later assault, and (3), the possession of airfields on Attu would bring the northern Kuril Islands under observation and aerial bombardment. So far as was known, there were about 2,500 Japanese on Attu. Originally, the Japanese had had their main base on Chichagof Harbor; later, because the entrance to this anchorage was narrow and rock-strewn, they had transferred their landing operations to the more commodious Holtz Bay, a few miles to the west. American reconnaissance reports indicated that the last transport to get through to Attu had arrived on March 10; after the supply convoy was turned back in the Battle of Komandorski, the only reinforcement received by the Japanese on Attu was a trickle of supplies carried in by submarine.

Aside from the hideous climatic conditions, there was no reason why the recapture of Attu should have been particularly difficult or costly. The enemy garrison was not large; it had no major fixed defenses; it had only sporadic and ineffectual air support; it had no naval support. Nevertheless, the operation proved both difficult and costly, due in the main to inexcusable errors of judgment by highly placed officers in the American command who cannot be satisfactorily identified.

As already noted, there were two forces in the Alaska-Aleutians area with equipment and experience suited to the local conditions: the small body of scouts (Castner's Cutthroats), which could serve as commandos, and the regular troops of the Alaska Defense Command. But in December, 1942, the American high command selected the Seventh Division (a regular Army division) to make the assault on the first Aleutian objective.* The Seventh was at that time training in the desert near San Luis Obispo, California, evidently in anticipation of duty in North Africa. There was considerable time left in which the division might have been re-trained under

---

* At that time, the first objective was expected to be Kiska; the decision to bypass it, and proceed first to Attu, was not made until March.

more northerly conditions of climate and terrain, but it was moved only to Fort Ord, near Monterey, in Latitude 36° 30′ North. Attu is in 53° North. True, the Seventh Division training program was modified, but the climate, the terrain and the conditions were wrong. Shortly before the men were embarked from San Francisco, on April 24, they were issued new boots: a 12-inch, all-leather, high-laced blucher type. They were issued a so-called "Alaska field jacket," cloth on the outside, with a heavy wool lining like a piece of blanket, an extremely small collar—and no hood.

If there had never before been any Americans in the Aleutians, if there had been no knowledge of the conditions which would be encountered, the issue of this gear might have been slightly excusable. But the scouts had long ago developed an outfit suited to the local conditions; the Navy had issued "shoe-pacs" (rubber bottoms, high leather tops), and parkas with large hoods. The "Alaska field jacket" had never been seen in Alaska until the ill-clad men of the Seventh Division reached Cold Bay on April 30, and it would have been better if it had never been seen there at all.

The landing had been set for May 7, but the convoy was held at Cold Bay by bad weather until May 4, and the schedule was set back a day. The entire force, including battleships, cruisers and destroyers (Rear Admiral Francis W. Rockwell had his flag in the *Pennsylvania)* was reconnoitered by the Japanese, and the garrisons on both Attu and Kiska were alerted. But on May 8 the "soup" around Attu was impenetrable; the force steamed off to the north, into the Bering Sea, to wait for clearing weather. Gradually, the Japanese relaxed their vigil, and by May 11, when the force again bore down on Attu, the enemy troops had reverted to a normal routine from which they were jolted by the salvoes of the *New Mexico, Idaho* and *Nevada,* as well as the flagship.

H-hour had been set for 7:40 A.M., but it was 4:20 P.M. before the first troops reached the shore of Massacre Bay. There was no Japanese opposition at the beaches; the greatest difficulty was to get the boats in through the shifting, fickle fog to their designated areas.

The Seventh Division was commanded by Major General Walter Brown, but the landings were under Colonel Edward

P. Earle, commanding officer of the 17th Infantry Regiment. As assault troops he had the 2nd and 3rd Battalions of his own regiment, and the 2nd Battalion of the 32nd Infantry Regiment. Also in the combat team were three batteries of 105-mm. artillery.

This was the main landing, but the battle plan provided for a sort of double envelopment. The 1st Battalion of the 17th, commanded by Lieut. Colonel Albert V. Hartl, went ashore more or less simultaneously on Red Beach, on the north side of the western arm of Hôltz Bay. This force was to drive southward while the main force drove northward up Massacre Valley: a junction was expected to be made in 36 hours, and the Japanese would then be penned into the eastern peninsula of the island where they could be destroyed. Seven-eighths of the area of Attu lay west of the Holtz Bay-Massacre Bay line; this was to be a no man's land. But to make sure that the enemy in the Holtz Bay area would be denied any chance of escape into this no man's land, a minor subsidiary landing was to be made west of Colonel Hartl's Red Beach, at Austin Cove, by a provisional battalion consisting of the 7th Scout Company and the 7th Reconnaissance Troop, under Captain William Wil-

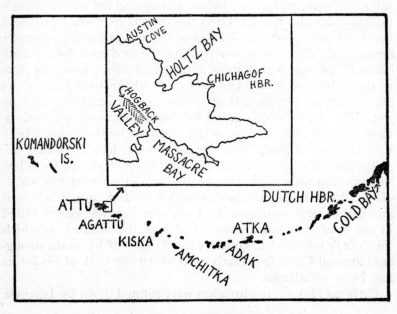

loughby. A fourth, and much smaller, landing was to be made by one platoon detached from the Reconnaissance Troop, at Alexei Point, east of Massacre Bay—to protect the flank of the main southern landing force and to give Colonel Earle information as to Japanese dispositions around the eastern capes.

Of the two battalions first ashore in the southern landing force, the 3rd (landed on Yellow Beach, on the left) was to advance up the floor of Massacre Valley, while the 2nd (landed to the right, on Blue Beach) was to advance up a ridge known as the Hogback which forms the northeastern wall of the valley for much of its length.

The advance during the first evening was rapid, if tedious. The infantrymen soon found that their feet were soaked from plodding over the tundra which holds water like a sponge. The artillerymen found that their heavy equipment broke through the crust of the tundra (formed by the roots of sub-alpine vegetation) and churned uselessly in the black gumbo beneath. They emplaced their guns wherever they could find a solid base, and fired the first shots of the campaign, within an hour after landing, when an enemy morter was located. The infantrymen advanced unopposed up the valley for distances ranging from a mile to a mile and a half before it was decided to consolidate positions for the night. Then the defects in their equipment became more apparent. A foxhole dug in the tundra promptly became half-filled with water. The fog and rain (often combined in a savage Scotch mist) kept the humidity hovering close to the saturation point, and boots or "Alaska field jackets" set out to dry on the stumps of willow shrubs remained soaking wet. The water-logged ground delayed the moving up of rations from the beach. But as the northern twilight closed in, a halt had to be made: the Japanese were looking down the Americans' throats from crannies and caves in the rocky ridges surrounding the valley. One patrol, in platoon strength, which made a foray to the northeast was driven back, but it achieved one noteworthy result: on the body of a Japanese officer killed in the operation was a detailed plan of the manner in which the enemy intended to conduct the defense of his main stronghold around Chichagof Harbor, to which the bulk of his forces had been withdrawn.

Early on May 12, the invaders were pinned down by Japanese

fire from the surrounding heights; there was confusion on the beach, which further hindered the movement of supplies; liaison between the various commands and command posts ashore was bad; worst of all, communications broke down between the forward company command posts and Colonel Earle's post. Colonel Earle went forward in person, accompanied only by a scout, to check on his forward elements. Hours later, a search party found his body. The scout had been severely wounded. Colonel Earle had enjoyed the confidence of the men, and at first an effort was made to keep the news of his death from them. This, of course, encouraged the spread of rumor and gossip, which must have had as bad an effect on morale as the knowledge of the commander's death. His place was taken by Colonel Wayne C. Zimmerman, who had been General Brown's chief of staff.

For six more miserable days and nights the southern landing force was unable to advance up the floor of the valley. The number of casualties going back to the aid stations was increasing at an alarming rate, considering the lack of progress. Some were men wounded by Japanese fire, but more were men suffering from trench foot or exposure, the result of their improper equipment, and cases of what used to be called shell shock were fairly numerous.

It was clear that so long as the American forces were on the valley floor, and the enemy on the heights above, progress would be either impossible or prohibitively costly. On the 14th, it appeared that this fact had been recognized by the command, and when the 3rd Battalion again attacked through the valley, it was supported by other elements on the ridges on both flanks. But the tactical situation still was improperly understood, and the elements on the flanks were too weak. As a result, the attack again faltered. The 3rd Battalion had suffered such heavy casualties that Colonel Zimmerman withdrew it for a rest, and put the 2nd Battalion of the 32nd Infantry in its place.

On the 15th and 16th, two more attacks were made with the new order of battle, but they were beaten back as decisively as the earlier ones. The big guns of the American fleet lying offshore could not find the enemy's artillery and mortar emplacements. Air support proved impracticable: on the fourth day of the stalemate, Wildcat fighter-bombers, flying from an escort carrier, tried pin-point bombing of Japanese positions in the narrow pass ahead of the Americans. The pilots were unable to maneuver, boxed in as they were between mountains, overcast and the ground directly below them, and two crashed in flames within a few minutes.

Meanwhile, various measures had been taken to bring the wearing engagement to a decision. On May 14, General Brown had asked that the ultimate reserve, consisting of units of the Alaska Defense Command, being held at Adak, be embarked and committed. Admiral Rockwell approved the suggestion, and on May 17 the 1st Battalion of the 4th Infantry was shipped from Adak, landing at Massacre Bay on the following day. However, by this time General Brown himself had been relieved of his command. It was the first case (a subsequent instance at Munda has already been mentioned) of an Army general being relieved in the midst of an engagement by a Navy or Marine Corps superior. There were to be several others. Major General Eugene M. Landrum stepped into command; as his principal advisers he had Colonel Stewart, of the Alaska Defense Command, and Colonel Lawrence Castner (as chief of staff and deputy chief of staff respectively). These changes brought into the top staff positions men who had an intimate knowledge of Aleutian conditions. Landrum ordered the troops out of the valley and onto the flanking ridges.

The most decisive change of all, however, was effected by the Japanese under the prodding of the northern landing force under Colonel Hartl. On May 16 the northern forces had seized the ridge overlooking the western arm of Holtz Bay, and the Japanese commander, Colonel Yasuyo Yamasaki, recognized that this made his extreme right flank vulnerable. Instead of ordering his troops to make the usual suicide stand where they stood, he calculated that he could exact a higher toll of the attackers if he withdrew his men to the heights overlooking the eastern arm of Holtz Bay, where the terrain would again favor them against the attackers. So he shortened his entire line—and incidentally made it possible for the southern landing force under Colonel Zimmerman to walk, during the evening of May 17, unmolested through Jarmin Pass, before which they had been stalled for a week. In the next valley beyond the pass, the men from the south effected a junction soon after midnight with Hartl's men * from Holtz Bay. This was the junction which the battle plan said was to be effected within 36 hours; it had taken six and a half days.

Up to this time there had been two American forces, one driving to the south, the other driving to the north, with little communication between them, no coordination and no physical contact. Now that the physical contact had been made, the direction of the fighting also changed: both forces swung to the east, though the southern force's line of advance was somewhat north of east. This lay through Clevesy Pass. A fairly large proportion of the Japanese troops were suffering from what seemed to be a kind of shell shock; when the Americans closed in on their positions, they would lie in their foxholes or gun pits screaming insanely and often pounding the ground with their fists. They would not permit themselves to be captured, yet they did not commit suicide when they had every opportunity to do so. The majority of these cases had to be killed because they reached for weapons when they were about to be taken prisoner. As one American enlisted man put it: "Sure, we got plenty prisoners, but they get cold too quick." Another peculiarity of the Japanese defense was the skill with which Colonel Yamasaki withdrew considerable numbers of men from positions which he was about to lose. In this way he retained a sizable force, even after many days of a hopeless, losing fight.

The only help which reached the defenders of Attu consisted of two flights of aircraft sent from the northern Kurils on May 22. One, consisting of torpedo bombers, made a vain attack on the gunboat *Charleston* and the destroyer *Phelps,* off Massacre Bay. The other, consisting of 16 level bombers, was intercepted by Lightning fighters from Amchitka and forced to jettison its bombs at sea. Nine of these planes are claimed as having been shot down.

It was shortly after this date, when the southern force had broken through into Chichagof Valley, that the American command decided to use heavy bombers (B-24 Liberators) in direct, close support of ground troops. So far as the writer is aware, this was the first occasion on which this had been at-

* The northern landing force by this time had been increased by the addition of the 3rd Battalion of the 32nd Infantry, and the two-battalion team, with artillery, had been taken over by Colonel Frank L. Culin.

tempted: it was to be tried later at Cassino and in Normandy, and always with the same dreadful result. Panels of colored cloth had been laid out on the ground in front of the American lines, and smoke shells were fired during the bombing to give the bombardiers every possible guidance. The first flights bombed effectively and accurately, within 200 yards of the American positions, but a later flight mistook its bearings and dropped a string of 500-pound bombs in the midst of the American forward companies. Immediately—perhaps taking their cue from the fall of the bombs—two Lightning fighters darted in and strafed the same area. The casualties resulting from this double error have not been disclosed.

From May 22 through May 28 the action on Attu followed a set pattern: making the utmost possible use of artillery preparation, the entire American force, now numbering about 12,000 (with perhaps half that number directly engaged) advanced over difficult ridges and against stubborn resistance. But there was an immense advantage in that the attackers were not pinned down on a valley floor, naked and exposed to fire from above. They were meeting the Japanese on more nearly equal terms, but with a growing superiority in numbers and still greater superiority in firepower.

By evening of the 28th, all the surviving Japanese (except for stray snipers) were penned into the area around their main camp at the mouth of Chichagof Valley, fronting on Chichagof Harbor. They were under heavy pressure from the west, southwest and south; the American right flank, southeast of the Japanese, was comparatively weak. General Landrum decided to launch an all-out attack on the morning of the 29th. But while the American commander was making his decision, so was the Japanese commander.

Colonel Yamasaki had left perhaps a thousand men, of whom many, up to 300, were wounded. He might have stayed where he was, as so many Japanese commanders have done in similar circumstances, and let his men die where they stood, each trying to exact an American life in forfeit for his own. Yamasaki was too resourceful and imaginative a commander for that. He reasoned rightly that at this stage of the campaign the American forces would be extended to the full, in an offensive attitude. His scouts told him that the American right flank was weak.

He reasoned that American artillery emplacements far behind the front lines were likely to be lightly defended by infantry. He decided upon a plan so bold that it has been widely condemned as ludicrous or insane. Actually, it would seem better not to underrate the enemy; on this occasion his plan was such that if it had succeeded it would have been considered incredibly brilliant. Too much attention has been given to the incidental features of the plan. Yamasaki ordered the seriously wounded to commit suicide, while the lightly wounded were to take part in the attack with whatever weapons they could wield. Also, as the counter-attack developed, atrocities were committed in American aid stations which have distracted attention from the fact that to reach these aid stations, far behind the lines, Yamasaki's men had to achieve considerable military success.

From the starting point of the Japanese counter-attack to the American artillery emplacements around Engineer Hill was a distance of eight miles. Yamasaki ordered his men to jump off at 3 A.M. on May 29, break through the American lines, and—without stopping to mop up—capture the artillery positions and turn the guns on the American beachhead at Massacre Bay. In its early stages, the attack had some success on which Yamasaki cannot have counted: Company B of the 32nd Infantry was withdrawing from its positions on the floor of Chichagof Valley to a battalion kitchen in the rear when it was set upon by a horde of screaming Japanese. The completeness of the surprise is attested by the fact that this company was pulling back to get hot food: no counter-attack had been expected. The company was thrown into disorder. So were many other American units on the line of the Japanese advance. Aid stations and field hospitals were overrun, and the wounded slaughtered along with the doctors and corpsmen.

The frenzied enemy troops were pouring down toward the positions of the division engineers and the 50th Engineer Regiment when the alarm was given in their bivouac area. The important thing to remember in evaluating the effectiveness of Yamasaki's plan is that by this time his men had covered no less than five miles of the eight miles they had been assigned to regain, to reach the American artillery. The engineers, who had not been expected to have to fight as infantrymen, reached for whatever small arms were available, formed an emergency line, and soon found themselves engaged in the closest kind of fighting. Service troops and cooks joined in the struggle. As the murky daylight brightened, it was clear that the force of Japanese counter-attack had spent itself against the engineers' line. Isolated enemy parties reached one or two of the American howitzer positions, but fell just short of their goal of turning American guns upon American troops. The bulk of the credit for stemming the attack must go to the engineers.

All through the day of the 29th and the morning of the 30th, disorganized Japanese remnants were being mopped up far behind the "front." During the afternoon of the 30th, the Chichagof camp area was occupied against negligible resistance. The Battle of Attu was officially ended on June 2. Hundreds of Japanese had committed suicide by holding grenades to their heads or hearts.

In all, 2,300 Japanese died in the futile defense of Attu. Only 29 were taken alive. There were 3,000 American casualties, but most of these were wounded (1,135) or invalided out suffering from trench foot or exposure incurred through wearing faulty equipment; 400 were killed or missing.

In the case of Attu, as in the case of Tarawa, it would be idle to pretend that there were no lessons to be learned. The most gratifying feature of the operation and its aftermath was that the lessons were learned. For the recapture of Kiska (which had a garrison estimated at 10,000 men), a far larger force was assigned; it was shipped to Alaska and trained in local conditions, and it was properly equipped with suitable footwear and parkas. The softening up of Kiska by air bombardment far exceeded that of Attu.

The great expeditionary force arrived off Kiska on August 15, and sent assault troops ashore after a tremendous naval bombardment,* only to find that there were no Japanese in the landing areas. Still, there were some American casualties: due to faulty liaison, patrols fired on groups which appeared to be out of position, and were only later identified as American. Under cover of fog, the entire Japanese garrison had been evacuated from Kiska. (The suggestion that so large a force had

---

* Contributing battleships were the *Pennsylvania, New Mexico, Idaho, Mississippi* and *Tennessee.*

been removed by submarine is silly.) The strategy of attacking Attu first, and isolating Kiska, thus paid an enormous dividend. The Japanese were driven from the Western Hemisphere; the northern flank of the vast Pacific front was secure, and steps were promptly taken to bring the war home to the Japanese in their outlying northern islands. The williwaws persisted, but the artificial fog was lifted from the Aleutians.

VII. Playing Leapfrog

WITH THE CAMPAIGN on New Georgia ended, except for the mopping up of enemy remnants on the west coast between Munda and Bairoko, the South Pacific command was confronted with a strategic problem. Up to this point, its progress (first to Guadalcanal, then to the Russells and New Georgia) had been dictated by geography, by the short range of fighter aircraft and by the smallness of the forces available. Having regard to these considerations, the command had had no choice but to advance "island by island," in a process which had come to be known derisively as "island-hopping." But now the command had a choice: it could either continue the island-by-island progress, and deliver its next attack upon Kolombangara, or it could begin a leapfrogging movement and deliver its next attack upon Vella Lavella, thus bypassing Kolombangara with its large enemy garrison and powerful defenses.

One of the oldest of military maxims could be quoted as an argument against leapfrogging: "Never leave a powerful enemy force in the rear of your own forces." But such maxims had been developed in land warfare, fought under conditions totally different from those found in the archipelagoes of the Pacific. Furthermore, one could cite a fundamental of military strategy in favor of the leapfrogging method—that which concerns economy of force. For it was clear that if Kolombangara were to be frontally assaulted, the force required would be considerably greater than had been required at Munda.

Vella Lavella, unlike Kolombangara, was very lightly held by the Japanese. In the last days of the battle for Munda, there were reports that 300 additional Japanese had been garrisoned in the southwestern part of the island, but they were quickly reported to have been transferred elsewhere. It did not appear that the permanent garrison of the island numbered more than 300 men, or 500 at the outside. Its terrain was less forbidding than that of Kolombangara; it held excellent sites for airfields of moderate size, and the natives were known, from the experience of the *Helena's* survivors and the co-operation they had given the coast watchers, to be extremely well disposed to Americans and Britons.

Rear Admiral Wilkinson and Lieut. General Millard Harmon both recommended to Admiral Halsey that Kolombangara be bypassed, and that the scene of the next invasion be Vella Lavella. Halsey approved, and at the very time the capture of Munda was announced (August 7), the plan for the occupation of Vella Lavella was ordered set in motion. However, before it could be executed there was to be another brush with the Tokyo Express which the Japanese, having lost the fight on New Georgia, were now running to reinforce Vila. Barge traffic had been heavy for weeks, and PT boats had been busy trying to interrupt it, but during the night of August 6-7 the enemy elected to send in larger ships, and to cover them with a force containing a light cruiser (or large flotilla leader) and three destroyers.

As usual at this stage in this campaign, Allied intelligence was excellent, whether based upon reconnaissance or other sources of information. Long before the Japanese naval force had left the protection of the network of bases in the northern Solomons, a force of six American destroyers had been assembled at Tulagi, and conferences with representatives of the amphibious force command had been held aboard the flagship of Commander Frederick Moosbrugger, who was to be commodore of the force, while the ship lay off Koli.

Shortly after noon on the 6th the force cleared Savo and set out on a westerly course into the Solomons Sea. The weather favored the young commander: it was as foul as any the Solomons can produce, with thunder storms in unbroken succession along the route past the Russells, past Buraku, past Tetipari and Rendova to the waters south of Gizo Strait. It was 10 P.M. when the force turned north for the run through the narrows. Moosbrugger ordered a reduction of speed after a while, because he did not want enemy coast watchers on Gizo or Ganongga to see the bow waves or the wakes.

After some time on a northerly course, the force turned southeast into Blackett Strait, in case the Japanese had barges in there. There had been plenty of them on recent nights, and they had proved to be fast, heavily armed and even armored —more than a match for the plywood PT boats which at that time had nothing heavier than a 20-mm. gun to use against the barges. (As a result of several disasters and countless near-disasters in this war against the barges, PT boats began to be armed with 40-mm. and even 75-mm. guns.) As it happened, there were no Japanese barges in Blackett Strait at this time, so Moosbrugger turned back to the northwest and headed out into the wider waters of Vella Gulf.

He was heading due north, toward the Slot, when at 11:35 P.M. Dean Savage, the lookout at the masthead of the flagship, said: "Looks like a white wake, bearing 359 degrees." Moosbrugger again changed course, to leave the Japanese on his port hand. Within a few minutes, four targets were discerned, in column. The order, "Stand by to fire torpedoes to port," was given. The Japanese continued to approach without deviating from their course—a fair indication that their radar for detecting the presence of American ships was not as good as the American radar. The angle opened until the targets were almost fair on the port beam, and then Moosbrugger gave the order: "Execute—fire torpedoes!"

When the tin fish from the tubes of six destroyers were well launched on their runs, Moosbrugger circled to starboard. One of the enemy ships was illuminated by the flash of an explosion against its side, then another and another. It appears that three vessels were hit by torpedoes, including the light cruiser or flotilla leader, and the flames from this vessel silhouetted the fourth vessel in the squadron, which up to this time was undamaged.

On his new course, Moosbrugger bored in to attack with gunfire. The six destroyers opened up with their 5-inch rifles, firing over the starboard beam. The Japanese had been taken by surprise, and it took them a long time to answer—a fatally long time, because in the meanwhile the American ships compounded the damage done by the torpedoes. At first the Japanese were so confused that they fired automatic weapons into the air, evidently believing that they had been bombed. By the time they recovered their wits, their desperate answering gunfire was not good enough to do anything better than bracket Moosbrugger's flagship. At least twice, the lookouts aboard the American destroyers reported torpedoes approaching, but there were no hits.

Forty-five minutes after the first American torpedoes had been fired, the largest of the Japanese ships blew up. The water was covered with oil, much of it burning, and blobbed with the heads of Japanese sailors trying to escape its choking clutch. Moosbrugger stayed around the scene for almost an hour and a half, vainly hoping to intercept the transports which the enemy warships must have been covering. He ordered his ships to pick up Japanese survivors, but the enemy sailors pushed life rings away and swam off, screaming imprecations.

As is the case with so many of these night engagements, the precise damage inflicted upon the enemy is not known. Moosbrugger reported that the whole Japanese force had been destroyed, but when Admiral King's report was issued in Washington, eight months later and 12,000 miles away, it said merely that "the three Japanese destroyers were believed sunk." The lot of a successful commander in a night engagement is not a happy one. But Moosbrugger's outstanding performance was recognized by his immediate superiors, who at once recommended him for promotion. In no other recorded instance has so junior an officer been entrusted with the command of such a large force.

The move into Vella Lavella was laid on for August 15. There has been a great deal of misinformation issued from official sources as to the nature of the operation. Admiral King says that "the island was not occupied by the Japanese"—a statement which is palpably untrue. Immediately after the first troops had gone ashore, General MacArthur entered the claiming stakes with the assertion that the island had been "seized." As was to be shown over a period of two months, there is a world of difference between setting troops down upon a fringe of coastline and "seizing" an entire island. This fact, however, is more immediately apparent to the combat infantryman who faces death or mutilation from enemy fire than to those in command of the communiqués.

It had been expected that the greatest threat to the occupation would come from Japanese air power based in the northern Solomons. This expectation was fully realized. All the efforts of the Thirteenth Air Force, and Navy and Marine Corps air groups associated with it, could not keep the enemy's fields completely non-operational. The airfields on Banika and the newly captured field at Munda, together with the emergency strip at Segi, were invaluable in bringing air cover close enough to the front so that the enemy's most determined air attacks were broken up. It is interesting to note that the planes of Fighting Squadron 12, led by Lieut. Commander Joseph C. ("Jumping Joe") Clifton, were detached at his request from the *Saratoga* and based temporarily at Guadalcanal so that they could participate in the central Solomons offensive. In their first assignment over Kolombangara they met no opposition, but they stayed to take part in the actions which developed over the Vella Lavella beachhead.

During the afternoon of August 14, the force which was to occupy Vella Lavella left the rendezvous area in Iron-Bottom Bay. The troops, comprising the 35th Infantry (25th Division), were embarked in destroyer-transports, protected by destroyers whose names have come to personify these campaigns up the Slot: the *Nicholas, Radford, Taylor, O'Bannon* and *Chevalier*. At dawn on the 15th, the infantrymen were set ashore on the southwestern part of Vella Lavella, and the absence of effective Japanese opposition gave rise to the premature and over-optimistic assertion that the island had been "seized."

The enemy's reaction in the air was reasonably prompt: an extraordinary assortment of antiquated planes from land fields and seaplane bases in the Buin-Shortland area and from fields farther north on Bougainville and Buka was assembled and thrown into action against the landing craft which followed the APDs to the beach, carrying equipment and supplies. It was in repelling one of these attacks that Fighting Squadron 12 first distinguished itself. The enemy command knew it could not retain air control in the northern Solomons, and was unwilling to commit large numbers of new aircraft in a lost cause, but made frequent and heavy attacks, by both day and night, with what it had.

During the afternoon of August 17, the American command got word of the approach of an enemy force containing numerous barges, escorted by four destroyers. Captain T. J. Ryan, Jr., using the *Nicholas* as his squadron leader, was detailed to intercept the Japanese, taking with him the *O'Bannon, Taylor* and *Chevalier*. A Catalina flying boat, assigned to provide reconnaissance for the task force, reported the position of the Japanese to Captain Ryan at 11:35 P.M., but at the same moment a Japanese reconnaissance seaplane reported the position of Ryan's ships. The enemy was able to strike first: several planes attacked with light bombs, but none of the American destroyers was hit. Out of bombs, the Japanese aircraft followed the formation and marked its path with flares, although the night was brilliant with moonlight.

The enemy ships had not turned away, as might have been expected. At 12:45 A.M. they were advancing on a collision course, but two minutes later the Japanese commander changed his mind and his course. Captain Ryan had to engage in a stern chase to bring the opponent under his guns. He planned to tackle the destroyers first, and then work over the barges on his way back, since these slower craft would not have been able to escape. It proved impossible to maneuver into position for a torpedo attack, and the leading American destroyers had fired only a few rounds of shells when Japanese aircraft again appeared and tried to break up the attack. They concentrated on the *Nicholas,* as leader, and obtained some near misses. However, Ryan's destroyers were able to set at least two of the enemy ships on fire, without being themselves hit, before the decision was made to abandon the chase and return to pot some sitting ducks.

Deserted by their escort, the barges were virtually helpless against vastly superior firepower. The destroyers were able to use both their main 5-inch batteries and their rapid-fire 40-mms., and the enemy craft were smothered in a hail of explosives. How many were destroyed is uncertain, but it is improbable that any escaped. If these men and their supplies (which included gasoline) were intended to reinforce the Japanese garrisons on Vella Lavella, there can have been few who reached shore alive—and still fewer who were fit for action. At the moment Ryan was beginning to retire, his squadron was attacked for the third time by enemy aircraft, which shook the *O'Bannon* with near misses. But that was as close as they got.

Most of the task of clearing Vella Lavella fell to the 14th Brigade (under Brigadier L. Potter) of the 3rd New Zealand Division, which was landed on September 18. The Japanese had fallen back before the American assault troops, but had not been run to earth where they could be destroyed. The New Zealanders made small leapfrog movements around both coasts and caught the Japanese in a pincers on October 5. The following night, when Potter's men were preparing an assault, the bulk of the Japanese (estimated at 500 men) were evacuated by barge. When the New Zealanders closed their pincers on October 9, there was nothing in between the two arms.

Although the campaign on Vella Lavella was dragging on far longer than had been expected, and was resulting in the killing of comparatively few Japanese, it was achieving its strategic purpose. The Japanese had seen the futility of attempting to maintain their positions on Kolombangara, and were trying to evacuate their garrisons. Moreover, now that Arundel had been secured and had become the site of several powerful artillery batteries, the enemy on Kolombangara was given added, and more tangible, reason for wanting to leave. The rain of shells upon his encampments around Vila made the area untenable.

Throughout the latter part of September and into early October there was frantic enemy barge traffic by night through the waters between Kolombangara, Vella Lavella, Choiseul and Bougainville. At the turn of the month, the Japanese decided that more effective measures must be taken to bring the evacuation to a quick conclusion. A convoy containing eleven ships, including the escorting destroyers and gunboats, was detected moving south from the Buka area toward Bougainville Strait, and was attacked by Liberators of the Thirteenth Air Force. One destroyer is believed to have been sunk, and other ships were damaged. For a few nights the Japanese again relied on barge traffic. But during the first three nights of October, Admiral Wilkinson assigned destroyer squadrons, including one commanded by Commander Alvin D. Chandler from the *Nicholas,* to the task of destroying these barges, which had proved too tough for the PT boats to handle except at the risk of heavy losses. The destroyers illuminated the narrow straits off southern Kolombangara with star shells, and usually found a chain of barges sneaking along close inshore. In one night they sank 20 barges, killing the personnel with which they were crowded, or throwing them into the water to make their way as best they could to an unfriendly shore. In the three nights, more than 40 barges were sunk. Considering the overcrowding common aboard Japanese craft, at least 4,000 men must have been involved in the attempted evacuation, and perhaps many more.

The enemy decided to make another major effort, with a large convoy, lavishly escorted, during the night of October 6-7. During the afternoon of the 6th, the destroyers *Selfridge* (flag), *Chevalier* and *O'Bannon,* under Captain Frank R. Walker, were returning to Tulagi after an uneventful sweep up the Slot when they received radio orders to reverse course. Allied reconnaissance had detected a Japanese force southward bound, divided into three groups: first, a light cruiser (or flotilla leader) and four destroyers; second, four destroyers, and third, a group of large landing craft or similar personnel carriers. Admiral Wilkinson was having difficulty in assembling a force of sufficient power to meet the Japanese concentration, but decided to use Walker's three destroyers, and three others commanded by Commander Harold O. Larson. The latter's squadron was to rendezvous with Walker, and pass under his command, some time before midnight.

Unfortunately, Larson's squadron was delayed. Unfortunately, also, the Japanese had reconnaissance planes out which discovered Walker's destroyers and made an accurate tally of their number in the light of numerous parachute flares. The Japanese had the advantage in that their forces were already concentrated, while the Americans' were still divided.

The *Chevalier* reported the first contact; the enemy force was steaming down the Slot, and at this time was due west of the heavily outnumbered and outgunned American squadron. Soon it resolved itself into two columns, each containing four destroyers, and one of them headed by the cruiser or flotilla leader. The Jap personnel carriers were still over the horizon somewhere. Captain Walker maneuvered his force so as to leave the enemy to starboard, and prepared for a torpedo attack. The Japanese appeared to be trying to box the Americans between their two columns, but before they could achieve this, Walker gave the order: "Fire torpedoes." The projectiles were fired simultaneously from the destroyers, each of which had ten tubes. Three Japanese ships, including the largest, were reported hit by torpedoes. As soon as the tin fish had finished their run, Walker ordered his ships to open with their guns. His flagship engaged a destroyer which fell out of place in the formation, her erratic course marked by the flames shooting from her hull. The *Chevalier* had a destroyer dead in the water, and quickly reduced it to a flaming hulk, torn by internal explosions. The *O'Bannon* concentrated on the largest enemy ship, which her captain, Commander Donald J. MacDonald, believed to be a light cruiser. Fires spread relentlessly through her hull, and then, says MacDonald, she "blew up with the most terrific explosion it has ever been my pleasure to observe." The destroyer which had been the *Chevalier's* target also "burned furiously and then blew up with a terrific explosion," MacDonald reported. The two other destroyers in the first Japanese column were both hit, and withdrew to fight their fires, but not until they had engaged in a gunnery duel with the American cans, repeatedly bracketing them but failing to score direct hits.

The tenor of American success was broken when the *Chevalier* was suddenly illuminated by the blinding flash of a torpedo striking her port side amidships. She was cut in two, and her stern half swung into the path of the *O'Bannon*. MacDonald could not maneuver out of the way, nor could he arrest the motion of his own ship sufficiently to avoid collision. The *O'Bannon's* bow crashed into the *Chevalier's* after engine room, doing more damage than it took. Temporarily, MacDonald lost steering control, which greatly complicated his task of maintaining gunfire against the retreating Japanese ships, assessing and controlling his own damage, and standing by the remnants of the *Chevalier,* which were beginning to sink rapidly, in order to pick up survivors. About this time, also, the *Selfridge* received a hit on the bridge which blew at least six men overboard, just when she had been preparing to make a second torpedo run against the Japanese.

MacDonald ascertained that while the *O'Bannon's* bow was buckled, the only large hole could be virtually closed by patching with timber. With this job in hand he again turned his attention to the *Chevalier,* whose captain, Commander George

R. Wilson, signaled: "We are going fast." MacDonald still could not maneuver the *O'Bannon* directly alongside the *Chevalier's* remains, so he ordered the boats lowered to pick up survivors—just as three Japanese bombers swooped down to attack. They missed the American ships, but the water already was filled with men abandoning the *Chevalier,* and many must have been injured by the near misses. At this critical moment another surface force was reported approaching: fortunately, it proved to be the squadron under Commander Larson, who undertook to stand off the surviving Japanese and give the *Selfridge* any assistance she needed, leaving the *O'Bannon* to care for the survivors of the *Chevalier.* In all, 85 per cent of the latter's complement were taken aboard the *O'Bannon,* although many were frightfully burned or otherwise injured, and several died shortly after they had been picked from the sea by the *O'Bannon's* men, scores of whom jumped overboard to help in the rescue work.

The battle went on, with the *Selfridge* credited with hits on at least one of the Japanese destroyers in the second column, and Larson's destroyers completing the rout. The judgment of South Pacific headquarters was that three Japanese warships, including the largest, had been sunk, and possibly a fourth, while at least two had been heavily damaged. The enemy retired, having accomplished his mission; the *O'Bannon* retired at a fraction of her normal speed; the *Selfridge* retired with her wounds—and was passed on the way to Tulagi by a Catalina flying boat bearing the six men blown from her bridge during the battle. They had been picked up from a raft blown overboard by the explosion which cast them into the sea. Despite the cost, it was a notable victory for the "tin-can navy."

No name has been formally conferred on this engagement; it is sometimes known as the Battle of Choiseul. However it may be named, this encounter effectively ended Japanese attempts to evacuate their personnel from Vella Lavella and Kolombangara. Most of the men they could hope to save had already been taken off or drowned in the attempt; any effort to rescue the remnants would be too costly. Evidently the enemy command in the northern Solomons was still anxious to buy time, for in the first days of October it took the extraordinary step of challenging the overwhelming Allied air supremacy over

Vella Lavella, in order to drop supplies by parachute to the beleaguered troops who were being compressed into an ever smaller pocket by American and New Zealand columns.

The Japanese jig was already up on Kolombangara, however. On October 6, elements of the 27th Infantry and the 169th Infantry were landed on the southern part of the island, and advanced against token opposition to the area of Vila. This key position was occupied within four days, during which 600 Japanese had to be rooted out of holes, run down and killed, in the fixed pattern of Pacific island warfare.

On Vella Lavella, where about 300 Japanese had been killed by Americans and New Zealanders, organized resistance ended by October 12; two days later, General MacArthur was able to proclaim: "The entire New Georgia group of islands now is in our hands." The campaign which had faltered so often since the first easy landings at Rendova on June 30 was at last crowned with success.

From northwestern Vella Lavella, it was only 60 miles to the network of Japanese bases in the Shortland area: Faisi, Poporang and Ballale. It was only 75 miles to the still more important network on the south coast of Bougainville: Jakohina, Buin, Kahili, Kara and Tonolei. There was a line of Allied air bases stitched up the Solomons chain to Vella Lavella: five fields on Guadalcanal, two in the Russells, three on New Georgia (Segi, Munda and Ondonga) and Barakoma on Vella Lavella. But the high command felt that it was necessary to carry air support still closer to the beachheads where the main fighting in the northern Solomons was to be, against a Japanese force on Bougainville and Buka which was variously estimated at 25,000 to 50,000 men.

The next stepping stone along the route was in the Treasury Islands, 50 miles northwest of Vella Lavella, and almost equidistant between that newly captured base and the objective on Bougainville (later disclosed to be the Empress Augusta Bay area). Consequently, at dawn on October 27, after the usual preliminary warship bombardment, elements of the 8th New Zealand Brigade went ashore on Mono Island, largest of the Treasury group (it is about seven miles in diameter), and also on Stirling, an islet to the south of Mono. The Japanese had mortars set up to cover the beaches, but most of their small

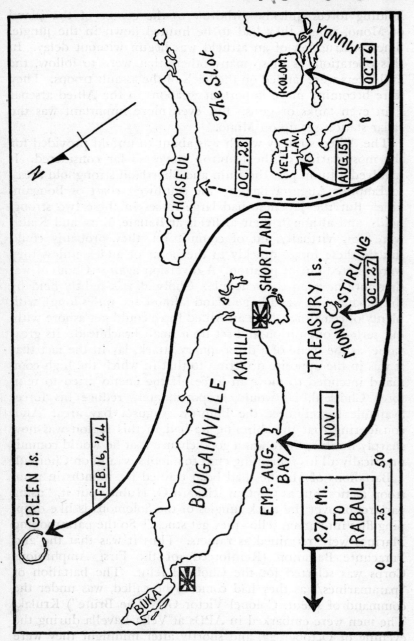

holding forces quickly withdrew to the center of the island of Mono, where they had to be hunted down in the jungle. The construction of an airfield was begun without delay. In this operation, as in so many others that were to follow, the bulldozers were landed on the heels of the assault troops. They were becoming more important weapons in the Allied arsenal than even tanks or guns. But even more important was the radar station set up on Mono.

The Allied strategy which was about to unfold provided for the most daring of the leapfrog moves so far considered. It involved a jump past the Buin and Shortland stronghold areas, to Empress Augusta Bay, on the southwest coast of Bougainville. But the Japanese had large forces in these two strongholds, and although their airfields at Ballale, Kara and Kahili were now virtually out of commission, they probably could shuttle these forces quickly to the point of attack unless they were feinted out of position. A diversion against Choiseul was therefore next on the schedule. Choiseul was lightly held by the Japanese; it was a large island (almost 100 miles long), with plenty of coastline where an Allied force could get ashore without serious opposition and set up a small beachhead. Its great value, as the scene of a diversionary attack, lay in the fact that it was in the opposite direction to that in which the high command intended to move in force. If the enemy tried to reinforce Choiseul, he would proportionately reduce his forces available to reinforce the Empress Augusta Bay area. And, considering that the shipping he had in this region was now sharply limited, there was a good chance that he would commit practically all his remaining craft to a fool's errand on Choiseul.

Battalions of Marines had been trained for months in paratroop tactics, but as Captain Richard G. Hubler put it, "using paratroops over the thick jungles of the Solomons is like dropping flies into green jello—they get stuck." So the paratrooping Marines were retrained as raiders. Thus it was that the 2nd Parachute Battalion (Reinforced) of the First Amphibious Corps was selected for the Choiseul feint. The battalion of "paramarines," as they had come to be called, was under the command of Lieut. Colonel Victor G. ("The Brute") Krulak. The men were embarked in APDs at Vella Lavella during the evening of October 27, and shortly after midnight they were set ashore at the abandoned native village of Voza, roughly midway down the southwestern coast of Choiseul. Higgins boats left behind for local operations were run into hiding places beneath the overhanging trees of the Zinoa Islands while the paramarines prepared to push inland at dawn. The Japanese detected the operation—as it was hoped that they would —and reacted quickly by bombing and strafing the Higgins boats, but without causing serious damage.

Krulak's men pushed inland a short distance to a knoll which could be reached only by a single trail, so steep that men had to climb it virtually hand over hand. Foxholes were dug, and a defense perimeter was set up. Patrols found about 200 Japs at a barge harbor called Sangigai, seven miles southeast of Voza, and a somewhat smaller number at Warrior River, 18 miles northwest of Voza. Somewhere on the island there were 3,500 others.

To worry the Japanese as much as possible, it was announced by the high command that "strong American forces" had landed on Choiseul, and Krulak made plans to launch simultaneous attacks against both the enemy concentrations within range, to heighten the illusion of a large, mobile force. A combat patrol sent toward Sangigai shot up one Japanese barge found on the beach en route, killed a few of the enemy—and let the rest escape to tell their story.

At dawn on October 30, two companies (about 200 men each) set out for Sangigai, one along the beach and one, led by Krulak personally, traveling by a parallel, inland route. The Japanese at Sangigai were panicked by the attack launched by the American shoreward company, and ran directly into the fire of the inland company. In an hour and a half of confused fighting in the dim, irreligious light of a diabolical jungle, the enemy fled, leaving 72 dead. There were seven Marines dead and 12 wounded. The barge base was wrecked before the two companies hurried back to their little fortress, carrying their wounded. The terrain was so rough that 24 men were assigned to each stretcher, eight men to work in three shifts.

At dawn of November 1, more than two companies of the paramarines were embarked in Higgins boats and set ashore beyond the Warrior River mouth—three miles to the northwest of it. Their object was to raid the Japanese camp there and to bombard a supply dump on Guppy Island with mortars. Both these missions were accomplished, 42 enemy dead were counted, whereas only two Americans were killed, one was missing and two were wounded. The re-embarkation at Warrior River proved difficult, in the face of enemy fire, and one Higgins boat was lost, but air cover and the assistance of PT boats turned the trick.

The feint on Choiseul appeared to have succeeded, because that night Tokyo broadcasts spoke of a landing on Choiseul by 20,000 American Marines. However, the local Japanese commander would be certain soon to discover that all the American attacks had been made in less than battalion strength. The only hope was that he might already have asked for reinforcements from Bougainville, and that these would be dispatched before he discovered his error. This seems to have been the case. The American command decided on November 2 that its assault forces at Empress Augusta Bay were securely ashore, and therefore the Choiseul feint had served its purpose. Supplies were dropped by air to the paramarines that same day, and plans were made to remove them at midnight, November 3. The evacuation was carried out a couple of hours behind schedule; a few hours later (at dawn) the Japanese launched a heavy assault on the knoll which had served as Krulak's base.

During the night of October 31-November 1, the largest Allied invasion force yet seen in the Pacific ploughed through the waters of the Solomons toward southern Bougainville. (There were extensive naval operations in support of the forthcoming invasion, but it will be more convenient to consider them later.) The commander of the entire amphibious operation was Rear Admiral Theodore S. Wilkinson. The commander of the invading troops was Lieut. General Alexander A. Vandegrift, who had remained in the South Pacific to command the First Amphibious Corps after the death of Major General C. D. Barrett. (Vandegrift already had been ordered to Washington to become Commandant of the Marine Corps.) The great majority of the assault troops were comprised in the 3rd Marine Division, under Major General Allan Hal Turnage, and included the 3rd, 9th, 12th (artillery) and 21st Marine Regiments, with the Raider Battalions attached.

The transports and their supporting craft stayed as long as

possible on a course which would have carried them to the Buin-Shortland area. This was to deceive the Japanese into believing that this great force was going to make a frontal assault on the main centers of Japanese strength. Finally, the invasion armada swung to the northwest, on a course which would bring it to the coast of Bougainville at Empress Augusta Bay. Shortly after 5 A.M., November 1, it was lying offshore. There was, as yet, no reaction from the enemy.

At 5:47 a destroyer fired two rounds on to the beach in the hope of drawing counter-fire from the Japanese, and thus inducing them to disclose the positions of their batteries. There was no answer. At 6:01 all the warships within range began shelling the beach line. Still there was no answer. At 6:30 the warships' gunners raised their sights and began firing on more inland positions, while the transports and their covering craft kept up the drumfire on the beach. Beneath an umbrella of Navy and Marine Corps Corsairs (F4Us), Army Airacobras (P-39s) and Royal New Zealand Air Force Warhawks (P-40s), the tactical bombers came in: Avengers carrying one-ton bombs, and Dauntless dive-bombers with 1,000-pounders. For the first time, the Japanese reacted: with anti-aircraft fire against the bombers. As usual, it looked as though there could be nothing left alive on the beach.

As usual, this appearance was deceptive. When the first waves of assault troops began moving in toward the beach at 7:30, the Japanese who had held their fire so well snapped into action. Their main concentrations were on Puruata Island, just off Cape Torokina, and on the cape itself. These were on the right flank of the invading Marines. On the left flank, the Japanese were present in much less strength, and the beachhead in that sector was secured on schedule.

In the immediate vicinity of Cape Torokina (the sector of the 3rd Marine Regiment, under Colonel George W. McHenry), Japanese artillery, mortar and automatic-weapons fire against the landing craft and the troops crossing the beach was so heavy that the first two assault waves were effectively destroyed, and unable to secure a beachhead. The third wave thus became, for all practical purposes, a new first wave. It, too, took heavy casualties, but its members were able to scratch a toehold in the edge of the jungle. Carrying parties bringing in fresh supplies of ammunition for the assault troops had to fight their way ashore. It was not until late afternoon that the southern beachhead, in the Cape Torokina sector, could be considered secure.

The extent to which enemy air power in the northern Solomons had been crippled was shown this day: not a single Japanese tactical aircraft appeared to challenge the Allied fighters on patrol or to attack the invading ground forces. It was not until hours later that the first enemy reaction in the air developed, and this was produced by multi-engined aircraft which had had to fly from fields on New Britain and New Ireland, hundreds of miles away.

During the night, the Japanese tried their habitual tactics of trying to infiltrate the American lines, but there was no concerted enemy counter-attack on a major scale for several days. In the meantime the Navy's Construction Battalions had begun work on an airfield on November 3. (The field was first used on November 24.)

Since the 3rd Marine Regiment had taken the heaviest beating on D-day, it was soon withdrawn from the immediate vicinity of Cape Torokina, and assigned to the extreme left flank, where things were quieter. Ironically, this was the sector where the Japanese decided to make their first substantial counter-attack. Down from the north, by barge, came 500 to 600 enemy troops with enough rations for only one day: they were supposed to over-run American positions within that time, and thereafter live on captured supplies. The Marine company on the far left of the regimental sector took the full brunt of the Japanese attack, delivered with a 3-to-1 superiority in numbers, and was forced to fall back. Reinforcements halted the Japanese onrush, but it took more than 24 hours and a number of Sherman tanks—the first mediums used in the South Pacific, which would have been so welcome at Munda—to turn the Japanese attack into a retreat.

The invasion was now a week old, and the 37th Division under Major General Robert S. Beightler was brought in. Eventually, the plan was for the Fourteenth Corps to take over the entire operation. There was bitter attritional warfare for many weeks, with especially sharp fighting at the end of the third week in November (the engagement known as the Battle of

Piva Forks). But the beachhead was expanded, despite the difficulties of terrain, and more airfields were begun. Just before Christmas, the Americal Division, under Major General John R. Hodge, was landed to relieve the 3rd Marine Division. The Fourteenth Corps of Major General Oscar W. Griswold relieved the First Amphibious Corps of Major General Geiger. In March, the Japanese assembled what was, for them, a heavy concentration of artillery. More surprising, they carried it by hand (in disassembled form) up and down mountain trails which were all but impassable for an unburdened man. The American perimeter at Empress Augusta Bay was still too small: the enemy's artillery was able to bring at least one of the airfields under fire. (If the perimeter had been expanded to give the airfields immunity from artillery, it would have had to be manned by a much larger force.) The Japanese infantry succeeded in denting the perimeter temporarily, and by this time, a total of 8,000 Japanese dead were said to have been counted on Bougainville. It remains only to be added that 18 months later, when the tide of war had swept thousands of miles beyond Bougainville, Allied troops were still fighting the bypassed Japanese there, and dying in its jungles. But by this time the job had been turned over to the Australians.

There was an abundance of naval activity in the northern Solomons at the time of the invasion of Bougainville. Simultaneously with the extension of amphibious operations to the area around southern Bougainville, cruiser forces pummeled enemy positions on northern Bougainville and on adjacent Buka Island, to guard against reaction from that quarter. There were large American naval forces, including carriers, available to support the Empress Augusta Bay landing, but most of them were not intended to be used for close support. The major part of this burden fell upon a task force commanded by Rear Admiral Aaron S. Merrill, and comprising the *Cleveland, Columbia, Denver* and *Montpelier,* with two divisions of destroyers under Captain Arleigh Burke.

These ships laid down the heaviest fire on the Empress Augusta Bay beaches before the landing, and then withdrew to prepare themselves for the expected surface action. One division of destroyers, directly under Captain Burke, went all the way back to Hathorn Sound (between Kolombangara and New

Georgia) to refuel; Merrill took the cruisers and the other destroyers toward Vella Lavella, where they cruised during the
middle of the day. They were squared away by 1 P.M.

Japanese naval forces previously reported around Rabaul
included five cruisers (two heavy, three light) and ten destroyers. This morning, an American scout plane saw four cruisers
and six destroyers entering St. George's Channel, between New
Britain and New Ireland. It was not clear whether they were
a part of the forces previously reported, or an addition to the
total enemy strength in the area. Merrill was ordered to intercept any attempt by any or all of these forces to attack the
vulnerable beachhead and the vulnerable transports lying offshore there.

It was not long before Merrill got word that an enemy task
group containing four cruisers and six destroyers was advancing
on a southeasterly course. He had several factors to consider.
His first responsibility was to protect the beachhead. By traveling far out to sea to meet the enemy, he could have plenty of
room to maneuver. His was the only cruiser squadron left
which was available for this duty, and it behooved him to take
no unnecessary chances. If he elected to stay closer to the
beachhead and engage the enemy there, he could reduce the
chances of his being detected, because he could travel at lower
speed. Merrill chose the latter.

Burke's destroyers rejoined the cruisers at dusk. The evening
was uneventful, but at 2:22 A.M., November 2, some minelayers retiring from Cape Moltke reported that they were being
followed. A Japanese snooper plane had been watching them
during their operation, and now, the squadron leader *Renshaw*
reported, he was "bringing my snooper with me."

Five minutes later Merrill's ships, on a north-northwest
course, made contact with a group of enemy ships, 38,000 yards
away, on a west-northwest bearing. Two other groups were
quickly detected. At first it was believed that the center group
contained four cruisers, and that the destroyers were on each
flank. Merrill ordered Burke in at once to make a torpedo
attack, and ordered the other destroyer division, under Commander B. L. Austin, to work out a torpedo solution and prepare to follow Burke's division. Merrill was determined to
take no needless risks with his cruisers, because the Japanese

were using a 24-inch torpedo with a warhead twice as powerful as that of the standard 21-inch "fish." (It is likely that these were the torpedoes which sank the *Helena* and severely damaged the *Honolulu, St. Louis, Leander* and *Australia* with single hits.) Merrill planned to open fire when Burke's torpedoes were running through the Japanese formation, throwing it into confusion. Actually, he opened at 2:45, three minutes earlier than intended, because one of the Japanese columns was already turning out of the path of the torpedoes.

The range was 18,000 yards—long, but by no means excessive, for the 6-inch guns of which the *Cleveland*-class cruisers had 12 each. The Japanese did not reply at once: they were launching seaplanes to spot for them. Then their fire was heavier than expected, for there were groups of ten splashes made by 8-inch shells, from two heavy cruisers of the *Tone* class. Merrill's ships were outgunned.

The Japanese warships fired star shells and their seaplanes dropped parachute flares. The night, which had been rough, rainswept and hideously black, was now rough, rainswept and hideously light. The Japanese gunnery was excellent; their salvo dispersion was slight; they dropped salvoes consistently close to the American ships; there were several straddles with close patterns. There was no denying that the Japanese deserved to score more hits than they did. But the old rule that while "good gunnery can give you straddles, only God can give you hits," worked in the Americans' favor. Perhaps, as Merrill put it, it was "because we led purer lives." However, he did not put his entire reliance upon pure living as a defense: he kept the force zigzagging constantly at high speed, laid smoke, and had star shells fired with fuses set to go off just short of the Japanese ships, so that the glare would blind enemy gunners engaged in visual range-finding. (Such tactics would be virtually useless against radar range-finding.)

At the beginning of the action, Merrill had succeeded in crossing the enemy's T. American gunners and torpedomen alike scored heavily on several Japanese ships and the enemy admitted the loss of a light cruiser and two destroyers, while others must have been seriously damaged. Thirty-one Knot Burke chased them half way across the Solomons Sea (the action had begun only 30 miles off Cape Torokina), trying to pick off cripples, before he was obliged to give up the pursuit. The American force had no ships sunk. Of the cruisers, only the *Denver* had suffered substantial damage, from three shell hits. The nose cap of one 8-inch shell penetrated an unarmored part of the *Columbia's* side and lodged in the canvas locker (still known, anachronistically, as the sail locker). The destroyers had fared little worse: The *Spence* had taken a shell hit near the waterline and was slowed by water getting into the fuel tanks; the *Foote* had suffered most severely of all the American ships, taking a torpedo which evidently had been intended by the enemy for one of the American cruisers.

The engagement was a clear-cut defeat for the Japanese: they at no time were anywhere near gun range of the soft-shelled targets in Empress Augusta Bay.

At 8 A.M. a group of Japanese aircraft attacked one of Merrill's destroyer divisions, and at 8:10 no less than 67 enemy planes attacked the rest of the force. They did no damage, and several were shot down.

Although it was ineffective, the strength of the Japanese strike showed that Rabaul and its chain of airfields was still potent and could not be lightly challenged. Admiral Halsey now had two carriers in his Third Fleet and he would have liked to use them to challenge Rabaul. But despite all its bombing and alleged punishment at the hands of General MacArthur's fliers, Rabaul was still considered too formidable for the aircraft which could be flown from two carriers, especially when one of them was a light carrier carrying only 40 planes or so in a composite squadron. Therefore, Halsey ordered Rear Admiral Frederick C. Sherman to take the *Saratoga* and the *Princeton* into position for launching an attack on the Buka and Bonis airfields, a hundred miles north of Empress Augusta Bay. These neutralizing raids were executed on November 2, and had scarcely ended when Sherman received orders from Halsey to attack Rabaul, after all. It had been decided that with so great a concentration of enemy warships in Simpson Harbor, the danger to the Empress Augusta Bay beachhead was too great.

Why it took Sherman's force three days to get into position for the Rabaul attack has not been disclosed. But it was not until the morning of November 5 that the *Saratoga's* Air Group 12, under Commander Howard Caldwell, and the *Princeton's* group reached the air over the enemy fortress built around the great volcano of Rabaul. It had been found possible to send in almost a hundred planes, because land-based Navy fighters had been sent out from Munda to maintain the combat air patrol over the carriers during this crucial period when their own planes were away.

The fighter pilots of Lieut. Commander "Jumping Joe" Clifton's squadron had had no experience in combat save that won over Vella Lavella; now they were outnumbered, 2 to 1 or 3 to 1, by Japanese fighters who used every trick in the book to draw them off from the bombers they were assigned to protect. Under Clifton's vocally boisterous but highly effective leadership, the fighters fulfilled their mission superbly. Half the enemy fighters were listed as destroyed, and one-fourth as damaged. Only three American planes were lost. The dive-bombers and torpedo planes had a field day. The former claimed one enemy cruiser sunk and five damaged; the torpedo plane pilots listed two cruisers and two destroyers sunk, as well as four merchantmen; the high command's distillation of these reports came out as six cruisers and two destroyers damaged.

As of November 5, Rabaul seemed to be still tough, but by no means impregnable. Flushed with the success of his first carrier operations in more than a year, Halsey signaled urgently to Admiral Nimitz at Pearl Harbor and got temporary reinforcements: three carriers (*Essex, Bunker Hill* and *Independence*) under Rear Admiral Alfred E. Montgomery could be spared for just a few days before heading back north for the impending invasion of the Gilbert Islands.

It was November 11 when the two task groups were in position, about 200 miles from Rabaul. Once again, land-based Navy fighters had been called up to cover the carriers while their own fighters were away. The approach of the American air groups had been carefully and thoroughly scouted by the Japanese. Rabaul had been fully alerted in every department: most of the warships had fled the harbor, most of the merchantmen were under way, the enemy's aircraft had got off the ground, there was a cloud of fighters overhead, the most dreaded anti-aircraft concentration in the Southwest Pacific was up to its usual standard. Even the weather was on the enemy's side: there was a heavy overcast over Simpson Harbor. Small wonder that one wit, in Bombing Squadron 9 (flying from the *Essex*) radioed back to his carrier: "Rabaul in sight—notify next of kin." As it developed, seven American planes were lost, but the Hellcat fighters exacted a toll of 24 Japanese planes, and several ships were heavily damaged, including destroyers, while a light cruiser was believed to have been sunk. It could have been much worse.

And it was much worse when the carriers began to retire. About 1:30 P.M., no less than 120 Japanese aircraft began to stream out of the western sky to attack the American task force. There was a mad scramble to get the maximum number of American fighters off the decks; then there was a madder scramble in the air as these fighters tried to gain sufficient altitude before the Japanese dive-bombers could attack. Some of the American bombing planes still in the air were caught in the anti-aircraft fire of their own ships. The Japanese tried every technique and tactic they knew; many came close, but none scored a direct hit. More than 50 were listed as shot down, for a loss of only three American aircraft. Participants in the engagement put the Japanese loss at a minimum of 90 planes, and probably more than a hundred. There had been a lot of shooting in 60 excited minutes.

In their communiqués at this period, the Japanese began to sink American ships wholesale. Within two weeks, Tokyo had "sunk" or "damaged" no less than 96 American or Allied warships, and those "sunk" included several battleships, several carriers and several cruisers. There was no word of truth in these assertions. The only loss at this time was the destroyer-transport *McKean*. The Emperor of Japan was involved in the hoax, and awarded a rescript to Admiral Osami Nagano, chief of the naval general staff, for these purely fictitious feats of derring-do.

With the establishment of a firm foothold at Empress Augusta Bay, the eastern arm of an amphibious pincers closing on Rabaul had been forged. The final blows shaping it were struck by American destroyers and cruisers.

On November 16, Captain Arleigh Burke was operating with four destroyers and his usual verve off Bougainvile and Buka. His ships pumped 101 tons of shells into Buka Passage airfield and the installations surrounding it. When daylight came,

Japanese torpedo planes attacked the squadron ineffectively, but there was not an enemy surface ship to be seen.

The situation had changed slightly by November 25. Burke's destroyers encountered an enemy force containing four destroyers and two larger vessels, which may have been either flotilla leaders or light cruisers. The action was joined 90 miles southeast of Rabaul at 1:50 A.M. and continued until Burke's ships were running out of ammunition. The purpose of the Japanese foray has never been established. Burke knew at once that he was outnumbered and outgunned, but was fortunate in having the enemy ships divided into two groups of three, so that he could tackle each in turn. The first attack was made with torpedoes, and Burke believes the Japanese were unaware of his presence until two of their destroyers were struck by torpedoes. These vessels disappeared from the Americans' view so quickly that they are believed to have sunk immediately, leaving few if any survivors. The third ship in the nearer enemy force was then brought under gunfire, since it had stayed on an even keel despite two reported torpedo hits. Burke detached one of his destroyers to finish off the cripple, and started north at top speed in pursuit of the three vessels which still had not been seriously damaged. It was not until this time that the first Japanese torpedoes were fired at Burke's ships, and all missed.

The three American ships remaining with Burke concentrated their fire on the largest of the Japanese vessels. "I knew we were getting hits with our 5-inchers from 7,000 yards but he wasn't slowing down," Burke said later. "Our boys were firing so fast that many collapsed from gas fumes in the gun mounts, and from sheer exhaustion. Finally we got close enough so that I knew the shells from all three ships were hitting him. He was burning and exploding all over. Just as we prepared to open up with torpedoes again, he sank with a terrific explosion."

The cripple, meanwhile, had been polished off, and a fifth Japanese ship had been damaged. The sixth, if hit, does not appear to have been critically damaged, because she did not slacken speed. An hour and 40 minutes had passed, and the chase had led straight to the mouth of St. George's Channel. There were only 12 shells left for the forward gun of his flagship, and other gun mounts were almost as low. Reluctantly, faced with the exhaustion of his ammunition and a shortage of fuel, Burke had to call off the chase.

Burke and his ships were in action again off the east coast of the northern Solomons on December 20, shelling a Japanese bivouac area at Tinputs Harbor. Three days later, a cruiser and destroyer force shelled Buka and Bonis airfields, and on the 27th the Kieta area, which included a long-abandoned airfield, was shelled.

Weeks before American and New Zealand forces executed the last leapfrog operation of the Solomons campaign (moving into the Green Islands, north of Buka, on February 16, 1944), the tedious process begun at Rendova had served its strategic purpose. Rabaul, completely exposed on the east, was being reduced to impotence by a similar campaign waged against it from the west. There can be no doubt that the campaign through the Solomon Islands was strategically necessary. For without it, the task of neutralizing Rabaul would have been ten times more difficult. Success in the Solomons, too, had a bearing on the later decision to bypass Truk. There can be no doubt that the high command was obliged to conduct the early stages of the Solomons campaign on an "island-by-island" basis. And there can be do doubt (although there will inevitably be criticism of certain phases of the operation) that the decision to conduct the later stages of the Solomons campaign on a leap-frogging technique saved thousands of lives and shortened the war against Japan by many months.

VIII. Closing the Pincers on Rabaul

WHILE THE SOUTH PACIFIC forces under Admiral Halsey were engaged in the bitter-end, time-consuming process of securing their hold on Guadalcanal in the closing months of 1942, the Southwest Pacific forces under General MacArthur were engaged in an almost identical campaign in Papua, near the southeastern tip of New Guinea. The immedate objectives, Buna and Gona, had no value except in so far as they represented bases denied to the enemy, for only with difficulty could they be developed into bases from which further Allied offensives could be launched.

In the first months of 1943 offensive activity on the ground was limited to a push northwestward along the coast from Buna and Gona, through some of the worst terrain in the world. In the air, however, this period was more noteworthy. The air forces, under Lieut. General George C. Kenney, were growing steadily, if slowly, and were beginning to interfere seriously with the Japanese supply line running from Rabaul, down the northwest coast of New Britain, through Vitiaz Strait to their bases in Huon Gulf—Lae and Salamaua. The Japanese were faced with the necessity of building up these bases despite constant aerial harassment. Furthermore, they were engaged in an abortive land campaign around Wau, 50 miles south of Lae, which constituted a drain upon their already inadequate supply system.

It was in these circumstances that the Japanese felt obliged to make a major attempt to reinforce their Huon Gulf positions. During the morning of March 1 a Liberator bomber on patrol sighted a Japanese convoy of seven troop and cargo transports, with an escort of three large and four small destroyers, heading southwest down the coast of New Britain. Its position at this time was roughly opposite Talasea, in the middle of the concave coast line. The weather was foul: the overcast extended from a height of many thousand feet almost down to the surface of the sea, which was whipped by heavy rain. Only a chance break in what was otherwise 10/10 cover enabled the Liberator crewmen to get a glimpse of the enemy force. Air attack under such conditions was out of the question. However, Kenney had no intention of letting these ships get anywhere near their destination before striking at them. During the night, every squadron in the region was alerted and every plane fit to take the air was loaded with bombs and bullets.

March 2 dawned with some improvement in the weather: there were fairly numerous breaks in the overcast. The enemy ships had advanced by this time to Vitiaz Strait. There, Kenney loosed his storm. While Lightnings flashed overhead, Flying Fortresses thundered in beneath the overcast. The first wave scored five hits on a vessel estimated at 10,000 tons, leaving it afire and awash. A 6,000-ton ship, hit amidships, caught fire, split in two and sank, while a third vessel of this size was hit in the bow. The second wave of B-17s scored a hit on the bow of one of the larger escort ships. The third wave of heavy bombers, including both B-17s and B-24s, is credited with several hits on all four of the smaller transports, two of which were believed to have been seriously damaged. When the day's strikes ended, four Japanese destroyers were clustered around one of the larger transports, evidently trying to rescue the personnel it carried. The enemy's attempt to protect the convoy with an air umbrella had failed dismally: thirteen of his fighter planes had been shot down, with slight or negligible loss to the Allied fighters.

The next day, March 3, the battle reached its climax. The Japanese ships had passed through Vitiaz Strait and were emerging into Huon Gulf. At 10:10 A.M. they were attacked by a large force of Mitchell medium bombers (B-25s) carrying 500-pound bombs. In all, there were nine reported hits and several near misses on seven ships, including a destroyer. Within ten minutes, the assault was renewed by a force of Beaufighters belonging to the Royal Australian Air Force, which also was under Kenney's command. They strafed four transports and supply ships. Within an hour, the day's third attack was delivered by another force of Mitchells. By this time the enemy had called up fighter planes, but only six arrived in time, and one of these was shot down. One large merchantman ("6,000 to 8,000 tons") was hit and was believed to have been left in a sinking condition; hundreds of Japanese crowded into lifeboats and clustered on rafts were strafed.

It appears that by this time the Japanese had chosen to join two convoys: the one which had already been so badly mauled, and another group of five auxiliaries (personnel and supply ships) escorted by three destroyers. The weather was continuing to improve, and the Japs had advanced closer both to their destination and to the fields from which Allied aircraft were flying. Between 3 and 3:30 P.M. there were no less than six attacks, in this order: a formation of A-20s (Havocs); a lone B-17; a squadron of B-25s; a squadron of B-17s; a squadron of B-25s and a final squadron of B-17s.

It is impossible to unscramble the results of individual attacks. Three merchantmen were described as "exploding" at various times. Destroyers were hit repeatedly, and left dead in the water, heavily afire. There were numerous engagements with enemy fighter aircraft, but most of these were taken care of by a top cover of Lightning fighters, while a few fell victim to the gunners of Mitchells and Forts.

By the last light of a memorable day, American reconnaissance planes took inventory. All they could find were three cargo ships, all burning, one large destroyer and one small one, both damaged, in a sea covered by wreckage, oil slicks, lifeboats, rafts and swimming men. A fourth enemy merchantman is said to have sunk during this reconnaissance. In this day's heavy fighting, the Fifth Air Force lost three fighters and one B-17.

The next day, there was no trace of the damaged merchantmen, and they were presumed to have sunk. B-17s are credited with having polished off the two crippled destroyers. All the 12 transports and supply ships in the convoy were written off as sunk, along with all their ten escorting warships. However, some observers say only 15 ships were sunk. It was believed that an entire Japanese division of 15,000 men had been destroyed. Scores of enemy aircraft had been shot down, smashed on the ground at Lae, or so crippled as to be of little further value. And all this had been wrought by 136 Allied aircraft, of which only four had been lost.

The Battle of the Bismarck Sea was one of the most outstanding successes, if not *the* most outstanding success, ever achieved by aircraft alone against armed ships with some air cover. It was not, as some expansive Army Air Force supporters claimed, comparable with the Battle of Midway. Its importance was obscured, rather than clarified, in the florid phrases of General MacArthur's communiqué: "We have achieved a victory of such completeness as to assume the proportions of a major disaster to the enemy. . . . Our decisive success cannot fail to have the most important results on the enemy's strategic and tactical plans. . . . His campaign, for the time being at least, is completely dislocated. . . . A merciful Providence must have guarded us in this great victory." (The communiqué failed to mention Lieut. General Kenney.)

In the broad, strategic sense, the claims made in the communiqué were true, but the effects of the victory were not immediately apparent. The Japanese had, in the Huon Gulf area, sufficient supplies to continue fighting, on a reduced and defensive scale, for many more months. Since the enemy was showing his usual stubbornness in feeding his dwindling supplies and reinforcements into the Wau area where he had no hope of any real success—the best he could hope to do was to buy a little time—the Allied high command decided to encourage him in this wasteful process. The Wau campaign was kept active; during months of attrition, the Japanese were compelled to siphon out more and more of their troops from Lae and Salamaua. The Japanese persisted in their ill-advised policy after the fighting had swept well beyond Wau, to the vicinity of Mubo, where there was a small, jungle air strip, a few miles south and slightly west of Salamaua.

The push on Salamaua from Mubo would be extremely difficult to supply, and would be in danger of being outflanked by the Japanese in the coastal area to the east. So part of the Allied strategy called for landings on the coast at Nassau Bay, east of Mubo, and turning the tables on the Japanese in the intervening triangle, who would find themselves outflanked. Late in June, Company D of the 2/6th Battalion of the 17th Australian Brigade sent forward advance elements which made a daring reconnaissance of the Nassau Bay area. During the night of June 30-July 1, the 1st Battalion of the 162nd Regimental Combat Team of the United States Army landed on the beaches of Nassau Bay. The Japanese had a defensive perimeter there, and refused to be drawn off by a "mustard plaster" diversionary attack launched by the Australians. There were numerous casualties among the invading Americans, but a toehold was secured, and after 48 hours heavy artillery was landed, and then the success of the operation was never in doubt.

The following stages of the campaign in this area were extremely complex, because of both the geography and the Allied strategy: it was desired to draw off as many Japanese as possible from Lae to Salamaua, and if possible kill them on the approaches to Salamaua, and thus leave Lae vulnerable to envelopment from the rear or from the skies. The Japanese cooperated well. The 162nd Infantry and both the 15th and 17th Australian Brigades had heavy fighting all through the first half of July, by which time the Mubo sector could be considered secure. But the same dreary process was continued for almost six weeks more. The story of the campaign is studded with the names of forgotten pinpoints in the jungle, for which men died, often in seesawing operations in which a position might be captured and lost half a dozen times: Old Vickers, Mount Tambu, Komiatum, Charley Hill and Scout Ridge. The capture of Mount Tambu on August 19 was regarded as decisive in the campaign for Salamaua, and the honors for its seizure went largely to the 17th Brigade. The brigade was replaced in the line by the 29th Brigade. On August 26, Major General E. J. Milford, commanding the 5th Australian Division, took over operational command of all troops in the Salamaua drive, from Major General S. G. Savige, of the 3rd Australian Division. At this stage, Australian troops were within two miles of Salamaua airfield.

On September 4, 1943, the Allied command showed, on a modest scale, what could be done on a vast island such as New Guinea by envelopment tactics. With the support of American naval forces and landing craft, the Australian 9th Division was landed a few miles east of Lae on the north coast of Huon Gulf. The Japanese in both Lae and Salamaua were thus cut off from reinforcement or escape by sea, as Huon Gulf fell under Allied control. The 9th Division had a dual mission: some elements were to drive westward along the coast, into Lae; others were to strike out eastward, toward Finschhafen by way of Hopoi Mission.

But this was only a part of the plan. Lae was to be subjected to double envelopment, and since there was no feasible approach from the west by land, the western arm of the attacking forces would have to be brought in by air. Twenty miles southwest of Lae there was a large grassy area in the Markham Valley. On September 5, Australian pioneer troops who had marched for five days from a forward Allied air base reached this area, around Nadzab, where the Japanese had an emergency landing strip which was no longer operational. The Australians had an appointment to meet some Americans who were due to drop in during the morning.

Before noon, the sky was filled with transport planes of the Fifth Air Force. Hundreds of officers and men (led by Colonel Kenneth H. Kinsler) of the 503rd Parachute Regiment parachuted to earth, while General MacArthur watched the operation from an accompanying plane. The American paratroopers were veterans in their dangerous calling, although this was the first time they had been used in combat operations. (It also was the first case of aerial envelopment in the Pacific war.) Light equipment was parachuted with the combat troops; when the strip had been repaired sufficiently to allow aircraft to land, heavier equipment was flown in. Meanwhile, hundreds of men of the Australian 7th Division also had parachuted in—after only a week's training and a single practice jump. It is remarkable that there were not more casualties.

On September 11, the Australian 5th Division marched into Salamaua to find that it had been abandoned by the Japanese. There was nothing left in the place that was worth defending. It should be noted that at this time the Japanese were not indulging in the suicide stands which they later made on cut-off islands in the central and western Pacific. Instead, the enemy remnants melted away into the jungle and the mountains, hoping to reach further defensible positions. There was little possibility of evacuation by barge from Lae and Salamaua, because Huon Gulf was under Allied control. However, there was

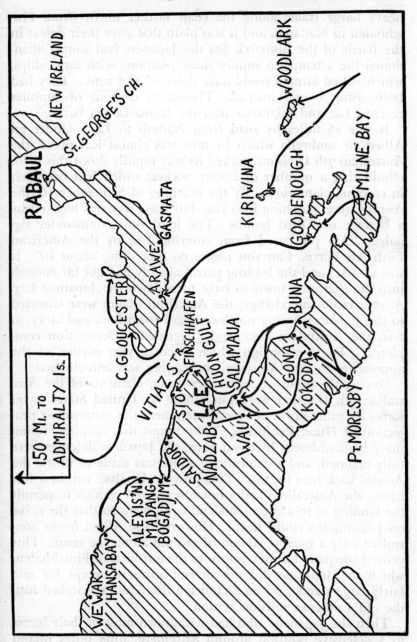

RABAUL

NEW IRELAND

ST. GEORGE'S CH.

WOODLARK

GASMATA

KIRIWINA

GOODENOUGH

MILNE BAY

ARAWE

C. GLOUCESTER

VITIAZ STR.

FINSCHHAFEN

SIO

HUON GULF

LAE

(HUON GULF)

SALAMAUA

NADZAB

WAU

BUNA

GONA

KOKODA

Pt. MORESBY

SAIDOR

ALEXIS'N.

MADANG

BOGADJIM

WEWAK

HANSA BAY

150 MI. TO ADMIRALTY Is.

heavy barge traffic along the coast farther north (from Fin-schhafen to Madang), and it was plain that after their defeat in the Battle of the Bismarck Sea the Japanese had simply aban-doned the attempt to supply these positions with large ships, which Allied airmen could have detected and sunk. They had been using barges instead. Thousands of tons of supplies reached Lae and Salamaua after the Bismarck Sea battle.

It was 26 miles by road from Nadzab to Lae. Under an Allied air umbrella which by now was almost leak-proof, the Australian 7th Division worked its way rapidly down this road, eliminating a number of enemy pockets which had been left in coconut plantations. By the morning of September 16, the Aussies were marching into Lae, but their way was blocked by a barrage of Allied bombs. The local unit commander sig-naled: "Am prevented from entering Lae by the American Fifth Air Force. Can you please do something about it?" It was 11 A.M., and the leading patrol already had got far enough into the shattered town to have torn down the Japanese flag. After a radio interchange, the American planes were diverted to the Japanese fleeing northwestward from Lae, and at 12:30 P.M. the Australian commander signaled: "Occupation com-pleted." For a campaign which began a year earlier, at the approaches to Port Moresby, the ending was anti-climactic.

During the night of September 22-23, elements of the Aus-tralian 9th Division were put ashore by United States naval forces six miles north of Finschhafen, near the easternmost pro-jection of Huon Peninsula. They found that despite prelim-inary bombardment by naval guns, the Japanese defenses were fully manned, and a determined effort was made to throw the Aussies back into the sea. This proved abortive: within a few hours, the Australians had a beachhead deep enough to permit the landing of reinforcements and equipment so that the drive on Finschhafen could begin. However, the Allied forces con-trolled only a narrow ribbon of ground along the coast. This proved adequate for an advance to the outskirts of Finschhafen, which the Japanese did not defend strongly except for one fairly large stand, and on October 2 the Aussies marched into the old Lutheran mission station.

Then the Japanese, who had withdrawn most of their forces to a defensive position around Sattelberg, nine miles inland

and 3,000 feet up in the hills, struck with the utmost ferocity. Not only did they descend from their hill-top fastnesses; they sent in a considerable force of assault troops by barge, and succeeded in landing some of them on the same Scarlet Beach where the Aussies had landed ten days earlier. One of the most savage local actions of the campaign was fought in this area for the next five days, with 3,000 Japanese estimated killed. The enemy were rooted out of their retreats around Sattelberg and Wareo in November, with the aid of medium tanks (in this case, the British "Matildas").

The Japanese still held the northern shore of Huon Peninsula, with concentrations at Sio and Saidor. While it was not considered necessary to wait for the reduction of these positions before undertaking the invasion of New Britain, it was obvious that they would have to be taken out eventually, or Allied control of Vitiaz Strait would not be complete. Consequently, plans for their capture were made, although action was to develop first on New Britain. (Sio was taken by Australian 9th Division forces which then moved along the coast to Saidor, and affected a junction on February 10, 1944, with patrols of the United States 32nd Division, which had been landed on January 1.)

In considering the extraordinary advance of Australian and American forces under General MacArthur, from the threshold of Port Moresby to the shores of Vitiaz Strait in little more than 12 months, too much importance cannot be attached to the rôle of Allied air forces under Lieut. General Kenney. The speed of the advance was, in fact, determined as much by the speed with which air forces could be built up as it was by the terrain and the build-up of ground forces and service forces. Kenney defines the role of the air forces as having been "to help ground troops get the land on which we build airdromes and advance the bomber line, from which we help them go ahead to get some more land for more airdromes, and keep the process going."

While this was, substantially, the pattern of the advance from Huon Gulf to Saidor (and later from there to the western tip of New Guinea) it did not precisely fit the campaign to neutralize Rabaul. This great base at the northern tip of New Britain, with five airfields lying around it in a crescent, was 300 miles from the nearest fields under direct Southwest Pacific command (Finschhafen or Woodlark Island), and 200 miles from the Torokina and Piva fields on Bougainville, under the immediate command of Admiral Halsey. The operation which General MacArthur was planning—the invasion of the south coast of New Britain at Gasmata—would produce a kind of "paradox of ranges": Rabaul would remain uncomfortably far from Allied bases until a field was captured at Gasmata, but the Japanese themselves, flying from Rabaul, would not have to travel anything like as far as Allied aircraft—they could content themselves with attacking Allied invasion forces at or off the beachhead. It was clear that Rabaul must be knocked down for a long count before an invasion of any part of New Britain could be attempted; then, when an airfield on New Britain was secured, Rabaul could be knocked out completely. Rabaul had been a target for Allied bombers since the middle of 1942, but it was not until November 2, 1943, that it was subjected to an assault of major proportions. Then, in 12 minutes, about 300 tons of bombs were dropped, mostly on or near shipping in the harbor. Hits were claimed on 41 vessels, totaling 114,000 tons, while 68 aircraft were destroyed in combat and 13 on the ground. The town of Rabaul was set afire. (A major factor in the success of Kenney's bombers against shipping was the improvement, by the late Major William Benn, of skip-bombing, which had originated in Europe where it was called mast-height bombing.)

By the end of November, it had been discovered that the Gasmata area was held by a large garrison of enemy troops who had excellent prepared positions, and it appeared for a time that the invasion of New Britain would have to be indefinitely postponed until a much larger force could be assembled. At this time, the only assault troops available to General MacArthur and Lieut. General Walter Krueger, commander of the Alamo Force (forerunner of the Sixth Army), were the 1st Marine Division* and the 112th Cavalry Regiment (dismounted).

Rear Admiral Daniel Barbey, commander of the Seventh

---

* After the Guadalcanal campaign, there had been difficulty in finding a suitable rest and recreational center for the Marines. They finally were sent to Australia, and became temporarily available to MacArthur.

Amphibious Force under Vice Admiral Kinkaid, persuaded General MacArthur and his staff that a landing could be effected at Cape Gloucester, at the western extremity of New Britain, which would insure control of Vitiaz Strait and help to fence in Rabaul. It was decided that a preliminary landing should be made, however, on the south coast of New Britain, between the Strait and Gasmata. The point selected was Arawe, where a necklace of islands around Cape Merkus provided a good harbor, and where an air strip was available. Control of Arawe, and its conversion into an Allied base, would make it possible to cut the barge traffic between Gasmata and Vitiaz Strait, and compel any Japanese shipping bound for Gasmata to enter the Solomons Sea farther east—waters now dominated by Allied sea and air forces.

As a diversion within a diversion, it was decided that while the main force went ashore on the western side of Cape Merkus, a company commanded by Captain Edward Wright should land on the east side of the cape, at Umlingolu Plantation. The idea was that this landing, to be made in the dark several hours before the dawn operation at Arawe, would deceive the Japanese as to the invaders' true intentions. Furthermore, if Japanese forces later tried to escape eastward from Arawe, they would be cut off by Wright's men.

The 150 under Wright's command were unloaded from a destroyer transport into 16 rubber boats and paddled in toward shore. They passed over a dangerous reef, with the aid of a high tide. They were within 30 yards of the beach when the enemy cut loose with a murderous crossfire from machine and 25-mm. guns concealed along the shore. The landing had to be abandoned. More than 30 men had been lost, and a similar number wounded, from the original 150. Umlingolu Plantation had to be taken from the land by the main force moving across the cape.

At Arawe itself, the landing was effected as planned. At 6:15 A.M., cruisers in the covering force opened fire, followed by destroyers closer inshore. At 7 A.M., naval fire was lifted from the designated beaches and shifted to adjacent areas. Meanwhile, the Japanese were subjected to a new form of bombardment: two amphibious trucks (DUKWs, or "ducks") leading the buffaloes and alligators into the harbor, were loaded with men operating bazookas. In 15 minutes, the miniature rockets were considered highly effective. At 7:15, the buffaloes and alligators raced for the beach, the former firing as they went, and landed the assault troops. It is not surprising that enemy opposition was so light: there had been few Japanese here in the first place, and they had been softened up by 356 tons of bombs the previous day. By afternoon of the 15th, the cavalry-men were consolidating their positions. The only Japanese air attacks to this time had proved ineffective.

The forces landing at Arawe were under the command of Brigadier General Julian W. Cunningham. Within six days, the Arawe air strip was captured, and the operation could be considered a success. Later, elements of the 158th Infantry were moved into the area.

The landings at Arawe had been effected simultaneously with an exceptionally heavy aerial attack on the Gasmata area, with 248 tons of bombs. This served the dual purpose of keep-ing the Japanese guessing about Allied intentions toward Gas-mata, and also reducing the enemy's ability to reinforce his Arawe defenses from Gasmata. Aerial assaults against the Cape Gloucester area since December 1 had resulted in dropping 2,000 bomb tons by December 23, and almost 3,000 tons two days later.

By this time there can have been no possibility of strategic surprise in a landing at Cape Gloucester. During Christmas Day, the Japanese must have detected a great troop convoy and naval covering force proceeding through Dampier Strait * but even at this stage there remained the possibility of tactical surprise. The Japanese could not be sure precisely where the Allied forces would land.

As it developed, the landing was to be a double operation, aimed at the envelopment of the air base on Cape Gloucester. The assault troops of the 1st Marine Division, commanded by Major General William H. Rupertus, were to go ashore at two points (Yellow Beach 1 and Yellow Beach 2) on Borgen Bay, east of the cape, and at a point (Green Beach) south of the cape. As these two forces approached, the defenders would

---

* Vitiaz and Dampier Straits are twin channels between New Britain and Huon Peninsula. They are divided by Umboi Island, and have a combined width of about 75 miles.

be cut off from overland reinforcement, and eventually trapped. The Japanese had been well prepared with beach defenses near the air base but far less well prepared in the areas where the Allied command had chosen to land. In these sectors, the strongest point was an eminence known as Target Hill, 450 feet high, overlooking Borgen Bay.

Before dawn on December 26, Australian cruisers under the command of Rear Admiral V. A. C. Crutchley opened fire on Target Hill and adjacent strips of beach. A few minutes later, American destroyers joined in. Shortly after 7 A.M., the covering warships lifted their fire and the battering was taken up, without pause, by Liberator heavy bombers of the Fifth Air Force. These in turn were followed by Mitchell medium bombers and Havoc attack-bombers in low-level and strafing missions. Rocket ships added their quota of explosives to the destructive hail. At 7:43 (two minutes ahead of schedule) the first Marines hit the beach. They found that the scattered Japanese defenses had been so shattered by 300 tons of shells and a similar weight of bombs that the enemy had all but abandoned them. The establishment of the beachhead was relatively easy. The assault waves in this sector were from the 7th Marine Regiment, under Colonel Julian W. Frisbie.

An attempted Japanese air attack during the morning was beaten off by covering fighter planes. The naval bombardment force already had withdrawn, depriving the enemy of one choice group of targets, but in the afternoon a more determined aerial assault was launched. It is presumed to have come from airfields around Rabaul, although these had been subjected to tremendous interdictory attacks by the Thirteenth Air Force, flying from Solomons bases in Admiral Halsey's command. Almost a hundred planes must have taken part in the operation, for 61 were reported to have been shot down. In return for these heavy losses, the Japanese were able to sink only the destroyer *Brownson,* with the loss of more than a hundred lives. Other vessels were damaged, mostly by near misses.

The Japanese were never able to organize truly effective resistance on the ground, but their defending forces were of high quality and they were greatly aided by the normally swampy terrain which was made still more formidable by torrential rains. It took the Marines four days to cover about five miles to the air base. Even this slow advance would have been impossible without heavy mechanized equipment (notably medium tanks and alligators) and a large quantity of medium artillery. Supply was so difficult that the Marines often had to ration their use of bullets and grenades. Co-ordination was so difficult in the almost trackless jungle that one American unit narrowly escaped extermination by their own 75-mm. guns. But at the end of the fourth day the first air strip was won, and by noon of the fifth day the second had been secured. Two battalions each from the 1st Marine Regiment (Colonel William J. Whaling) and the 5th (Colonel John T. Selden) were responsible.

As was so often the case in jungle campaigns against the Japanese, early successes against light resistance were followed by savage and protracted battles. At Arawe, before the end of December, the 112th Cavalry was driven from the air strip—a fact which the Allied command did not acknowledge until it could announce that the objective had been retaken. The recapture involved the landing of specially trained American Indian "Bushmasters" of the 158th Infantry, who completely demoralized the Japanese by their tactics. At Cape Gloucester, the heaviest fighting developed early in January, 1944, east of the air base. Marine veterans of Guadalcanal asserted that they had never fought in worse conditions than in the battle for Hill 660, which fell to the 3rd Battalion, 7th Marines, on January 13.

During the next month, progress was gradually accelerated on both the north and south coasts. On the north, the Marines advanced eastward to Rottock Bay and pushed inland, while from Arawe the Army forces moved northward until the two services effected a junction in the middle of the island. The western tip of New Britain was thus secured about February 23, with more than 7,000 Japanese reported killed in the process. During March, the pace was quickened still more: the Marines pushed along the coast and then made an amphibious hop to the area of Talasea, an air base on the Willaumez Peninsula. This was captured on March 8. A month later, the enemy abandoned the Cape Hoskins airdrome, still farther east, and also the major air base at Gasmata on the south coast. The Japanese by this time were in full, if slow and orderly, retreat toward the Gazelle Peninsula on which their once-great stronghold of Rabaul was situated. The enemy was encouraged to believe that the Allied forces would pursue him and besiege him there. Actually, Rabaul was by this time neutralized, and could be left for subsequent disposition at a time of the Allies' choosing. For the pincers had closed on it with the conquest of the Admiralty Islands.

As early as January, plans had been set in train for the occupation of the Admiraltys, but at that time it had been intended to launch the invasion in April. The 1st Cavalry Division, commanded by Major General Innis P. ("Bull") Swift, had been ordered to submit a plan for the operation to Lieut. General Krueger as commander of the Alamo Force, but before its planning was well along, in mid-February, it was ordered to be ready to go in at a moment's notice. Some aviators snooping over Los Negros, the smaller and more easterly of the two important islands in the Admiralty group, had failed to detect any sign of Japanese occupancy. General Krueger, a tough old campaigner who took nothing for granted, was highly skeptical of the alleged enemy withdrawal. A compromise was agreed upon: the 1st Cavalry would execute a reconnaissance in force against Los Negros with elements of the 5th Cavalry Regiment on February 29; if a beachhead could be made good, reinforcements would be fed in as fast as they could be shipped from the staging areas.

General MacArthur decided to accompany the expedition making the reconnaissance in force—an extraordinary procedure for a theater commander. The landing point selected was in Hyane Harbor, which had a narrow entrance easily commanded by any guns which might be mounted on the two enclosing peninsulas. Fortunately, the enemy was not prepared to bring to bear anything heavier than automatic weapons (probably 25-mm. and 37-mm.) against the landing craft as they moved through the narrow entrance. Otherwise, the first waves of assault troops might well have been annihilated. For General Krueger had been right: the Japanese were still present on Los Negros in fair numbers. Destroyers covering the landing were able to lay down heavy fire on the peninsulas, and the first assault waves got ashore with casualties which were officially described as "light."

The landing point had been well chosen in one sense: most of the Japanese prepared positions were farther south, toward Momote airfield. The dismounted cavalrymen, having met little opposition on the beaches, fanned out at once, giving the enemy no time to regroup, and advanced upon the airfield directly along the north-south coastal road, and also in a flanking movement by an interior road. By nightfall, against only scattered opposition, the cavalrymen had seized the entire airdrome except for one taxiway and two revetments. General MacArthur, exposing himself in a manner nothing short of foolhardy, since he wore khakis with insignia and his "scrambled-eggs cap," where other officers wore jungle greens and no insignia, had inspected the swiftly captured field and re-embarked on a destroyer.

It was well that the commanding general left when he did, for that night the Japanese showed what they were capable of when their numbers and determination had been under-estimated. There were 5,000 Japanese on the island, and only a thousand Americans. There were small infiltration attacks throughout the night, and a full-scale attack launched just before dawn was "repulsed with heavy losses." The cavalrymen's second night ashore was much the same as the first, but on March 2 the balance of the 5th Regiment was landed and the situation became somewhat less precarious. After noon on March 3, the entire regiment launched an attack, supported by a 75-mm. howitzer battalion, and extended the perimeter. However, much of these gains was lost during the night in another savage Japanese attack.

Reinforcements were urgently needed, and arrived just in time: elements of the 7th Cavalry Regiment, which relieved those units of the 5th which had made the first landings. On March 6, part of the 12th Cavalry Regiment was due, and in anticipation of its arrival, to secure an ample landing beach, an attack was launched during the night of the 5th which succeeded in recapturing most of the ground previously lost. From then on, the outcome of the fighting on Los Negros was never in doubt, although it lasted three weeks more. Its early, uncertain stages have been recounted in some detail because there is a great tendency in grandiloquent communiqués to give the impression that an operation such as this is a walkover for the forces engaged. Nothing could be more unfair to the men who fight these actions under the most appalling climatic conditions, many of whom are wounded, and all of whom see their friends killed beside them in overcoming what may be officially known as "negligible resistance by disorganized enemy remnants." All the 5,000 Japanese had to be killed on Los Negros, which was supposed to have been abandoned.

The Admiralty Islands were important not only because of their airfields, not only because of their position flanking Rabaul, but because they contained in Seeadler (Sea Eagle) Harbor one of the finest anchorages in the Southwest Pacific. This body of water, ten miles long with an average width of five miles, is enclosed by the eastern tip of Manus (largest island in the group), the curve of Los Negros and the islets of Koruniat, Ndrilo and Hauwei, which are properly extensions of the northern peninsula of Los Negros.

On General Swift's orders, reconnaissance patrols were sent ashore on Hauwei, the Butjo Lou Islands and Bear Point on Manus itself, to find suitable emplacements for division artillery. The technique first used at Munda was to be used again at Manus. Bear Point proved unsuitable; the Butjo Lou Islands were unoccupied and available; Hauwei proved to be a tough nut, and the patrol landed there was almost lost when the Japanese sank its only landing craft. Most of the men were rescued by PT boat. The next day, March 12, the 2nd Squadron of the 7th Cavalry was assigned to capture Hauwei and make it available as an artillery platform. The operation was completed in about 48 hours: not until then did General Swift order the assault on Manus begun, with the 2nd Cavalry Brigade combat team, under Brigadier General Verne D. Mudge, to make the landing at Lugos Mission on March 15.

The regiments comprising the brigade were the 7th, which fought under Custer at the Little Big Horn, and the 8th, which boasts more Medals of Honor than any other regiment in the United States Army. The landing was considered one of the most perfectly timed and co-ordinated in the Southwest Pacific campaign. Actually, General Swift noted that it was a minute and a half late because a heavy sea slowed the landing craft—"not too bad." Naval and air support were excellent, as was the weather, and the Japanese made their contribution to the favorable picture by staying away in large numbers. The landing was made about two miles west of Lorengau airdrome and, as at Momote, the cavalrymen immediately advanced both along the coastal road and by an interior flanking route. The artillery support from Hauwei and the Butjo Lou batteries was extremely effective in disorganizing the defenders, as was also the continuing bombardment (available on call) from destroyers in the great harbor. Even captured artillery was turned upon the defenders of Lorengau airdrome.

During the first day, the American forces approached to within striking distance of the field, and at dawn on the 16th the 1st Squadron (Reinforced) of the 8th Regiment launched an all-out attack. The Japanese defenses were thick and well prepared in the immediate vicinity of the field, and its capture consumed three days, with the 2nd Squadron of the 8th, and elements of the 7th, also committed. Lorengau town was taken shortly thereafter. Although mopping-up lasted another month, Manus, with the magnificent anchorage of Seeadler Harbor, soon became one of the greatest bases in the area.

What should have been the climax of the campaign to pinch off the Bismarck Archipelago proved to be anti-climactic. In January, plans had been laid for an invasion of New Ireland at a point near Kavieng, second only to Rabaul as a major Japanese base in the area. It had been agreed that this should be executed by Marines from Admiral Halsey's command. The men were in the Russell Islands, and were expecting to be embarked early in March, when word was received that General MacArthur had moved into the Admiralty Islands and that his reconnaissance in force had been turned into full occupation. This wiped out the strategic need for a landing on New Ireland, and the plan was abandoned.

However, Halsey's Third Amphibious Force, under Rear Admiral Theodore S. Wilkinson, was ready to go; so was the Marines' regimental combat team * under Brigadier General Alfred H. Noble. The St. Matthias Islands, east of the Admiraltys and 75 miles northwest of Kavieng, were selected as the

---

* The four Raider Battalions had been formed into the 1st Raider Regiment in 1943; on February 1, 1944, this was reconstituted as the 4th Marine Regiment, to replace the "China Marines" lost in the Philippines, and the designation of "Raider" disappeared.

target, and on March 20 the Marines went ashore on Emirau, an island in the group where the Japanese had maintained a sizeable force at one time. Nearly all had pulled out and the island, eight miles by five, flat, and suitable for the construction of airfields, was quickly secured. Simultaneously, the bombardment force, including battleships, which had been originally detailed to support a landing on New Ireland, was sent to neutralize Kavieng and to make sure that the Japanese there could not interfere with the St. Matthias operation. About a thousand tons of shells were poured into Kavieng by old battleships, including the 14-inch-gun *New Mexico* and 16-inch ships of the *West Virginia* class. Thereafter, Kavieng was never a threat.

The occupation of the St. Matthias group had the effect of closing the pincers tight around the Japanese concentrations in the Bismarck Archipelago. It was estimated that there were 50,000 of the enemy cut off in Rabaul, on the Gazelle Peninsula of New Britain, and on New Ireland. To have assaulted them frontally would have required the mounting of an offensive far greater than the Allied forces in the Southwest Pacific were then capable of. It is true that the pinching-off technique left these large enemy forces to be dealt with later by Australian troops in a campaign which was not less bloody or exhausting because it attracted little public attention—rather the reverse. But by pinching off Rabaul and Kavieng, the Allied command made it possible to proceed swiftly and immediately with the advance along New Guinea toward the Moluccas and Mac-Arthur's great goal, the Philippines.

IX. Flyspeck Islands

THE ENTIRE CENTRAL and western parts of the Pacific appear, on the map, to be liberally sprinkled with flyspeck islands. Most of them are arranged in groups, such as the Carolines and Marshalls, and this fact has a marked effect on their military value: islands within the same group can support each other through the overlapping of aerial reconnaissance ranges, and the concentration of aircraft from several islands to support whichever one is singled out by the enemy for attack. However, there are some isolated flyspecks, which have a value of their own: Marcus, never occupied, within historic time, by any people other than the Japanese; Wake, which the Japanese seized from the United States in December, 1941, and Nauru, which they seized from the British at about the same time.

These outposts had the advantage, for the Japanese, of affording bases from which reconnaissance planes could operate far beyond the range they would have from the large island groups. They were the perfect exemplars of the "unsinkable aircraft carrier," so deeply appreciated by the Japanese warmongers even before they began the war. But these outposts also had an advantage for the United States during the transition from defensive to offensive warfare: they could be attacked with little danger of reinforcements arriving, either by air or by sea, before the attacking force had finished its task and begun to withdraw. In the late summer of 1943, the Pacific command was in need of such targets.

It had some new weapons which needed blooding.

On June 1, high-ranking officers on CinCPac's staff had trooped out, in twos and threes, on the top "deck" of the headquarters building at Makalapa, carrying binoculars which they focused on an aircraft carrier moored off Ford Island. Any aircraft carrier was something of a novelty at Pearl Harbor in those days: the Navy had only two afloat in the Pacific, and the *Saratoga* had been in the South Seas for months, while the *Enterprise* had been under repair at Pearl. But it was not only the scarcity value of carriers which excited the interest of these officers. The new arrival was the first of a new class of carriers, embodying all the latest improvements in hull construction, in the design of her power plant, in armor and armament, and in facilities for handling the maximum number of aircraft in minimum time. It was the *Essex*. Soon there would be more like her: one which had been begun as the *Bonhomme Richard*, but had been launched and completed as the *Yorktown*, perpetuating the name of the smaller carrier lost in the Battle of Midway, and one which had been begun as the *Cabot* and completed as the *Lexington*, perpetuating the name of the first American carrier lost in action, in the Battle of the Coral Sea.

Almost as noteworthy as the *Essex* herself were the planes assigned to fly from her deck, in Air Group Nine, under Commander John Raby. The Navy had started this war with the Grumman Wildcat fighter (F4F-3 and later models), which had a 1,200-h.p. engine and a level speed of little more than 300 m.p.h. Now it was to be superseded by the Hellcat, another of the phenomenally successful Grumman family (F6F-3), with 800 more horsepower and rated at 400 m.p.h.

Besides the big, new battle carriers there were new carriers of a smaller class, intermediate between the *Essex* type and the converted merchantmen or escort carriers. The intermediate type were of the *Independence* class: their hulls were of the same dimensions as the *Cleveland*-class light cruisers. Some had actually been laid down as cruisers, but little work had been done before they were reclassified as carriers, and they were modified from the engine rooms up. They had an insignificant island on the starboard side of the flight deck, and funnels trunked out horizontally. They could carry only half as many planes as the *Essex* type, and could not handle them as easily or as fast as their bigger cousins. But they had this great advantage over the jeep carriers, as the escort carriers were called by the men who served in them: they were just about as fast as the battle carriers, new battleships and cruisers, whereas the jeeps (of which there are several classes with varying speeds) could make only 18 knots.

The first of the cruiser carriers to reach Pearl Harbor were the *Independence* and the *Princeton*. They had aboard them Air Groups 22 and 23 respectively.

All the individual pilots, radiomen and bombardiers in these carriers' air groups had received the rigorous training which has made United States Navy aviators the most skilled fliers in the world. But carrier aviation is so complex that it was felt necessary to give all these air groups a warm-up against isolated targets before they were precipitated into a major battle in an area where the enemy could be expected in strength. So the flyspeck islands came in handy.

In mid-August, two task forces were organized: one, under Rear Admiral Arthur W. Radford, including the *Princeton* (flag) and *Prince William,* was dispatched to cover landing operations at Howland and Baker islands, and the construction of an airfield at the latter. These particular flyspecks were American territory, but the small parties of meteorological observers stationed on them had been withdrawn shortly after Pearl Harbor: the Japanese in the Gilbert Islands were threateningly close, and it was adjudged more important, with the limited forces available, to build up islands which there would be a better chance of defending—such as Canton, in the Phoenix group, Wallis Island, Samoa and the Fijis. The Japanese did not contest the re-occupation of Howland and Baker.

The other task force left Pearl Harbor in small groups on August 22 and 23. Under Rear Admiral Charles A. Pownall, with his flag in the *Yorktown,* it comprised the *Essex, Independence, Indiana, Nashville* and *Mobile,* and ten destroyers. Scuttlebutt * had it that the task force was to cover the recapture of Wake Island. That seemed to be regarded as a minimum objective. It was eight days before it was made known that the target was Marcus Island.

Marcus Island was unknown until 1864, when it was visited by the ship *Morning Star.* The next caller appears to have been the U.S.S. *Tuscarora* in 1874. The Japanese eventually claimed the islet, which is shaped like a right-angled triangle with the corners rubbed away by the sea. The east and south sides are about a mile and a half in length; the northwest side,

---

* Ships' gossip; so called because it is exchanged most freely at the drinking fountain, or "scuttlebutt."

slightly longer; the area is estimated at about 740 acres. The only information about Marcus was what the *Enterprise* fliers had picked up by observation and camera during their brief raid on the morning of March 4, 1942. The island was known to have an airfield, and it was believed to consist of three strips paralleling the coasts.

The task force was little more than 100 miles north of Marcus, and within about 900 nautical miles of Tokyo, at 4 A.M. on September 1. It was time for the carriers to turn into the wind and begin launching planes. But there was no wind for them to turn into. The sea was flat, and over it a light mist was draped. To create a strong enough wind across their flight decks, the carriers were pushed beyond the 32.5 knots with which they are officially credited, to whatever their maximum speed might be. The cruisers could keep up, and the destroyers were not even forced, but the *Indiana* was outpaced and fell behind, eventually disappearing over the horizon. The take-off into this dead calm and surface mist would be dangerous. There was considerable risk of striking the upper works of cruisers and destroyers. So the latter put on their masthead lights: it looked like a Christmas lighting display, but out of season and out of place, so close to Tokyo.

The *Yorktown's* planes took off first. Forming up was difficult, but toward the end of the take-offs the mist became thinner, and since it was limited to a thin layer directly above the surface of the sea, pilots had uninterrupted vision into the upper air from the high flight decks of the carriers. The last to leave the *Yorktown* was Commander James H. Flatley, an expert in the lethal arts, who had flown against the Japanese in the first tentative carrier operations of the war. Now he was flying a specially fitted Hellcat, with two extra gas tanks. It was his duty to lead the entire group (from all three carriers) to Marcus, directing the squadron commanders on the choice of targets. With Air Group Five on the way, the *Essex's* Group Nine and then the *Independence's* 22 took off. It was still pitch-dark, but the mist cleared, and Sirius shone in the southwestern sky with such brilliance that its greenish light was reflected from the sea.

At 6:03 A.M. the leading pilots sighted Marcus. There are several claimants to the honor of having been first. However, it is certain that Lieut. Commander Richard Upson, commanding Torpedo Five, was the first to lead his division into attack. The Japanese had a radar station on Marcus, but it had given them no warning. The task force and even the air attack group had approached undetected. There were lights burning on the still-sleepy islet. Upson decided that if he switched on his lights, the Japs would think a group of their own planes was approaching, and would not use their anti-aircraft. The idea was excellent, but just as Upson's division was in position to begin its run, the second division from the same squadron reached the area and prepared to shoot down these "enemy" planes with their lights on. Fortunately, identification was established just in time.

Marcus proved to have only two runways, one along the northwest side of the island and one along the south side. On the former there were a few objects which might have been aircraft: they were soon unrecognizable. On the south strip there were seven shapes which, as the light increased, were unmistakably Mitsubishi OB-01s (fast, twin-engined bombers, often used as torpedo carriers, and known to Allied airmen as Betties). Commander Flatley ordered the skipper of Fighting Five, Lieut. Commander Charles L. Crommelin,* down to strafe these aircraft which the Japanese were trying to man, in the hope of getting them off the ground. Four Hellcats, each with six .50-caliber machine guns spitting, swooped down and strafed the Betties. Within ten minutes, all were burning furiously. Not a Japanese plane got off the ground.

In the center of the island were the barracks area and administration building. This group of structures was attacked so often, on Flatley's orders, that the fliers nicknamed it "Flatley Square." Farther north was the radar tower, and near it was the radio transmitter mast. Both were ruined, but the Japanese evidently had an auxiliary transmitter, as events showed.

Although they had no opposition in the air, so that their qualities as fighters could not be displayed, the Hellcats proved themselves magnificent strafing planes, highly maneuverable in the face of the spasmodic anti-aircraft fire which the Japanese eventually threw up. The Avenger, which had been carrying

---

* One of five famous brothers, all in the Navy, four of them aviators.

2,000-pound bombs for months in operations from land bases, was flown from carrier decks with this heavy load for the first time in this operation. Many of their heavy bombs (sometimes mistakenly called "block-busters") were fitted with delayed-action fuses to go off after six, 12, 24 and odd hours. This had an amusing result later.

In mid-morning, the first attack group had to return to the carriers to refuel and re-arm. Jimmy Flatley, an intense, bantam-sized man with a deeply religious nature, who brings the fervor of a crusader to the business of Jap-killing, stayed on until his gas began to run low, and then turned over the group command to Commander John Raby, who had flown out later from the *Essex*.

Losses were light. An Avenger from the *Yorktown*, piloted by Lieut. J. W. Condit, had trouble and was compelled to make a forced landing. He and his two crewmen got out into their rubber boat and their position was reported by *Essex* pilots. Eventually Admiral Pownall (whose code name on the TBS was the descriptive nickname "Baldy"), gave permission for the *Nashville* to fly off her two seaplanes in an attempt to rescue the three lost fliers. But they could not find the raft. The task force, which contained half the carrier strength of the United States Navy as of that date, could not be endangered to save the lives of three men, and began to leave the area. There is a widely circulated story, probably untrue in details but valuable as a clue to the character of the *Yorktown's* commanding officer, as to what happened next. The story has it that the skipper, Captain Joseph J. ("Jocko") Clark, went to Pownall and asked permission to fly off another group of carrier planes to search for Condit and his men. The admiral thought that the risk was too great. At this point "Jocko" breathed fire, stuck out his thick lower lip more than usual, announced that he didn't care whether he was "broken" for it, but "Those are my men and this is my ship, and we're going after them." Pownall consented to the search, but the men were never found. However much the story may have been adorned in re-telling, it explained why "Jocko," now a rear admiral who has been in command of a task group (larger than the entire task force of which the *Yorktown* was a unit on September 1, 1943), is idolized by his fliers.

Two fighter planes were lost with their pilots. A third

fighter, flown by Lieut. Mayo A. Hadden Jr., had to make a forced landing in the path of a destroyer which had been assigned to pick him up. The Hellcat, with its high stalling speed, is one of the toughest planes for a water landing, but Hadden did it neatly, half a mile ahead of the can. Aboard the surrounding ships we watched, tense, to see whether he would have time to get clear of the plane before it sank. A breeze had made up, and the sea was choppy. Hadden raised himself out of the cockpit, threw his parachute pack in the water, walked along the left wing and stepped into the water as the plane sank. The process took exactly ten seconds by my watch. It took little more than a minute for the destroyer to eat up the intervening half mile, although she had to slow down to pick up Hadden. Life rings were thrown to him, but he pushed them away. (Later he said he had mistaken them for sharks.) Then a life net was lowered, and he climbed up to safety and a change of uniform.

Early in September, great preparations were being made for amphibious forces to take the offensive. The *Yorktown* and *Essex* had only two days in Pearl Harbor before they were dispatched to the Pacific Coast on what Secretary Forrestal calls "a logistic mission": they were to act as transports for ground forces and vehicles.

There were to be two more warm-up operations before the big offensive. Two new cruiser carriers had arrived, the *Belleau Wood* and *Cowpens*. The former was worked into a task force with the *Lexington* and *Princeton* which set out under Admiral Pownall to test out the defenses of Tarawa, in the Gilbert Islands—and incidentally to gather information for future operations.

It is necessary, in considering these raids, to go back for a moment to the development of a secret base in the Ellice Islands. This group, lying just south of the Gilberts, had been a no man's land for ten months when, on October 2, 1942, a Marine Corps landing group from Samoa disembarked at Funafuti. This atoll, roughly in the center of the Ellice Islands, was dangerously exposed to Japanese attack, and American forces to support it were far away and far between. Therefore, its development was kept secret. By April, 1943, it had been built up to the point where Liberator bombers could be staged there. Thus the first raid on Nauru was made possible. This flyspeck island, valuable to the Japanese for its phosphate deposits, also had air strips which made it a major nuisance to the American command. A score of B-24s flown up from Wallis Island staged at Funafuti on April 19 and bombed Nauru during the night. They may have inflicted serious damage, but the Japanese soon decided where the bombers had come from, and on April 22 they made a night reprisal raid on Funafuti. There were no revetments for the 19 Liberators on the island at the time; it was due mainly to luck and bad Japanese marksmanship that only one was severely damaged. As it was, the base personnel suffered casualties. But Funafuti was strengthened, and the Japanese made no attempt to dislodge the garrison. In September, the more northerly atoll of Nanumea was occupied. This outpost served as an aircraft detection station and made Funafuti more secure. On the night of September 18, the largest bomber forces yet based in the Ellices were flown off to attack Nauru and three atolls in the Gilberts: Apemama, Tarawa and Makin.

Tarawa received the bulk of the bomb tonnage (60 tons dropped by 25 planes of the Seventh Army Air Force, Colonel William A. Halzapfel commanding the group). Before they could get away from the target area, the heavy bombers were attacked by enemy fighters, of which six were claimed as shot down, while nine other planes were listed as probably destroyed on the ground.

At dawn on the 19th, the carriers arrived, commanded by Admiral Pownall. Commander Leonard P. Southerland, commanding Air Group 16, directed the attack, which was concentrated against Tarawa. Throughout the operation, in which 80 tons of bombs were dropped, not a single Japanese plane was air-borne. Consequently, the Hellcat again missed the opportunity to prove itself against air-borne opposition. However, the enemy's anti-aircraft fire was intense: it accounted for two Dauntless dive-bombers, one Hellcat and one Avenger. Two inter-island steamers of about 700 tons each were sunk, and considerable damage was done to ground installations. At Makin, where part of the *Princeton's* Group 23 was in action, three four-engined seaplanes and another patrol plane were destroyed. At Apemama (which had no airfield), camps were strafed. On the 20th, land-based planes returned to assess the damage inflicted by the carriers. They found that the airfields had not been knocked out, because fighters rose to intercept them. But they got pictures on the basis of which it was believed that 50 to 60 per cent of Tarawa's ack-ack positions had been knocked out, and about 30 per cent of other installations. This somewhat optimistic view may well have been a major factor in the American command's estimate of the strength of Tarawa as a target for invasion.

The last warm-up was as large as the first two combined: all three of the available large carriers (*Essex, Yorktown* and *Lexington*) were combined with three of the cruiser carriers (*Independence, Belleau Wood* and *Cowpens*) into the largest carrier task force ever assembled by the United States Navy. It should be noted that the force was twice as numerous, and almost twice as powerful, as the one which had played the decisive rôle in the decisive battle of the Pacific war—Midway. Its planes were vastly superior. Rear Admiral Alfred E. Montgomery, who had had his flag in the *Independence* during the strike at Marcus, was the commander of the task force this time. Rear Admiral Arthur W. Radford, with his flag in the *Lexington*, commanded one of the component task groups.

The objective was Wake Island, which, like Marcus, was deep within the zone which the Japanese Navy was supposed to dominate, far closer to Japan than to the United States, and closer to Tokyo than to Pearl Harbor. It had been greatly strengthened by the Japanese, being covered with barracks for thousands of troops, with oil storage facilities and with gun emplacements, both coastal and anti-aircraft. Its airfield accommodated far more planes than the Marines had ever had there in December, 1941. The Japanese had even busied themselves dredging a channel into the lagoon.

The last hours before dawn on October 5 were pitch-dark and stormy. It was difficult and dangerous for the planes to circle the task force while forming up in preparation for the first strike which was made at dawn. Torpedo planes (carrying high-explosive and incendiary bombs) went in low enough to avoid interception. But the Japanese evidently had had some warning of the impending attack, for they had flown fighters off their three air strips, and had them waiting at medium altitude.

When the Hellcats arrived to cover the Avengers, they got their first taste of aerial combat.

The Japanese had 27 Zero fighters (all, apparently, of the early model known as "Zeke") in the air, and they had also taken the precaution of getting seven bombers off the ground. The Hellcats had the dual job of shooting down the Jap planes in the air and of strafing those on the ground before they could take off. Fortunately, they were numerous enough to accomplish both tasks. Lieut. Commander Paul D. Buie, who was commanding Fighting 16, from the *Lexington,* said later: "We had so many planes over the island, I had to elbow my way in to get a shot at a Zero." Since there were not enough Zeroes to go around, some Hellcat pilots had to do without. But the score was a striking proof, afforded in its first 20 minutes of combat flying, of the Hellcat's efficiency: 30 Jap planes were shot down. There was no certain case of a Hellcat being shot down by a Zero; the few Hellcats which were lost were all believed to be victims of anti-aircraft fire.

The day's second strike was made by the dive-bombers, taking as their principal targets the coast defense guns and anti-aircraft batteries. While they were at work, fresh squadrons of Hellcats covered them, and some strafed the crews of enemy ack-ack positions. The third strike, also by dive-bombers, was flown off well before noon, and was timed to coincide with the bombardment of Wake from both north and south by two groups of cruisers. The ships' gunnery at first was not good, and its results were overshadowed by those of the dive-bombers' attacks. This wave of planes had been ordered to go after oil storage facilities and ammunition dumps, so when any of the planes got a hit, the effects were instantly visible. A seaplane from one of the cruisers, which had been spotting the fall of shells, was shot down by three Zeroes which appeared from a passing cloud. Lieut. Alfred M. Roberts, the pilot, and Radioman George W. McCarthy bailed out, and as they floated down toward the sea they were attacked by the Zeroes with machine-gun fire. Both were wounded, but not seriously. The planes which came to their rescue were Hellcats, led by Lieut. Commander Edward H. ("Butch") O'Hare, hero of the Battle of Bougainville. All three Zeroes were quickly shot down, and a destroyer picked up the injured men from the seaplane. The cruisers resumed their gunnery, got the range more accurately, and kept on pounding Wake after the last carrier strikes for the day had ended.

Wake was such a small target—only four square miles, including Peale and Wilkes islets, which adjoin Wake Island proper—and there were so many fires burning that aviators having their first experience of this type of operation believed the objective had been obliterated. But Commander Southerland took a more sober view. During the night, the tenacious, persistent Japanese effected a partial recovery: either they flew in more planes from the Marianas and Taongi, or they produced some from roofed-over revetments around Wake's triple air strips.

During the first carrier strike on the morning of October 6, several of the Japs' new stock of planes were destroyed on the ground. Ten bombers were believed to have been shot down out of a force which was approaching Wake, presumably with the object of attacking the carriers. The enemy's light anti-aircraft guns were still firing from Wake. But the targets were not as numerous as they had been the day before. The cumulative effects of the continued bombing and shelling became apparent. Barracks, storehouses, power plants, water distillation plants—all were set afire or destroyed. The Japanese expected a landing, and scuttled a ship in the entrance to the lagoon. But the task force retired, unscathed, during the afternoon. Its planes had dropped 320 tons of bombs. Its cruisers had fired 373 tons of shells; its destroyers, 81 tons. As against 30 Japanese planes shot down and 31 destroyed on the ground, 13 American aircraft had been lost, including eight of the new Hellcats. Counting the two-man crews of the four Dauntless dive-bombers and the seaplane shot down, 18 American airmen had lost their aircraft, but seven of the 18 had been picked up by destroyers. The next day, Navy Liberators led by Commander John K. Hayward were over Wake to assess the damage. They attacked at low level, but even so the anti-aircraft fire was weak and ineffectual, and there was no air-borne opposition. The carrier planes and the cruisers had done their job. The carrier task force, first developed by the United States Navy, first used successfully by the Japanese against Pearl Harbor, was beginning to come into its own, once again under American leadership, as the most mobile air force in the world.

However, not all the critics were satisfied. Major Alexander P. de Seversky wrote, on October 25, 1943:

> "Combined forces similar to those that pummeled Wake, if used against a well-defended objective like Japan proper, would be foredoomed to destruction by the enemy's heavy land-based bombers even before they entered the main Japanese waters."

In the light of subsequent events, that statement makes interesting, but unconvincing, reading.

x. The Human Machine

To THE GREAT MAJORITY of officers and men in the Pacific offensive, the commander of the Fifth Fleet was not a man but a legend. To those who have had no contact with him, and to many who have served close to him, he has the reputation of being the hardest man in the Pacific, whose only saving grace is that he is slightly less hard than CominCh King. To members of the naval aviation service, he is "that goddam' battleship admiral" who commits the high crime of allowing gunnery ships to finish off Japanese vessels which have been crippled in air attacks. To those who have served aboard his flagships he is a somewhat remote, decidedly austere individual who does his exacting job with neither flurry nor flourish, and asks only that others do their jobs almost as well as he does his. To countless graduates of the Naval War College he is a brilliant tactician who can strip the inessentials from a problem with his mental scalpel and operate cleanly on the living tissue beneath.

Raymond Ames Spruance is all of these, and something more: he is an incredibly efficient piece of machinery in human form. Early in life he dedicated himself to the task of becoming an admiral who would be competent to command in what Harold and Margaret Sprout call "the new order of sea power": an order of sea power in which technology is as important as human prowess and skill, in which the performance of an internal combustion engine may be more important than the quality known as "guts" in a commanding officer.

Raymond Spruance spent his infancy and high school days in Indianapolis. Between the ages of six and 13 he lived in South Orange, N.J., with a grandmother and three maiden aunts. His behavior was so proper that it seems to have satisfied even this exacting board of examiners: he was quiet, reserved and intensely studious. He was the same when he went back to Indianapolis, to his businessman father and literary mother, and attended Shortridge High School. He collected postage stamps and confined his athletics to walking. And because he had already begun to make a fetish of physical fitness and hardness, he slept with all the windows of his bedroom open.

Raymond Spruance graduated from high school in three years and then went back to live with his aunts while he took a year's course at the Stevens Institute of Technology in Hoboken. This completed, he and his family decided that he should try for an appointment to the Naval Academy. He had two strings to his bow: his mother knew Senator Fairbanks of Indiana, who was asked to obtain the appointment, and Raymond took a competitive examination in New Jersey. He won this, and wanted to go to Annapolis from New Jersey since this would represent the results of his own efforts. But he was persuaded to accept the Indiana appointment to avoid giving offense to the family's political connections. The preference he had then has continued to characterize Spruance: unlike many admirals, he has never been the creature of any Congressman or group of Congressmen, and he has none of them eating out of his hand. He has got along on cold merit, without political pull. When he was nominated, and quickly confirmed, for promotion to full admiral, he was the youngest four-star officer in the Navy.

During the long years between graduation from Annapolis and flag rank, nobody outside the Navy or his family circles ever heard of Raymond Spruance. The most spectacular thing about him was his determination to do everything in an unspectacular but ultra-efficient way. In World War I he was assistant engineer officer at the New York Navy Yard, and had duty in London and Edinburgh in connection with Allied efforts to improve and coordinate their fire control systems. No other officer has been recalled so often to the Naval War College to serve as an instructor. Because of his mastery of tactics and his skill in the various branches of engineering on which a modern navy is dependent, Spruance spent half his time ashore in the interval between the two world wars.

In 1938, Captain Spruance was given command of the battleship *Mississippi*. Broadly speaking, the commanding officers of large warships fall into two classes: those who run a taut ship, and those who run a happy ship. Spruance found a compromise: a "clean and happy ship." He did not believe in tautness for its own sake, but he did believe that cleanliness and tidiness were indications of the men's pride in their floating home. In wartime, Spruance still insisted upon neatness and order, not for their own sake, but because without them there could be no efficiency.

One of the sternest tests of a man's capacity for command is his ability to delegate authority to competent subordinates. Spruance has this ability in a high degree. If an officer assigned to him does not measure up to his standards of competence, the officer is quickly transferred. Consequently, Spruance is surrounded with men in whom he has confidence. He is not known ever to have lost an hour's sleep, even on the eve of battle, through inability to delegate tasks to the proper subordinates.

Commanding officers of United States Navy ships often burn themselves out with worry because they will not leave the bridge while the ship is at sea, and in many cases will not retire to their sea cabins (abaft the bridge) during the night. Spruance was never one of these. Once the *Mississippi* was going through a tricky, narrow strait at night. It was still peacetime, but nine captains out of ten would have stayed on the bridge all night, hovering nervously over the officer of the deck, or perhaps taking the con (control) themselves. In the middle of the passage, Spruance turned to the navigator and said: "You're the navigator and you ought to know where we are and where we're going. You do it. I'm going to turn in."

His first combat duty was to command a division of cruisers when it formed part of the fast carrier task force under Vice Admiral William F. Halsey in raids on the Gilbert and Marshall Islands. It was not until midsummer of 1942 that Spruance received a command involving vital decisions which could affect the course and duration of the war against Japan. Halsey was in the United States, taking treatment for a skin ailment, when Nimitz was making dispositions to meet the expected attack on Hawaii, which was to begin at Midway. Vice Admiral Frank Jack Fletcher, the next senior officer who had been entrusted with the command of carrier task forces, was on his way to Pearl Harbor aboard the *Yorktown*, damaged in the Battle of the Coral Sea. Nimitz decided to send out the *Enterprise* and *Hornet* first, with Spruance in command of the group. They left Pearl Harbor on May 28. The *Yorktown,* which had arrived the day before, was given emergency repairs in record time, and sailed on the 31st. She caught up with the Spruance group just as battle was joined off Midway on June 4, and Fletcher took command. But that afternoon the *Yorktown* was mortally wounded, depriving Fletcher of a ship in which to fly his flag, so Spruance took over for the remainder of the battle.

This phase of the Battle of Midway was the pursuit. The enemy had been trounced, and was withdrawing in confusion. Naval aviators have had a field day, criticizing Spruance because, like Jellicoe at Jutland, he failed to catch the retiring enemy forces and destroy them. Since Spruance is not an aviator, many naval aviators regard him as the proper butt for criticism. But as usual in such cases, the aviators ignored half the factors which Spruance had to weigh. These were: the American task force was reduced to two carriers, and neither of these had anything like its full complement of planes or pilots; the heaviest gunnery ships in support were cruisers; the destroyers were running short of fuel, and refueling in these waters, infested as they were with Japanese submarines, was highly dangerous; the *Saratoga* was on the way with replacements for the air groups, but could not reach Spruance until the Japanese would be far to the west of Midway, beyond the umbrella of land-based aircraft from that island, and nearing an umbrella of their own, raised from Wake or Marcus. Naval aviators who are most insistent upon the primacy of carriers in this war should be the first to concede that Spruance would have been foolhardy in the extreme to take undue risks with the *Enterprise, Hornet* and *Saratoga,* which were then the only operational American carriers in the Pacific. (The *Wasp* and *Ranger* were still in the Atlantic.) It might not have been true of Spruance, as was said of Jellicoe, that he could have lost the war in an afternoon, but he certainly could have lost the striking power of the United States Navy in that short space of time.

There can be no doubt that all these considerations passed through Spruance's brain, which assessed the several factors in the equation with the same precision as an electrical computing machine. Much of June 5 was spent on a wild goose chase after a Japanese carrier, reported by aerial reconnaissance, which proved to have been an optical illusion. The attacks on June 6 were a little more rewarding: enemy cruisers were heavily hit and one or two were sunk. Reconnaissance planes were still hunting for the Jap transports. But shortly after noon, the *Yorktown* was sunk, a thousand miles to the east, by a Japanese submarine. Spruance decided that enough had been lost, and enough had been risked, for a problematical gain. He went back to Pearl.

Whatever less-informed critics may say, Admiral Nimitz, who had all the facts at his disposal, was so well satisfied with Spruance's performance that he recommended him for the Distinguished Service Medal and made him his chief of staff and Deputy CinCPac. For more than a year, Spruance worked in total obscurity and anonymity. He went, literally, underground —into one of the basement offices at Makalapa. There he had an ordinary desk and a swivel chair, which he rarely used. He had a couch for visitors only. For himself, he had the floor to pace, and a stand-up desk.

Spruance used to walk to headquarters from the house on the hill which he shared with Nimitz. He used to spend nine-tenths of his working day standing up at his high desk. Sometimes a visitor would be asked to sit down, but Spruance would carry on the interview in the midst of his walking. Unlike some more highly publicized commanders, who pace their offices like a caged tiger, Spruance walked slowly and easily; the mannerism was no affectation, but a simple preference. As often as not, the visitor would be left standing, which was actually more comfortable for him since it brought him up to the same eye-level as the admiral.

Spruance had such a deep-seated aversion to publicity that he tried to persuade Nimitz to keep war correspondents away from the fleet. In this, fortunately, he was over-ruled. In spite of his own feelings about their place in the scheme of war, Spruance was both courteous and patient with newspapermen, and later he often had them aboard his flagship. An excellent example of Spruance's smooth way of handling things was afforded during an interview at Pearl Harbor. There was an urgent phone call, which Spruance excused himself to answer. When he turned to me again, the fatuous public relations officer tried to end the interview, telling Spruance that there were several officers waiting to see him. The admiral answered that he knew perfectly well who was waiting for him, and that he had not finished. He picked up the thread of his explanation at the exact point he had left it to answer the telephone. About 20 minutes later, he finished by neatly wrapping up the points he had discussed, and then turned to the waiting officers.

In the late afternoon of a day at Pearl Harbor, Spruance used to pull on a pair of the "inside-out" (split leather) high shoes issued to Marine Corps enlisted men, and set off for a walk. Sometimes it would be a seven-mile hike with Nimitz to a beach, followed by a three-mile swim, with a jeep for the return trip. Sometimes it would be just a ten-mile hike. Anybody invited to accompany him came back footsore and feeling that he had been subjected to a cruel and unusual punishment, in violation of his constitutional rights and to the great detriment of his physical constitution. The only officer who came near to keeping pace with Spruance was Nimitz. Yet when I asked Spruance about his propensity for walking the feet off his friends, he denied it with a straight face.

Spruance is the same height as Nimitz (5 feet 9½ inches), but 20 pounds lighter. Nearing 60, he still does not wear glasses; his brown hair is suffused with gray, but still dark. The face is strong and cold: the chiseled nose is long and slightly hooked; the mouth is thin and straight; the jaw line is truculent; the piercing eyes are bluish gray. Somehow, they give the impression of a man determined to be fair, of one who would neither seek nor show favor. It is a countenance that would look well on a Supreme Court justice.

When he had his flag in a carrier, Spruance used to take his pedestrian exercise on the flight deck—800 feet of glorious walking space. Later, when he had his flag in the *New Jersey*, he had to be content with a third of that—the length of the foredeck. So long as there was no immediate danger of enemy attack, he would take part of his walk clad in bathing trunks. (Sun-bathing is forbidden in combat areas because of the danger of flash burns.) Aside from walking, swimming is his only recreation; symphonic music and reading are his only relaxation.

Unlike his good friend Halsey, with whom he alternated command of the main striking force of the Pacific Fleet, Spruance has never bothered to tell a breathless public anything of his views on strategy. But within the naval service he is a little more communicative. He told a writer for the *Jerseyman* (ship's newspaper of the *New Jersey*):

"This job we have to do out here cannot be handled by any one branch of the service. It requires the complete coordination of surface and air forces, troops and submarines. The whole plan of action may seem complicated, but boiled down to its essentials, all you need is teamwork and the proper use of the weapons at hand. . . .

"When any new weapon comes along—like the airplane—we always go through a stage in which there are many who believe that the new weapon is going entirely to supplant the old. But eventually the new weapon takes its place in the arsenal, just where it belongs. Of course, all the old weapons develop and change to fit changing circumstances. But the object of Navy tactics is to use all of the weapons that you have at your command, to inflict the maximum loss upon the enemy, with the greatest conservation of your own forces."

In Spruance's mind, conservation is not merely the antithesis to expenditure; it is the antithesis to waste of any kind. If he goes out with a balanced fleet, and the aviators have plenty of action, some losses and an abundance of glory, he considers it wasteful to have the heavy-gun ships along as a sort of supercargo. If there is a chance to use gunnery ships to finish off enemy craft crippled in air attacks, he will use them for that purpose—and damn the torpedoes of criticism launched by the aviators.

XI. Terrible Tarawa

IN THE SUMMER of 1943, before the Fourteenth Corps had captured Munda, while an expedition was being mounted for the re-occupation of Kiska, while planning was in progress for the landings on Bougainville, Admiral Nimitz accepted a recommendation from his staff that the offensive against Japan should be begun through the Central Pacific, as well as the North and South Pacific. The starting point (after Baker had been built up) was to be in the Gilbert Islands, a snaking line of 16 atolls lying across the Equator, about 400 miles west of the International Date Line. Vice Admiral Spruance was relieved of his duty as chief of staff and Deputy CinCPac, and named ComCentPac (Commander, Central Pacific). The planning for the invasion of the Gilberts went on, while other offensives were unfolding on either flank, thousands of miles away.

Not much was known about the Gilbert Islands as a military objective. It was about New Year's Day, 1942, that the Japanese moved in and settled down for a long stay. By February 1, aviators from the *Yorktown* (part of Admiral Halsey's first raiding carrier force) found no appreciable shore defenses at Makin, the only atoll in the Gilberts to be attacked that day. Reconnaissance photographs taken so soon after the Japanese had moved in were, of course, useless in the summer of 1943.

Thereafter, the Gilberts were unmolested until August 17, 1942, when the submarines *Nautilus* and *Argonaut* landed a combat team from the 2nd Marine Raider Battalion, commanded by Lieut. Colonel Evans F. Carlson, of *"Gung Ho!"* fame. Again, Makin was the objective. The raiding party virtually annihilated the garrison of 300 or so Japanese, and withdrew with moderate casualties. The neighboring atoll of Little Makin was not even scouted.

Two months later, the cruisers *Portland* and *Juneau* were on their way out to the South Pacific (the *Portland* soon to be crippled, the *Juneau* to be sunk) when it was decided to give them gunnery practise against the Japanese in the Gilberts. On October 15, under Rear Admiral Mahlon S. Tisdale, the two ships steamed into the archipelago from the southeast. The *Portland*, with nine 8-inch guns, took on the central atolls of Maiana, Apemama and Tarawa, while the *Juneau* paid its respects to the southern atolls, in the Kingsmill group. The *Portland* had no opposition and little to shoot at around the first two targets. It had just worked up to a position west of Betio, at the southwestern tip of Tarawa, and had started to get the range on some attractive shipping in the lagoon, when Admiral Tisdale ordered the force to withdraw.

After that, the Japanese in the Gilberts were let alone until the Army's Seventh Air Force bombers started coming over from Funafuti. Then, from Baker Island, the offensive was stepped up. The Navy's Bombing Squadron 137 (flying Venturas) and Photographic Squadron Three did their utmost, along with the Army planes, to obtain a maximum of information through photo-reconnaissance. The carrier strike of August 19, 1943 (above) contributed some more. The substance of it was that the Japanese had made Betio islet, on Tarawa atoll, the king-pin of their Gilbert Islands defenses. There they had eight 8-inch guns, in twin mounts. They had plenty of anti-aircraft, up to 5.5-inch; plenty of blockhouses, some tank traps and many small defensive positions. How many was not known; nor was it known how well they had been dug into the ground. These were matters which could not be ascertained by aerial reconnaissance. The use of other methods of gathering information would seem to have been indicated.

The natural defenses of Betio were almost as formidable, and as little known, as those installed by the enemy. The atoll of Tarawa had not been the subject of an oceanographic survey since the visit of Lieutenant (later Commodore) John Wilkes, U.S.N., in 1841. His charts were still in use, 102 years later. In the meantime, the coral polyp had been busy, making Wilkes's charts inaccurate.

There have been defects in the charts of all the Pacific islands which have been fought over in this war, but for the most part they have not proved serious. It was to be otherwise at Tarawa.

Even more important than the soundings were the tides. In most of the Central Pacific, there is not much tidal rise and fall—generally less than two feet. But the depth of water over the reef inside the lagoon of Tarawa, on the course to Betio, was never more than 5½ feet, even at high water on a spring tide. On a neap tide it would be a foot or so less. With a strong southeast wind driving the water off the coral shelf, it would be still less. It might not be enough to float a Higgins boat.

In the preliminary planning for the invasion of the Gilberts, two principal methods were considered. Army spokesmen advocated preliminary seizure of islets, which were understood to be lightly held, within artillery range of the ultimate objectives on islets which were known to be strongly held. Marine Corps spokesmen advocated landings directly on the main objectives. The difference in viewpoint exemplifies the widely held view that "Army officers are long on strategy and short on tactics; Marine officers are short on strategy and long on tactics." The tabloid characterization is too general and over-simplified to be entirely true, but it has a large element of truth in it, and goes far to explain certain features of the Pacific war. The Army argued that its use of near-by artillery at Rendova had reduced the cost of taking Munda; the Marines retorted that it had taken more than five weeks to reduce Munda. Both statements were true, and they were not mutually exclusive.

After the broad outlines of the campaign for the Gilberts had been determined by the higher staffs, the details were worked out by the division commanders directly concerned. For Makin atoll, this meant Major General Ralph C. Smith, of the 27th Division (Army); for Tarawa, Major General Julian C. Smith, of the 2nd Marine Division. The latter's chief of staff was Colonel Merritt A. Edson, who had leaped to fame at Tulagi and Guadalcanal, and the operations officer was Lieut. Colonel David Shoup. The Marine division had been in New Zealand for the better part of a year, most of its elements having been in action on Guadalcanal; headquarters was in a room of the Windsor Hotel in Wellington. The problem of the reefs was given earnest consideration. If it should happen that there was not enough water to float a Higgins boat, the whole enterprise might end in costly failure. Major Henry C. Drewes, commander of the division's amphibious tractor battalion, experimented with these vehicles on New Zealand beaches, and it was decided to use them for the first time in combat. Hitherto, they had been used for lightering cargo ashore from ships at bases where there was insufficient wharfage, such as Espíritu Santo.

On November 1 the division sailed from Wellington and began its tortuous course to Tarawa. On the way the convoy picked up a powerful escort of old battleships, including three which had been damaged at Pearl Harbor and an appropriate screen of cruisers and destroyers. It stopped at one of the American-held islands while the landing was rehearsed. The trial was most satisfactory. There was ample water for the Higgins boats.

Most of the men in the force thought that their objective was Wake Island. On November 14, Rear Admiral Harry Hill issued an order to "Give all hands the general picture of projected operation," and this was done with welcome thoroughness.

The convoy zigzagged back and forth across the Date Line so often that most of the men lost track of the day. D-day was described as November 20, but even this was deceptive: it was the approximate Pearl Harbor equivalent of a time and date which should have been expressed in terms of the place where the action occurred. The misuse of November 20 as the "West Longitude Date" for the landing on Tarawa has become so widespread that it is indicated in parentheses after the correct, East Longitude date, in this account, and the dates before and after D-day are similarly indicated.

By the time the men aboard the transports knew what their destination was, the area was already under preliminary attack by Seventh Air Force and Navy planes. At first, beginning ten days before the invasion, the aerial blows were scattered throughout the Gilberts and Marshalls, for two reasons: (1), to destroy enemy strength, especially air power, in all the neighboring islands, so as to prevent reinforcement of the points to be attacked, and (2), to avoid singling out the invasion objectives and thus giving the enemy precise forewarning. It was not until D-minus-four that Tarawa came in for especial attention. Then, for two days, it was heavily bombed by Army Liberators from Funafuti. On D-minus-two, they shared the work with air groups from carriers commanded by Rear Admiral Alfred E. Montgomery and Rear Admiral Van H. Ragsdale. As early as D-minus-three, Seventh Air Force Liberators were able to fly low over Betio, strafing as well as bombing; no enemy planes were airborne and the attackers suffered no damage from "weak anti-aircraft fire."

This refrain, "weak anti-aircraft fire," was repeated over and over in the next three days. Carrier pilots saw no Japanese above ground, and the islet appeared from the air to have been completely devastated. Some of these deceptive impressions reached the assault troops aboard the transports. By now they were hot for battle, partly because, for two weeks, they had been closely confined in torrid quarters with humidity near the saturation point—conditions which try the souls of men. After so much misery, they wanted a fight. Some of their officers were foolishly over-optimistic. Colonel Edson was one of the few who refused to place too great reliance on the ability of preparatory bombardment to destroy well-protected defenses. Admiral Hill allowed this message to be circulated: "It is not our intention to wreck the island. We do not intend to destroy it. Gentlemen, we will obliterate it."

Tarawa was indeed to be virtually obliterated, but not in the easy, arm's-length bombardment, as some thought.

It was 3:45 A.M. on Sunday, November 21 (Saturday, November 20, W.L.D.) when the transports hove to off Tarawa's western face, where the lagoon was open to the sea with no intervening island strips such as there were on the other coasts. About 5 o'clock a Japanese light blinked a demand for the recognition signal. Receiving no reply, the island commander, Rear Admiral Keiji Shibazaki, took appropriate measures.

The longest-range guns on the island had been the eight 8-inch rifles made by Vickers, reported to have been removed by the Japanese from Singapore, and set up on Betio in four twin mounts: one pair at the northwest and one at the southwest corner of the islet; one midway along the north shore, near the base of the pier (see map) and one on the eastern promontory. The one near the pier is said to have been knocked out by a direct hit from a 1,000-pound bomb dropped by a flier from the *Chenango*, but the others were still operational as D-day came and H-hour approached. At 5:07 one of them opened fire. The first shell fell near the transports. Other enemy guns joined in. Shells began to rain in the transport area, where Higgins boats already were milling around, some loaded, some waiting to be loaded. The first casualties at Tarawa were from near misses which threw mountains of water over some of the boats.

At 5:12, the flagship *Maryland* opened counter-battery fire and was joined by two other battleships. The enemy guns fell silent after 20 minutes. But the unscheduled bombardment continued until 5:42. The carrier planes were almost due. They did not appear. Instead, Japanese guns opened up again. One transport was being bracketed consistently: it was only a matter of time before she must take a direct hit. Others were being splashed by near misses. At 5:48 the order was given for the transports to withdraw, out of range. The boats already in the water must follow them as best they could. H-hour would have to be postponed (it had been set for 8:30). At 6 A.M. the battleships opened fire again, both to cover the transports' withdrawal and in an effort to silence the stubborn shore batteries. They ceased at 6:13, when the first carrier strike arrived. The planes dropped all their bombs in nine minutes, and at 6:22 the gunnery ships resumed their work. They stood in to within a mile of the shore for destroyers, and three miles for battleships. At these close ranges, the shells traveled almost horizontally, and had such a low trajectory that they were likely to ricochet from a hard, rounded surface, such as an enemy gun emplacement covered with a steel cupola. At a greater range, while the accuracy would have been reduced, the shells would have fallen almost vertically; this "plunging fire" would have had far greater penetrating power and less chance of richocheting.

At 7 A.M. a small minesweeper entered the lagoon, under orders to lay a smoke screen. She was brought under heavy fire by shore batteries. Her commanding officer, a lieutenant, found a strong breeze blowing from the southeast over Betio, so that any smoke laid would be in the faces of the assault troops. On the TBS, he recommended to the task force commander that the plan to lay smoke be abandoned. It was. This meant switching the landing to an alternative schedule which had been worked out for use in such a contingency.

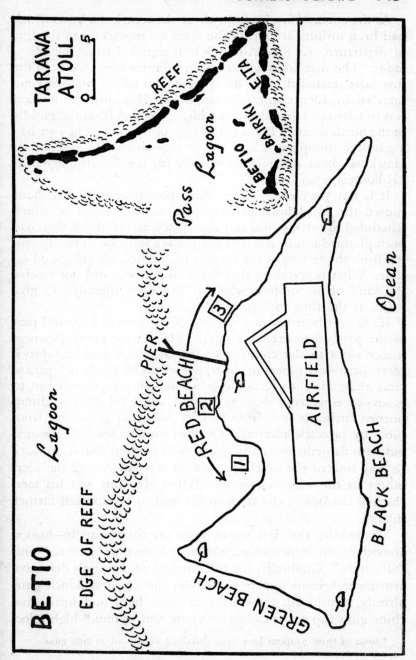

As the enemy's fire from the shore slackened, the boats which had been milling around in the open sea moved up to the line of departure. At 8:20 Admiral Hill signaled from the *Maryland*: "The first boats will leave 15 minutes late." At 8:30 the first boat started in, carrying a scout and sniper platoon commanded by Lieutenant William Deane Hawkins. Its mission was to seize the 1,400-foot pier which extended from the middle of the north shore of Betio to the edge of the reef. The pier had a gasoline dump on it and two storage sheds. At 8:37, while Hawkins's boat was picking its way in, the flagship signaled: "H-hour is 0900" (9 A.M.).

It is not yet clear whether these postponements of H-hour caused the breakdown in coordination, as a result of which scheduled air strikes did not take place at the times they had been planned for, or whether there was a separate difficulty arising from the failure of the carriers to get their air groups off on time. What is certain is that the assault troops did not receive the kind of air support which it had been intended to give them, at the time intended.

Hawkins's boat reached the end of the pier at 8:55 and part of the platoon secured the ramp. There were many Japanese sniper nests in the crannies of the coconut-log-and-coral-rock pier; there were others in the upper works of wrecked Japanese craft alongside the pier. The scout and sniper platoon had to clean out as many of these as it could, while the gasoline dump burned furiously—not from hits by American guns, but from those by Japanese mortars. The two storehouses were cleaned out with flamethrowers and the 32-man platoon started to work its way toward the beach, some men traveling along the pier, others in the water alongside. When Hawkins and his men reached the beach, the warship fire had to be directed farther inland.

Meanwhile, the first waves were on their way in—loaded aboard amphibious tractors, variously known as "amtracs" and "alligators." Gradually, the full strength of Tarawa's defensive armament became apparent. Besides the 5.5- and 8-inch guns already mentioned, there were mortars, light and heavy machine guns (up to .50 caliber), 25-mm. and 37-mm.* high-veloc-

* Some of these weapons have been described as 20- and 40-mm. guns.

ity guns, 70-mm. field pieces, 75-mm. mountain guns, 75-mm. high-velocity dual-purpose guns, 80-mm. anti-boat guns, and 127-mm. dual-purpose guns in twin mounts. Some had been knocked out, but by no means all—perhaps not even a majority.

For the landings, the central part of the north shore had been designated as Red Beach. The westernmost sector, or right flank, was Red Beach 1, assigned to the 3rd Battalion, 2nd Marine Regiment. Adjoining it, and extending as far east as the pier, was Red Beach 2, assigned to the 2nd Battalion, 2nd Regiment. The pier formed a "party wall" between this and Red Beach 3, assigned to the 2nd Battalion, 8th Regiment, extending eastward to a point opposite the eastern end of the airfield.

The first three assault waves of these three battalions reached the shore with comparatively few casualties between 9:10 and 9:17 A.M. Lieutenant Hawkins's platoon was by this time heavily engaged with a Japanese machine-gun emplacement a few yards inland from the end of the pier. The beach proved to be only about ten yards wide—less in many places—and was separated from the main part of the islet by a sea wall, four feet high, faced with coconut logs. The first troops flopped on the beach, under heavy fire from snipers and mortars: any who tried to scale the wall were met by a hail of machine-gun fire.

While the amtracs had been standing in to the beach, Japanese 37-mm. or 40-mm. guns had begun to fire on the Higgins boats farther out, in which the fourth wave of assault troops was boated. About 9:25 the commanding officer on Red Beach 1 reported that the boats coming in on his right flank were being held up on the reef, and that the troops who had started to wade in were under heavy fire. While precise figures can never be obtained, it seems likely that half the fatal casualties on Tarawa were incurred in this phase of the battle. The brisk southeast wind, which had rendered the use of smoke inadvisable, had also blown the water off the shelving reef, so that Higgins boats ran hard aground as much as half a mile offshore. Strafing attacks by carrier planes, which were to have been directed against the enemy gun emplacements, did not develop at the most opportune time. And there were more operational enemy guns than there should have been: the original air support plan had called for the dropping of 1,500 tons of bombs, and although the total eventually reached 700 tons, it was considerably under that at the time of the landings.

There were several instances in which a direct hit by a mortar or a medium shell on a landing boat killed all but two or three of the 20 or more occupants. There were many more cases in which casualties ran as high as 25 per cent. There were many casualties among the men wading in, in water up to their necks, loaded down by heavy equipment, in the face of murderous fire from automatic weapons.

With more men gaining the shore and attempting to push inland, the warship fire had to be lifted almost entirely. More and more Japanese manned their guns. Major Drewes, commander of the amtrac battalion, was killed in one of those vehicles. Lieut. Colonel Herbert R. Amey Jr., commander of the 2nd Battalion, 2nd Regiment, was killed in shallow water as he was about to gain Red Beach 2. The alligators which had carried the first waves to shore were already carrying wounded back to the boats. Since the boats could not traverse the reef, the alligators were pressed into a sort of ferry service.

Over the battlefield droned a Kingfisher observation plane (from one of the gunnery ships) piloted by Lieut. Commander Robert A. MacPherson. Shortly after 10 A.M., when there was little more gunfire for him to spot, he radioed to his task group commander: "Can't something be done about that blockhouse?"—a blockhouse near the center of the island in which many guns appeared to be sited. The task group commander (he has not been identified) acknowledged receipt of the message, but nothing was done about the blockhouse.

The commander of the landing forces (Combat Team 2) was Colonel David Shoup, who started ashore before 10 o'clock. He had not reached the pier when the 2nd Battalion, 8th Regiment, reported that it had pushed inland as far as the airfield (actually, to one of the taxiways) on the left flank. It was 10:08. But that local, rapid progress was not typical. At 10:18 the 3rd Battalion of the same regiment was ordered to get its boats up to the line of departure. It was none too soon. The 2nd Battalion of the 2nd Regiment, on the center beach, was in grave difficulties. Colonel Shoup had reached the pier (narrowly escaping death from a near miss while wading in) and set up temporary headquarters. At 11:05 he called for the 3rd Battalion, 8th Regiment, to land on Red Beach 3 and cut across the base of the pier to support the left flank of the hard-pressed battalion in the center. At 11:45 the center battalion still had not received the requested support, and Shoup had to reassure its acting commander: "Third Battalion is landing to your rear and catching hell." At 11:58, the acting battalion commander described his situation succinctly as "bad," but more help was on the way. Seven minutes later, two companies of the 1st Battalion, 2nd Regiment, landed on the center beach and gave direct support, more quickly and effectively than the 3rd Battalion of the 8th had been able to.

Colonel Shoup got ashore at about this time, on the center beach, just west of the pier. He saw for himself what havoc had been wrought by the Japanese fire: the two battalions of the 2nd Regiment originally committed were "disorganized"—a strong word in the technical, military usage. He set up his command post in a dugout at the edge of the beach, and went to work to straighten out the situation. The 2nd Regiment was now entirely committed on the right flank: the 3rd Battalion on Red Beach 1, the 1st and 2nd Battalions on Red Beach 2. Shoup ordered the latter two to attack toward the airfield to obtain a bridgehead, as distinct from the narrow toehold on the beach which at that time was all the marines had. On the left flank (Red Beach 3), the 8th Regiment was pinned down; the cut-up remnants of its 3rd Battalion were for the most part absorbed into the 2nd, although some men whose boats had drifted west of the pier in the effort to pick a hole through the curtain of fire and gain the beach stayed there and fought with the 2nd Regiment.

Early in the afternoon, medium tanks began to go ashore. Few though they were, they gave confidence to the foot troops (light tanks already had proved a failure, here as elsewhere), and they quickly cut a swath through to the taxiways of the airfield. The trouble was that not enough combat infantrymen could be put ashore. All afternoon, reserve teams were kept in their boats, milling around just out of range of the Japanese fire. Five hours after the first landings, the issue was in doubt. At 3 P.M., the commander of the battalion on Red Beach 1 reported by radio to Colonel Shoup that he was still in a landing boat offshore and consequently out of contact with his men fighting on the beach. General Julian Smith had to order him: "Land at any cost, regain control of your battalion and continue the attack."

On the basis of reports from Makin that the enemy garrison there was much weaker than that at Tarawa, General Holland Smith decided in the late afternoon to release the 6th Regiment, constituting the balance of the 2nd Marine Division, which had been held in corps reserve, to General Julian Smith for use at Tarawa. The question whether it should be used on other islets in the atoll was still not determined. For one thing, it was uncertain what strength the enemy had on these other islets. Before 6 P.M., General Julian Smith issued an order for the division reconnaissance company to make landings before midnight on Buota and Eita islets, but the order was not received by the reconnaissance company commander until after midnight, when it was too late to execute it.

As dusk fell, General Julian Smith ordered Colonel Shoup to consolidate his holdings and dig in in anticipation of a night attack. Colonel Shoup still had received no report from the 3rd Battalion, 2nd Regiment, on his extreme right flank. All he knew was that on Red Beach 2 the 1st and 2nd Battalions of the 2nd Regiment held positions as much as 150 yards inland; in the center, where his command post was situated, the beachhead was only about 50 yards deep; on the left, the 8th Regiment held Red Beach 3 to a depth of only 30 yards in many places. Both regiments were scattered along the beach, with many men pinned down below the sea wall, unable to penetrate inland at all.

The situation that night was touch-and-go. If the Japanese had launched a determined, well-coordinated counter-attack, they might have pushed the marines back into the lagoon. Evidently they lacked the cohesion to do so. While many of their strongpoints still held out, their communications above ground had been destroyed. Fires burning on the islet illuminated the pier and the approaches to the beach, over both of which American landing parties were trying to carry in supplies. Ammunition, rations and water had to be manhandled ashore under constant fire from the islet. There was also mysterious enfilading fire from positions out in the lagoon. The hulks of two wrecked Japanese ships are popularly supposed to have harbored the snipers and machine gunners who kept up this fire, but Robert Sherrod reports that some of it came from abandoned American tanks and amtracs—the Japanese swam out and manned them. For the marines on Betio it was a night of unmitigated hell.

Dawn of D-plus-one (November 22 [November 21, W.L.D.]) found the 1st Battalion of the 8th Regiment trying to land on Red Beach 2. This was the last reserve of the two regiments committed; all that was left was the 6th Regiment, now being held as division reserve. The first waves suffered the same frightful casualties as had the original waves on D-day. Colonel Elmer Hall, the regimental commander who directed the battalion landing, held off the later waves, reporting that it was "Impossible to land vehicles and equipment because of heavy enemy fire." Nor was this the only setback in the first light of the new day: enemy mortars got the range on the area where the medium tanks had been parked for the night. Most of the tanks escaped. Lieutenant Hawkins, whose scout-sniper platoon had manned a defense perimeter during the night, set out in the morning to clean out Japanese machine-gun nests along the beach. He was wounded, but continued the work in cooperation with tanks, and his section knocked out three pillboxes. Shortly afterward, he set out again on a similar mission. This time, he was mortally wounded in the shoulder by a shell which severed an artery. The Medal of Honor was awarded, posthumously, and while he lay dying his comrades were engaged in the capture of the air strip which now bears the name of Hawkins Field.

The battle to take this airfield was complex and confused. No straightforward combat narrative has been compiled, setting forth its progress step by step.* The most striking feature of the early hours of D-plus-one day is the fact that casualties among the marines seeking to land on the islet were proportionately as heavy as on D-day. The Japanese had not lost enough emplacements to effect a material reduction in their

---

* Of the extensive literature on the campaign, *Tarawa: The Story of a Battle*, by Robert Sherrod (Duell, Sloan and Pearce, New York, 1944) remains the best general account—amazingly accurate when one considers that it was compiled within a few weeks after the engagement. *Betio Beachhead*, by Four Marines Who Were There (G. P. Putnam's Sons, New York, 1945), suffers from official supervision, but discloses many important details.

volume of fire. Moreover, the coconut palms from which snipers had been shot on D-day were now reoccupied. Fortunately, much sniper fire was inaccurate. Unfortunately, so was much of the air support given by Hellcat fighter-bombers from the American carriers.

When the battle was exactly 24 hours old, Colonel Shoup sent a message to General Julian Smith: "Urgently request rations and small-arms ammunition landed on beach." As the sun rose higher and beat directly through the shredded palms upon the naked beach, the shortage of drinking water became as serious as the shortage of ammunition. (The scarcity of food was not yet serious: under the emotional stress of combat, many men will go two days without thought of food.)

At 10:30 A.M. General Smith asked Colonel Shoup whether the two regiments now entirely committed would be sufficient to take the island. He still was undecided whether to commit the 6th Regiment elsewhere (on other islets). About this time, forward elements advanced across most of the air strip, but at 11:30 Shoup could only report that his situation was still critical. The center (Red Beach 2) was in trouble, and the colonel asked to have a battalion of the 6th Marines put ashore there—in rubber boats, so that they would not be grounded on the reefs, and would present a low target. The few tanks operating were in great demand; so were the flame-throwers of the 18th Regiment (Engineers).

Shortly after noon, the pace quickened. Elements of the 2nd and 3rd Battalions of the 2nd Regiment, pushing along the islet from the right flank, reached the beach at the western tip of Betio. This opened up the possibility of effecting new landings on the western shore, which had been designated as Green Beach, under less direct and less heavy fire from the enemy. Part of the 6th Regiment was at once ordered to make such a landing. Almost simultaneously, another combat team from the 6th was ordered to go ashore on Bairiki islet, off the eastern tip of Betio, to prevent a Japanese withdrawal in that direction. The landing areas on Bairiki had been designated as Blue Beach. About this time, too, the 1st Battalion of the 10th Regiment (Artillery) got ashore on Red Beach, in the center of the original landing area, and set up its guns to support the accelerating advance. This period, approximately 30 hours after the first waves landed, was the turning point of the battle for Betio. Japanese fire against the pier was cut down until, shortly before sunset, mobile guns towed by jeeps were landed on it and trundled along it to the land.

A destroyer stood inshore and fired about 80 rounds of 5-inch bombardment ammunition at the big central blockhouse which had attracted Lieut. Commander MacPherson's attention the previous morning. The bombardment ammunition, fired at close range (with a flat trajectory) was ineffective against the several feet of reinforced concrete, coconut logs and sandbags of the blockhouse. Armor-piercing ammunition used at a greater distance to gain the penetrating effect of "plunging fire" might have done more good.

The night was quiet, by comparison with the night which had preceded it. Before dawn of D-plus-two day, a lone nuisance raider dropped eight bombs—four on the American positions and four on the Japanese. As Keith Wheeler, of the *Chicago Times,* put it: "He was absolutely impartial." One marine was killed and several were wounded.

The 1st Battalion (commanded by Major William K. Jones) of the 6th Regiment moved out at dawn from Green Beach, at the southwestern tip of the islet, and tackled the enemy positions facing the south shore. This had been designated as Black Beach, and the decision not to land upon it had been wisely taken. The artillery and machine-gun emplacements were even stronger and more numerous than elsewhere on the islet. However, they faced the sea, and the marines were able to approach them from the side or the rear. The actual elimination of the positions was more difficult than the approach. Marines with sub-machine guns or flame-throwers had to expose themselves while they got close enough to pour bullets, grenades or flame into the firing slits. Often, all three were required, and because the underground positions were divided into chambers, each pillbox or blockhouse had to be treated two or three times, because the first treatment did not kill the Japanese in the rear chambers.

The 3rd Battalion (Lieut. Colonel Kenneth McLeod) of the 6th Regiment also was landed on Green Beach and began to advance eastward along the main axis of the islet. To pave the way for the ground troops, ship and air bombardment was maintained on the long, narrow eastern tip, where the enemy had many large, well-built blockhouses. The marines were spread out over the rest of the islet in such a confused pattern that it would have been unsafe to give them fire support. Every marine position, except those on the beaches, had Japanese behind it.

The battle plan for the day provided for rectifying this confusion. The two large pockets of Japanese, southwest and southeast of the pier, were to be cleaned out by the 8th Regiment. At nightfall, it should be possible for the 8th to establish a secure line down the eastern end of the air strip, joining up with the 6th Regiment near the south shore. There was no major hitch in the unfolding of this plan. More tanks had been landed, and these, along with 75-mm. guns on half-tracks, gave the marines the close fire support they needed against the formidable pillboxes. One hitch developed in the landing of General Julian Smith, who left the *Maryland* in the late morning, intending to set up his divisional command post on Green Beach. His Higgins boat grounded a hundred yards offshore, and the general had to wade. Then he found the location unsuitable for a command post, and re-embarked in an amtrac to go around to Red Beach. The amtrac was crippled, and the driver wounded, but the general transferred to another and finally joined Colonel Shoup in the command post of Combat Team 2.

By 7 P.M., the battle plan had been executed. The marines had a fairly straight line running from north to south near the eastern edge of the airfield, and the surviving Japanese were pinned in the eastern end of the islet. They had no hope of escaping to Bairiki, because the 2nd Battalion of the 6th Regiment had landed there the previous night. The only possible avenue of escape had been closed.

One of the most remarkable features of the Betio battle is the fact that on this third night the Japanese were capable of organizing a determined counter-attack, although they had failed to do so on the preceding nights, when they might have profited more. This was no "banzai charge": it was launched by men firing sub-machine guns, firing rifles and throwing grenades in the hope of causing the marines to open fire and thus betray their positions.

In this first phase, the enemy drove a wedge between Company A and Company B of the 6th Regiment. Each company held its positions, but with nothing to spare: 1st Lieut. Norman K. Thomas, commanding Company B, notified Major Jones, the battalion commander, that another such attack would carry through his lines. Jones told him that he could not spare reinforcements, and that Thomas simply had to hold. Jones did, however, send water and ammunition up to Company B, using the medium tank "China Gal" as a transport. Also, destroyer fire was called for, to be laid on the area from which the Japanese had attacked. The 5-inch shells fell within 50 yards of the marines' lines. Undoubtedly this delayed the second phase of the attack, and it may have broken the Japanese cohesion, for the assault which began shortly after 11 P.M. had more of the elements of a banzai charge. Some of the Japanese appeared brandishing sabers. One got into the foxhole where Lieut. Thomas had his command post. Thomas killed him with his pistol butt. The second attack was beaten off: again, with nothing to spare.

The Japanese spent hours reorganizing, and tried a variety of tricks to get the marines to betray their positions. At 4 A.M. the final phase began. By this time, the banzai aspect was still more pronounced. Some of the attackers were naked, except for a G-string, and carried only a saber or a knife. There were countless close-quarter fights, of the type in which the marines excel. In the morning, about 300 Japanese bodies were counted in front of the battalion's positions. Company B had held, as ordered, but at great cost. The battalion was relieved by the 3rd Battalion, which had landed on Green Beach and had passed through the intervening 2nd Regiment.

At 8 A.M. of D-plus-three day (November 24, local date, or November 23, West Longitude date), the 3rd Battalion jumped off. The Japanese on this sector had shot their bolt during the night. The marines drove down the remaining, narrowing half of Betio islet in a little under five hours with only 34 casualties (nine killed, 25 wounded). The remaining Japanese were numerous, but exhausted and ineffective. In the area through which the 3rd Battalion of the 6th Regiment passed, 475 enemy dead were counted. Fourteen prisoners were taken. A few minutes after the 6th reached the eastern end of Betio, the last Jap pocket on Red Beach 1, which had been holding out for three days, was cleaned out by the circling 1st Battalion of the 8th Regiment.

It was 1:12 P.M. when General Julian Smith declared the islet of Betio secure: 76 hours, 12 minutes after the first landing by the scout and sniper platoon of Lieutenant Hawkins. "Secure" is a relative term: for several days and nights, odd Japanese continued to appear from the ruins in which they had been entombed; they tried to exact one or two American lives before they themselves were killed, and a few of them succeeded. But the islet was secure enough for the Stars and Stripes to be run up, alongside the Union Jack brought by the returning British Resident Commissioner. Within 24 hours, the assault troops began re-embarking, to be relieved by garrison troops. A day later, the Seabees had repaired the air strip sufficiently for Ensign W. W. Kelly to fly in a Hellcat from Commander Bernard M. Strean's Fighting Squadron One, ferried in by the *Nassau* and *Barnes*.

Strangely enough, the precise cost of the capture of Tarawa will never be known. The Marine Corps assault troops lost 984 officers and men dead or missing, and had 2,072 wounded. In addition, the Navy Medical Corps lost two officers and at least 27 enlisted men, and two or three times as many were lost from among the coxswains of landing craft, gunnery observers and fliers from the carriers. The best approximation possible is that the total dead numbered 1,100. Later (on November 28), 32 more marines were to be killed in mopping up the last Japanese pocket on the atoll: 200 men who had gathered on the northern islet of Buariki.

Two questions about these heavy casualties have caused the campaign for Tarawa to stand out in the annals of the Pacific war: (1), why were they so heavy, and (2), could they have been reduced? There is wide agreement on the answer to the first question: the Japanese positions were better dug in and better protected than had been expected; the mischance which brought a stiff wind to carry the water off the coral shelf northwest of Betio left the first landing elements hideously exposed; after the landings, the Japanese fought, as they have always fought, to the death.

Could the casualties have been reduced?

It is the writer's opinion that other atolls in the Gilbert Islands should have been invaded first, to permit the building of airfields from which Tarawa (and Makin, of which more later) could have been brought under much heavier and more intensive aerial attack. It is the writer's opinion that the indirect approach to Betio, from other islets in the Tarawa atoll, might have served to reduce the casualties, as it did later at Kwajalein and Eniwetok. It is clear that the preliminary warship bombardment was not heavy enough, and that the air support was not as heavy as had been intended, nor was it always delivered at the right time. These are largely matters of experience. There is no doubt that plunging fire with armor-piercing shells would have done more damage to the well-casemated Japanese positions than short-range fire with bombardment ammunition. But in this connection it must be remembered that the invasion of the Gilbert Islands represented the first sortie by the United States Fleet into a Japanese preserve; Admiral Spruance properly insisted that his ships retain their quota of armor-piercing shells, against the possibility of a fleet engagement with the enemy. Hindsight makes it clear that this precaution was unnecessary, but hindsight was not available before the invasion of the Gilberts began.

The worst that can be charged against the leadership in the Tarawa operation is a series of errors of judgment arising from lack of experience in this kind of attack (it was the first atoll ever to be reduced by amphibious forces) and to lack of information about the objective. However, naval and marine officers who have tried to cover up the question of responsibility by asserting that the preliminary bombardment was as heavy as it could have been, and did as much damage as it could have done, are doing their cause a disservice. Such statements are simply not true. Never again, after Tarawa, did the assault troops go ashore after so little preparation by guns and aircraft. It is more constructive to point out that the lesson of Tarawa was learned than to pretend that it did not exist.

While the battle for Tarawa was raging, there was action also at Makin, but of a very different sort. Makin atoll lay 120 miles north of Betio, and apparently had not been strengthened by the Japanese, despite the attack on it in August, 1942, by Carlson's Raiders: the garrison still consisted of about 300 combatants and an equal number of laborers, mostly Koreans. It has not been disclosed whether the weakness of the defenders was known before the attack was launched. If it was, the effort expended was disproportionately great. The covering fleet was similar in size to that at Tarawa, and was under the personal direction of Rear Admiral Richmond Kelly Turner, the Navy's top amphibious force commander. Distant cover, against the possibility of Japanese attack from the Marshalls, was provided by the carrier task group under Rear Admiral Charles A. Pownall. Close cover was provided by a group under Rear Admiral Arthur W. Radford, further supported by escort carriers under Rear Admiral Henry M. Mullinix, with his flag in the ill-fated *Liscome Bay*.

Before dawn on November 21 (November 20, W.L.D.), battleships, cruisers and destroyers laid down an immense barrage on Butaritari, the main islet in the atoll. This is about eleven miles long, so the effect of the bombardment was far less concentrated than on Betio. The Japanese had had forewarning of the attack, from a reconnaissance plane report the night before, and no doubt the entire garrison went underground when the firing began. It is doubtful that any of them were killed by it. However, there were several deaths and a number of injuries among the 1,700 natives who had no underground shelters to hide in.

Coordination between the amphibious force and the naval aircraft was better than at Tarawa, and the landing beaches were bombed and strafed by carrier planes as the first waves of amtracs stood in toward the beaches. The assault troops comprised the 27th Division (three regiments of the former New York National Guard), under Major General Ralph Smith. The main burden of the fighting was to be borne by the 165th Regiment, better known by its World War I designation of the "Fighting 69th," under Colonel Gardner Conroy, but the first landing was made by a company combat team of the 105th Regiment (upstate New Yorkers, nicknamed "Apple-Knockers"), under Major Theodore Bradt. It landed on the north shore of Butaritari. The plan was to divide the Japanese and to prevent their sending reinforcements to the west against the major landing by the 165th. Bradt's vehicles encountered little fire on their way to the beach and drove quickly inland, capturing a large blockhouse where a score or more of the enemy are reported to have been killed. Later, the 2nd Battalion of the 165th, under Lieut. Colonel John F. McDonough, landed in this area, using the 105th's beachhead as a springboard.

Meanwhile, the 1st and 3rd Battalions of the 165th landed at the broad western tip of the island. There were two half-submerged hulks off-shore; the Japanese emplaced there let the first wave reach the beach, and then opened fire on the rear and flank of the second wave. Admiral Turner sent a destroyer into the lagoon, and its guns demolished the hulks at close range. Tanks (medium and light) followed closely on the first waves of infantrymen. Some of the troops had to wade in 300 yards, but there was no comparison with the scene at Betio.

The two battalions found only snipers and small, isolated parties of Japanese at the western end of the island, and soon began to advance toward the east. The main enemy strength was in the center, and comprised an area about a mile long, 300 to 500 yards wide, bounded on both east and west by formidable tank traps. It was believed that the majority of the Japanese would make a stand there. By early afternoon, the western landing team was ashore, with command posts set up. The 1st Battalion had had some opposition in landing; the 3rd ("Shamrock") Battalion, under Lieut. Colonel Joseph T. Hart, had had little. The 3rd was accompanied by Lieut. Colonel James Roosevelt, U.S.M.C.R., second in command to Carlson during the 1942 raid, now present as an observer.

The main weight of the advance was channeled down the north shore road of the island. When the first substantial opposition developed, Colonel Conroy found it necessary to expose himself in giving orders for resumption of the attack, and he was killed instantly by a Japanese marksman. Lieut. Colonel Gerald W. Kelly took over as acting regimental commander. Progress was rapid: the 2nd Battalion's landing on the north shore, and the advance eastward by the 1st and 3rd, caught the Japanese in the West Tank Trap in a trap of American design. The defense line for the night was set up farther east.

During the second day, the 2nd Battalion took up the advance, and gained about half a mile through a network of well-casemated Japanese positions. As at Betio, it was found that the tanks' 75-mm. shells bounced off the cupolas of the enemy positions, or exploded harmlessly against them. The only effective weapon was the satchel charge of TNT, which was often inserted in the firing slits by means of a long pole. Snipers were numerous in the vegetation, which was unusually luxuriant for a low islet. An unexpected difficulty arose from the fact that the natives' taro pits proved effective tank traps. At nightfall, it was estimated that 250 Japanese had been killed; it seems doubtful that all of these were combatants, but there is no reason to believe that more than about a hundred enemy combatants were left alive. The American line for the night was still 300 yards short of the East Tank Trap.

At dawn of D-plus-two a heavy artillery barrage was laid down on the area around the tank trap, but it appears to have been wasted, for there were no Japanese in this sector when the 3rd Battalion passed through the 2nd and took over the advance. In fact, the 3rd simply walked through the East Tank Trap unopposed, and kept on walking for three and a quarter miles beyond it, without even coming under sniper fire. This night, Company I (on the left or lagoon side) and Company K (on the ocean side) held the front. The battalion command post was in Company I's sector. By chance, the line had been established within 50 yards of prepared Japanese defenses. This fact was not known to Colonel Hart, for the advance had been continued too long, almost until dark, and there had been no daylight left to reconnoiter the area ahead.

The events of this night have been greatly exaggerated. The Japanese staged one of their infiltration attacks, similar to that during the same night on Betio (described above). Expert analysts like Lieut. Colonel S. L. A. Marshall are satisfied that some of the Japanese gave themselves Dutch courage by drinking sake between different phases of the attack, which may justify the label of "Sake Battle" which has been attached to the engagement. But it was not otherwise especially remarkable. Several men in the crews of the forward guns were killed or wounded; many showed great resourcefulness in meeting an attack of a type with which they were unfamiliar. About 30 Japanese appear to have been killed during the night.

On the morning of D-plus-three, it was plain that the Japanese had expended themselves in the night attack. There was no more organized opposition as the 169th swept on to the eastern end of Butaritari. Major General Ralph Smith reported to Major General Holland Smith, "Makin taken," just two hours before Major General Julian Smith made a similar report on Tarawa. Actually, as at Tarawa, there was a little cleaning up still to be done.

Simultaneously with the landings at Tarawa and Makin, a third atoll in the Gilberts had been invaded. This was Apemama, made famous by Robert Louis Stevenson. There were few Japanese on the atoll, but they saw that the invading force also was small, consisting only of a company of marine scouts, landed by submarine. They resisted fiercely for a while, and one American was killed and two were wounded. A larger force was embarked at Tarawa and headed for Apemama.

While it was on the way, Captain Jones, commanding the scout company, persuaded a destroyer on screening duty off Apemama to lay down a barrage on the Japanese defense area. The day the reinforcements arrived, Captain Jones found that some of the Japanese had been killed in the bombardment and the rest had obligingly committed hara-kiri.

There were no Japanese in the rest of the Gilbert Islands. The archipelago was secure, and provided a foothold for the next leapfrog move through Micronesia. In addition to the casualties on land, already enumerated, the attacking forces had lost the escort carrier *Liscome Bay*.

While the land fighting on Makin and Tarawa was raging, the Japanese had sent down many air attack groups from the Marshalls. In several cases the pilots had bored in as far as the fringe of the anti-aircraft curtain, only to decide that the risks were too great, and then turn tail. Even these abortive attacks became less numerous when the land fighting ended—perhaps because the surface craft then had greater freedom of movement—but then Japanese submarines began to be reported, especially in the waters around Makin.

At dawn on November 25 (November 24, W.L.D.) the escort carriers in Rear Admiral Mullinix's group had their crews at general quarters, as is usual at twilight in dangerous waters. The air crews were at flight quarters, for it was planned to fly off search groups at sunrise. At 5:13 A.M. a lookout cried:

"Here comes a torpedo!" The *Liscome Bay* was capable of only 18 knots, and was not particularly maneuverable, despite her twin screws.* There was no time for Captain Irving D. Wiltsie (who had been navigator of the *Yorktown* when she was sunk at Midway) to maneuver the *Liscome Bay*. The torpedo hit amidships, and immediately set off a series of explosions (in the magazines or gasoline storage, or both) which were more damaging than the original explosion of the torpedo itself.

Observers on near-by ships could not imagine how any one could be left alive on the *Liscome Bay*. The little jeep carrier was a mass of flames and explosions: the deck of a battleship 1,500 yards away was littered with debris from the stricken ship. But many men did survive the first explosions, and soon obeyed the order of Lieut. Commander Bodler, who appeared to be the senior surviving officer, to abandon ship.

The sea was covered with gasoline and oil which were ignited by a blazing aircraft which fell over the side as the ship canted to starboard. Many of the men in the water were killed in this fire, and some of the survivors were terribly burned, while others were injured by underwater explosions. One of the destroyers had the extraordinary record of having rescued survivors from the original *Lexington* and *Yorktown* as well as the *Hornet*, but those great ships had died slowly: the tinder-box *Liscome Bay* was an inferno from the moment she was struck until, 20 minutes later, the shattered hulk sank by the stern. In this case, the rescuers found their task infinitely more heart-breaking, and numerically less rewarding: only about 200 officers and men were saved; 54 officers and 658 men were lost, including Admiral Mullinix and Captain Wiltsie. The *Liscome Bay* was the first escort carrier lost, and the only carrier of any class lost in 1943.

Although no other ships were sunk, there was one other notable loss in the Gilberts campaign. Lieut. Commander Edward H. ("Butch") O'Hare, who had been awarded the Medal of Honor for shooting down five Japanese bombers in a few minutes and saving the old *Lexington* off Bougainville in February, 1942, was flying in the Gilberts campaign as the

---

* She was one of the smallest (480-foot) class of escort carriers, built in the Kaiser yards at Vancouver, Wash. She had been in commission only two and a half months when the invasion of the Gilbert Islands began.

skipper of a composite squadron. During the night of November 28 (November 27, W.L.D.), the Japanese sent down one of their torpedo strikes, and O'Hare went up, leading a flight of night fighters to protect Admiral Radford's task group. What happened is unclear, and presumably never will be known. The night fighters made an intercept, and shot down two or three of the Japanese attackers, driving the rest away. O'Hare turned off, perhaps to pursue one of the enemy, and was never seen again. Lieut. Commander John L. Phillips, who had been flying wing on O'Hare, saw a splash like that of a plane striking the water. The inference that it was O'Hare's plane is inescapable, but in the absence of exact proof, the Navy listed O'Hare as "missing." Admiral Radford is of the opinion that in the action in which O'Hare gave his life, the night fighters saved the carriers from "certain torpedo hits."

XII. Giant Atolls

THE INVASION of the Marshall Islands had been decided upon by the Joint Chiefs of Staff before the recapture of the Gilberts was actually undertaken, and a general directive concerning the operation had gone out from CominCh King in Washington to CinCPac Nimitz at Pearl Harbor. The tentative plans drawn up by King's staff provided for beginning the conquest of the Marshalls at the beginning—in the eastern or Radak (Sunrise) chain, containing the frontline positions facing out upon the ocean which the attackers must cross. Naturally, the Japanese had elaborately fortified several of the individual atolls in this chain: Wotje, Maloelap and Mili. Two islands in the western or Ralik (Sunset) chain must be grouped with these three for military purposes: Rongelap, at the northern end, and Jaluit, at the southern end. These protected the flanks of the eastern front.

But CinCPac's staff was beginning to question whether it was necessary to begin at the beginning. Why not by-pass the outer islands named above, and strike at once, deep in the rear, to Kwajalein and Eniwetok? While these were great Japanese bases, it was probable that they did not have the same highly perfected beach defenses as Tarawa and the islands in the eastern Marshalls. To advance directly into the western Marshalls, and descend upon Kwajalein, after the recapture of the Gilberts would be leapfrogging on a gigantic scale never before contemplated. It would be extremely dangerous: an amphibious force lying off Kwajalein would be exposed to attack by Japanese aircraft flying from the north (Wake), from the northwest (Eniwetok and Ujelang), from the southwest (the Carolines), from the south (Nauru)—and from all the by-passed islands to the east, unless these could be neutralized in advance. Could these positions be neutralized? Air officers on

Admiral Nimitz's staff and his new war plans officer, Rear Admiral Forrest Sherman, assured him that they could. Nimitz approved a new plan, providing for beginning the invasion of the Marshalls at Kwajalein.

Now it was up to the airmen to make good on their promise to inhibit interference from the islands which were to be by-passed, and to soften up the island or islands to be invaded. This phase of the operation overlapped the securing of the Gilbert Islands. A constant source of irritation during the Gilberts campaign had been the persistence of the Japanese on Nauru. This flyspeck had been repeatedly bombed, but its air base was regularly and promptly repaired by the enemy so that a few planes could fly off to attack the American fleet off the Gilberts. It was decided to administer a knock-out blow to Nauru. A mixed task force containing the carriers *Bunker Hill* and *Monterey* was assigned for the purpose. For once, the carriers' planes played a relatively minor role. Rear Admiral Willis A. Lee, the outstanding "battleship admiral" in the new, air-minded navy, took all six of the 35,000-ton battleships (*North Carolina, Washington, South Dakota, Massachusetts, Indiana* and *Alabama*) within gun range of Nauru, and tried to sink it. Each big ship fired 200 or more rounds of 16-inch ammunition. Nauru did not sink, but it never fully recovered from this onslaught, and small, regular raids were sufficient to keep it neutralized thereafter.

The atolls to the north and west of the Gilberts consisted of small broken ribbons of land, where the Japanese could disperse their installations widely. Bombardiers also had a difficult task: overs or shorts would be almost certain to fall in the water, probably killing some fish which the Japanese would gladly accept for their next day's rations.

After Tarawa was secured, there was an opportunity for one heavy blow to be struck by the carriers before they had to return to Pearl Harbor. It was a double blow, at Kwajalein, well to the west, and at Wotje, in the eastern chain. The task force was under the command of Rear Admiral Charles A. Pownall, with a group under Rear Admiral Alfred E. Montgomery. Kwajalein was by far the more juicy target. Here, air groups flying from the *Lexington* (II), *Yorktown* (II), *Enterprise, Essex* and other carriers not yet identified, took the Jap-

anese by surprise, on December 4. The enemy had just sent
in a major convoy of reinforcements and supplies. A dozen
transports—unhappily, they already had been unloaded—were
lying at anchor at the south end of the lagoon off Kwajalein
islet. At the north end, off the twin islets of Roi and Namur,
were a light cruiser and a large tanker. Another light cruiser
was in transit across the lagoon. Most of these ships had been
sunk or damaged before the Japanese could fly off fighter planes
or get the range with their anti-aircraft.

Actually, however, the strike might have been of more benefit
to future operations if the enemy ships had not been there.
Many bombers which had been assigned targets among the
ground installations were unwisely diverted to attack the shipping. One result was that the Japanese were able, somewhat
belatedly, to get off a larger number of aircraft than otherwise
would have been the case. At least 50 planes, including many
torpedo bombers, were left undamaged. The American attack
ended within an hour, and the carriers turned away at high
speed. But the Japanese planes caught up with them and subjected them to a 5½-hour attack. Although many of the attacking aircraft were shot down, the *Lexington* was hit by a torpedo
on the starboard quarter. She was able to return to base under
her own power.

For the next six weeks, the task of keeping the Marshalls
neutralized devolved upon land-based air forces. At this time,
all those in the area were under the command of Rear Admiral
John H. Hoover. There were Army planes from Major General Willis H. Hale's Seventh Air Force; Navy planes from
Fleet Air Wing Two (to be followed by Marine Air Wing
Four). The Seventh Air Force alone dropped 1,750 tons of
bombs in these six weeks. Every airfield in the Marshalls was
rendered 20 per cent to 80 per cent inoperative. Equally important, thousands of photographs were taken both by the bombers
and by special photo-reconnaissance planes using new devices
to permit effective photography at night.

On January 5, 1944, the bombing of targets in the Marshalls
went on a one-a-day schedule. Thereafter, the enemy knew
what was coming, but he did not know precisely where it was
coming.

The forces assigned to the invasion were so great that they

had to be assembled at various points around the compass from Kwajalein, and dispatched at their several speeds on a schedule which would get them to the objective in the proper order. Some came from the Aleutians, some from the West Coast, some from Hawaii, some from the Ellice Islands and some from islands farther south and west. Vice Admiral Raymond A. Spruance was in command of everything in the expedition, whether it floated or flew. His principal subordinate for the naval forces was Rear Admiral Marc A. Mitscher, with his flag in the *Yorktown*. Under Mitscher were four admirals, each commanding a task group of carriers. The organization of the command for the amphibious forces was dictated by the geography of the objective.

Kwajalein is shaped into so narrow a ribbon, which in turn is cut into so many short pieces, that it makes a perimeter no less than 230 miles long. The whole formation, a mighty monument to the puny polyp, is the world's largest atoll. Since the atoll is 80 miles long (measured inside the crescent-shaped lagoon) and its principal "land masses" are 50 miles apart, the amphibious forces for its capture were divided into two distinct units. Rear Admiral Richmond Kelly Turner exercised both the over-all amphibious command and the direct command of the southern force assigned to the islet of Kwajalein, which gives its name to the entire atoll. Operating closely under Turner was a minor attack group, led by Rear Admiral Harry W. Hill. To the north, assigned to take the' islets of Roi and Namur, was the second major attack group, under Rear Admiral Richard L. Conolly.

The extraordinary effectiveness of the preliminary aerial campaign against the islands is attested by the fact that not one of the hundreds of American ships engaged was attacked by any Japanese surface, submarine or air craft during the voyage.

Despite the thoroughness of this preliminary effort, no chances were taken. All the islands where the Japanese were known to be in any strength were designated as targets for both land-based and carrier-based bombers on January 30. From their southern atolls, Admiral Hoover's planes struck at every island within reach: Mili and Jaluit, Wotje and Maloelap, and both ends of the Kwajalein atoll. The more northerly atolls had, in addition, the honor of having entire carrier task groups assigned to their discomfiture. The group under Rear Admiral Samuel G. Ginder did its best to flatten Wotje; the group under Rear Admiral J. W. Reeves hammered Maloelap. To make triply sure, heavy cruisers under Rear Admiral Ernest G. Small (the *Pensacola, Salt Lake City* and *Chester*) divided their attentions between these two atolls. A third carrier group under Rear Admiral Frederick C. Sherman worked over Kwajalein islet, while the fourth, under Rear Admiral Montgomery, took on the job of reducing Roi and Namur.

Eniwetok was off to the northwest, and would have been immune under this set-up. So during the night of January 30-31, the carrier groups were redistributed. Only Admiral Montgomery kept his assignment unchanged. Admiral Sherman pulled out from Kwajalein and went off to work over Eniwetok. To fill the void off Kwajalein, Admiral Reeves steamed west from Maloelap. And to make sure that the Japanese on Maloelap would derive no benefit from his departure, the group under Admiral Ginder was divided, and one half took on Maloelap while the remainder continued to devote their attentions to Wotje. Again, Admiral Small's 8-inch-gun cruisers were lobbing shells into these familiar targets. (The *Salt Lake City* had bombarded Wotje in the first American offensive action of the war, on February 1, 1942, while the *Chester* had bombarded Maloelap.)

But the real weight of the growing offensive was now being poured on the strongpoints at Kwajalein. Having given his carrier airmen a day in which to ruin any aircraft the enemy might still have around, and to ruin his shore batteries, Admiral Spruance moved up his bombardment force. In all, there were 15 battleships in the area, but two, the *New Jersey* (wearing Spruance's flag) and the *Iowa* were assigned as a screening force to cover the carriers. In the remaining 13 there were ships which had been damaged at Pearl Harbor: the *Maryland* (16-inch), *Tennessee* and *Pennsylvania* (14-inch). One, the *Colorado,* had been on the West Coast at the time of that attack. There were ships which had been in the Atlantic when war came to the Pacific: the new *North Carolina* and *Washington* (16-inch) and the old, but rebuilt, *Idaho, New Mexico* and *Mississippi* (14-inch). There were ships which had not existed as fighting units two years earlier: the *South Dakota, Massachusetts, Indiana* and *Alabama.*

Only five large carriers have yet been identified as having been in the four task groups mentioned: the *Saratoga, Enterprise, Essex, Yorktown* and *Bunker Hill,* and only two light carriers, the *Princeton* and *Cowpens.* But there must have been enough, together with the 15 battleships, to make Admiral Spruance's force the greatest concentration of modern capital ships ever assembled. Supporting the battleships and combat carriers were escort carriers, vulnerable and relatively slow, but effective in areas where enemy air power had been erased. Five have been identified: the *Corregidor, Sangamon, Suwanee, Chenango* and *Nassau.* There were cruisers and destroyers galore. Among the former there have been named: the new heavies, *Baltimore* and *Boston;* the veterans *Wichita, New Orleans, Indianapolis, Louisville, San Francisco, Portland, Minneapolis;* the little anti-aircraft ships *San Juan, San Diego* and *Oakland,* and the new, heavily-armed lights, *Mobile, Santa Fe* and *Biloxi.*

The plan was to flatten everything that the Japanese had on the islets of Roi, Namur and Kwajalein before landings were begun. To achieve this plan, 2,500 tons of bombs and shells were rained upon the two square miles of Roi and Namur in the 48 hours beginning at dawn on January 30; an equal tonnage was dropped on the similar area of Kwajalein islet. As a further insurance, the Army's plan for an indirect approach to the main objectives was to go into effect on the morning of February 1.

In the first, dark hours of that morning, the first American warship to penetrate Kwajalein in a generation was inside the lagoon. It was a destroyer, seeking to knock out shore batteries by firing from their rear. However, the destroyer itself was caught in a crossfire (possibly including overs from American ships outside) and was soon ordered out again.

The assault troops for the southern islets comprised the Army's 7th Division, the victors of Attu, commanded by Major General Charles H. Corlett. Their first objectives were four islets lying northwest of Kwajalein itself: Ninni and Gea, flanking Gea Pass from the ocean to the lagoon, and Ennylabegan and Enubuj, flanking South Pass. Aerial reconnaissance had indicated that all these islets were very lightly held, if at all. The Reconnaissance Troop (a cavalry unit) of the 7th Division had been ordered to take Ninni and Gea. For this purpose it was divided into two groups, each accompanied by half an infantry company.

The night was pitch black, and a variable rain was falling when the first landing craft were hoisted over the sides of the transports. The infantrymen were loaded into these; the cavalrymen into rubber boats. The landing craft towed the boats to within 800 yards of the shore. The northern force of cavalrymen, under Captain Paul B. Gritta, which had been ordered to take Ninni, landed on an islet about 4 A.M. Gritta's men were not met by enemy fire: they waded through three feet of water from the point where their boats grounded, about 20 yards out. They began to reconnoiter the island.

The southern group, under Lieut. Emmett L. Tiner, landed on Gea as planned, but failed to cover the entire islet in their first sweep across it in skirmish line, and so missed the few Japanese who were holed up near the east shore. The islet had to be combed again: one American was killed, another wounded, and about 30 Japanese were killed. That ended the resistance on Gea, which is 600 yards long and 400 yards wide.

By sunrise, Gritta had all his men ashore, had killed four and captured two Japanese, and was preparing to clean out two more pockets, when division headquarters notified him by radio that he had captured the wrong islet. In the dark, his force had gone ashore on well-named Chance Island,* a mile northwest of Ninni. The high command (Admiral Turner and General Corlett) was not concerned about any stray islets, but only about securing the land on both sides of Gea Pass, to win a protected channel into the lagoon for subsequent operations. Gritta was ordered to re-embark his men and get over to Ninni at once. The cavalrymen left in their rubber boats at 10 o'clock; the infantrymen remained to hold Chance Island. The cavalrymen combed Ninni, and by 2:30 P.M. were able to report that there was not a Japanese on it. Gea Pass was safe for shipping. Meanwhile, the infantrymen on Chance Island had stirred up a hornet's nest of Japs. They were ordered to change

* Originally known as Gehh Island.

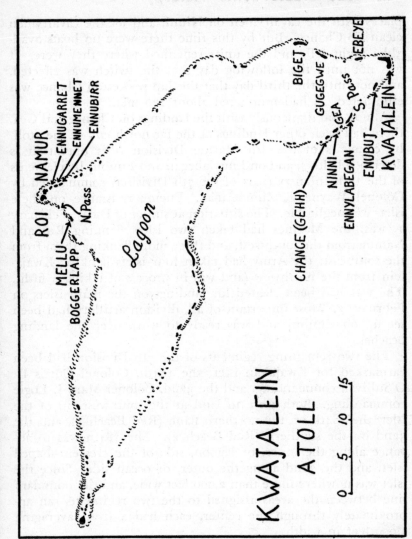

places with the cavalrymen on Ninni, and let the cavalrymen clean up Chance. But by this time there were no boats available; night fell, and the units remained where they were. It was not until the following day that the switch was effected, and not until the third day that the Jap pocket on Chance was eliminated. It had numbered about 120 men.

Almost simultaneously with the landings on Chance and Gea, there had been other landings at the far north end of the atoll, by elements of the 4th Marine Division (this operation is described below), and on Ennylabegan and Enubuj by elements of the 17th Infantry (part of the 7th Division) commanded by Colonel Wayne C. Zimmerman. Enemy resistance on these islets was negligible. The situation at sunset of D-day, February 1, was: the Marines had taken two islets flanking Roi and Namur from the southwest, and three more flanking them from the southeast; the Army had taken four islets flanking Kwajalein from the northwest (and was in process of taking a fifth). The way had been cleared for landings on the main islets on February 2. Most important of all, division artillery had been set up on Enubuj and was ready to work over the landing beaches.

The two remaining regiments of the 7th Division had been earmarked for Kwajalein islet: the 184th, Colonel Curtis D. O'Sullivan commanding, and the 32nd, Colonel Marc J. Logie commanding. Both were to land at the southwest tip of the islet, the 184th on the northern flank (Red Beach 1), and the 32nd on the southern (Red Beach 2). The 184th was to advance along the inner, or lagoon, side of the crescent-shaped islet, and the 32nd along the outer, or ocean side. Since the islet was nowhere more than 2,000 feet wide, and the boundary line between the areas assigned to the two regiments ran approximately through the center, each had a front averaging 1,000 feet in width.

The assault waves were loaded into landing vehicles (both unarmored "alligators" and armored "buffaloes") from LSTs lying well out from the reef, near Enubuj. In two main columns they traveled southeast to the two designated beaches, under a protecting barrage fired from Enubuj. There was no enemy interference as the tracks of the amphibious vehicles ground up to the sand, and many of the men were able to jump ashore, dry. A striking contrast with what had happened at Tarawa! The 32nd, on the right, had virtually no opposition. The 184th found a few pockets of Japanese holding out in what was left of a coast artillery position. Companies L and K cleaned out the enemy quickly and efficiently. It was 9:30 A.M. when the landings began; within an hour the beachhead was secure. Before noon, supplies started to arrive, borne by "ducks" (amphibious trucks).

Also before noon, Admiral Turner ordered the attack groups inside the lagoon, for greater protection against possible submarine attack. The offensive was rolling in high gear. It looked as though, when the tanks and other heavy weapons got ashore, the job of eliminating the surviving Japanese on the islet would be easy. But as it happened, the tanks ran into greater difficulties than had the infantrymen, many of them getting stuck in shell craters.

The tank men's experience was typical, in a broad sense, of the difficulties that the infantrymen later found themselves confronting. The islet had been so wracked by bombing and gunfire that most of the features so carefully modeled on the relief maps with which the men had been briefed were no longer recognizable. There remained craters, underground chambers or passages, and innumerable piles of rubble in which an enemy could hide if he did not mind living like a rodent. The palms and brush had been torn and burned by explosive.

Even so, progress was good during the first day on Kwajalein islet. The two regiments kept well abreast and advanced almost a mile before establishing defensive positions for the night. From subsequent events it is clear that the advance was continued until too late an hour: there was not enough daylight left for the companies holding the line to reconnoiter the ground ahead of them, or to establish sufficiently close contact with companies holding adjacent sectors. Toward midnight there was a downpour lasting about an hour, and as soon as the rain stopped the Japanese attacked, behind a barrage of light mortar fire. Company L, holding the extreme left flank on the lagoon side, had its positions overrun in a confused action in which panic resulting from enemy infiltration was a major factor. However, the yardage lost was not great, and on the morrow it was quickly re-won.

The second day of fighting on the islet produced further gains of up to three-fourths of a mile on the flanks, and somewhat more in the center, where the airfield was captured. The battle plan called for the two regiments to continue their advance abreast and to reach the tip of the islet by the end of the third day. The event was different. Early on the morning of D-plus-2, the 184th reached an area in which there were several Japanese blockhouses which no prior reconnaissance had revealed. There had been bomb hits and shell hits all around them, but this factor had simply made them harder to detect, for they were nestling in a landscape which seemed to have been turned upside down. The only weapon which would eliminate the Japs in their chambered underground positions was a satchel charge containing 25 pounds of high explosive. And this had to be delivered inside the blockhouse—no mean feat.

At 12:30 P.M., at a conference of the assistant division commander, Brigadier General A. V. Arnold, and Colonels O'Sullivan and Logie, it was decided to let the 184th concentrate on cleaning up the unexpected enemy strength in the blockhouse area. Then the 184th was to be pinched out; the 32nd would wheel around it, and take over the entire front for the remaining half-mile or so to the northeast tip of the islet. The amended battle plan got off to a fairly good start, but soon bogged down again: the landscape had been made unrecognizable by the preliminary bombardments. Maintaining contact between squads was difficult enough; between platoons and companies it was often impossible.

Defense positions for the third night again were set up hastily as darkness was falling, but this time the situation contained a more serious element than it had before. Now, there were sizable pockets of Japanese holding out behind the forward positions of the 32nd Regiment. The Japanese sallied out during the night and created a good deal of confusion, and caused some casualties.

The fourth day did not begin auspiciously. There was a traffic jam where the 184th was being pinched out, and then, when the 32nd really got going for what was expected to be the winning drive, the terrain became even more difficult. There were estimated to be about 500 Japanese left alive in the last 650 yards of the islet. It appears that at least half were suffering from the effects of concussion, such as burst ear drums, and many were more seriously wounded. They were concentrated now in the area which had taken the heaviest bombing and shelling of all—for these had continued, ever since the day of the landings, on areas remaining to be occupied, and this was the third day after the landings. All through the area were Japanese corpses, or what remained of them: few were in one piece. Despite these obstacles, the infantrymen quickly recovered from the morning's poor start, and by midafternoon one platoon of Company G, advancing along the beach (the left flank) reached the tip of the islet. All that remained was for Company F to clean out the small, quarter-circular pocket remaining. On the basis of a report that this could be done by 4 P.M., word was passed up the chain of command to CinCPac himself at Pearl Harbor, that Kwajalein islet had been completely occupied by this hour.

It was not quite so simple. The Japanese remaining were in just as tough, underground positions as any of those who had been killed during the march up the island. They exacted more casualties before they were wiped out by American fire or committed suicide. In the last few minutes, tanks were needed to support Company F on the right flank. It was all over at 7:20 P.M.

On Kwajalein islet, the 7th Division had lost 177 men killed and had had 712 wounded. Japanese dead * totaled 5,000. The ratio in fatal casualties was 28 to 1 in favor of the attackers, as compared with a ratio of 5 to 1 at Tarawa. The difference must be attributed to two factors: the immensely heavier preliminary bombardment, the close bombardment from Enubuj, and the fact that after the first exposed landings at 9:30 A.M. on February 2, all other landings had been made under the protection of surrounding positions held by American forces.

The day before the battle ended on Kwajalein, the 1st Battalion of the 17th Infantry was embarked in LSTs from Ennylabegan and ferried across the lagoon toward Ebeye, the next islet north of Kwajalein on the east side of the perimeter reef. Ebeye had been worked over the day before by heavy gun-

* Including the island commander, Rear Admiral Monzo Akiyama.

fire and aircraft; it was given another hour-long shelling by cruisers and destroyers on the morning of the 4th before the 1st Battalion transferred to alligators and buffaloes and went ashore at the south end of the islet at 9:30 A.M. Ebeye is a mile long and 250 yards wide. The Japanese had been induced, by the heavy fire of warships from the ocean, to concentrate on the lagoon side; there they had an extraordinarily elaborate system of "spider holes"—fox holes covered over with palm fronds, which were almost indistinguishable from the rest of the terrain, because it was plentifully decorated with the tattered foliage of what, until a few days before, had been proud trees. For the rest, the operation was like that on Kwajalein islet, but on a smaller scale. It took two days. Ebeye was declared secure at the same time as Kwajalein.

Still there were three islets in the southern group to be reduced: Loi, Gugegwe and Bigej, in that order northward from Ebeye. On February 6, elements of the 17th Regiment which had been in reserve on Ebeye were re-embarked on LSTs and landed by LVTs on Loi; from there, they repeated the move to Gugegwe. The Reconnaissance Troop which had taken the westerly islets on D-day was embarked in destroyer transports and moved across the lagoon to Bigej, and elements of the 184th which had been in reserve on Kwajalein were shipped by LST to Bigej, in support of the cavalrymen. Resistance on all these islets was nominal and they were secured in one day.

Thanks to a new technique in battle reporting,* this campaign is probably the best recorded of any in a war which has been called the best reported of all wars.

The twin islets of Roi and Namur, joined by an artificial causeway, were alike in that the greatest dimension of each was about a mile. They differed, however, in that Roi was a bare, treeless waste, with a triangular airfield in its center, while Namur had a heavy growth of coconut palms, a few other trees, and the inevitable *Scaevola* bushes. The base of Roi's isosceles airfield was a runway 4,300 feet long and 265 feet wide; the other sides were runways 3,600 feet long and 195 feet wide. The Japanese had been clever enough not to clutter up the causeway with telephone poles too close to the

* *Island Victory*, by Lieut. Colonel S. L. A. Marshall (The Infantry Journal, Inc., Washington and Penguin Books, New York, 1944).

road, so airplanes could taxi over it from Roi and find concealment in dispersal bays on the edge of Namur's groves.

The commander of the northern attack group had not been
called "Close-In" Conolly for nothing. His battleships lay within easy range of the target, lobbing in 16-inch shells with relentless precision. The air base having been rendered inoperative
in the preliminary aerial bombing campaign, it was no longer
a target. There was one patch of bare ground in which there
were no installations. The gunfire is reported to have been so
accurate that no shells were wasted on this area.

The transports and landing ships were lying off the northwest shoulder of the atoll—the lee side, in the prevailing winds.
H-hour was not so early for the 4th Marine Division, under
Major General Harry Schmidt, as for the Army troops in the
south. The first objectives for the Marines were Mellu and
Boggerlapp, two islets to the southwest of Roi, corresponding
roughly to Gea and Ninni among the southern objectives. Between them was a pass into the lagoon; north of Mellu was the
more important North Pass.

The first landing was made at 9:51 A.M. on February 1. The
Marines advanced, firing, but there was no overt resistance
until later in the day, when a pocket of Japanese had to be
cleaned out, at a cost of some casualties. At 10:10 A.M., the
next assault wave hit the second islet. There was no resistance
whatever, and within 20 minutes it was declared secure.

With two passes into the lagoon covered by the Marines'
support artillery on these two islets, Admiral Conolly sent
landing craft in during the early afternoon. To make sure that
they suffer as little interference as possible from the enemy on
Roi and Namur, he took his battleships to within 2,000 yards
of those strongholds and laid it on with both main and secondary (5-inch) batteries. "Close-In" Conolly was outdoing
himself. The landing craft met as little opposition as might
have been expected in the circumstances, and ploughed across
the three-mile stretch of coral-studded water to the islets flanking Roi and Namur on the southeast: Ennugarret, Ennumennet
and Ennubirr. The third of these landings was not made until
6:24 P.M. In less than two hours, despite the handicap of darkness this islet was secured.

Throughout the day, the only noteworthy Japanese counteraction had consisted of a few rounds of ineffective artillery fire. During the night, supplies were built up for the American artillery emplaced on Mellu and Ennugarret. Just as in the southern part of the atoll, the stage was set for the main drama.

During the morning of February 2, Roi and Namur were subjected to a final, shattering bombardment by every weapon within reach: heavy bombers, carrying one-ton bombs; Avenger planes from the carriers, also bearing one-ton bombs; Dauntless dive-bombers with lighter missiles; Hellcats on strafing missions, during which they often dropped belly tanks containing enough gasoline to serve as incendiary bombs; battleships, cruisers and destroyers. The islets were covered with a pall of smoke and dust, in which the only distinguishable features were the darker columns of smoke from burning fuel dumps. Meanwhile, the landing teams were preparing for the assault. Destroyers, transports, LSTs and landing craft entered the lagoon and formed up in the area between the two strings of captured islets, south of the designated landing beaches.

About 11 A.M. the LSTs dropped their bow ramps. Alligators and buffaloes, running almost awash, scuttled to the beaches like vastly enlarged water-bugs. Before noon, the first assault wave was ashore. There had been no active opposition to the landing itself. The enemy was incapable of offering any.

The 23rd Marine Regiment had been assigned to take Roi. The southwestern part of the islet's shore was the landing beach for Landing Team 1, built around the 1st Battalion, and commanded by Lieut. Colonel Hewin O. Hammond. The southeastern sector was allocated to Landing Team 2, built around the 2nd Battalion, commanded by Lieut. Colonel Edward J. Dillon. The regimental commander was Colonel Louis R. Jones.

On the southwestern sector, the scattering of dazed Japanese who had survived the bombardment climbed from their pillboxes and spider holes as soon as Landing Team 1 advanced up the beach, and fled to equally shattered but more substantial positions inland. The Marines' skirmish line advanced at record speed: within 30 minutes, one platoon charged a thousand yards through scenes of unprecedented ruin and desolation, and reached the northwest tip of the islet.

Landing Team 2, on the right, did not have it quite so easy.

There were some machine guns still firing from pillboxes near the shore. These impeded the advance until they could be outflanked and destroyed by grenades, satchel charges, flame-throwers or bazookas. Other enemy groups were hiding in ruins and bomb craters. The advance quickly gained momentum, however, and carried to the long southern runway.

At 3 P.M. the two skirmish lines presented such an irregular front that Colonel Jones ordered them pulled back to an east-west line roughly bisecting the islet. It would be more economical to launch a final attack on a well-organized front, with tank support. The tanks were Sherman mediums, each with a 75-mm. gun. The attack got under way at 3:15. It went forward at a slow, measured pace. Thoroughness now, rather than speed, was most to be desired. While it was in progress, a campaign of extermination had to be undertaken in the area which had been regarded as already secure. Roi's air strips had had an elaborate drainage system. Concrete drains, some of them as much as two feet wide and three feet deep, were interconnected, and finally ran down toward the lagoon to empty. The covering slabs of concrete were pierced at intervals by three-inch slots. At countless places these top slabs had been smashed by bombs or shells, opening a rubble-strewn way into the drains. The Japanese showed a rodent-like capacity for scurrying into these drains, armed with a rifle or sub-machine gun. Then they sniped at the surrounding Marines. Every section of drain between possible entrance points had to be hosed out with automatic rifle fire or flamethrowers. The process required three days.

The onslaught across the island required only two and a half hours. Everywhere there were little knots of Japanese, putting their lives up at auction, but nowhere was there a concentrated stand. The preliminary expenditure of steel and explosive paid a big dividend in record time. At 5:40 P.M. Colonel Jones was able to report to Major General Schmidt: "The island is secured."

Namur was tougher. It contained the majority of the large administration buildings for the garrison of all Kwajalein atoll. Although these had been smashed by the bombardment, there were enough jumbled masses of reinforced concrete to provide excellent hiding places for the enemy. The remnants of the coconut groves also helped him.

The 24th Marine Regiment (Colonel Franklin A. Hart) had the assignment to take Namur. Its assault elements were, from left to right on the southern beaches, the 3rd Battalion, under Lieut. Colonel Francis H. Brink, and the 2nd Battalion, under Lieut. Colonel Austin R. Brunelli. Little opposition was encountered on the beaches proper, but it developed quickly when the push inland began, and the enemy maintained considerable pressure against the area where the Marines were trying to enlarge their beachhead.

Seabees who had landed with the third wave of assault troops, in the expectation that the beach would be quickly secured to permit them to begin their normal duty of construction, found themselves engaged, alongside the Marines, in destruction of the enemy.

There were enough Japanese left on Namur, with enough cohesion, to be able to launch a counter-attack at 4:15 P.M. It failed to push the Marines' line back. By sunset the line was within a quarter of a mile of the ocean at the northeast corner of the islet. The tenacity of the Japanese was shown at a point where there was a pile of riddled, rusty oil drums. Sniper fire had come from there, early in the afternoon, so demolition charges had been set which appeared to make it impossible for any human being to survive, either in or under the pile of drums. But twice during the afternoon the process had to be repeated: either the Japanese had filtered back, or they had been hiding all along in holes in the ground, underneath the drums. The range at which most Japanese were killed was not more than ten yards. Many individuals were killed in hand to hand combat, with the bayonet or even the stock of a rifle.

There was intermittent gunfire and rifle fire throughout the night of February 2-3. Nevertheless, the unloading of supplies continued on the southern beaches. About 5:30 A.M., a force estimated at 200 Japanese launched a counter-attack, and inflicted many casualties before it was beaten off. By daylight, it was found that many pillboxes which had been cleared the previous evening were again tenanted. A methodical attack was launched, with tanks co-ordinated with infantry, against the last Japanese strongpoints in the northeast corner of the islet. By 3:45 P.M.

it was declared secure, and Major General Schmidt held an impressive flag-raising ceremony. While this was in progress, a Japanese ammunition dump blew up with what was probably the greatest single explosion of the campaign. The gigantic, mushrooming column of smoke aptly supplied an exclamation point to mark the end of the most successful operation of its kind ever undertaken.

The 4th Marine Division had lost 194 men (129 killed and 65 missing); 436 had been wounded. The Japanese dead, including the island commander, Rear Admiral Michiyuki Yamada, totaled 3,479, according to the best available count—actually an approximation, since many corpses were dismembered. The 91 prisoners represented almost three times the usual proportion of one per cent.

The total cost of the conquest of Kwajalein atoll (both Army and Marine Corps) was 356 officers and men killed or missing. The number of Japanese killed was put at 8,500, for a ratio of 24 to 1.

The difference between the four days taken to secure Kwajalein islet and the two days taken to secure Roi and Namur appears to reflect the differences in the terrain and in the strength of the enemy rather than the traditional difference in method between the two American services. For at Roi and Namur the Marines were using the same technique of close artillery support from adjacent islets as was the Army at Kwajalein.

The over-all success of the operation was so striking that Admiral Turner said, even before it was completed: "Maybe we had too many men and too many ships for this job, but I prefer to do things that way. It saved us a lot of lives." When the American forces killed the last, shell-shocked defenders, the greatest problem on the islets was one of sanitation. Fortunately, this had been anticipated. The corpses were assembled as quickly as possible and buried. Lime was used in great quantities, along with sprays to control disease-bearing flies and insects.

The task of clearing the islets of wreckage and rehabilitating them as American bases was immense. Bulldozers pushed hundreds of tons of debris into shell craters, or wherever else it would be out of the way. Construction began at once.

The small native population had suffered surprisingly little during the military operations. Most of them had been transferred by the Japanese to islets where there were no military installations. The new American civil government, headed by Captain E. C. Ewen, U.S.N., set aside such islets for the natives, contracted for the men's labor, and organized a market in which the products of native craftsmen were available to souvenir-hunting garrison troops at fair prices.

The most serious question in connection with the coming of American domination to the Marshall Islands was in the realm of international law. The first proclamations of military rule posted in the name of Admiral Nimitz declared that the authority of the Emperor of Japan was "suspended." There were two faults in this. One was the assumption that the Emperor had any authority, other than the fact of illegal occupation, at the time of the American landings. Japan had withdrawn from the League of Nations in 1935, and had thereby lost the right to remain as the mandatory power in the Marshalls. The second defect in the proclamation was the use of the word "suspended." It should have been "ended." Whether the mandated islands are to pass under American sovereignty or under an international trusteeship, for the protection of the peace of the Pacific and the welfare of the natives, was then, and remains, immaterial. The vital point was, and still is, that there shall be no idea of restoring the "suspended" authority of the Emperor of Japan, for whom the State Department had such a tender regard in 1944.

Although the conquest of Kwajalein atoll has been described as the first military operation in the wresting of the Marshalls from Japan, Kwajalein was not the first atoll to be occupied. The southern attack group of Admiral Turner's forces, under Rear Admiral Harry Hill, was busy on January 31 and February 1. With a landing team drawn from the 106th Infantry (Army) it arrived off Majuro on the 31st. This atoll, roughly midway between Makin (the northernmost U.S. base in the Gilbert Islands) and Kwajalein, had been known for 30 years to have great possibilities. The Germans, who held it from 1899 to 1914, had been planning to make it their main naval base in the Central Pacific. They had not got beyond the blueprint stage when the Japanese seized all the Marianas, Caroline and Marshall Islands for what was then believed to be the benefit of the Western Allies. It was known that the Japanese had been busy there during World War II. How strongly they held Majuro was not known.

Reconnaissance on January 31 brought no Japanese opposition, and it was clear that Majuro was not garrisoned in strength. But still it was not known how weakly they held it. On the morning of February 1 the transports and landing ships sailed into the lagoon through Calanin Channel, putting out reconnaissance parties in rubber boats as they went. There were no Japanese on Calanin islet, and none on Darrit, to the east. Only a few rounds had been fired when it was decided to call off the bombardment. The scouts swarmed from one islet to another, and collected the grand total of three Japanese. The native chief added a 200-pound hog as a mark of respect and esteem—and gratitude, because the Americans showed a willingness to pay for souvenirs, a characteristic which the Japanese had not displayed.

The remarkable thing was that the enemy had substantial installations on Majuro: well-built, concrete barracks; a small railway with abundant rolling stock; construction machinery, and the makings of a seaplane base. Apparently they had withdrawn the garrison for the defense of atolls which they believed to be more directly threatened. To Admiral Nimitz's command, the most valuable thing about Majuro was the hole in the doughnut: its lagoon, six by 21 miles, is one of the best anchorages in the Pacific. Majuro was quickly developed as a way station for the fleet. Its principal function was to supply fuel, and its principal clients were the fast carrier task forces.

With the seizure of Majuro and the conquest of Kwajalein, American forces in the Marshalls held positions from which the neutralization of the bypassed islands to the east could be maintained economically, and they were reasonably secure against counter-attack from the west or southwest. In the northwest, however, there remained a source of danger: Eniwetok atoll. Next to Kwajalein and bypassed Jaluit, Eniwetok was probably the most strongly garrisoned of the Marshalls under the Japanese regime. If it had fewer shore batteries, beach defenses and combat troops, this was because it was not a forward position, but a rear base, invaluable for staging supplies and equipment to the more easterly islands, but most important of all as an aircraft staging point. Every Japanese plane flown to the eastern Marshalls and the Gilberts was believed to have landed en route at the 4,000-foot air strip which literally overhung the water on both the ocean and lagoon sides of the heart-shaped islet of Engebi.

The atoll of Eniwetok is roughly circular (about 20 miles in diameter), with its principal islets: Engebi at 12 o'clock, with small islets flanking it to 11 o'clock on the west and to 3 o'clock on the east; Parry islet at 4:30; Eniwetok islet at 5:30. The two major entrances to the lagoon are East (or Deep) Passage at 4 o'clock, and South (or Wide) Passage at 6 o'clock.

All the islets and the two anchorages had been attacked by Rear Admiral Sherman's carrier planes at the turn of the month, simultaneously with the landings on Kwajalein. Engebi's runway was pocked with a hundred craters and littered with blocks of torn-up concrete; fifteen twin-engined bombers were obliterated; five supply ships were forced aground in flames. Four float planes at the Parry islet seaplane base were wrecked. After this mauling, Eniwetok would not require the attentions of so vast a carrier fleet as had been used for Kwajalein.

However, it was essential that Japanese interference from bypassed islands, or from the threatening bastion of Truk to the southwest, should be shut off. In mid-February, Admirals Spruance and Mitscher set off for Truk, with all the available fast battleships, three-fourths of the fast carriers and appropriate numbers of cruisers and destroyers—the force which became famous as Task Force 58. They hit Truk on February 18 (see Chapter XIV). While they were busy in this area, land-based bombers were staging the first raids of the war on two other supposed strongpoints in the eastern Carolines: Ponape and Kusaie. Liberators from Midway attacked Wake Island. Divisions of cruisers steamed up and down the bypassed eastern Marshalls. Their efforts were complemented by those of Dauntless dive-bombers and Warhawk fighters from the Gilberts.

With the enemy thus pinned down by every feasible means of attack, an American force set out to take Eniwetok. Admiral Turner was in over-all command; Admiral Pownall had the carriers, including the *Saratoga;* Admiral Hill commanded the attack group. For Engebi, which was to be the first objective, the assault troops were the 22nd Regiment of Marines (Colonel John T. Walker commanding), reinforced by the Fifth Corps Reconnaissance Company and the Corps Tank Battalion.

D-day was February 18, East Longitude date, coinciding with the carrier assault on Truk. The attack group approached from the southeast, and steamed boldly into the lagoon after South Passage was cleared by minesweepers. The first islet passed was Eniwetok, and the opinion of observers aboard Admiral Hill's flagship was that the enemy had "few works and only a semblance of fortifications there." In consequence, Eniwetok islet was given little attention by the bombardment

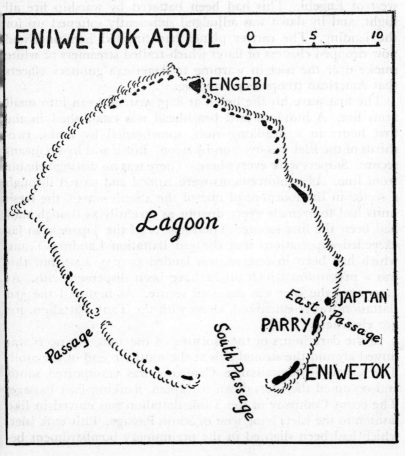

ENIWETOK ATOLL   0   5   10

ENGEBI

Lagoon

JAPTAN

East Passage

PARRY

South Passage

Passage

ENIWETOK

force. The importance of this omission became evident later. Parry, the next islet to the north, was considered more formidable, and was given correspondingly more attention. Next was Japtan. At the north was Engebi.

The preliminary bombardment was a repetition of every other in this atoll campaign. Not a single shore gun answered. During the day the Corps Reconnaissance Company was put ashore in landing vehicles on Aomon and Buziri, two islets southeast of Engebi, and wiped out the handful of defenders. The company then began to work northwest toward Engebi, to set up artillery. At 1 A.M. of the 19th, the Scout Company of the Tank Battalion set out in rubber boats to seize islets west of Engebi. This had been battered by warship fire all night, and by dawn was adjudged sufficiently softened up for the landing. The carrier planes had finished bombing, and now dropped clusters of flares which trailed streamers of white smoke over the islet in warning to American gunnery officers that American troops were landing.

The first wave hit the beach at 8:45 A.M. and ran into small arms fire. A hundred-yard beachhead was established in the first hour; in a headlong rush, spearheaded by tanks, two-thirds of the islet was overrun by noon. But it was by no means secure. Snipers were everywhere. There was no distinguishable front line. As reinforcements were landed and passed through a sector in the footsteps of one of the assault waves, the fresh units had to grenade every dugout as carefully as though they had been the first ashore. The tenacity of the Japanese so far exceeded expectations that the 3rd Battalion Landing Team, which had been in reserve, was landed at 9:55 A.M., but this was a precaution which might have been dispensed with. At 4:50 P.M., the islet was declared secure. At nightfall the 3rd Battalion was re-embarked, along with the Tank Battalion, for use elsewhere.

In the dark hours of the morning of the 20th, a pincers was forged around the strongholds at the southern end of the atoll. The Corps Reconnaissance Company was transported south and occupied the islets down to Japtan, flanking East Passage. The Scout Company of the Tank Battalion was moved in like fashion to the islets lying west of South Passage. Eniwetok islet, which had been slighted in the preliminary bombardment because it was supposed to be so lightly held, was the objective. It had been decided to land about half way down the western shore, and to fan out north and south from the beachhead.

The assault troops for this operation were the 106th Infantry (Army), commanded by Colonel Russell G. Ayers. (For the entire Eniwetok operation, the 106th was brigaded with the 22nd Marines under Brigadier General Thomas E. Watson, U.S.M.C.) The 3rd Battalion of the 22nd was in reserve. The first Army men landed at 9:18 and found the beaches only lightly defended. But as they turned north and south, they discovered that the dense growth of bush held far larger numbers of Japanese than had been expected, and they were in better condition to resist than had been their compatriots on Engebi. They had sufficient cohesion to withdraw in fairly orderly fashion to a succession of defense lines which they had constructed across the narrow island. The reserve of Marines was committed before nightfall.

By this time the American forces held a substantial part of the islet's waist. Landing of the battalions' mortar companies and of regimental artillery was slowed by the narrowness of the beaches. Perimeter defenses were set up for the night, and the ground troops were given some protection against Japanese counter-attack by the warships, which lay close inshore and kept their searchlights playing on the perimeters all night. A few Japanese snipers nevertheless infiltrated the American lines. But there was no counter-attack in force. At dawn the Army had all its artillery ashore, and by evening of the 21st, with close support from artillery, warships and carrier planes, the southern end of the islet had been cleared. By the afternoon of the 22nd, the push to the north was completed, and Admiral Hill went ashore to officiate at the raising of the flag. Two battalion commanders of the 106th, Lieut. Colonels Harold I. Mizony and Cornett Winslow, apologized for the delay in securing the islet. It was not their fault, nor their men's. The fault lay in preliminary reconnaissance and staff work, and in the higher echelons of the command for not having ordered sufficient bombardment. It is only fair to add, however, that this omission was made good, so far as possible, by the close cooperation of naval ships and aircraft after the landings had been made.

In most islands, the job of cleaning out the last Japanese has been compared to a rat hunt. Colonel Ayers suggested that on Eniwetok it was "more like a prairie dog hunt. The Japs dug in on this island just like prairie dogs hole up in western Nebraska." During the night of February 21-22, two Japanese who had emerged from spider holes (or prairie dog holes) had been killed just outside Ayers's command post.

During the last stages of the Eniwetok operations, the heavy warships had been softening up Parry islet. For this, the 22nd Marines were used, with the 3rd Battalion re-embarked from Eniwetok as reserve. The Japanese garrison on Parry had been on the hot seat for five days, fully aware of events at Engebi and Eniwetok, and with no hope of reinforcement. Not a Japanese airplane broke the sky; not a Japanese ship was afloat anywhere within a radius of hundreds of miles to support them. Theoretically, they should all have been killed or wounded, or shocked into readiness to surrender, before the first Marines stepped ashore. But they were ready with machine guns when the assault waves appeared.

It was not the Japanese who drew first blood. By one of those tragic accidents which are inseparable from war (they have occurred in every part of the Pacific and in every part of the European theater where American troops have been engaged, and they have occurred also among the forces of other nations), three LCIs heading for the beach were fired upon by an American destroyer. After a board of investigation had sifted the incident, Admiral Nimitz reported that both the LCIs and the destroyer had been off their assigned positions. Thirteen men aboard the landing craft were killed and 46 were wounded.

During the landings, an American battleship was so close inshore that rifle fire from the Japanese garrison carried across its decks. But the LCI gunboats were still closer inshore, using their concentrated armament to silence the Japanese machine gun nests and permit the Marines to gain a foothold. Parry was much smaller than Eniwetok, but it was heavily overgrown with brush, and the Marines (reinforced by a defense battalion which had been designated for the permanent occupation of Eniwetok islet) were confronted with the same "prairie dog" elusiveness of the enemy as the Army had been on Eniwetok.

It was secured at 7:30 P.M. The conquest of the atoll was complete.

There were 29 other atolls in the Marshalls. All but four were quickly occupied against nominal resistance or no resistance whatever. Four remained: Jaluit, Wotje, Mili and Maloelap. On February 2, Admiral Turner had said: "We can either take them or leave them to wither on the vine." They were left to wither, and for 18 dreary months, Marine Corps and Army aircraft flew bombing and strafing missions over them. The native population of Wotje was evacuated by destroyers late in 1944; others were removed later from other atolls. The Japanese garrisons had no supplies except what had been stockpiled and the trickle that came in by submarine. Their officers, at least, must have listened to the radio and must have known how far the tide of American conquest had surged past them. But there was no disposition to surrender. The term "withering on the vine," which had a certain popularity in the early months of 1944, had become a sour and sorry jest by 1945. The Japanese in the Marshalls still had not withered when their homeland surrendered.

XIII. Admiral of the Ocean Air

It was a bleak day in February, 1942. The newly commissioned aircraft carrier *Hornet* turned into the wind to conduct an experiment never before attempted in the history of aviation: the launching of medium bombers from a floating runway little more than 800 feet long. The two B-25s were successfully flown off. There was no more interested spectator than the commanding officer of the *Hornet,* Captain Marc A. Mitscher, who had been a party to virtually all the great innovations in the development of American naval aviation.

It was a similarly bleak day in April that same year when the *Hornet* turned into the wind, 800 miles from Tokyo. There were sixteen B-25s on her deck, under the command of Lieut. Colonel James H. Doolittle, who was far from confident about the take-off. Mitscher gave his personal assurance that the Navy would get the big Army planes off the deck, and Doolittle was satisfied. Mitscher was not the kind of man to give such an assurance unless he was certain that he could fulfill it. And he did.

What happened to Doolittle's pitiful little bombing force over Japan and on the way to China was no fault of Mitscher's. The Navy had been something less than lukewarm about the whole project of bombing Tokyo with such a force at this stage of the war, and Mitscher, who had to risk his ship at a time when the United States Navy was desperately short of carriers in the Pacific, might have been expected to be one of the least enthusiastic. Granted that the material damage done by Doolittle's fliers to the Japanese war machine was negligible, Mitscher nevertheless believes that the attack paid big dividends: that it threw the Japanese into such panic that they kept large air forces tied up for defense of the home islands, instead of sending them, as intended, to support the invasion of Australia.

There are many who will disagree with Mitscher as to just how effective the Doolittle raid was in achieving this result, but there is none whose opinion is entitled to more respect.

It is given to few men to play so large a part as Mitscher has played in the development and proving of a new arm of naval warfare. It is not that he was first in the field: America's first naval aviator died an untimely death; the second, Vice Admiral John H. Towers, probably deserves more credit than any other man for keeping the infant of naval aviation from being strangled in the Navy Department's red tape entanglements. But after war came to the Pacific, Towers's duty was on land: Mitscher had command at sea of the Fast Carrier Task Forces of the United States Pacific Fleet—the greatest concentration of mobile, long-range destructive power in the history of war. When the fast carriers and their supporting craft operated as part of the Fifth Fleet (being then known as Task Force 58), they were under the over-all command of Admiral Raymond A. Spruance. When they operated as Task Force 38 of the Third Fleet, they were under Admiral William F. Halsey. Spruance is no flier, and Halsey won his wings late in life. When the fleet put to sea, it was Mitscher who was admiral of the ocean air.

The Marc A. in front of Mitscher's surname stands for Marc Andrew, and not for Marc Antony, as the romantic-minded have rashly concluded. He was born in Hillsboro, Wisconsin, but when he was two years old the family moved to Oklahoma, then Indian Territory. Young Mitscher's ambition was a perfectly natural one for a boy raised on the plains around Pawhuska: he wanted to go to West Point, and be commissioned in the cavalry. However, there were many boys in the region with similar ideas, and some had more influence. There was nothing for Mitscher to do but to accept the appointment to the Naval Academy, which was going begging.

He was 19 when he entered, five feet seven inches tall, and barely topped 120 pounds. He played on the baseball team, and wrestled as a flyweight. There had been only one other appointee to the Academy from Oklahoma, one Peter Cassius Marcellus Cade, Jr. He had "bilged" the year before Mitscher arrived, but the upper classmen insisted that the second Oklahoman always begin answers to their questions by repeating the name "Peter Cassius Marcellus Cade Junior" as fast as the syllables would roll off his tongue. At that time Mitscher felt some resentment toward Mr. Cade (or at least toward the parents who named him); today all that he bears as a result of the experience is the nickname "Pete."

As is so often the case, there was nothing in Pete Mitscher's Academy record to suggest that he would one day wear three stars and occupy a distinguished place in American naval history. He was content to be a "2.5 man," where a rating of 4.0 was to be desired. He is frank to say that he graduated at "the wooden end of the line." Naturally, the Bureau of Navigation paid little attention to the desires of so undistinguished a young officer. In the last month at the Academy he had happened upon an English book dealing with aviation, and he asked to be assigned to the Navy's infant aviation branch. He was refused. Soon, he renewed the application, and was again refused. Ensign Mitscher was transferred from the old armored cruiser *Colorado* to destroyers. Nobody was more surprised than he was when, in 1915, the Bureau had a change of heart and ordered him to Pensacola for training as an aviator.

Mitscher was Naval Aviator No. 32. In World War I, he flew patrols from New York and Montauk, and was given command of the new training station at Miami. His name first became known to the public at the time of the Navy's elaborate effort to annex the record for the first transatlantic flight. Only one of the four NCs that left Newfoundland ever got to the coast of Europe, and that one was not Mitscher's: his came down off the Azores, lost because of a sudden change in the weather. In Mitscher's mind, the only lesson of that complex and ambitious undertaking was one that "any damn' fool should have known to begin with—the place for direction-finding equipment is on a ship or on shore, and not on a plane that vibrates the way ours did in those days."

He came to public notice again when flights of Navy planes made the record long hops from San Francisco to Honolulu and from San Diego to Panama: Mitscher organized and led those pioneer flights, then slipped back into obscurity, but into a position of vastly more importance for the future of American naval aviation, as Assistant Chief of the Bureau of Aeronautics under Admiral Towers. In 1941 he was given the carrier

Hornet to commission, and had her out in the Atlantic on shakedown when the Japanese struck at Pearl Harbor.

After she had launched Doolittle's B-25s against Tokyo, the *Hornet* and the accompanying *Enterprise* turned back to Pearl, and soon set forth again, still under Admiral Halsey's command, for the Coral Sea where battle appeared inevitable. As might have been expected, the distances involved were too great, and the task force missed the engagement in which the *Lexington* was lost and the *Yorktown* damaged. With the foreknowledge that the Japanese would strike next at Midway, the task force returned to Pearl and again was prepared for immediate sailing. Mitscher received his commission as a rear admiral, and the *Hornet* received the new commanding officer, Captain Charles P. Mason. Just how Mitscher managed it is not clear, but he succeeded in retaining command of the *Hornet* during the decisive battle of Midway. It was from her deck that Torpedo Squadron 8 flew to its doom; it was from her deck also that other and more fortunate flights were launched, which contributed much to the decisive defeat of the Japanese in the most crucial engagement of the Pacific war. After that, Mitscher left the ship and put on his stars.

Mitscher went a long way around to arrive at his most important duty. During the invasion of Guadalcanal and the long-drawn-out struggle to hold the bridgehead there, Mitscher was Commander, Fleet Air, South Pacific, first under Vice Admiral Robert Lee Ghormley and then under Admiral Halsey. In March, 1943, he was ordered up to Guadalcanal as Commander, Air, Solomons, and arrived at the beginning of April in the midst of one of the most furious air battles of the 18-month Solomons campaign.

It was at Guadalcanal that I first met Admiral Mitscher. His headquarters was in a Dallas hut in the ravine between Henderson Field and the Lunga River, where General Vandegrift had had his headquarters in the hottest days of the campaign for "Bloody Island." At any time, Mitscher looks somewhat older than his years, because of his baldness and his sunken mouth. But at Guadalcanal, during the campaign for New Georgia, he looked 15 years older. (He was then 56.) Months of shore duty had told on him; so had the climate during the Southern Hemisphere summer. Mitscher practically never raises his voice above a whisper, but he will raise it to a normal conversational tone—the equivalent, for him, of a shout—to express his dislike of the tropics. The strain of conducting a campaign with insufficient forces, drawn from three services, with the inevitable problems of coordination resulting, also had told on him.

One of the things which had made Mitscher sick at heart, and anxious to get out of the Solomons, was the series of Japanese atrocities against some of his fliers who were shot down. He has no children of his own, but he has an all-embracing regard for the youths who have borne the brunt of the aerial phases of World War II. Often, in speaking of their courage and their accomplishments, he will find himself at a loss for words. The cruelties which some of "his boys" suffered at the hands of the Japanese left Mitscher with such a deep and bitter and personal hatred of the enemy that he now finds it difficult to refer to them as other than "little ------ bastards." And in his careful speech, such expressions do not appear by accident.

Mitscher's appearance at Guadalcanal was deceptive. He had decided that in that filthy, tropical climate there was nothing to be gained by rushing around, so he was conserving his energy. He was never too pooped to pitch horseshoes, with one of his staff officers, against Vice Admiral Aubrey W. Fitch and one of his staff. Pitching left-handed, Mitscher hung up so many ringers that he sounded like a blacksmith at work. Also, he could always put aside that apparent fatigue when reports came in to him of the day's strikes. If things had gone well, all of Mitscher's restraint could not conceal his bubbling pride in "those boys." If things had not gone so well, Mitscher would recount the handicaps under which "those boys" were operating: often at extreme range, against superior numbers, or against targets difficult to identify, and so on. The combined Army, Navy and Marine air forces which Mitscher commanded were pitifully small, but when he turned over the command to Major General Nathan F. Twining, those pitifully small forces had taken the measure of the Japanese in the Solomons. Mitscher had earned a rest, and some relief from the tropics.

Meanwhile, the first of America's new crop of aircraft carriers (of both the *Essex* and *Independence* classes) had reached the Pacific with the new Hellcat fighter planes. While he was on the West Coast, commanding Fleet Air, these carriers began to write the history of the new-style war across the Pacific—writing in bullets and bombs. It was not until after the far-from-perfect operations at Tarawa and Kwajalein in November and early December of 1943 that Mitscher was ordered back to sea duty.

For neutralizing raids during the invasion of Kwajalein, Admiral Spruance took the bulk of the fleet, and Mitscher had command of the carriers. The first target was Truk. Mitscher says that all he knew about Truk was what he had read in the *National Geographic Magazine*—"and the writer had been mistaken about some things." The Japanese also had a lot to learn about Truk when Mitscher's airmen had finished with it.

The *Intrepid* having been damaged, Admiral Spruance decided to accompany her back to Pearl in his flagship, with another carrier to supply air cover. Mitscher was to go on to the Marianas, seemingly a still more daring assignment, with the seven carriers remaining, their battleships, cruisers and destroyers. This was one of the few occasions on which Mitscher had an opportunity to show his skill entirely independently, without a fleet commander over him. His personality began to show through the usually terse, official language of fleet signals before he was well away from Truk: "I cannot tell a lie. D-day is Washington's birthday." That quiet brand of humor is typical of the man. Invariably described as "wry" or "gnomelike" because of his appearance and manner—the manner of a wizened Puck—he has the faculty of enjoying himself hugely while scarcely showing it.

He also has the faculty of working out the most complex tactical problems without appearing even to be concentrating. He usually has the air of a man dreaming about trout or salmon fishing in the Pacific Northwest. Sometimes he is, but more often he is thinking less of "the big one that got away" than of the "little ------ sonofabitch" that got away from the combat air patrol. To outguess the enemy, he put himself in the position of this lone Japanese pilot, and asked himself what he would do in such a case. He startled his staff officers by asking each, on different occasions, "Well, what would you be doing now if you were that little ------ sonofabitch?" Time and again, Mitscher seemed uncanny in his ability to read the enemy's mind: in that, undoubtedly, lay one of the greatest sources of his strength as a commander of roving, oceanic air forces.

He had, besides, a glacial calm in emergencies which helped to cool off even the most excitable officers around him. Faced with critical decisions, when the lives of scores or hundreds of men depended on his picking the right answer with a minimum of delay, Mitscher remained unperturbed, still talking in the almost inaudible monotone that drives subordinates crazy until they get used to it, and easing the tension with some touch of dry humor or a homely figure of speech used when it is least expected.

Most of Mitscher's humor is of this type. He speaks so slowly that his staff officers think ahead, trying to finish the sentences for him in their own minds—only to discover that he has been aware of their mental processes, and has deliberately shifted to another tack for the pleasure of watching their confusion. Despite the constant use of an opprobrious expression to refer to the enemy, Mitscher is far less profane in his speech than Halsey or many another admiral. Indeed, the only other vulgarism to which he is addicted is "Goddamnittohell," uttered so smoothly and softly that it explodes in the listener's mind afterward, like a delayed-action fuse.

Above all, Mitscher is utterly unaffected. Like most carrier men, he is a member of the "brown-shoe navy." Somehow, his shoes are always freshly shined, no matter what the conditions in which he may be traveling. Aboard his flagship, he perched on a high stool, fitted with arms, on the flag bridge, and always faced aft. A carrier running at speed under any conditions creates considerable wind of her own; if she is heading into the wind to launch or recover planes, the current across her flight deck often exceeds 40 or 50 knots. Mitscher's explanation of his facing aft is crushingly simple: "Only a damn' fool faces into the wind."

The only trivial legend that has sprung up about him concerns his ability to light a cigarette, under any wind conditions, with a single wooden match. His deflationary reply to any one expressing wonderment is: "After all, I'm a sailor."

It is not for any of these external characteristics, pleasant though they may be, that aviators revere Pete Mitscher. It is because he was so whole-souled in his devotion to the fight in which he was engaged, and to the men engaged in it with him. Once or twice he asked official photographers to take his picture with some young pilot who had just distinguished himself in combat, and in each such case he insisted that the picture was not to be given general release in the Navy's publicity service. He wanted a print for himself, because he genuinely felt a pleasurable glow of reflected glory from the company of the young hero.

Mitscher's utter devotion to "those boys" was shown in the final stages of the far-flung operation known as the First Battle of the Philippine Sea, when he ordered the lights turned on. Scores of fliers were saved who otherwise must have been lost. It is small wonder that naval aviators worship Mitscher in a quiet way. They would be ingrates if they did not.

To the American people, Mitscher remains less well known than Spruance, and far less well known than Halsey, who is somewhat more photogenic and cannot open his mouth without uttering some derision of the enemy which is considered "good copy" by most newspapers and press associations. Mitscher has served with equally satisfactory results under both the four-starred fleet commanders. It would be idle to pretend that he has always been in agreement with either of them. When the archives are opened, and the signals exchanged between the flagships * during the two battles in the Philippine Sea can be examined, I believe that Mitscher will emerge as the officer who was most consistently right, even when he was overruled. No doubt he has made mistakes; he seems to have been over-impressed by the seriousness of the Jap threat to his force when he first tackled the Marianas in February, 1944, and at other times to have under-estimated the danger from proximity to land-based enemy aircraft. With due allowance for these matters, Mitscher's record of accomplishment has a luster which outshines that of colleagues and competitors alike. If there had been no Pete Mitscher to take command of its fast carrier task forces, the Navy would have had to create one.

*As fleet commander, Halsey and Spruance flew their flag in a gunnery ship (cruiser or battleship); Mitscher, as commander of the fast carrier task forces, flew his flag in a carrier.

XIV. Air Power Goes Cruising

In the old days of imperialist expansion, rival imperialist powers used to have to contend for command of the sea. The last clear-cut struggle of this kind, prior to World War II, was in the Napoleonic wars, after which British sea power dominated the world's oceans, all but undisputed, for a century.

Thus, it was not until the Japanese struck at Pearl Harbor that a modern version of the classical contest for command of the sea, as envisaged by Mahan, developed in sea power's machine age. Perhaps even more important than the fact that this contest was waged with superheated, high-pressure steam, rather than with sail, is the fact that it came when command of the sea could no longer be exercised by old-fashioned fleets of surface ships, but demanded control of the air above the seas, by aircraft.

Before the war, the Japanese had boasted openly that they would control the Pacific, or most of it, with aircraft based upon their "unsinkable carriers"—the countless flyspeck islands of Micronesia. They made good that boast for a period of two years during which no American battle fleet ventured into the huge quadrant lying west of the International Date Line and north of the Equator. In those two years, the only forces which penetrated the cordon thrown around their conquests by the Japanese were fast carrier task forces engaged on hit-and-run raids. These, gratifying as they were, and valuable as they were in gaining information and experience for the United States Navy, were far from being a challenge to Japanese command of the western Pacific.

In the United States there was a large and highly vocal school of thought which contended that Japan could never be deprived of her sea command except by land-based air power. The idea was that fleets of super-bombers must be built, capable of crossing the Pacific from bases in western North America. The aircraft carrier was dismissed as an out-of-date stopgap. Perhaps this school of thought would have been right if America's enemy in the Pacific had had the same technical skill and industrial potential as the United States. But fortunately, the Joint Chiefs of Staff did not overrate the enemy in this regard. They went ahead with a great program for the building of aircraft carriers and the manufacture of aircraft suitable for operation from carriers.

One thing was certain: the showdown, when it came, would not involve parallel lines of battleships slugging it out with their main batteries. Battleships might be present, and might play an important part, but battleships alone would not be decisive.

It would be an unequal struggle, between opponents of widely differing characteristics. The Japanese, constituting a second-rate nation in the industrial sense, had discovered in the Solomons and New Guinea that they could not afford to compete with the United States in an aerial war of attrition. They simply could not replace aircraft fast enough. They had shown in the Tarawa and Kwajalein campaigns that their disposition of land-based aircraft was inadequate when they were on the defensive (although it had worked well enough when they were winning): the theory of great chains of "unsinkable carriers" was that they should be mutually self-supporting. Thus, if the United States Navy attacked Tarawa in such strength as to knock out all aircraft based in the Gilberts, and even some of those in the southern Marshalls, still there should have been enough in adjacent island groups to knock out the American carriers, drive off the gunnery ships and transports, and so save the attacked position. The theory was sound; but the Japanese were discovering that it was a theory which became invalid when a poor nation tried to apply it.

The struggle for command of the sea, then, was to be waged between Japan, with an unlimited supply of unsinkable carriers but a sharply limited supply of aircraft, with an outmoded, unbalanced fleet, and on the other hand the United States, with no unsinkable carriers in the region where the campaign must be fought, but with a seemingly unlimited supply of aircraft to fly from the decks of carriers so numerous as to be almost expendable, and with the world's newest, heaviest and fastest line-of-battle ships.

Since the Japanese had avoided a decisive engagement when they could have had one for the asking, it was up to the American command to set the time and place and determine the manner in which the decision was to be had. The American commanders made their choice at Kwajalein, while the air was still heavy with the stench of battle. Admiral Nimitz visited the scene, and conferred with Admirals Spruance and Turner. It was decided to run off the Eniwetok operation at once (instead of waiting a couple of months, as originally expected). To make it impossible for the Japanese in the Caroline and Marianas Islands to interfere with the capture of Eniwetok, it was decided to send the bulk of the United States Pacific Fleet, organized into the Fifth Fleet, to strike at the Carolines and Marianas.

Thus, the crucial decision to seek a showdown on the command of the sea came as an incidental by-product of the invasion of Eniwetok. The Pacific Fleet was now big enough to permit Nimitz to send Spruance on an errand of this magnitude, and at the same time keep enough ships in the Marshalls to cover the invasion of Eniwetok, although some naval forces were still tied down in the far northern Pacific and some were in the South Pacific under Admiral Halsey, besides those in the Southwest Pacific under General MacArthur.

The Fifth Fleet steamed back, in the first week of February, to its newly acquired base in the lagoon of Majuro atoll. There it was refueled and resupplied, and soon it put to sea again. Only the highest officers knew what the target was to be. Spruance was in over-all command, with Rear Admiral Marc A. Mitscher in command of all the mobile air power mustered in Task Force 58. In an air encounter, Mitscher would have tactical command. (When the Fifth Fleet was organized and operating as a carrier striking force, with the battleships distributed to protect the carriers, the entire fleet would be known as Task Force 58.)

Task Force 58 was divided into three groups, each containing three carriers, under Rear Admirals John W. Reeves, Alfred E. Montgomery and Frederick C. Sherman. The first target was to be Truk. No name in the Pacific evoked more awe among

Allied fighting men. Partly because of its geography, partly because the Japanese had striven so hard to exclude all foreign sightseers even during the years of peace, Truk had become a bogey. It had been reconnoitered only once, soon after hostilities began, by Australian flying boats, and then had not been visited by Allied forces until February 4, 1944, when two Marine Corps photo-reconnaissance Liberators flew over it at a height of more than four miles.

It was partly on the basis of their pictures, showing major Japanese fleet units at anchor, that Nimitz decided to send Spruance out to attack Truk. It was also largely on the basis of their visit that the Japanese decided to get their major fleet units out of there. The feeling of awe must have been mutual. When word was passed through the American fleet giving the name of the target, there was consternation. As Lieut. Commander Philip H. Torrey, commanding the Essex's Air Group 9, expressed it later to Lieutenant Oliver Jensen: * "My first instinct was to jump overboard."

The task force steamed undetected through all the areas in which the Japanese might have been expected to have surface or aircraft searches. It was the morning of February 17, East Longitude date, when the carriers reached the launching area about a hundred miles northeast of Truk. Among the carriers engaged were the *Yorktown* (Admiral Mitscher's flagship), with Air Group 5; the *Essex*, with Air Group 9; the *Enterprise, Bunker Hill, Intrepid* and *Belleau Wood.*

It was 6:35 A.M., and still pitch dark,† when the carriers turned into the wind to launch the fighter sweep which would first bring the war home to the Japanese at Truk. At 6:49 the Hellcats began to take off, and within a few minutes there were almost 80 of them in the air. They had rendezvoused and were well on their way to the target when, at 7:14, the Truk radio went off the air: the Japanese had received their first warning. Whether they got the word from a patrol plane or from one of their aircraft detection stations (radar) is not known. At 7:50, when the fight was joined, the enemy had a fair number of Zeroes in the air, and more were taking off. The Hellcat

* *Carrier War,* by Lieutenant Oliver Jensen, U.S.N.R. (Simon and Schuster, New York, 1945.)
† The ships were on West Longitude dates and had not set back their clocks.

pilots, directed by Commander Edgar E. Stebbins, skipper of Air Group 5, had to concentrate first on the enemy planes already air-borne, and this gave the Japanese an opportunity to get more planes off the ground than would otherwise have been the case. (Stebbins himself, whose mission as fighter director was not supposed to involve dog-fighting, had to turn aside to shoot down a Zero which was bothering him.)

The fight for local command of the air over Truk was a wild mêlée. There were plenty of Zeroes, but numbers no longer meant anything in the Pacific air war, because Japanese planes and tactics had become markedly inferior. The Zero, although modified by this time and equipped with such safety devices as self-sealing gas tanks, still caught fire if hit squarely by a single burst of .50-caliber slugs. The new Grumman fighter was far more rugged and could take ten times as much punishment. Some Japanese pilots showed, by their handling of their planes, that they were experienced and expert, yet their performance in combat was often downright stupid.

There was extremely heavy anti-aircraft fire. However, this was of little use during the American fighter sweep, because the Japanese gunners would have been just as likely to hit Zeroes as Hellcats, and in any case a fighter plane cavorting through the skies at 350 m.p.h. is no easy mark. A precise breakdown of the figures is impossible, but it seems certain that about three-fourths of the 127 enemy aircraft shot down over Truk this day were destroyed in the preliminary fighter sweep, plus an indeterminable proportion of the 77 destroyed on the ground. Only a handful of American planes were lost—and by no means all of their pilots.

Little more than an hour after the fighter sweep had begun, the dive-bombers (both Dauntlesses and Helldivers) and Avenger torpedo bombers arrived to perform a major operation on Truk and such shipping as remained there. It is important to understand the make-up of Truk: it is neither a simple mountain-top island nor a simple atoll. Instead, it combines the best features of both. There is a perimeter reef, averaging almost 40 miles in diameter, which serves as a breakwater and forms a magnificent anchorage, with six passes through the reef which are navigable for ocean-going craft; in the center of the lagoon is a cluster of mountain-top islets. These enclose an inner anchorage; they have sufficient land area to hold a large garrison (the Japanese are estimated to have had 50,000 men there); they contain excellent sites for waterfront installations such as a navy requires, and they might have been designed by nature for the siting of big guns.

Since most of their own aircraft had been knocked down, the Japanese gunners were able to go into action unfettered when the American bombers arrived. But they were by no means free from interference, because fresh waves of American fighters accompanied the bombers, and strafed the enemy gun positions. Although many pilots had flak holes in their planes, few were lost.

At 10:45, Admiral Spruance received a report from the aircraft director over the island that six ships, described as cruisers and destroyers, were fleeing toward North Pass. Before Spruance could take any action on the report, aircraft from the *Yorktown* attacked the fleeing squadron and apparently hit three ships, one of which, described as a *Katori*-class light cruiser, was either sunk or so badly damaged that she abandoned the attempt and hid among the islands in the lagoon. Only five ships got through the pass.

At 11:15, Spruance put into effect his plan to give the gunnery ships a mission separate from that of the carriers, but complementary to it. His flagship, the 45,000-ton battleship *New Jersey*, fell out of her position in a carrier task group, followed by her sister ship the *Iowa*, two cruisers and four destroyers. This force hauled off to the west, to intercept the Japanese. Spruance himself took tactical command of the force, every ship in which was capable of considerably more than 30 knots. Shortly after 1:15 P.M., a lone Zero rigged as a fighter-bomber dropped out of the broken cloud cover and released a small bomb which narrowly missed the *Iowa*. It was the only air attack on the formation, and the Zero got away.

Spruance detached the two cruisers and sent them to the south (closer to Truk) to finish a laggard Japanese warship, variously described as a light cruiser and a flotilla leader, which had been damaged in previous air attacks. This left four targets fleeing westward, in the path of the two American dreadnaughts and their screen of four destroyers. These were a light cruiser, with part of its superstructure blown away by bombs;

a destroyer or flotilla leader which apparently had escaped damage; a damaged destroyer, and a 443-ton minelayer which was burning. One or more of the destroyers or torpedo-carrying cruisers fired spreads at extreme range against the American ships: both the American cruisers and the *Iowa* had to dodge torpedoes.

The little minelayer was blown to bits by the secondary (5-inch) batteries of the *New Jersey;* two American destroyers finished off the damaged Jap destroyer; both battleships fired at ranges of 30,000 to 35,000 yards on the enemy ship which had hitherto escaped damage, and although she may have been hit, her speed of 35 knots or more was not affected, and she made good her escape. The burning light cruiser was sunk by the combined fire of the two battleships. In one of those errors inseparable from war, a Dauntless dive-bomber was shot down by the *Iowa's* gunners before its friendly identity was recognized.

Rather than return to Task Force 58 on the same course he had followed on the way out, which might have led him into a submarine trap, Spruance decided to take the force all the way around Truk. Although his bag of enemy ships was small considering the force at his disposal, he had demonstrated more clearly than any other fleet commander how gunnery ships could be used in conjunction with carrier aircraft to reduce the number of enemy cripples, some of which escape after nearly every naval action.

Many aviators aboard the American carriers were bitterly critical of Spruance because he allowed his gunners to finish off cripples which the aviators seemed to regard as their private property. This attitude is regrettable, to say the least. No one, even aboard the battleships, would deny the aviators credit for 90 per cent or more of the damage done to the enemy at Truk. The morale of ships' gunners (especially aboard battleships), who too seldom had a chance to use their guns against the type of targets for which they were intended, was of just as much concern to Spruance as the aviators' feelings. And properly so.

One of the clear-cut victories of the operation was credited to Torpedo Squadron 17, six of whose planes caught an ancient light cruiser of the *Tenryu* class, 25 miles southwest of Truk. One torpedo hit under the bridge; there must have been other hits, and the ship was being abandoned when the planes had to leave the scene.

During the night, American carriers' air groups were usually inactive, except for reconnaissance, but this operation was to provide a notable exception. Lieut. Commander William I. Martin, commanding Torpedo Squadron 10, had worked for a year on the idea that torpedo planes equipped with the latest electronic devices (radar) could be used more effectively against enemy shipping in darkness than in daylight. This theory was to be given its first practical test at Truk. However, Martin himself had been injured in a fall, and was unable to lead the squadron, so Lieutenant Van Eason took command of the 12-plane flight, which divided into two elements when it reached Truk.

The Japanese promptly detected the planes' approach, but the anti-aircraft fire was all at high elevation, while the torpedo planes bored in low. In turn, the two sections attacked shipping lying at anchor off the island of Moen, each plane dropping four 500-pound bombs fitted with delayed-action fuses—a precaution necessitated by the adoption of the mast-height technique. Of the 48 bombs dropped, 13 were direct hits and seven were listed as probable hits; one plane was lost, and several returned damaged (the Japanese got the elevation when the attack had been in progress for some time). With this limited effort and at this small cost, eight Japanese merchantmen were sunk and five ships, including a destroyer, were damaged. The percentage of hits was four and a half times as great as in the average daytime strike.

The Japanese were also busy during the night. Truk's own air squadrons having been shot out of the skies or pinned to the ground, reinforcements were called up from other bases in the Caroline Islands. Here was an opportunity for the theory of mutually self-supporting, unsinkable carriers to prove itself: the Japanese should have been able to muster enough planes to offer a serious threat to the 700 or so aircraft distributed among the American carriers, but were able to produce less than a dozen. In night torpedo attacks they scored their only success of the operation against American surface ships: one hit near the stern of the carrier *Intrepid,* which temporarily deprived her of steering control.

At daylight, the air groups from the eight undamaged carriers returned to the assault on Truk, but the operation was not long continued, because of optimistic reports of damage to shore installations and shipping. Not a single Japanese plane took off from Truk's airfields to challenge the attackers. It was computed that besides the 204 enemy planes destroyed the previous day, 50 had been damaged on the ground. The final tally of ships struck listed 23 vessels definitely sunk. These included two light cruisers, three destroyers, one ammunition ship, two oilers, two gunboats, eight cargo ships and five unidentified. (The Japanese were amazingly honest in reporting their losses, conceding the sinking of two cruisers, three destroyers, 13 freighters, and the destruction of 120 aircraft.) The Navy counted six additional Japanese ships as probably sunk, and eleven as damaged—for a grand total of 40. Only 19 American planes were lost, and several of their pilots and crewmen were saved.

In this operation was the first indication that sea-going air power, if mustered in sufficient strength with enough planes aboard enough carriers protected by enough battleships and screening units, could seriously dispute the Japanese command of the sea in the western Pacific. If Truk could be manhandled in this way, it was a fair presumption that the Marianas could be given the same treatment. Spruance ordered Mitscher to go ahead, minus two battleships, the *Intrepid* and another carrier which Spruance led back to Pearl Harbor.

Saipan was to be the principal target, lying only 1,450 statute miles from Tokyo. (Truk was 700 miles farther away from the enemy capital.) On the way to the northwest, Mitscher's signal to the fleet, "I cannot tell a lie. D-day is Washington's birthday," was only a half-truth, because his ships were still operating on West Longitude dates; it would be February 23 at Saipan before his carrier planes could cut down any Japanese trees. However, action did develop on February 22, East Longitude date. At 2 P.M. a Japanese plane slipped through the combat air patrol; the pilot saw as much as he needed to see of the fleet formation, and made good his escape. Mitscher anticipated the worst, and alerted the whole of Task Force 58 with the strongly worded signal: "We have been sighted by the enemy. Get ready to fight your way in."

The attack began about 11 P.M. The Japanese sent in wave after wave of flare-carriers and torpedo planes, and the night was further illuminated by the lavish anti-aircraft fire of the ships. How many attackers there had been was impossible to tell, but when dawn broke it was computed that 14 had been shot down. The carriers by this time were preparing to launch the fighter sweep which was intended to pin down any additional Japanese planes on their home fields, but before the Hellcats could begin to fly off, there were more attacks. A twin-engined bomber (Betty) was hit several times on its mad course through the task force, and appeared certain to hit the *Belleau Wood* in a suicide finale. Unaccountably, it soared over the deck, and then it was disintegrated by a crossfire of ack-ack from the carrier, a battleship, a cruiser and a destroyer. The *Yorktown* and the *Essex* had similar narrow escapes. The Japanese claimed one carrier as sunk, another as damaged, and three large warships damaged, "of which two were most probably aircraft carriers." It remains only to add that no American ship was sunk or damaged.

When the fighter sweep reached Saipan, the weather was foul, with a 300-foot ceiling. Perhaps it was partly because of the bad weather, but it must have been mainly due to stupidity, that the Japanese still had their fields packed with planes, despite the ample warning they had had. Less than half got off the ground: 29 were shot down, and 87 were listed as destroyed on the ground (at both Saipan and the adjoining island of Tinian, to the south).

Few enemy ships were found. One cargo ship was sunk; another was damaged and apparently beached, and a third was set afire. A patrol craft was blown up, and seven other small ships were damaged. For the rest, the day-long operation consisted of bombing and strafing hangars, runways, ammunition dumps, fuel stores and seaplane ramps. The enemy was surprisingly weak in an area where he might have been expected to show strength. At Guam, the captured American island farther south, no attack had been planned, but a squadron of fighters from the *Bunker Hill,* far off their assigned course, strafed a new airfield the Japanese had built, and took photographs which proved valuable later in the year.

The final score in the air was: Japanese aircraft destroyed, 135; American aircraft lost, six.

Task Force 58 by now had gone far toward proving the thesis that command of the sea could be seized from Japan with the ultra-modern, sea-going, mobile air force built around aircraft carriers. It had earned a rest, and Mitscher had earned the vice admiral's three stars which were conferred upon him.

But if command of the sea as far west as Truk and the Marianas could be gained by this means, why not command of the sea as far west as Palau and the Philippines? The Japanese had been keeping much of their fleet in southern waters, and Palau was one of its major bases (now that Rabaul was closed). General MacArthur was planning a major leap westward along the New Guinea coast, and even though by March, 1944, he held an outpost in the Admiralty Islands, all his operations farther west would be in danger of outflanking from Japanese positions in the Carolines. Palau had to be the next target.

Task Force 58 again was the chosen instrument of destruction, but its composition was somewhat changed after the Marianas strikes. There were more carriers, including the *Princeton* and the *Monterey,* and Admiral Spruance was present again, with his Fifth Fleet staff. Truk was within reach of heavy bombers striking from either Eniwetok, in Nimitz's command, or the Admiraltys, in MacArthur's area, so it was decided to harry it from both directions, to keep the Japanese quiescent and incapable of interference with the passage of the fleet. This was one of the first instances of close co-operation between the two theaters in tactical matters. There was one detail, however, which must have been the result of an accident, and not of joint planning: three days before the carrier strike was due at Palau, one of MacArthur's B-24 reconnaissance planes worked over the island group and alerted the fleet units which were then anchored there. The great majority of these got safely away, although one battleship is said to have been torpedoed by an American submarine.

If it had not been for this untimely reconnaissance, the damage done to the Japanese navy at Palau must have been far greater. None of the ships in the lagoon at the time of the carriers' arrival was allowed to escape, because a squadron of

Avenger torpedo planes laid mines in the passes leading into the lagoon.

Task Force 58 had been detected by enemy patrol planes during the last day or so of its approach to the target, and the night of March 29-30 (East Longitude date) was marked by the usual Japanese torpedo attacks, which were unsuccessful. Palau had been thoroughly alerted, and when the first fighter sweep descended upon it at dawn, there were about 30 Japanese fighters in the air. They were hopelessly outnumbered; ten were shot down by a single squadron (Fighting 5) and the rest were divided, somewhat unequally, among the other squadrons represented.

When the dive-bombers and torpedo bombers arrived, shipping was the top-priority target, and the Hellcats sent in to cover the bombers were able to join in the attacks on Japanese surface craft. The only warships present were three destroyers and one craft of unspecified type. The three destroyers were trying to escape while Avengers were laying mines in the main channel. Two were turned back, one of them was later sunk in the lagoon, while the third slipped through the minefield and seemed about to escape when eight Avengers carrying torpedoes caught up with it. The aircraft torpedo has not been a successful weapon in the Pacific war, so Lieut. Commander Richard Upson, commanding the squadron from the *Yorktown*, felt justified in expending all eight against the lone destroyer. Five of them hit it simultaneously, and the target disappeared instantaneously.

While the carrier's crews patched damaged planes and made ready for the second day's strikes, the Japanese also were busy. From some nearby field, probably in the Philippines, they produced 40 or more fighters which flew to Palau during the night and were in the air again, ready to defend the smoking, battered base, when the American planes arrived. If any of them escaped, nobody knows where they went. When the day's work was done, 22 auxiliaries and cargo ships (including five tankers) were listed as sunk, and 16 as damaged. Of enemy aircraft, 114 had been shot down, and 36 destroyed on the ground, while 49 were classified as "probably destroyed." The American carriers lost 25 planes, but the growing daring of the Navy's rescue operations resulted in the saving of all but 18 airmen. At one time a submarine had so many fliers fished from the sea crowded into its cramped quarters that the commanding officer signaled: "Forming airedale club in forward battery."

The closing phases of the three days' strikes against the western Carolines were devoted to three minor positions lying northeast of Palau—on the route of the fleet's withdrawal. The most important of these, theoretically at least, was Yap, lying 325 statute miles from Palau, and noted chiefly as a cable station which caused dissension at Versailles. The weakness of Yap showed how little genius the Japanese have for building up bases except in cases of the utmost urgency. They appeared to have no anti-aircraft guns on the island (properly, a close cluster of islands), and nothing heavier than rifle fire greeted the American planes which destroyed the radio and cable station and set fire to everything that looked inflammable. The only sign of recent construction was an airfield, still uncompleted. Not a single Japanese plane appeared to dispute the skies with the carrier air groups.

Some planes which had been assigned to Yap were diverted to Ulithi, about a hundred miles to the northeast. There was a radio station there, but little else. On April 1, Woleai atoll, southeast of Yap and 675 statute miles due east of Palau, was the target for a fairly large strike by fighters and bombers. The American fliers found eleven Zeroes on the runway and two twin-engined bombers; all were strafed and prevented from taking off. A radio station, fuel and ammunition stores and a few small buildings and vessels were bombed and strafed. Task Force 58 steamed back to its base, unmolested.

Command of the sea had been gained, by winged sea power, and the time had come to exploit it. On April 13, Task Force 58 set out again, with Mitscher flying his flag now in the *Lexington*. Its mission was without precedent in the Pacific: to support amphibious operations in a separate theater, the Southwest Pacific Command of General MacArthur. (Previously, Nimitz's carriers had been used only in support of Nimitz's own amphibious assaults.) D-day for the troops was April 22 (East Longitude date); the carrier air groups were to begin operations on April 21.

It is safe to say that if the Japanese had dispatched a large fleet toward American-held positions, it would have been detected soon after leaving port, and several days before it could reach its destination. But Task Force 58 steamed for a week through waters which the Japanese were supposed to patrol, and was not detected until April 20. Even then, it was not attacked. That same day, Lieut. General Kenney's bombers delivered the last of their preliminary strikes against the three Japanese airfields in the Hollandia area on the north coast of Netherlands New Guinea—Hollandia itself, Cyclops and Sentani. The next day, the carriers were off the coast and took over the assignment.

As is always likely to be the case in war when one side holds an overwhelming advantage, the event was anti-climactic. The enemy had withdrawn everything that he could, even the bulk of his ground forces, from the region, because Kenney's land-based fliers had already seized command of the air. The enemy carefully refrained from sending in gunnery ships or carrier-borne air forces, because Mitscher's mobile air force had seized command of the sea. D-day was noisy, but not otherwise noteworthy from the point of view of Task Force 58: hundreds of tons of bombs were dropped, and tens of thousands of rounds of .50-caliber ammunition were fired. But all this expenditure of explosives was for the purposes of insurance.

The same procedure was followed on April 23, and when the advancing ground troops ran into a pocket of opposition, they were given tactical support from the carriers. Mitscher sharply rejected a suggestion that this would be a good time for the Navy to go off hunting its favorite quarry—the Japanese fleet—and insisted that so long as his assignment was to support Mac-Arthur's troops in a landing, he would stay there and do nothing else. But during the afternoon of the 23rd, MacArthur released the naval force; his beachhead was secure and Kenney's land-based air forces would be able to cope with any counterblows the Japanese might deliver.

Task Force 58 steamed away to the east, refueled, and then set out for Truk. It was shadowed all the way by Japanese snoopers, of which six were shot down, but no doubt they had radioed the fleet's position and course before being "splashed." Although the Japanese had conceded command of the sea to Task Force 58, they were not yet ready to concede command of the air over Truk, and they had brought in an estimated 200 bombers and fighters since the February assault.

The fighter sweep was launched before dawn on April 30 (East Longitude date) from a position about 75 miles southwest of Truk. About the time it reached the target area, 15 Japanese planes which apparently had taken off from Satawan, in the Nomoi group, southeast of Truk, were detected approaching the carriers. Eight Hellcats from the combat air patrol intercepted them nine miles off the starboard beam of the force, and all but four of the enemy planes were shot down. These four broke through the screening destroyers and cruisers, although it seemed that they were flying through a solid wall of anti-aircraft fire, and got into position to launch torpedoes. Evidently they had been damaged or their bombardiers had been wounded, for two of them flew across or over the *Yorktown's* bow, with torpedoes still attached, before they succumbed and fell into the sea. A third was shot down astern of the *Lexington;* only one succeeded in launching its torpedo, and this missed the cruiser at which it was aimed. The attack was completely abortive.

Since there were no ships worth mentioning left at Truk, the target of the American carrier planes was the complex of shore installations. Mitscher was anxious to show what his force could do; he went so far as to admonish the pilots: "Plaster it [Truk] with everything you have—including empty beer bottles, if you have any." Sixty enemy fighters which had constituted the combat air patrol at the opening of business that day were all shot down; an equal number was destroyed on the ground. The bomb tonnage dropped was heavy enough to satisfy even Mitscher's craving for destruction: in this first day, the *Yorktown's* Air Group 5 flew 227 sorties and dropped 110 tons of explosives. Other large carriers did almost as well, and the cruiser-class ships contributed their quota. Hangars, barracks, warehouses, fuel dumps, repair shops and all the other paraphernalia of a great base, such as Truk had been, were left in flames. The only effective opposition the enemy was able to offer consisted of heavy anti-aircraft fire.

The next day (May 1, East Longitude date) was much the same. Air strikes against Truk were slightly diminished in intensity because one group of carriers had been detached during the night and dispatched to the southeast to support a bombardment force under Vice Admiral Willis A. Lee in an attack on Satawan.

In many ways, the most notable feature of the two-day strike on Truk was the rescue service for fliers forced to land in the sea because of flak damage to their planes. This service had been highly developed during the February strike, when King-fisher (OS2U) seaplanes catapulted from cruisers made daring water landings within range of Japanese shore batteries to pick up fliers from life rafts. (One, piloted by Lieutenant [j.g.] Den-ver Baxter, landed inside the lagoon to pick up Lieutenant [j.g.] George M. Blair. Baxter thus became the first Allied flier to land at Truk.) Destroyers had been busy with rescue work, as always during these strikes, and Lieutenant John M. Sullivan had had the good fortune to be rescued by *The Sullivans*, the only United States warship named for a family, which had 23 other Sullivans aboard.

The arrangements for rescue work during the second strike were even more elaborate. A submarine had been added to the team, following the successful experiment with this technique at Palau. The sub in this case was the *Tang*, commanded by Commander Richard H. O'Kane, and it was kept frantically busy answering dozens of calls from pilots reporting that their companions had force-landed on the water. The *Tang* had to stay on the surface, never safe from the danger that a trigger-happy American flier would mistake her for a Jap, and never safe from Japanese shore batteries which took her for what she was. Somehow, she survived these equal hazards, and actually engaged an enemy shore battery in a gunnery duel. One King-fisher picked up a downed fighter pilot, but then the rescue plane itself capsized in the heavy seas, and a second Kingfisher had to pick up the original survivor and the crew which had saved him. The pilot of the second plane, Lieutenant (j.g.) John A. Burns, transferred his cargo to the *Tang* and both set out on more errands of mercy. The *Tang* picked up a *Yorktown* pilot from Kuop Reef, which he had reached by paddling all night. (He had been shot down in the first day's strike.) The climax came when the *Tang* rendezvoused with Burns's King-fisher and found that the little "bug" had picked up no less than nine passengers. They were taken aboard the *Tang*, and so were Burns and his radioman. The Kingfisher had been so battered as to be incapable of taking off, and O'Kane sank her with gunfire. In all, the *Tang* took 22 fliers aboard in two days off Truk.

On May 2 (East Longitude date), Task Force 58 was retiring to the east, and its air groups joined the gunnery ships in a combined bombing and shelling of Ponape, 440 statute miles from Truk. Ponape is an island formation of the same type as Truk, but the central mountain-top island is larger than any in the Truk lagoon, and the surrounding lagoon is smaller. Consequently, the gunnery ships did not have to lie so close to the reef as would have been the case if they had been used to bombard Truk. The results of the action, although never described in detail, are reported to have been "excellent."

This mission completed, Task Force 58 left the combat area for a brief respite. In three months it had established a principle new in naval warfare: that a mobile, carrier-based air force, used in a properly balanced fleet so that it need fear no encounter with any enemy fleet under any circumstances, can seize command of the sea. In those three months it had seized command of millions of square miles of island-studded Pacific, from the Marshalls to the Philippine Sea. The only area in which the Japanese could still claim dominance was in their "inner fortress," where land-based aviation could fan out from coastal bases in support of surface fleets, including carriers. At a later stage in the great Pacific offensive, the fast carrier task forces of the Pacific Fleet would take command of the sea in the inner fortress also.

xv. The Isles of Thieves

THE CONQUEST of Kwajalein and Eniwetok in February, 1944, extended American control in the central Pacific hundreds of miles to the west. The sweeps by Task Force 58 showed that command of the air could be gained, over any of the enemy's island bases, so long as the carrier fleet could stay there to exercise command. But the carriers, even with the immense help of modern methods of refueling and resupply at sea, could not stay out indefinitely, so land bases still farther west were needed.

The most inviting were in the Marianas. This north-south chain of islands, 485 miles long and lying approximately on the 145th Meridian, East Longitude, had been called by Magellan the Islands of the Lateen Sails, and later the Islands of Thieves. Sold to Germany in 1899, and occupied (like the Marshalls and Carolines) by the Japanese in 1914, they were retained even after Japan's withdrawal from the League of Nations should have ended the mandate under which they were held from 1919 to 1935.

The islands which had thus fallen into the hands of international thieves were well situated for Admiral Nimitz's purpose. They were within 1,300 to 1,500 miles of the Japanese coast around Tokyo, and while this was beyond the range of any bombers then operating from Pacific islands, it was just within the range of the B-29 Superforts then coming into service. Best of all, capture of the southern Marianas would cut off direct air and sea traffic between Japan and all the islands to the south, the most important of which, early in 1944, were the Carolines with the strongholds of Truk and Palau.

Very little was known of Japanese dispositions and strength in the Marianas. The first reconnaissance pictures were taken by Task Force 58 fliers during the February 23 strikes; so far as has been disclosed, no more were obtained until April 18, when Saipan and Tinian were attacked by Liberator heavy bombers of the Seventh Air Force and Fleet Air Wing Two, from Eniwetok. The plan of battle must have been determined on the basis of very scanty information.

Except for the continuous chain extending through the northern Marianas, the Volcano and Bonin Islands and the Izu group just south of Tokyo, the southern Marianas were isolated from Japanese positions within range of tactical aircraft. Consequently, there was much less preliminary work to be done in neutralizing nearby bases than was the case in compact groups of islands such as the Solomons. On May 19 and 20, Marcus Island (about 700 miles northeast of Saipan) was attacked by carrier planes from a Fifth Fleet task group, and on May 23 Wake Island was bombed. At the beginning of June, land-based aircraft from General MacArthur's command, flying from bases in the Solomons, Admiraltys, Emirau and Hollandia, launched a neutralizing campaign against the western Carolines. Truk, Yap and Palau were the principal targets, but some attention also was given to Woleai, an atoll only 400 statute miles south of Guam, and the nearest base in the Carolines to the Marianas.

Saipan was selected as the first objective. Near the southern end of the chain (150 miles north of Guam), it was the largest of the group which had been occupied by the Japanese since 1914. Its 72 square miles of rugged terrain lent themselves well to the construction of underground fortifications in which the Japanese delight, and the fringing reef lying close inshore around most of the island was a major hazard in the first and most difficult stages of an amphibious operation. The Japanese had made little preparation during the first 29 years of their occupancy to repel an invasion, but during the last few months they tried to repair this omission. The likeliest place for a landing seemed to be the extreme north of the island's west coast, and they started concentrating defense works there. Pre-invasion estimates set the strength of the Japanese garrison at about 20,000.

The invasion and connected military operations were entrusted to the Fifth Fleet, under Admiral Spruance. Task Force 58, under Vice Admiral Mitscher, was in its familiar role as the spearhead of the attack. On June 11 the task force arrived in Marianas waters and flew off fighter planes to seize control of the air over the target area. This was achieved in the first sweep, when 124 enemy planes were destroyed on the ground or in the air at Saipan, Tinian, Rota and Guam. American losses were eleven Hellcats and eight pilots. On June 12, only 16 additional Japanese aircraft were destroyed, but two small cargo ships at Saipan and an oiler to the northwest were sunk. A convoy attempting to escape from the area toward the home islands was attacked, and an oiler, five cargo ships and nine escort craft were damaged. Another convoy brought under attack the next day was said to contain troop transports which were believed to have unloaded reinforcements at Saipan.

This was June 13, the day the fast battleships of Task Force 58 were withdrawn from the carrier groups and set to work bombarding the west coasts of Saipan and Tinian. They fired their main batteries (each containing nine 16-inch guns) and secondary batteries (twenty 5-inch guns) for almost seven hours, and under cover of this bombardment fast mine-sweepers cleared the waters for the assault ships which were to follow, and underwater demolition teams worked along the beaches to remove obstacles which would impede landing craft.

On June 14, the fast battleships returned to duty with Task Force 58, and their place off the coasts of Tinian and Saipan was taken by pre-Pearl Harbor battleships which Navy men now refer to as "OBBs." Great destruction was wrought in the target areas. The morning of June 15 opened with a still heavier bombardment by the OBBs and their attendant cruisers and destroyers and rocket ships. Escort carriers had arrived to send their planes in further support.

The entire amphibious force, including the support ships, was under the command of Vice Admiral Turner. Lieut. General Holland M. Smith headed the Fifth Amphibious Corps; the assault troops were to be the 2nd Marine Division (Major General Thomas E. Watson, with Brigadier General Merritt Edson as assistant division commander), and the 4th Marine Division (Major General Harry Schmidt, with Brigadier General Samuel C. Cumming as assistant division commander); the area reserve was the Army's 27th Division (Major General Ralph Smith). The invasion of Guam had already been decided upon, and was scheduled to follow that of Saipan within a few days; the troops for this operation had been embarked, and were passing sweltering days and nights aboard ship (in the vicinity of Eniwetok), waiting for a decision as to when they should be committed.

For the landing beaches, the American command had selected a portion of the Saipan coast where the Japanese had not expected an assault, because the reefs extended farther west there than they did in the northern sector. A partial element of surprise was therefore obtained. The northern landing beach, assigned to the 2nd Marine Division, was 1,500 yards long, on the west coast between the capital, Garapan, and the town of Charan Kanoa, but nearer the latter. The southern beachhead, assigned to the 4th Marine Division, also was 1,500 yards long, and included the town of Charan Kanoa, extending to the vicinity of the sugar mill south of the town.

Because the establishment of the beachhead was costly, it has been generally assumed that the Japanese were manning the beach defenses in strength. Actually, although the 48-hour battleship bombardment had made the beach positions untenable, the Japanese had excellent prepared positions farther inland, with an abundance of mortars and artillery well sited to permit them to lay down a heavy fire on the beaches.

H-hour had been set for 8:40 A.M., June 15: the first waves were eleven minutes late when they hit the beach. The first and the two succeeding waves encountered comparatively light enemy fire, especially on the left flank, but just when it seemed that a beachhead could be secured cheaply, the enemy opened up with greatly intensified mortar and artillery fire. The result was that the fourth and fifth waves had heavy casualties in the landing craft, and soon the rain of fire upon the beach itself was so heavy that many who had reached shore safely (and who should therefore have passed the greatest danger) were killed or wounded. These casualties (mostly caused by shell fragments) were so heavy that in the first ten hours after the landings, the 2nd Battalion of the 6th Marines (2nd Division) had four commanding officers: the first two were wounded, and the third was only a temporary replacement.

The invaders made fair progress during the first day, but the yardage gained was of less importance than the price paid.

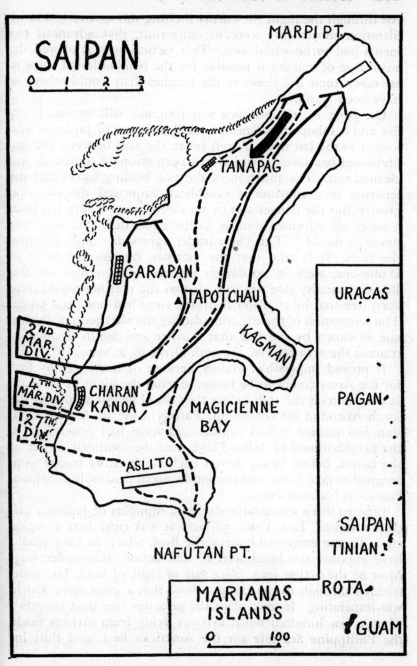

SAIPAN

0   1   2   3

MARPI PT.

TANAPAG

GARAPAN

▲ TAPOTCHAU

KAGMAN

2ND
MAR.
DIV.

4TH
MAR. DIV.

27TH
DIV.

CHARAN
KANOA

MAGICIENNE
BAY

ASLITO

NAFUTAN PT.

URACAS

PAGAN

SAIPAN
TINIAN

ROTA

GUAM

MARIANAS
ISLANDS

0   100

All through the night the enemy shelling was so severe, and infiltration movements were so dangerous, that advanced elements had to be withdrawn. This tactical retreat offered the advantage of making it possible for the bombardment ships to lay down their fire closer to the beaches than would otherwise have been feasible.

On June 16, the advance was resumed, still against heavy fire and stubborn resistance by small numbers of Japanese who fought to the last man. About noon, the area between the two divisional beachheads, which had been strongly contested, was cleaned out. The junction of the two landing forces and the securing of a continuous beachhead improved the situation greatly, but the danger was by no means past. There has been a lot of misinformed writing to the effect that "the issue was never in doubt." This cheer-leader approach simply obscures the facts. It is true that the marines, on the afternoon of D-plus-one, were in no danger of being driven into the sea. But the casualty rate was so high that the marines would have been defeated by attrition if drastic steps had not been taken. The seriousness of the situation during the afternoon of D-plus-one is shown by the fact that Turner and Smith decided to commit the area reserve, the 27th Division, at once.

It proved impossible, mainly because of heavy enemy fire, for the Army troops to be landed during the night of June 16. It was noon on the 17th before they could be put ashore, at the southern end of the beachhead. Patrols of the 4th Marine Division had pushed inland rapidly and some had penetrated to the neighborhood of Aslito Field, near the southeast corner of the island, before being driven back. The Army troops were assigned to take Aslito and the southeastern peninsula of Saipan, known as Nafutan Point.

June 19 was a memorable day: vast numbers of Japanese aircraft attacked Task Force 58, and it was clear that a major effort by the enemy to destroy the fleet, which in turn would have exposed the beachhead to destruction, was under way. Most of the action took place out of sight of land, but word trickled through to the troops ashore that a great naval battle was impending. It took place the next day (see next chapter), when a few hundred naval aviators flying from carriers made the Philippine Sea safe for the American fleet, and thus insured the success of the campaign for the southern Marianas.

It was the same day, June 20, that the Army troops captured Aslito Field, which was renamed for Commander Robert H. Isely, a carrier group commander shot down over the field on June 12. The 4th Marine Division by this time had pushed through to Magicienne Bay, north of the airfield, and had wheeled to the left, to advance up the east coast of the island. Elements of the 27th Division were passed through the marines and assigned to the central sector. This created an unnatural order of battle, with the 2nd Marine Division on the left, moving up the west coast and the west slope of the mountainous spinal column; the 27th Division elements in the center, and the 4th Marine Division on the right. The Army and Marine Corps forces are trained differently and carry out even standard operations in different ways. There is always occasion for friction when elements of two such different forces have to fight side by side, and co-ordinate many of their operations.

It did not take long for the friction to develop. The Army men had been trained not to advance against defended positions until there had been time to bring up artillery and soften up the enemy. The Marine Corps had trained its men to hit hard, hit fast and keep going. The result of this difference in method, possibly aggravated by a difference in the quality of officers, was that the American front line repeatedly sagged in the center, where the Army troops advanced more slowly. The Marine Corps elements on each side just as repeatedly found themselves in danger of being outflanked. The upshot was that in the heat of the moment and of battle, Lieut. General Holland Smith relieved Major General Ralph Smith as commanding general of the 27th Division, and replaced him temporarily with Major General Sanderford Jarman. The incident did not become generally known until several weeks later, and then only the Marine Corps version was published. The ill will which it generated was enormous. Until the Army's side of the case can be properly presented it is impossible to arrive at a fair judgment in the matter. It may be that Ralph Smith was advancing more slowly than the exigencies of the campaign dictated; it is certain that he was advancing more slowly than Holland Smith had dictated. And it is equally certain that

Holland Smith was not nicknamed "Howlin' Mad" because of any sweet reasonableness.

Fortunately, while the generals were bickering the enlisted men and field officers were getting on with the war. Extensive use of land mines and booby traps by the enemy, and repeated nuisance raiding at night by small numbers of planes failed to slow the advance appreciably. Ten days after the landings, the left flank was securely anchored in the southern outskirts of Garapan town. On June 25, the 1st Battalion of the 2nd Marines (2nd Division), commanded at this stage by Lieut. Colonel R. M. Tompkins, succeeded in scaling Mount Tapotchau, the highest peak on the island (1,554 feet) and in establishing positions near the summit. For some unaccountable reason, the Japanese who had bitterly resisted the advance up the ravines, gave up the summit more readily. However, at least five major pockets of enemy troops had been bypassed in the advance to the peak, and the job of cleaning them out of their caves and inter-connecting tunnels required many days and many American lives. At the same time as the 2nd reached the top of Tapotchau, the 4th Marine Division cleaned up Kagman Peninsula, the more northerly of the two arms which enclosed Magicienne Bay.

North of Tapotchau the island begins to narrow, and there was not enough room for three divisions abreast; with the capture of the peak, the 2nd had completed the major part of its mission, so the 27th pinched it out by advancing at an angle to the west coast while the marines on the left flank mopped up Garapan. The entire island was honeycombed with underground positions. The Japanese had machine-gun nests at every turn along the foot trails, and 3-inch anti-tank guns along the winding, narrow road which led to the northeastern peninsula. Many of their heavy guns were in caves, mounted on tracks so that they could be propelled to fire a few rounds, and then withdrawn before the grasshopper planes (Stinson Sentinels, or L-5s) could radio word back to the artillery as to the enemy guns' location. The establishment of an operational air base at Isely Field, as far back as June 22, had done much to facilitate the campaign, but had not changed its essential nature. On June 26 the Japanese launched a severe counter-attack from one of the bypassed pockets on the slopes of Tapotchau; the next day they broke through the Army lines on Nafutan Point.

On July 4, Garapan was captured—or rather, its ruins were captured: only a couple of dozen buildings were standing in a town which had numbered 10,000 people. It was apparent that the campaign had not long to run. But this was equally apparent to the Japanese island commander, Lieut. General Yoshijo Saito, and to Vice Admiral Chuichi Nagumo, commander of Japanese naval forces in the Central Pacific. At 3 P.M. on June 6, through captured enemy orders, the American command learned that an all-out counter-attack was to be launched before dawn on the 7th. By this time, corps artillery had been brought so close to the front that it could give direct and effective support to the forces on the west coast, where the Japanese attack was expected. The most direct and effective way of using artillery in support of infantry in these circumstances would have been to lay down a crushing barrage during the night on the areas from which the Japanese would have to jump off. This was not done. No official explanation has been offered. The 27th Division's dispositions to meet the attack also appear to have been defective.

The number of Japanese making the attack was variously reported as 1,500, 3,000 or even 5,000. The first waves of Japanese who charged the American positions in the dark of the morning on July 7 carried rifles and sub-machine guns; but among the last elements were men with nothing but swords or bayonets lashed to broomsticks. The 105th Infantry on the extreme left flank broke under the attack, and some men swam out to the reefs offshore, while others fell back. Aid stations were overrun, and the wounded were killed, completing the analogy with the last charge on Attu a year earlier. Some of the attackers who had been poorly armed picked up American weapons and drove on.

Not until the Japanese had gained between 1,500 and 2,000 yards was the attack stemmed—by the artillery which was in danger of having its batteries overrun. A battalion commanded by Major William L. Crouch had moved up its 105-mm. howitzers only the night before, and was hardly in shape to repel an attack of this kind. The gunners fired horizontally into the oncoming Japanese masses, with fuses cut to four-tenths of a second, so that the shells exploded only 50 yards ahead of the guns. Even so, the enemy burst through the positions occupied by two batteries, causing 50 per cent casualties in one and 20 per cent in the other. At this stage, the Japanese were slowed by a combination of exhaustion and attrition. By dawn, they had lost the initiative; then the weight of American arms and reinforcements began to tell. The enemy was pushed back the entire distance of the advance, and the Americans regaining the bloody ground were appalled at the number of Japanese corpses with which it was littered.

Later, it developed that when the attack failed, Saito and Nagumo had committed suicide, the former having found his strength insufficient to enable him to take part in the operation. His strength was not even sufficient for him to take his own life neatly, and he had to be dispatched by an aide. Many lesser Japanese officers had killed themselves with some degree of ceremony, and greater numbers of enlisted men had done so with grenades held to their heads or chests.

Exaggerated stories of suicides among the civilians on Saipan were circulated in the United States, and seized upon with glee by Japanese propagandists as proof of their people's willingness to die.

However, it is now clear that the number who died voluntarily was far less than at first reported. The 25,000 civilians estimated to have been on Saipan included perhaps 5,000 from the home islands of Japan, and it was among these that the suicide rate was highest. Even so, considerably more than half survived. There were many deaths among the Okinawans, who constituted the largest element in the population, and among Chamorros, Koreans and Kanakas, but most of these deaths resulted from the acts of Japanese soldiers or were the unavoidable result of American military action.

With the cutting up of enemy troops into pockets near the north end of the island on July 9, organized resistance was declared to have ceased. This was true, in the sense that the enemy no longer had any cohesive force, but the fighting went on. One marine regiment was reported to have killed 711 Japanese on July 11 and 12. The mopping up went on intensively for weeks, and with diminishing intensity for a year. American casualties in the conquest of Saipan were 3,426 killed and

13,099 wounded. The number of Japanese killed or captured was put at 29,747.

The spotlight shifted swiftly from Saipan to fresh areas of conquest. As already mentioned, the operation to liberate Guam had been postponed, and while this was begun on July 21, it is more convenient to treat first of the conquest of Tinian, which began three days later. As late as July 7, Japanese artillery on Tinian had shelled Isely Field on Saipan, and it was clear that Saipan could never be really secure until Tinian was captured; moreover, the relatively flat terrain of Tinian offered one of the great strategic prizes of the Marianas campaign: sites for half a dozen 8,500-foot runways from which B-29s could fly to bomb Japan.

The enemy garrison on Tinian was estimated at about 9,000 men. Although the island as a whole is much lower than Guam or Saipan, it is a plateau surrounded by steep cliffs. This made the selection of landing beaches difficult. Intensive aerial reconnaissance during the Saipan campaign had revealed two very small beaches on the northwest coast, and the amphibious force command under Rear Admiral Harry W. Hill decided to use these. The disadvantage of their narrowness (the northern one was 65 yards wide, and the southern one 130 yards) would be outweighed by the relative absence of defenses, the fact that the Japanese would be surprised by a landing there, the fact that they could be covered by land batteries on southern Saipan, and the fact that the landing craft and landing ships would have only a short run to the unloading point.

For this was to be a shore to shore operation, the first on such a scale in the Pacific. The troops assigned to the assault were the two marine divisions which had fought on Saipan. Major General Clifton B. Cates had taken command of the 4th, which was to make the initial assault; the 2nd could not be fed in until the next day, because of congestion on the tiny beaches.

At 7:40 A.M. on July 24, the 25th Marines, reinforced to combat team strength under Colonel Merton J. Batchelder, went ashore from LSTs and LSDs (landing ships, tank, and landing ships, dock) on the 130-yard White Beach 2. The 24th Marines, under Colonel Franklin A. Hart, hit White Beach 1, which offered them only 65 yards. Both had been embarked at Saipan; by 11 A.M. they were across the beaches and enough material had been landed to permit the 23rd Marines (Colonel Louis R. Jones) to be brought in across the southern beach. Later in the day, a landing team built around the 1st Battalion, 8th Marines (2nd Division) was landed as division reserve. The enemy had indeed been surprised by the point of landing, and resistance at the beachhead was limited to small-arms fire by isolated groups of Japanese. Within a few hours, however, the enemy artillery and mortars got the range, and those which survived the incessant pounding by American warships and aircraft lobbed shells into the beachhead area. Seventeen of the invaders were killed this day.

During the night, this enemy barrage·built up to an insistent drumfire, and at 2:30 A.M. on the 25th, an ambitious counter-attack was begun. The Japanese island commander had brought up troops from the southern sector by forced marches, and they were thrown into action at once all around the 2,500-yard perimeter set up by the marines. However, the Japanese commander had dispersed his forces widely, and they were not strong enough at any one point to effect a breakthrough. After dawn, when the marines resumed the offensive, they had lost less than a hundred killed and had had 225 wounded; in front of their perimeter were hundreds of dead Japanese: the count was reported to be 1,241.

During the 25th, the 2nd Marine Division which had been loaded on transports instead of landing ships was disembarked over the two narrow beaches and wheeled left, to take Ushi Point (the nearest point to Saipan, only 2½ miles away across Saipan Strait) and then swing down the east coast of the island. The buildup of the beachhead was completed on the 26th, and both divisions broke out and scored extensive gains on the 27th. The 2nd took Ushi Point Airfield, and between them the two divisions captured a strip averaging three miles deep across the northern tip of the island. On July 28 the 4th captured Mount Lasso (560 feet), the highest point on Tinian, and the 2nd swept southward almost five miles. The race to the southern beaches was conducted at an average speed of about two miles a day by the 2nd Marine Division, and about three miles a day by the 4th, on the longer, bulging western coast. Taken from the rear after intensive bombing and bombardment, the prepared Japanese defenses around Tinian town did not prove especially formidable, and this area was secured on July 31. The next day, both divisions reached their objectives on the south coast.

As at Saipan, there was a confused situation regarding the civilian population. Large numbers had surrendered at first, and it was obvious that the great majority wished to surrender. However, the soldiery did not wish to permit them to do so, and there were several recorded instances of soldiers roping civilians together and killing them with demolition charges or by small-arms fire.

Final American casualties on Tinian were 314 killed and missing, and 1,515 wounded. The number of Japanese killed was put at 6,939, while prisoners taken boosted the total garrison troops accounted for to almost 7,500.

Unlike the conquest of Tinian, the liberation of Guam was a separate operation from the conquest of Saipan. Only the top command, vested in Admiral Spruance, was the same. Rear Admiral Richard L. Conolly was Admiral Turner's deputy in charge of the Third Amphibious Force; Major General Roy S. Geiger, U.S.M.C., commanded the Third Amphibious Corps, which consisted of the 3rd Marine Division (Major General Allen H. Turnage), the 1st Provisional Marine Brigade (Brigadier General Lemuel P. Shepherd, Jr.) and the Army's 77th ("Statue of Liberty") Division (Major General Andrew D. Bruce). The Provisional Brigade was an especially noteworthy grouping of experienced fighting men; besides the 22nd Marines, it included the four original raider battalions, veterans of Makin (1942), Tulagi, Guadalcanal, New Georgia, Bougainville and Emirau. Formed into the 1st Raider Regiment in 1943, these battalions had been reconstituted as the 4th Marines in February, 1944—perpetuating the designation of the original 4th or "China Marines" who were lost at Bataan and Corregidor.

In one respect, of course, the Guam operation resembled those in the rest of the southern Marianas: it was covered by forays of the Fifth Fleet, and especially its carrier component, Task Force 58, designed to isolate the battlefield. As early as June 23 and 24, Pagan in the northern Marianas was attacked by the fast carriers and battleships; on the 24th, also, a flyspeck in the Volcano Islands which later was to become a household word throughout America was first attacked and got its name into the fine print of the communiqués: Iwo Jima. On July 4, Iwo was attacked again along with the more northerly Peel and Hillsborough Islands (which appear in the communiqués under their Japanese disguise of Chichi Jima and Haha Jima) in the Bonin group. These operations, conducted by a task group under the command of Rear Admiral Joseph J. Clark, were notable for the fact that they carried American surface ships closer to the Japanese home islands than they had penetrated before. They were designed, primarily, to cut down Japanese air power in the chain of stepping-stone islands, and thus to prevent interference with the fleets and armies engaged in the southern Marianas.

On June 11 and 12, when the softening-up of Saipan began, Japanese installations on Guam were bombed and bombarded to prevent enemy interference with the impending operations to the north. On the 16th, battleships trained their guns on the airfields and nearby facilities; on the 19th and 27th, carrier planes were active. On July 5 the intensive preparation began, since D-day by this time had been decided upon, and thereafter the Japanese on Guam knew no peace until they found it in death or surrender. Through July 9, the load was borne by carrier aircraft; on the 10th, surface units appeared and subjected the island to bombardments which were maintained day after day (mainly by cruisers and destroyers) until the 16th. Then the battleships joined the attack, and stayed until long after the troops had gone ashore.

By the morning of D-day, July 21, no less than 10,000 tons of naval shells had been poured into Guam alone. The island was much larger than any previously invaded in the central Pacific, being 30 miles long and almost eight miles in average width, with an area of 225 square miles, but the areas subjected to bombardment represented only a small fraction of the total, and the shellfire was therefore far more concentrated than the dimensions of the island might suggest. The Japanese evidently had expected landings to be attempted in the immediate neighborhood of Port Apra, for most of their coast defense guns were so sited as to cover that area. Instead, the American

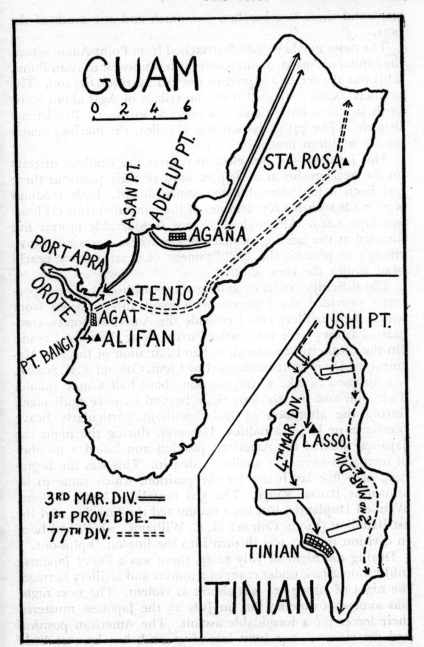

GUAM

0 2 4 6

STA. ROSA ▲

ASAN PT.

ADELUP PT.

AGAÑA

PORT APRA

OROTE

TENJO ▲

AGAT

ALIFAN ▲

PT. BANGI

3RD MAR. DIV. ━━━
1ST PROV. BDE. ━━
77TH DIV. ════

USHI PT.

4TH MAR. DIV.

2ND MAR. DIV.

LASSO ▲

TINIAN

TINIAN

command chose two beaches, one north and one south of the port.

The more northerly beach stretched from Point Adelup, near the capital of Agaña, about 3,000 yards southwest to Asan Point. This was the sector assigned to the 3rd Marine Division. The southern beach extended from the village of Agat about 3,000 yards to Point Bangi, and was assigned to the 1st Provisional Brigade. (The 77th Division was to follow the marines ashore on the southern beach.)

The Japanese did not elect to contest the landings directly on the beaches, for as at Saipan, most of their positions there had been made untenable by bombardment. Both landings were made within a few minutes of the scheduled time (H-hour was 8:30 A.M.). Although there was considerable mortar fire directed at the landing vehicles and beaches, it was not heavy enough to prevent the establishment of a satisfactory beachhead within the time allotted.

The difficulty lay in extending the beachheads. The topography provided the Japanese with many hill positions from which their artillery could enfilade the American forces, compressed as they were into narrow strips along the coastal roads. On the northern beachhead, the 2nd Battalion of the 21st Marines (3rd Division), commanded by Lieut. Colonel E. R. Smoak, was assigned to take a cliff position about half a mile inland. This cliff, and the 500-foot ridge beyond it, were both taken during the afternoon of D-day without particularly heavy resistance or large casualties. However, during the night the Japanese shelled the American position and killed a number of men who were only shallowly dug in. This was the beginning of a five-day battle for the position, which came to be known as Banzai Ridge. The 3rd Battalion (Lieut. Colonel Wendell Duplantis) had been committed the first day, and the 1st Battalion (Lieut. Colonel M. C. Williams), which had been in division reserve, was thrown into the line on D-plus-one.

During the night of July 22-23, there was a heavy Japanese infiltration attack under cover of a mortar and artillery barrage; the night of July 23-24 was almost as violent. The next night was somewhat quieter, but on July 25 the Japanese mustered their forces for a formidable assault. The American position had deteriorated, not from loss of ground, but because little territory had been won in four days of fighting, while there had been severe losses in manpower. The 1st Battalion, for example, had only 250 men left in the line. The main force of the Japanese counter-blow struck this battalion about 10 P.M. and within a short time it succeeded in penetrating the American line. The situation was not restored until dawn, when it was estimated that 500 to 700 men of the Japanese 18th Infantry Regiment and an additional attached battalion had been killed.

Thereafter, the situation improved, and this was due in large measure to the fact that the 3rd Marines, on the left flank of the division, had gained high ground in the vicinity of Fonte and had thus eliminated many of the positions from which the Japanese had enjoyed undisturbed observation of the invaders' lines. Simultaneously, the right flank of the division was extended southwest to Piti, and a short distance beyond the town a junction was effected with the 1st Provisional Brigade which had cut across the base of Orote Peninsula.

When the brigade landed on the 21st, the 4th Marines went ashore on the right flank at the southern extremity of the beachhead and pushed directly inland, while the 22nd Marines landed on the left flank and wheeled left (north) to cut off Orote. The experience of these two regiments closely resembled that of those to the north. The 4th, under Colonel Alan Shapley, took preliminary positions in the foothills of Mount Alifan, but during the night of July 21 it was subjected to night attacks on both flanks. In one sector northwest of Alifan, tanks fought tanks. A small position known as Hill 40 changed hands four times before the Marines secured it. (All the night actions in this campaign were fought under the unearthly glare of star shells fired by ships offshore to fall ahead of the American lines and to illuminate the Japanese positions.) The 4th succeeded in beating off all the Japanese attacks by dawn and in inflicting heavy losses, but its own combat effectives were cut down in the process.

The enemy's attacks on the 22nd Marines' sector were smaller but involved clever infiltration, which proved just as dangerous as the use of larger numbers. Three officers and 69 Japanese enlisted men got to the perimeter of Colonel Merlin F. Schneider's command post. Many were killed by 25 men of a reconnaissance unit under Lieutenant Dennis Chavez, Jr. The two regiments counted 600 enemy dead the next morning. At 9 A.M. the advance was resumed up Mount Alifan, and the 874-foot peak was secured by nightfall, despite extremely difficult terrain. Almost a thousand Japanese were said to have been killed in this advance.

On the morning of July 25, the 22nd Marines pushed off in the face of substantial Japanese fire from well-prepared pillboxes, and had to contend also with occasional tank sorties. Casualties were severe, but during the day the regiment succeeded in cutting across the base of Orote Peninsula to Apra. That night it was compressed into the narrow isthmus, its freedom of movement still further cut down by extensive marshes, and it was not favorably disposed for withstanding an attack. As the Japanese began their charge they were brought under fire by corps artillery using fragmentation shells, some of them being ranged within 70 yards of the American lines. The assault, which started at 10:45 P.M., lasted until dawn, when more than 400 enemy dead were counted.

By this time the main northern and southern beachheads had been joined, and the American lines extended in a continuous arc from the 3rd Marines' position just short of Agaña to that of the 77th Division below Point Bangi—a distance of about 9 miles.

On July 26, the Provisional Brigade shoved off to the west with its two regiments abreast, the 22nd on the right advancing along the north shore of the peninsula, and the 4th on the left. Progress was quick at first, but the opposition stiffened all that day and the next, until it was clear that the Marines had run into the main Japanese defensive positions on Orote. Tanks massed in front of the infantry had to blast a way through. The 22nd Regiment was nearing the old Marine Corps barracks and thus had a sentimental reason for pressing the advance. However, it was not until 3 P.M. on July 29 that this point could be captured. The 3rd Battalion of the 4th Marines had had a bitter, two-day fight to overcome defensive positions on two low ridges which lay across the approaches to the air strip. At 4 P.M. on the 28th the battalion overran the old Marine Corps rifle range and the way to the airfield lay open. With its capture on the 29th, the Marines broke the back of Japanese resistance on Orote and the peninsula was secured for all practical purposes. After two days of intensive mopping up, some troops could be withdrawn and employed to clear stray Japanese from southern Guam.

Meanwhile, the Stars and Stripes had been raised on Mount Alifan, formally ending two and a half years of Japanese occupation. Agaña had been captured on July 31, but what had been a picturesque little city of about 12,000 people was reduced by now to heaps of rubble and charred woodwork. When the Leathernecks had fought their way through the outer system of pillboxes and dugouts, they found that the enemy had abandoned the shattered town as of no further value to them. The 77th Division, which had followed the Provisional Brigade ashore, had fought its way inland north of Mount Alifan and in a highly creditable operation had captured Mount Tenjo, 1,020 feet high. The Army troops then pushed due east across the island, through roadless terrain, to the east coast near Port Pago.

The Japanese had chosen to abandon the southern half of the island. Even the small number of troops needed to guard a concentration camp was withdrawn and the 3,000 Chamorro inmates found freedom. By August 3 the enemy was compressed into the northeastern one-third of the island, and resistance began to stiffen. The 77th Division began to advance up the east coast, having effected a successful "swinging gate" operation with the 3rd Marine Division as the hinge. The Provisional Brigade at this time was in corps reserve. On August 6 the brigade moved north from Agaña to join the 3rd Marine Division in the drive up the west coast.

The only two remaining points at which the Japanese made major stands were Mount Santa Rosa, near the east coast in the 77th Division's sector, and at a road junction in the northwest on the Marines' front. The enemy could have staved off defeat at Santa Rosa for many days, but as in so many cases of this kind the Japanese did the unpredictable, and abandoned a fine set of defenses at Yigo, southwest of the peak. On August 10 all organized resistance was declared to have ended: the number of Japanese dead was put at 10,971, and only 86 prisoners had been taken. It appeared that the Japanese garrison, which had been believed to number 20,000, had been over-estimated. But by the middle of November the number of enemy dead was set at 17,238, and there were 463 prisoners. The mopping up of remnants which hid in the hills continued for twelve months after the island was declared "secure."

A remarkable feature of the campaign in the Marianas was the weight of artillery, including naval gunfire, employed to soften enemy positions before the ground forces attacked. In the capture of the three islands, naval fire support ships fired a total of 36,260 tons of 5-inch to 16-inch shells and 5-inch rockets. Before the landings on Guam, no less than 10,000 tons had been used there, and as the campaign wore on, Rear Admiral "Close In" Conolly kept his fire support ships close to the beaches, so that 4,400 tons more was expended before the island was secured. Considering that the Japanese put up such a spirited defense in spite of this pounding, it is easy to imagine that without it they would have fought far more effectively, and would have taken a heavier toll of the invaders.

On Guam, too, corps artillery under the command of Brigadier General Pedro A. del Valle, U.S.M.C., was particularly effective. It began to go ashore on D-plus-one day, and executed one firing mission that evening. The next day it was sufficiently well disposed to execute 14 missions, and on D-plus-three the number increased to 41. In most cases, the corps kept division and brigade artillery in a common pool, permitting mass fire support on a scale which would have been impossible if the artillery had been under the piecemeal control of the units to which it belonged.

A gratifying detail of the Guam campaign was the successful employment of the Army's 77th Division in a corps under Marine command. There was none of the recrimination which developed on Saipan, and Admiral Nimitz went out of his way to commend the 77th for its efficient, workmanlike performance.

In another respect, too, the recapture of Guam differed from the conquest of Saipan and Tinian: the great majority of the inhabitants were Chamorros, American "nationals" though not American citizens, and their loyalty was equaled only by the gratitude they showed upon being liberated from Japanese rule, which had been everywhere oppressive, and in some cases brutal and sadistic. There was no occasion here for stories of mass suicides; on the contrary, there were more Chamorros counted after the liberation than there had been in the 1940 census.

For the immediate task of prosecuting the war against Japan, the conquest of the southern Marianas and the neutralization of the rest of the chain represented a major turning point. Guam, which had been almost defenseless when the Japanese struck in December, 1941, was quickly built up into a base comparable with Oahu in Hawaii. Great airfields were created; so was a large and reasonably safe harbor, where hitherto there had been only a third-rate anchorage for a few vessels in Port Apra. Under the emergency of war, the Navy built up Guam without having to ask the consent of Congress.

The conquest of the southern Marianas was the last step in the central Pacific theater before the onslaught against the "inner fortress" of the Japanese. The only intervening islands, in the Volcano, Bonin and Izu groups, were so close to the enemy's homeland that they could be reached by fighter planes flying from Honshu, and so could be defended as though they were a part of the "sacred soil" itself. They could not be considered as oceanic outposts, in the same category as Tarawa, Kwajalein, Eniwetok, Saipan or Guam. The next step in the march on Japan must be an assault upon some one of these positions directly supporting the inner fortress—and no such step could have been taken without the prior capture of Saipan, Tinian and Guam.

XVI. Jutland, New Style

AFTER THE CAMPAIGN for Guadalcanal, the Japanese battle fleet lay low. Although the enemy had certain mental quirks which have caused many of his military decisions and actions to be treated as matters for mirth by American writers, he must be given credit for having examined the strategic situation carefully during the amphibious advance from the Gilbert Islands westward. The logical place for him to try to stop this advance would be in the Marianas. The logical way for him to try to stop the advance would be to throw in his mobile, carrier-based air force in coordination with land-based air forces operating down through the island chain. If he could knock out the American fast carrier task forces, the invasion force lying off the beaches of the target island (Saipan, as it developed) would be left relatively defenseless; if by chance he could get at the amphibious force first, by making an "end run" around the guardian carrier task forces, the latter would be left with nothing to defend.

The Japanese who was mainly responsible for working out a battle plan to carry out this strategy was Admiral Shigetaro Shimada, who was both Navy Minister and Chief of the Naval General Staff. In the late spring of 1944, he was careful to keep the bulk of the fleet at southern bases in the captured islands, far out of range of American snooper planes, and in an area which, in those days, was out of reach even for bold, massive raids such as those executed by Vice Admiral Mitscher against Truk, the southern Marianas and Palau. Reconnaissance of the Jap fleet's movements had to be carried out by American submarines.

The Japanese, however, could fly off search planes to comb vast areas of ocean for an approaching enemy. Thus it was that on June 10, when Task Force 58 was still hundreds of miles short of its target area, two Japanese snooper planes dodged through the combat air patrol and saw enough to give Tokyo a valuable advance warning. From the fleet's position, the Japanese would deduce that operations were to begin at dawn on June 12 if the target area was the southern Marianas. This would give them two nights and a day in which to send aerial reinforcements south to the threatened positions from the home islands. Mitscher decided to try to cancel the advantage the Japanese had gained from this early reconnaissance report; he put on speed, and determined to strike at the airfields in the southern Marianas as early as possible on June 11.

Heavy weather interfered, and the operation did not begin until dusk. The fighter sweep, executed by 200 or more Hellcats against airfields on Saipan, Tinian, Rota and Guam resulted in the destruction of 124 enemy planes, top honors for destructiveness going to the highly experienced Fighting Squadron Two, flying from the *Hornet,* and the inexperienced Fighting 15, part of a new air group attached to the *Essex.* The next day, when only 16 additional enemy planes were encountered in further fighter sweeps, it became clear that the speed-up plan worked out for Mitscher by his operations officer, Commander Gus Widhelm, and his deputy, Lieut. Commander John Myers, had succeeded. The carriers' air groups had got in their first blows before the Japanese could build up the island air forces to formidable strength, and they had messed up the runways and installations around the fields.

It was on June 12 that the American command first received warning from a submarine that the Japanese fleet was on the move. The next report is said to have come from another submarine off Halmahera, describing a Japanese force of six aircraft carriers, four battleships, eight cruisers and at least eight destroyers steaming north.

Mitscher and Spruance calculated how long it would take this force to reach the vital area around the southern Marianas, and must have received some reassuring word that the Japanese were delaying, because on June 14 two task groups of Task Force 58, commanded by Rear Admirals Joseph J. Clark and W. K. Harrill, were detached and sent north to the Bonins. These groups comprised the *Yorktown* (now carrying Air Group One), the *Essex* and *Hornet* and light carriers of the

Independence class. They ran into filthy weather and not many Japanese planes on the afternoon of the 15th; on the 16th, visibility was better and Japs were more numerous.

These two carrier groups were already on their way south when, at 3:45 A.M. on June 18, the Japanese fleet was again located, this time by the submarine *Cavalla,* Commander Herman J. Kossler commanding. Rather than attack at once, which might have won him credit for sinking an enemy ship but cost him an opportunity for valuable reconnaissance, Kossler submerged and let the enemy fleet pass over him. The parade took more than an hour; there were so many propellers that the submarine men could not count them. It was some time before Kossler could surface and radio his report to Spruance, by way of Saipan: the Japanese fleet was about 700 nautical miles almost due west of Guam, and was heading toward that island, at about 20 knots.

In flag plot aboard the *Lexington,* Mitscher and his chief of staff, Captain Arleigh ("31-Knot") Burke, calculated that it would be night before enough of the 700-mile gap could be closed to permit the American air groups to strike the enemy's carriers. Mitscher therefore asked Spruance whether he wished to force a night engagement, and received a negative answer. Spruance felt that difficulties in ship handling, aircraft operations and communications at night were so great as to offset the obvious advantages of attack under cover of darkness. However, Spruance assured Mitscher (whom he had put in tactical command of the entire force, since this was an air operation) that he would press the pursuit of a damaged or fleeing enemy at any time.

Task Force 58 was working to the west and south, but throughout the period before the battle (as was to be the case during and after the battle) it was handicapped by an east wind: every time a flight of planes was to be launched or recovered, the carriers had to turn into the wind and steam toward Guam. The task force was limited also by the directive under which Spruance was working. Its first duty was to protect the invasion forces off Saipan against attack by enemy air fleets. If, in performing this duty, Task Force 58 could sink the bulk or the whole of the Japanese battle fleet, that would be immensely gratifying to Admiral Nimitz, but it would be incidental. Much of the controversy about the conduct of the operation arises from ignorance of this basic fact.

There were other complications. Clark and Harrill's groups, coming down from the north, could not rejoin Mitscher until noon on the 18th. The American destroyers would soon need fuel. But most important of all: if Spruance had permitted Task Force 58 to be sent charging westward, as 31-Knot Burke advocated, the Japanese might make an end run around the force, and get between it and the soft-shelled transports off Saipan. It was all very well to argue, as the airmen did, that there were old battleships and escort carriers off Saipan, able to protect the beachhead and its supply ships. But to Spruance, this protection did not give the beachhead a sufficient margin of safety, and he was determined not to let himself be lured out of position, no matter how glittering the prospect.

It appears that after Task Force 58 regained its full strength, with Clark and Harrill's groups present, it turned to the northeast, for it is said that in the late hours of June 18, the opponents were steaming on parallel courses. During the evening, one of the Japanese ships broke radio silence, and although the message undoubtedly was in code, the receipt of the signal (regardless of its meaning) made it possible to plot the position of part, at least, of the enemy force. It was 335 miles away, to the west-southwest. Once again, Burke and Mitscher proposed to Spruance that Task Force 58 turn west during the night, to be in position for launching an attack on the Japanese at dawn. Once again, Spruance refused. This is the most questionable decision of the battle. If the position and course of the Japanese were known with reasonable certainty, as Burke and Mitscher believed, the chance that the enemy could make his end run during the night was negligible, and Spruance's decision was wrong. But the situation was not so simple: Spruance had received a garbled radio report from another submarine, giving a position for the Japanese fleet a full 80 miles away from its position as indicated by other sources. This message had not reached Mitscher, and later it was proved to have been wrong. However, it is not clear that an attack such as Burke and Mitscher advocated would have located the Japanese fleet and destroyed it the next morning.

For at dawn on June 19, search planes from the American

carriers could not find the Japanese ships. This fact is conveniently overlooked in all those accounts of the operation in which Spruance is blamed for having denied his airmen a chance to sink the whole Japanese fleet. They had the chance at this time—and could not find the fleet. Meanwhile, the submarine *Cavalla* commanded by Kossler was being rewarded for its skipper's patience in not attacking a day earlier. His sub was on the surface when the lookout saw Japanese planes; Kossler expected an attack and prepared to submerge. But the enemy aircraft went on about their business of landing on a carrier a few miles away. Kossler fired six torpedoes, of which three hit. The sub was heavily depth charged, and then Kossler heard four big explosions which he took to mark the end of the carrier. The Navy credits him with having sunk the carrier *Syokaku.*

It was about this time that Spruance asked Mitscher to send bombers to neutralize Guam and Rota airfields. Mitscher replied that he was unable to do so because of the shortage of bombs. It was not that the carriers had exhausted their bombs, but Mitscher expected to have to fight an enemy fleet within a few hours, and he had to keep a reserve of bombs for this purpose. Mitscher proposed instead to neutralize the air over Guam with a strong combat air patrol.

As it developed, Spruance had his wish, despite the shortage of bombs. About 9:30 A.M., Japanese planes were reported approaching the fleet. The Japanese are estimated to have had nine carriers (five large and four light), which would have an aircraft complement of up to 600 planes; some of the air formations came upon the Americans from the southwest, some from the west and some from the northwest. Other planes flew out from the east, apparently from Rota and Guam.

The decks of the American carriers were thick with planes, fully loaded with bombs and machine-gun ammunition. The fighters were ordered flown off at once to meet the enemy; the bombers were ordered off immediately thereafter to clear the decks of inflammables and explosives in case of bomb hits. In the case of the *Essex's* squadrons, at least—and possibly others— the bombers not only got out of the way but set out to do as much damage as they could. Commander James H. Mini, leader of Bombing 15, and Lieut. Commander V. G. Lambert, leading Torpedo 15, headed for Guam and loosed their bomb loads on Orote airfield despite the fact that no fighter cover was available for them. For the balance of the day, at least, Orote would be of no use to Japanese planes flying in from the carriers to refuel.

The most logical plan for the Japanese would have been to divide their air groups into two classes, one to attack first and refuel later at Guam and Rota, the other to refuel first and attack later, since this would reduce congestion at the airfields. It seems likely that this was the plan, for some of the enemy air groups tried to break through the combat air patrol and the surface screen to get at the American carriers, while others seemed intent on flying by, in tight formation, as though they had urgent business elsewhere—which could only be on Guam or Rota.

The battle in the sky was joined at about 10:40 A.M., and although the Japanese were present in great strength, with groups ranging from 40 to 75 planes, they proved fantastically ineffective. All the evidence indicates that this was the carrier air force which the Japanese had spent 18 months in training for just such an occasion: except for its weight of numbers it was miserably unimpressive. The fighters were not aggressive, and did little to protect the bombers. The Americans—better pilots flying better planes—had rich pickings. In the first hour, only a handful of Jap planes broke through the "cap" (combat air patrol) and the screen, and they did no damage. At one time, a fighter pilot from the light carrier *Cabot* saw no less than 15 enemy planes burning.

When it was clear that large numbers of enemy aircraft were trying to fly past the fleet and on to Guam, the policy initiated by Mini and Lambert of the *Essex* was made official: the officer who was in command of Air Group Eight was appointed coordinator of all bombing and torpedo squadrons then in the air, and ordered to use them against Orote. When he reached the air over the peninsula, enemy planes were trying to land despite the bomb craters, and American fighters were slashing at them. Among these were the Hellcats of Fighting 16, flying from the flagship *Lexington,* and those of Fighting Two, from the *Hornet.* Lieutenant (j.g.) Alexander Vraciu, already an ace with 12 planes to his credit, could have gone home weeks earlier, but had chosen to stay with Fighting 16 for another tour of duty. Now, in eight furious minutes, he shot down six Japanese planes over Orote; his score of 18 made him the Navy's leading ace. But for one day's work, his score of six was soon matched by Ensign Wilbur B. Webb, of Fighting Two, who tallied six definitely plus two probables.

The enemy groups continued to appear for almost three hours, the last being logged at 1:16 P.M. The action, incredible as it was, was utterly monotonous: in the end, 404 Japanese planes were listed as shot down, while many others must have gone down in the ocean; of more than 500 which must have been engaged, only 18 broke through the combat air patrol, and 12 of these were shot down by anti-aircraft fire from screening surface ships before they could drop; two torpedoes missed the *Lexington;* one bomber hit the *Indiana* (the only direct hit of the attack) but caused no casualties and no military damage; two bombers scored near misses on carriers, and fragments killed two American seamen and wounded others. These were the only casualties among the ships. Of the American air groups, 27 planes were lost to enemy action, but the pilots of nine of these were rescued.

Never, in the short history of naval air warfare, had the expenditure of so large a force produced such little gain. The cream of the Japanese naval air force had been skimmed off in a matter of hours. The Japanese carriers had failed in their mission; with only a handful of planes left aboard to maintain a combat air patrol, they were now useless hulks on the ocean, so far as strategic value was concerned. The greatest single day's victory in the air might be followed by the greatest victory of this war on the surface of the sea, if only the enemy carriers could be found.

But the Japanese ships proved elusive. Long-range searches flown from the *Lexington* and *Enterprise* failed to locate the enemy on the 19th; perhaps, if the American ships had charged off to the westward, their planes might have caught up with the quarry, but this would have left the Saipan beachhead exposed to another trick Japanese play, which Spruance was not willing to do. Moreover, his ships were short of fuel and bombs. There are conflicting reports as to whether any refueling was done during the night; presumably the explanation is that only part of the force was fueled.

After standing guard over the islands during most of the night, Task Force 58 at last turned west, in pursuit of an enemy who was "crippled and fleeing" within Spruance's definition—for the destruction of his air groups was a blow more crippling in the long run than superficial damage to ships.

All day, the carriers flew searches far to the west: the weather was comparatively clear, for the western Pacific, and the failure of experienced reconnaissance pilots to locate the enemy ships is difficult to understand. It was not until 3:30 P.M. that Lieutenant Robert Nelson of the *Enterprise* reported "a task force stretching beyond the horizon" in Lat. 15° 35′ N., Long. 134° 35′ E.—due west of Saipan, and just about as far from that island as from Luzon, 700 nautical miles to the west. An oil slick indicated that the Japanese had interrupted their refueling when the American scouts found them, and had spilled oil on the water from hastily disconnected hose couplings.

The range was extreme: about 400 miles. Only about two hours of daylight remained, the air groups would have to attack in twilight, fly home to the carriers in the gathering darkness, and land on the decks in a pitch-black, virtually moonless night, with little or no gasoline to spare for circling the ships in the landing pattern. But this was the opportunity for which Mitscher and every other American admiral had been waiting, and it was not to be let slip. The planes had been warmed up at intervals throughout the day on the American carriers' decks, and shortly after 4 P.M. they were off on the longest, and one of the most hazardous missions in carrier warfare. The pilots and air crew men had no illusions about their chances of landing in the drink instead of on a carrier's deck.

Dusk was settling when the first American planes sighted their prey at about 6:30 P.M. In the failing light, and with failing fuel, no target coordinator was able to scout the whole enemy force and bring back a coherent report of its make-up. The result is that no two participants in the engagement agree on what they saw or what they hit. There are variously reported to have been six to eight carriers, divided into two or three groups; there is no agreement as to the number of battleships, or their disposition. There is even disagreement as to whether each carrier had its individual screen, or whether they were bunched as in an American task group. With this confusion (most of it highly understandable, considering the circumstances in which the observers found themselves) it is useless to try to reconstruct the action in any detail.

On one point there is general agreement: the carriers had few or no planes on their decks, and the combat air patrol over them comprised no more than 30 to 40 planes. These were spottily distributed, so that some American air groups avoided air-borne interception entirely, while others were heavily engaged until the Zeroes could be shot down or driven away by the escorting Hellcats. This took some time, as the Hellcats had been separated in some cases from the bombers they were supposed to cover, but in the end 26 Zeroes were counted as splashed.

On one other point there is widespread agreement: the anti-aircraft fire thrown up by the enemy carriers and especially by their screen of gunnery ships was exceptionally dense.

Air Group Eight, led by Commander Shifley, is reported to have attacked a light carrier in one of the enemy's more southerly groups, and to have scored at least two hits on it with bombs before a torpedo plane from an *Independence*-class carrier made a hit. A *Kongo*-class battleship (either the *Kongo* herself or the *Haruna,* since the *Hiei* and *Kirisima* were sunk in the Battle of Guadalcanal) also was hit and had fires burning on her superstructure when the American fliers left the scene.

The *Wasp's* air group is reported to have attacked the Japanese fleet train, consisting of five or six oilers and about the same number of destroyers: two of the former are said to have been sunk, and two more set afire. A destroyer is reported to have been seen sinking after having its stern blown off by its own depth charges—detonated by skillful strafing.

Still more damage was done among the more northerly Japanese ships. The *Yorktown's* Air Group One reported nine or ten bomb hits on a *Syokaku*-class carrier (the identification is doubtful), which had been previously hit in the stern by four 500-pounders dropped by an Avenger from an American light carrier. The *Yorktown* fliers also are credited with hits on the *Hayataka* and her sister ship *Hitaka,* besides two cruisers and a destroyer. The *Lex's* Bombing 16 and Torpedo 16 are reported to have made eight hits on a large carrier variously described as a Hayataka and as the *Taiho* *, while Bombing Ten and Torpedo Ten from the *Enterprise* were running up similar scores on a Hayataka and a light carrier. Three planes from Torpedo 24 (flying from a light carrier) are reported to have made three hits with torpedoes amidships on a Hayataka.

Desperately short of gasoline, and many of them with flak damage, the American planes did not linger to assay damage. Their pilots concentrated on joining up with planes which seemed to know where they were going, for the long flight back to the darkened east. This ordeal has been described for the fliers of Air Group 16—and it was substantially the same for the other groups—in more detail than any other period of two or three hours in any combat operation.† Several planes had been shot down near the Japanese fleet, and surviving pilots and crew men were floating around in life vests or inflatable dinghies, with little apparent chance of being rescued. During the agonizingly long miles back to Task Force 58, with gasoline gauges falling ever close to the "Empty" mark, most of the fliers expected that they, too, would soon be in similar plight. And some of them were.

But the number of fliers thus lost was far less than might have been expected. (The number of planes lost was considerably greater.) There was tension aboard all the carriers, but the tension was greatest in flag plot aboard the *Lexington,* where Mitscher had the responsibility for saving as many as possible of the boys whose courage he so greatly admired. Commander Widhelm suggested that the ships' lights be turned on, for otherwise few of the planes would find their roosts. The blackout was the most strictly enforced of all rules aboard warships in a combat zone. To switch on the lights was to advertise the fleet's position to any Japanese submarine which might be in the neighborhood, and therefore to invite disaster for any of a dozen carriers, as many battleships, twice as many cruisers and three times as many destroyers: almost a hundred thousand men, and an investment of billions of dollars, on whose se-

* The *Taiho* had been sunk the previous day by the submarine *Albacore.*
†*Mission Beyond Darkness,* by Lieut. Commander Joseph Bryan, U.S.N.R., and Philip Reed (Duell, Sloan and Pearce, New York, 1945).

curity depended the ability of the United States Navy to pursue
the offensive.

On the night of June 15, two aerial torpedoes had missed the
Lexington by only a few yards. Mitscher did not need to be
reminded of the perils. Yet there were hundreds of his boys in
the air now, and many of them had had no training in night
landings. For a few minutes, Mitscher stood on the flag bridge,
weighing the advantages and disadvantages. Then he stepped
into flag plot, closed the light-lock door behind him, and lit a
cigarette. He flopped on the transom (leather settee), pushed
up the bill of his baseball cap and rubbed his forehead. Pushing himself up from the cushions, he turned to Captain Burke
and said: "Turn on the lights." Then he went out on the
bridge again.

As the word was passed over the short-range radio, search-
light beams stabbed the sky, the panel lights on the carriers'
decks flashed on, and the gunnery ships in the screen twinkled
with red and green running lights. But even this did not make
the task easy. Two *Essex*-class carriers look as like as two peas;
Mitscher ordered all pilots to land on the first carrier which
could take them. There were mad rushes to get into the
landing circle; over-strained pilots cut each other out or dis-
obeyed the landing signal officers and refused to be waved off.
Accidents resulted, and cluttered the decks with wreckage so
that planes which had been in the landing circle had to find
another carrier—and not all could wait their turn. Plane after
plane lacked the gas to stay in the landing circle for a half-hour
or more; these and many others force-landed in the water, their
pilots and crew men scrambling out to be picked up by the
nearest destroyer.

It was an evening of sheer horror for the vast majority of the
men in the returning planes and for those responsible for getting them safely down on a flat-top's deck. But when it was
over, the cost of the mission was not excessive, and Mitscher's
daring in turning on the lights had been amply justified.
Ninety-five American planes were lost, either to enemy action
or in water landings; however, all but 22 of their pilots were
saved, and all but 27 crew men.

With the aid of information from fliers who had been shot
down in the midst of the scene of battle, and were picked up

the next day by cruisers' float planes, CinCPac tried valiantly to assess the damage done to the enemy. But the task was hopeless. At first, it was believed that one Hayataka had been sunk and the other left burning, the Syokaku badly damaged and two or three light carriers hit. Eventually, it was established that the *Syokaku* and *Taiho* had been sunk by submarines and the *Hitaka* by carrier planes, but the important feature of the result of this battle was that the harm done to the enemy was under-estimated for many months—and this had a vital bearing on Admiral Halsey's decisions in a later engagement.

On the morning of June 21, searches were flown both from the American carriers and from Saipan, but the Japanese remnants which were sighted got away before the attack groups could catch them. In many ways, the encounter which came to be known as the (First) Battle of the Philippine Sea resembles the Battle of Jutland. In each case, command of the sea was at stake, both in the broad sense and in the narrow sense referring to command of the sea leading direct to the enemy's homeland. In each case, the more powerful fleet had as its over-all commander a man who weighed every risk, who wished to avoid a night engagement at all costs, and who had a horror of letting the enemy get between him and his bases. In each case, the subordinate was a man willing to throw the rule-book away and take great chances to win great gains.

More important: after the Philippine Sea battle, as after Jutland, the victor did not know to the full what damage had been done to the enemy, both materially and morally, so that the extent of the victory became only gradually apparent. Spruance deliberately forwent the opportunity to destroy the the Japanese fleet's main striking force, because he judged the risk to the Saipan beachhead—his dominating responsibility—to be too great. Despite the handicap imposed upon him by Spruance's caution, Mitscher succeeded in destroying the bulk of Japanese sea-borne air power. He did not succeed in destroying the fleet, but he did it more damage than was at first believed, and its carrier task forces were never again a serious threat to the American advance upon the enemy homeland.

XVII. Portrait of a Killer

THE QUALITIES of the men who were advanced to positions of leadership and high responsibility in the war against Japan are many and various. Among the "top brass" in the Navy, Nimitz is admirable and likable, but hardly the type to capture the imagination as a "beloved leader"; Spruance and Turner are estimable, but not easy to like (although for widely different reasons); Mitscher is eminently likeable, and naval aviators are crazy about him, but the feeling is somewhat clannish. Only Halsey has attracted national attention and become the darling of a large section of the public in the same way, if not to the same degree, as MacArthur of the Army. But in Halsey's case, something else is added: he is the idol of vast numbers of men in the fleet, most of whom have never seen him, know very little about him, and could not even tell you when he has commanded a fleet in action, let alone cite one of his victory-making decisions.

It is a case where the average sailor's conception of the man, which happens for once to be the same as the landsman's conception of him, has become more important than the man himself. William Frederick Halsey, alone among Pacific commanders, can set off spontaneous waves of cheering merely by appearing at a medal-giving ceremony. Alone among Pacific commanders, he has, by the very magic of his name and personality, buoyed the morale of hundreds of thousands of fighting men when it was sinking for the third time. A commander with such powers is a valuable man to have around in any navy.

Halsey was born in Elizabeth, New Jersey, in 1882. With his long line of Colonial (including Pilgrim) ancestors, it might have been expected that his family would have the connections to get him into Annapolis without difficulty, especially since his father was a commander in the Navy. But the family had moved about so much, following father, that its members scarcely had time to learn the name of the local Congressman before the next move. Young Bill, or "Pudge," as many of his relatives called him, failed to get an appointment in 1899, and went instead to the University of Virginia, where he studied a little medicine and played a lot of football. His mother won the ear of President McKinley, who appointed young Halsey to the Naval Academy in 1900.

By this time he had become known as "Bull," because of his appearance and his tactics on the football field, and Bull he has remained. Five feet nine, he played fullback at 150 pounds, so it was not his bulk that won him the nickname. Rather, it was the short neck and jutting jaw, which he thrust out deliberately, and his manner of charging down the field.

A "2.5 man," he graduated two-thirds of the way down his class. As the years passed, Halsey's service record differed from that of most officers of his age, in that he had piled up more years of sea duty. And a large proportion of this time had been spent in destroyers.

In World War I, he commanded a destroyer division and received a Navy Cross for "important, exacting and hazardous duty . . . offensive and defensive action, vigorously and unremittingly prosecuted." Halsey minimizes that award, on the ground that the Navy Cross was bestowed too readily in that war. In peacetime maneuvers, he commanded destroyers with characteristic dash, and there are many legends about the "damage" he did.

When he was 52 years old, Halsey decided that the airplane had an important future in naval strategy and tactics, and that therefore the thing for him to do was to learn to fly. Because of age and poor sight, he was not allowed to take the pilots' course, but started to qualify as an observer. Somehow, he managed to emerge as a pilot.

This, of course, does not qualify Halsey as a "naval aviator" in the minds of men who took up aviation when they were scarcely out of their 'teens. They believe that a man who learns to fly so late in life can never be really air-minded. Actually, Halsey has never flown a modern combat plane and has never flown on or off a carrier's deck. That is a young man's game, and he knows it. He flies an advanced trainer to get air time.

While Halsey's air record may not be good enough for the young Turks, it has been good enough for Admirals Stark, Richardson, Kimmel, King and Nimitz to entrust him with the command of all America's aircraft carriers, until he became too heavy with rank. In 1939 he commanded Carrier Division 1, embracing the *Saratoga* and the old *Lexington*. The next year, with the rank of vice admiral, he became commander, aircraft, battle force—meaning all the carriers in the Pacific Fleet.

At the end of November, 1941, there were, by good luck and bad management, only three carriers in the Pacific. The *Saratoga* was on the West Coast; Halsey set off with the *Enterprise* (flag) and the *Lexington* to deliver VMF 211, a squadron of Marine Corps fighter planes, to Wake Island. On the 28th, Halsey issued "Battle Order No. 1" to the force under his command, and went far beyond any current orders by Admiral Kimmel for preparedness. He ordered his ships and planes to sink or shoot down any Japanese surface or aircraft which might be encountered. What would have happened if Halsey, with a chip on his shoulder, had chanced upon either of the Japanese task groups then steaming toward Pearl Harbor, under the command of Vice Admiral Chuichi Nagumo, can never be known. But it is an interesting hypothesis for students of history to ponder.

Halsey's planes became involved in the aerial fighting over Pearl Harbor on the morning of December 7. The task force originally had been due to reach port on Saturday; heavy weather on the voyage from Wake caused the estimated time of arrival to be set at 8 A.M. on Sunday, the 7th. This was set back still farther when the destroyer *Dunlap* sprang a leak and had to reduce speed; the whole force slowed down with her. Thus the two American carriers were saved from the fate of the battleships in Pearl Harbor that fateful Sunday morning. If they had been present, they would have been the prime targets of the Japanese attackers, and it is unlikely that they could have escaped crippling damage, if not destruction. The accident of weather must be credited with having saved them; with having made possible the tentative, hit-and-run type of offensive in which they were soon engaged (after Nimitz replaced Kimmel), and with having created the situation in which "Bull" Halsey could appear at his best, as a dashing wartime commander.

Those first raids on the Gilberts, the Marshalls, Wake and Marcus were far from being "great raids," as they are so often described. They were needling operations, and the force which executed them was more like a needle point than the broad spearhead of swiftly advancing American naval power with which it was wishfully compared. Halsey was the ideal man to command the carrier task forces at this time. He showed sound judgment, and he had good luck in getting to and from his targets under the cover of dirty weather. The speed and skill with which Halsey got away from places where it would have been unhealthy to linger gave currency to the expression, "Haul ass with Halsey." There is nothing pornographic about it, although the nice-Nellie school has bowdlerized it to such inanities as "Haul with Halsey" and "All out with Halsey." In its original, saline form, the phrase means simply to leave a place by hauling one's posterior out of it as quickly as possible. In the bad old days of early 1942, American naval forces had to be expert in that maneuver.

Because of a painful and stubborn skin ailment, he was not available to command the carrier task forces when they set out to fight the most crucial battle of the war, off Midway. Here is another topic for students of naval history to beguile themselves with during the long winter evenings of peacetime: if the dashing, impulsive Halsey had been in command during the last stages of that battle, instead of the cautious, calculating Spruance, could the entire Japanese force have been destroyed?

Halsey went back to the Pacific in mid-September. There was an offensive under way at Guadalcanal, and it was not going well. On the 15th of the month, Nimitz stepped aboard the *Enterprise* at Pearl Harbor to present some decorations. He had just received word that the *Wasp* had been sunk that afternoon (there is a 20½-hour time difference between the Solomons and Hawaii). Nimitz, ever ready to push a subordinate into the limelight, told the men assembled: "I've got a surprise for you—Admiral Halsey's back." The men cheered as they had cheered him when he stood on the flag bridge of the *Enterprise,* returning from the first little raids. Here, if anywhere, was a commander who could pull a sinking campaign up by its bootstraps.

Nimitz sent Halsey south, intending to put him in command of the few precious carriers which were left. But while Halsey was on his way south, the campaign on Guadalcanal was still further mired in the mud around Henderson Field. Morale was ebbing in all the armed forces concerned. When Halsey got to Nouméa, then Allied headquarters for the South Pacific, he found orders awaiting him: to relieve Vice Admiral Robert Lee Ghormley, and take over as Commander, South Pacific. There is no question that this change in command was vastly beneficial to the campaign, if only for the effect it had on the men. It is no exaggeration to say that Halsey's assumption of responsibility was worth a division of battleships, so great was the men's confidence in him as a rough and tough scrapper.

It is well, however, to remember that Halsey did not take over at a time when American naval forces had just suffered a defeat: on the contrary, cruisers and destroyers under Rear Admiral Norman Scott had just won, in the Battle of Cape Esperance (October 12), one of the cleanest-cut victories of the war. Neither did Halsey's arrival usher in an era of greater victories: the Battle of Santa Cruz, on October 26, nine days after he took over, was a tactical defeat, and only a moderate strategic success. Moreover, there seems to be a popular impression that at this time Halsey was always in the van of American naval forces, with his flagship leading the fleet, and pacing his flag bridge impatiently waiting for the enemy to appear and be utterly destroyed. Halsey's duty was not to be with the fleet, but to be at headquarters, which happened to be a thousand miles behind the battle front. It is to Halsey's credit that he stayed where he was supposed to stay, except for periodic visits to the front.

Halsey's greatest weakness is his impulsiveness of speech. As 1942 gave way to 1943, Halsey was angered by the atmosphere of despondency which he thought he detected in Australia, New Zealand and the United States. Never given to profound thought on matters outside his immediate concern, he did not understand that the emphasis on the long war ahead was necessary to prevent a let-down in the manufacture of weapons upon which his campaign depended. He thought it was defeatism, and reacted violently.

In Auckland, New Zealand, he said: "When we first started out, I held that one of our men was the equal of three Japs. I have now increased this to 20. They are just monkeys, and I say 'monkeys' because I cannot say what I would like to call them." (When he is not speaking for publication, Halsey always calls the Japanese "the bastards," or, if he is irritated, "the dirty little ------ bastards.")

A few days later, back at Nouméa, Halsey went farther. He predicted that the war in the Pacific would end in 1943, with an Allied victory parade through Tokyo. Nothing could have been more unwise or ill-timed. It nourished the very apathy and over-confidence in the United States which responsible leaders were trying to combat. When 1943 ended, Halsey was still manning a desk at his headquarters in Nouméa; his forces, far from having covered the 3,500 miles between Guadalcanal and Tokyo, had covered only the 300 miles to Bougainville. His face should have been red.

Halsey is undoubtedly sincere in his hatred of the Japanese. His slogan for forces under his command was almost from the start of the war: "Kill Japs—kill Japs—kill more Japs!" This attitude was widely understood and appreciated among the men of the fleet and other forces which served under him. His bravado and carefree speech have not always been so deeply appreciated by his superiors. Nimitz at one time found it necessary to pen this defense of his subordinate: "He is professionally competent and militarily aggressive without being reckless or foolhardy. He has that rare combination of intellectual capacity and military audacity, and can calculate to a cat's whisker the risk involved in operations when successful accomplishments will bring great returns." In the battle off Leyte in October, 1944, Halsey stretched the cat's whisker to a fineness which proved uncomfortable for thousands of American naval men, and fatal to hundreds of them.

From the day he left the *Enterprise* at Pearl Harbor on May 26, 1942, until he stepped aboard the *New Jersey* on August 24, 1944, Halsey had no occasion to exercise a command at sea. Consequently, he had no part in the great struggle for command of the sea which was fought and won by the fast carrier task forces under Spruance and Mitscher. However, for the first two months of his sea duty as Commander, Third Fleet, Halsey had Mitscher serving under him as Commander, Task Force 38.

Halsey, who appears so tactless in his public utterances, must be given credit for having shown great diplomacy and tact during the difficult period when his South Pacific forces were operating under the "strategic direction" of General MacArthur. To Halsey, also, goes the credit for having first appreciated the weakness of the Japanese in the Philippines, which caused the invasion of those islands to be speeded up.

In his 63rd year, Halsey weighs about 20 pounds more than in his fullback days, and keeps fit by swimming (often in gaudy, printed trunks) or by playing deck tennis with members of his staff while at sea. He has an anchor tattooed on his right shoulder—the souvenir of a juvenile impulse. As fleet commander, his day begins with a cup of coffee at 6 A.M., followed immediately by a reading of the overnight accumulation of dispatches. During breakfast with the score or more staff officers who share his mess (two-thirds of his staff have to join the ship's wardroom mess), he reads the mimeographed sheet which passes for a newspaper in the far places where the Navy travels. Much of his time during the day is spent on the flag bridge, where he has a high chair behind the wind screen. In warm weather, he will be in khakis, with the shirt neck open, and no tie. (No commander ever earned the gratitude of hundreds of thousands of men more simply or more richly than Halsey, when he forbade the wearing of neckties in the torrid South Pacific.) If it turns cool, he puts on an aviator's leather flight jacket, with fleece lining; in wet weather, an oilskin with four stars and the letters "ADM" (for admiral) painted on the back.

There are many minor contradictions in Halsey's character. He is a fairly strict disciplinarian, but his bearing has been marked by the informality of destroyers, in which he shipped for so many years. Similarly, he likes to have his flag in the biggest battleship available, as befits a fleet commander, but he expects all ships to be handled with the nimbleness of a destroyer.

Although he claims to have learned his lesson from his rash

1943 prophecy, Halsey still delivers sweeping opinions on the slightest provocation.

Like so many commanders who make a profession of acting tough and talking tough, "Bull" Halsey is easily touched by an expression of feeling among his men. He cannot receive their cheers and applause without a moistening of the eyes. When he has been decorated for the achievements of his command, he has always wanted to pass the credit on to his staff and his men, but he cannot get up and make an after-dinner speech to express his feelings. Usually, all he can say is a single, gruff sentence, punctuated by a "hell" or a "damn." And the men understand perfectly. More than any other commander in the war against Japan, he is their idea of a fighting leader. And his childish whim of wanting to ride the emperor's white horse would have been all right with them, too. Fortunately, it was made clear to him when he set out for the surrender ceremony in Tokyo Bay, that he should be on his best peacetime behavior. The occasion for him to display his more rugged qualities had passed with the ending of hostilities.

XVIII. Paving the Way

IN THE FIRST few weeks of 1944, General MacArthur had succeeded in neutralizing the main Japanese bases in the Bismarck and northern Solomon Islands, and had broken through to the open coast of northern New Guinea which stretched a thousand miles to the westward. In those same few weeks, the Pacific Fleet had seized command of the sea as far west as the waters lapping the eastern shores of the Philippines, to which MacArthur had pledged, "I shall return." But the general's American and Australian forces, on the north shore of Huon Peninsula, were still 1,800 statute miles from the Philippines, and 2,400 miles from Manila. The way had to be paved with bases where Allied air power could be housed: each base captured or carved out of the jungle would be used first as a roost for the transport planes carrying equipment to enlarge the base itself; then, in order, would come fighter planes, light bombers, medium bombers and finally heavy bombers, and the total of their efforts would extend Allied control of the air (and, almost equally important, of the coastal sea lanes) a few hundred miles farther west so as to permit the ground troops to seize a new base and repeat the process.

The distances were forbidding, and so were the concentrations of Japanese. Wewak, near the center of the north coast of New Guinea, 200 miles east of the boundary between Dutch and Australian-mandated parts of the island, was perhaps the most important of the enemy's strongholds. As an air base it had long ceased to be operational; hundreds of Japanese planes had been destroyed on the ground there by Lieut. General Kenney's fliers as far back as August, 1943. But it was the headquarters of the Japanese Eighteenth Army, and Major General Charles Willoughby, MacArthur's intelligence officer (always generous in his appraisals of enemy strength) estimated that there were 60,000 Japanese troops in the Wewak area. There were other major concentrations at Hollandia, just over the border in the Dutch part of New Guinea, and at numerous islands offshore, and at Manokwari on the Vogelkop or "bird's head" peninsula at the western end of the great island.

It was clear that some way must be found to contain these forces without engaging in a showdown fight as a result of direct assault. The way had been foreshadowed in the landings at Empress Augusta Bay, in the western Marshalls, at Cape Gloucester, in the Admiralty and St. Matthias Islands. It had been shown that a large enemy ground force could be safely bypassed provided that it had no air force at its disposal, and provided also that Allied forces held command of the sea in the area, so that the enemy ground troops could not be reinforced or shifted to meet the Allies at whatever point they had chosen to attack.

General MacArthur decided to use this strategy to advance his troops and his air power 1,500 miles closer to the Philippines. It violated the ancient principle of not leaving a powerful enemy force unreduced in the rear of one's own positions. But the old terms need redefining in the light of the development of air power. In the days of land armies, or land armies with sea support, but prior to the development of aviation, the principle was certainly sound. However, modern warfare is not so much a matter of the employment of land armies as it is a matter of combined operations. A powerful land army can no longer be said to be a powerful military force unless it has the tools of air power at its disposal. (In coastal or oceanic areas the third element of surface sea power is added.) Before the development of aircraft as an effective military weapon, tens of thousands of Japanese at a place like Wewak would have been "a powerful enemy force."

But after the development of air power, they were not a "powerful enemy force" in the full sense of the term, because they were not a balanced force.

When the definitions are modernized, it is seen that MacArthur's strategy in New Guinea was not so startling for its daring. The chief point about it, which is greatly to the credit of the command, is that it was based upon an up-to-the-minute appreciation of what really constitutes "a powerful enemy force." The campaign has been popularized as a miltary adaptation of Willie Keeler's tactics: "Hit 'em where they ain't." The campaign also has been somewhat irresponsibly tagged as a series of "save-a-life" operations. It is true that it avoided heavy loss of life in assault operations, but this, while praiseworthy and gratifying, was incidental: if it had seemed strategically necessary to make frontal assualts, they would have been made, however costly.

The coastal leapfrogging campaign may be said to have begun after the securing of the Sio-Saidor area in January. This made the Huon Peninsula a safe base for Allied forces, and Finschhafen was built up into a major staging point. Meanwhile, although the Japanese Eighteenth Army still was represented in considerable strength at its old headquarters at Madang, it was being compelled to regroup (around Wewak) by the pressure of the Australian 8th Brigade advancing down the Ramu Valley. The Aussies captured Madang on April 23, just 24 hours after the Eighteenth Army had been effectively cut off by the first and greatest of MacArthur's flying wedge operations along the coast.

This was a triple amphibious operation, involving a single and double envelopment of Wewak. The single envelopment was to be achieved by a combat team, in brigade strength, commanded by Brigadier General Jens Doe, landed at Aitape, 90 miles west of Wewak. The troops employed were the 163rd Infantry (of the 41st Division) and the 127th Infantry (of the 32nd Division).

A still larger force was to leapfrog past Doe's combat team, and effect the double envelopment of Wewak by seizing Hollandia. Since the three airfields there lay behind a range of coastal hills, the objective had to be approached from behind each end of the hills, and this made it necessary to divide the assault forces into two groups, one to go ashore at Humboldt Bay, 23 miles east of Hollandia proper, and the other at Tanahmera Bay, eleven miles west of Hollandia. For these operations, the assault forces were the 41st Division (less the one regiment committed at Aitape) and the 24th Division.

To confuse the Japanese, in case their submarine or snooper planes detected any one of the three amphibious forces engaged, the great masses of ships rendezvoused north of the Admiralty Islands and set a course to the northwest, which pointed toward

Palau. During the night it divided, and the respective elements turned south toward Aitape and southwest toward Hollandia. The Aitape force had tactical air cover supplied by escort carriers; the Hollandia operation was lavishly supported by the air groups from Task Force 58, as previously described.

Allied intelligence had estimated that there were 15,000 Japanese in the Hollandia area; if so, the information was hopelessly out of date. The Japanese had evacuated most of their air force personnel to bases farther west where they might still be useful for a while.

The operation around Hollandia ran off so smoothly that the fleet was released from its support assignment earlier than had been expected, and the troops ashore made rapid progress against scattered pockets of opposition. Two of the three airfields which lay under the threatening shadow of Mount Cyclops were captured within four days after the first landings and the third, Hollandia itself, was captured on the fifth day. All were quickly put into operation for Allied planes. At this stage, only 300 Japanese had been accounted for: 274 killed and a score of prisoners. These probably constituted a majority of the Japanese who had remained in the area—a far cry from the estimated 15,000—although six weeks later the number of enemy dead was said to have reached 3,782.

At Aitape, where 3,000 defenders had been expected, there proved to be about a thousand. Fighting in their usual prepared positions and with their usual tenacity, these had to be hunted down in weeks of intensive operations. In the first ten days, 842 Japanese were listed as killed in this area. American casualties have not been disclosed.

As the American lines were extended east of Aitape, it became necessary to feed in more troops. These comprised the 112th Cavalry and the two remaining regiments of the 32nd Division. But the Japanese disliked being left to "wither on the vine," with no hope of reinforcement, relief or supply, in a country where it was impossible to live off local products, and where men weakened by semi-starvation quickly fell victim to tropical diseases. On July 11 they launched a counter-attack.

Before this attack could be considered crushed, the Allied command had to feed in most of the remainder of Major General Charles P. Hall's Eleventh Corps, including the 124th

Infantry (of the 31st Division) and the 43rd Division, now commanded by Major General Leonard Wing. The enemy attack on July 11 broke through the American lines west of the Driniumor and won back considerable ground. On July 14 the situation had been restored sufficiently to enable the Americans to counter-attack in their turn. They soon regained the west bank of the Driniumor, and held there until August 1. On this date a second attack carried across the river a distance of two miles to Niumen Creek, where the Americans again dug in. On August 6 an enveloping movement was begun, with parallel columns striking south along the banks of both the Driniumor and the Niumen, which resulted in the entrapment and destruction of a considerable Japanese force south of the village of Afua.

From then on, for almost a year, the campaign was like that on Bougainville. In September of 1944 the Australian 6th Division was landed in the area, and by November this veteran outfit assumed the responsibility for eliminating the surviving Japanese. It was not until June, 1945, that the Wewak campaign could be regarded as approximately ended, although it had been won in the strategic sense 14 months earlier.

After the securing of Hollandia and the immediate area around Aitape (excluding Wewak), the Allied command lost no time in pushing still farther west. An attractive and supposedly easy target was situated 150 miles west of Hollandia, in the Wakde Islands lying off Maffin Bay. One of the islands, Insumuar, had a 4,700-foot runway, and was so small that there was practically no room for elaborate defenses around the strip. The 63rd Infantry (of the 6th Division) and the 158th Regimental Combat Team landed on May 17 against light opposition on the mainland side of Maffin Bay, near the villages of Toem and Sarmi, and set up artillery which shelled Wakde Islands across the bay. Warships, under Captain Albert G. Noble, contributed an abundance of firepower, and by the morning of the 18th it appeared that there could not be a Japanese left alive on Insumuar. Brigadier General Edwin D. Patrick, commander of the combat group, sent troops across to Insumuar in a shore-to-shore operation, and the first elements walked across the airfield unmolested after a short, stiff fight on the beach. The Japanese, however, were simply playing

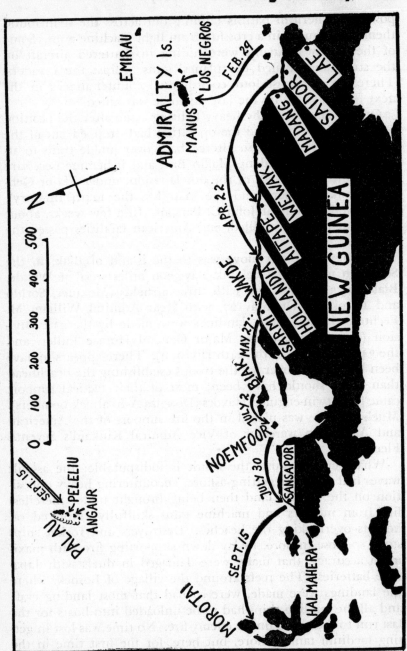

possum. American patrols fanning out across the strip found themselves caught in a crossfire from light machine guns. Some of the enemy remnants were hiding in shattered aircraft on the strip, and turned the planes' guns against the invaders. There were at least four co-ordinated counter-attacks in the next four days before the last Japanese was killed.

On the mainland, the heavy fighting came after the position had been "secured" and the operation had dropped out of the headlines. The Japanese filtered back over jungle trails to attack the beachhead along Maffin Bay, and it became necessary to commit the balance of the 6th Division, under Major General Franklin Sibert, and the 31st (less the 124th Infantry), under Major General John C. Parsons. In a few weeks, about 4,000 Japanese were killed, and American fatalities passed the 400 mark.

The next leapfrog move was to the island of Biak, in the Schouten group in Geelvink Bay, 200 miles west of Wakde. Biak was a large island, with three airfields (Mokmer, Sorido and Borokoe). On May 27, with Rear Admiral William M. Fechteler in command, landings were made by the 41st Division (Reinforced), under Major General Horace Fuller, and the 34th Infantry (of the 24th Division). There appears to have been less fighter cover for the troops establishing the beachhead than there should have been; most of their tactical support came from twin-engined Havocs (Douglas A-20 attack bombers). Much reliance was placed in the fire support of the American and Australian warships of Vice Admiral Kinkaid's Seventh Fleet.

Whatever the cause, the result is indisputable: the assault waves had difficulty getting ashore, encountering heavy opposition on the beaches and then being brought under merciless fire from mortars and machine guns skillfully emplaced on heights overlooking the beaches. Destroyers and rocket ships stood so close inshore, to lay down supporting fire with maximum accuracy, that many were damaged in duels with Japanese batteries. The reefs around the village of Bosnek, where the landings were made, were so bad that most landing craft and all the landing ships had to be unloaded into boats for the last run to the beach under enemy fire. No time was lost in getting medium tanks ashore, but here, for the first time in the

Southwest Pacific, the General Sherman with its 75-mm. gun was opposed by formidable Japanese tanks mounting a 47-mm., high-velocity gun.

The Japanese were forced back from the waterfront as successive waves of Americans gained the shore, but the enemy fell back to good positions along the inland cliffs. After three days, the beachhead still was not deep enough to be secure. The road westward to Mokmer airdrome lay under the cliffs, and when the American troops tried to force this route, even with the help of armor and continued fire support from the bombardment ships, they were exposed to relentless enfilading fire.

The attempt caused the recall of General Fuller, and his supersession by Lieut. General Robert L. Eichelberger, commander of the First Corps, who had first played this "Johnny to the rescue" role 18 months earlier, at Buna. Eichelberger sent a force inland, around the end of the escarpment, and with improved air support succeeded in outflanking the Japanese. Mokmer was captured eleven days after the first landings.

The enemy made a far more serious effort to retrieve the situation around Biak than at previous points along the New Guinea coast. Aircraft appeared in dozens, presumably from bases on Halmahera, to harass the invaders. A major attempt at reinforcement was apparently aborted when a "Tokyo Express" was put to flight by cruisers and destroyers under Rear Admiral Crutchley. Fifth Air Force fliers reported sinking four destroyers. It was not until June 19 that American ground forces were able to capture Sorido and Borokoe airfields, after the destruction of about 3,000 enemy combatant troops. Hundreds more were killed in the long mopping-up operations.

The Schouten group contained one more objective worthy of invasion and capable of conversion into a valuable Allied base: Noemfoor (or Numfor, in Anglicized spelling) Island, a hundred miles west of Biak. Roughly 15 miles by 12, Noemfoor commands the western entrance to Geelvink Bay. From its airfields, Allied fliers could complete the neutralization of Japanese Second Army headquarters at Manokwari, only 50 miles to the west. The island had been prepared for invasion by three weeks of daily bombing which culminated in a 230-ton strike on July 1. The next morning, before dawn, the invasion fleet appeared, with Rear Admiral Daniel E. Barbey in over-all command, and Fechteler in command of fire support ships which included the heavy cruiser *Australia,* the light cruisers *Phoenix* and *Boise,* seven destroyers, 200 PT boats and LCI rocket ships.

There was plenty of air support when the assault troops of the 158th Regimental Combat Team hit the beach near Kamiri airfield, in the northwestern part of the island, at 8:02 A.M. (two minutes behind schedule). The rocket ships laid down a creeping barrage ahead of the invaders, and destroyers stood inshore close enough to use their automatic weapons (40- and 20-mm.) against enemy gun positions ashore. The airfield was overrun by 9:50 A.M., and engineers of the Royal Australian Air Force were landed immediately to rehabilitate it for use as an Allied fighter strip.

On July 3, the 503rd Parachute Infantry Regiment (which had captured Nadzab ten months earlier in the first airborne operation in the Southwest Pacific) was parachuted down on Kamiri to reinforce the 158th R.C.T.—an extraordinary procedure, never adequately explained.

The rest of the campaign was swift and satisfactory. During the afternoon of D-plus-two (July 4), the second airfield, known as Kornasoren, was captured. Two days later, Kamiri was put into operation by the Aussie engineers, and a shore-to-shore operation was carried out, with naval support, to put troops ashore on the south coast near the third airfield, Namber. (The fact that the reefs did not prevent this movement suggests that they would not have prevented seaborne reinforcement of the 158th R.C.T. a few days earlier.) There was no opposition at Namber, and after five days the island was declared secure, with 410 Japanese listed as killed; later, the figure was raised to 2,000. American losses were not disclosed, but were said to have been "very light."

The effectiveness and value of the coastal leapfrogging technique were best demonstrated, perhaps, in the last operation of this kind in New Guinea. The Japanese were present in strength at Manokwari, about 170 miles west of Noemfoor, and at Sorong. But they were weak or absent in the intermediate stretch of coast, where the Allied command chose to land. This area, which included the mainland village of Sansapor and the islets of Amsterdam and Middelburg, had been elaborately prepared by aerial attack but was spared warship bombardment when Major General Sibert's 6th Division (less the 20th Infantry Regiment) went ashore on July 30, with Fechteler as amphibious force commander. The objectives were secured within a few hours.

There could be no more operations of this kind, because even the many possibilities offered by the vast island of New Guinea, 1,500 miles long, had at last been exhausted. It had taken 22 months to cover 1,500 airline miles from Milne Bay and to chop up the bulk of three Japanese armies. The accomplishment seems the more remarkable when it is not obscured by the orotund phrases of MacArthur's communiqués, which generally made it seem too easy, and gave little or no credit to the subordinate commanders who directed the execution of the plans, or to the tens of thousands of combat infantrymen, service troops, aviators, ground crews, naval personnel and Coast Guardsmen who actually executed the plans in the face of enemy fire.

In the direct path of MacArthur's return to the Philippines there now remained only the Molucca Islands, of which Halmahera is the most important; only Palau remained as a serious threat to his flank. Plans for the direct conquest of Halmahera were abandoned when it was decided that the strategic purpose could be achieved, much more quickly and less expensively, by landing on the smaller, less developed and less strongly defended island of Morotai, which lies within sight of the northern tip of Halmahera, only 14 miles away.

However, before either Morotai or Palau could be invaded, Japanese bases extending for hundreds of miles to the north, west and south had to be rendered impotent. The process was begun on August 31, when fast carriers under Rear Admiral J. J. Clark (who had commanded the *Yorktown* a year earlier) started a three-day series of attacks on the Bonin and Volcano Islands. This mission resulted in the destruction of 46 enemy aircraft and six ships; then the carriers headed south, and on September 7 and 8 their planes attacked Yap. (At this time, it was intended to invade Yap within two weeks.) At the same time, other fast carriers of the Third Fleet, operating under Vice Admiral Mitscher as commander of Task Force 38, subjected Palau to heavy air attacks. On September 9, the target was changed, and airfields on Mindanao came under the carrier planes' bombsights.

Within 48 hours, it was seen that the enemy was unexpectedly weak in the largest of the southern Philippine islands, so Halsey sent Mitscher north to test out the central (Visayas) area. The Japanese were surprised: 123 planes were destroyed before they could get off the ground, and 75 were shot out of the air (the original communiqué claimed double these figures), while five ships and 35 small vessels were sunk and six ships and 36 small vessels were damaged. One carrier task group was detached and sent south to complete the isolation of the selected battlefields by attacking Mindanao, Celebes and Talaud (between the Indies and Mindanao) on September 14 and 15. This operation was unsatisfactory because the command relationships had not been properly worked out. Throughout this period, land-based aircraft of the Fifth Air Force and the 13th Air Task Force had been ranging over the Moluccas, Celebes and Ceram, hammering the complex of enemy airfields in those islands.

On the morning of September 15, an 800-ship formation steamed into Morotai Strait. General MacArthur was aboard the *Nashville*, flagship of the amphibious force commander, Rear Admiral Barbey. With other bombardment ships, the *Nashville* spent some time off the northern peninsula of Halmahera, pouring shells into Japanese positions, before crossing the strait to join the main force off Morotai. The target area was at the southwestern extremity of the 40-by-25 mile island, and both landing beaches were at the base (although on opposite sides) of the finger-like Gila Peninsula which projects four miles southwestward from the main part of the island. A mile to the east of the landing beaches was Pitoe (also spelled Pitu) airfield, which the Japanese had abandoned.

Planes from escort carriers lying farther out gave tactical air support, and the bombardment ships, which included two Australian cruisers, unloaded 175 tons of shells on the beach area. The assault troops, drawn from the Eleventh Corps' 31st Division and the 126th Infantry (of the 32nd Division), waded ashore with no opposition save that offered by the treacherous coral reefs, which caused some injuries. Within two hours, the airfield was secured and General MacArthur was able to go ashore.

History repeated itself: the fight for Morotai began after the island had been declared secure. It was believed that 200 Japanese had taken to the hills of the interior; the American ground forces were concentrated in a narrow perimeter within a few hundred feet of the airfield, and through the closing months of 1944 the strip and the encampments around it were repeatedly infiltrated by Japanese raiding parties and regularly brought under mortar fire. Japanese parties were regularly ferried across at night by barge from Halmahera, and no amount of patrolling by PT boats could prevent the enemy's building up his forces on Morotai. By the beginning of December the bulk of the enemy's 211th Infantry Regiment had been landed and organized. These forces were in the interior, five to ten miles north of Pitoe and a second air strip which the Allies had built parallel with it. The threat by mid-December was so great that the 136th Infantry (of the 33rd Division) had to be brought in from New Guinea, and dispatched inland on December 26. In a bitter and difficult campaign ending January 14, 1945, the Japanese regiment was effectively destroyed, with 870 killed and ten captured. Casualties to the 136th were 46 dead and 127 wounded or injured in action. The Japanese commander, Colonel Ouchi, remained at large until July, when he was captured by Lieut. Colonel Jack McKenzie of the 93rd Division.

With the seizure of the beachhead on Morotai, General MacArthur had effectively bypassed Halmahera and the rest of the Moluccas, and stood within 300 miles of the southern Philippines. Simultaneously with the landing on Morotai there was the landing at Palau, and this was quickly followed by a series of carrier sweeps which changed the whole course of the war in the Southwest Pacific and drastically altered MacArthur's schedule for his return to the Philippines.

The entire amphibious operation at Palau was under the direction of Vice Admiral Theodore S. Wilkinson, but the first elements to go into action were the bombardment forces under Rear Admiral George H. Fort. The Palau group is about 70 miles long, and consists of one large mountain-top island (Babelthuap, in the most commonly accepted of many spellings) and half a dozen smaller islands of considerable elevation. The whole group is bounded by a fringing reef close inshore on the east, while to the west the reef is two to ten miles offshore, enclosing several large anchorages.

Babelthuap, with an enemy garrison estimated at 25,000, with elaborate defenses and plentiful supplies of weapons and ammunition, would have been costly to assault and offered no special advantage. The Americans needed a foothold on Palau to achieve three objectives: (1), neutralization of the Japanese base there; (2), use of airfields, and (3) use of an anchorage. Admiral Nimitz's war planners hit upon a highly unorthodox plan for gaining these objectives. Peleliu and Angaur islands, at the extreme southern end of the group, had either airfields or sites suitable for them, and if these could be seized and held, the locally based air power would be sufficient to neutralize the enemy on Babelthuap and the central islands. However, there was no anchorage near Peleliu. At the extreme north end of the group there were no small islands, but there was a good anchorage enclosed by Kossol and Cormoran Reefs. It was decided to clear this anchorage and to capture Peleliu and Angaur; the Japanese in the middle would be able to look out and observe Allied activity, but would be unable to do anything to prevent it.

Beginning on September 12, three days before D-day, Fort's bombardment ships subjected Peleliu, an island only six miles long by two miles wide, to the most intensive assault of its kind so far delivered. Pilots of the carrier planes who flew over the island during the last daylight hours of September 14 reported that it seemed deserted. One said: "It was like flying over an immense, broken graveyard. I looked for signs of life, but couldn't see any." There was a further three-hour bombardment on the morning of the 15th, but only a minute fraction of the garrison of 10,000 men was put out of action by the preliminary bombing and bombardment.

The assault forces were under several layers of command. Being drawn from the Third Amphibious Corps, they were under Major General Roy S. Geiger, U.S.M.C. The "expeditionary forces"—whatever that meant—were under Major General Julian C. Smith, U.S.M.C. Actually, the expeditionary forces at this time consisted of the 1st Marine Division (Reinforced), under Major General William H. Rupertus. The landing beaches selected were well to the south on the west side of

Peleliu, and lay southwest of the cruciform, two-runway air-field. The 7th Marine Regiment was assigned to the right flank, near the southern tip of the island where there were two peninsulas connected with the rest of Peleliu by the narrowest of isthmuses; the 1st Marines were to go in on the left flank, nearer the airfield.

As H-hour approached and the heavier bombardment ships lifted their fire, LCIs closed the beach and fired almost 10,000 rockets to smooth the way for the first waves. The marines transferred from the transports to amphibious tractors (alligators), in a marked improvement on the technique used at Tarawa, and headed for the beach under the cover of strafing attacks by fighter planes. Most of the first elements got across the reef and on to the beach without many casualties; then a group of amtracs got hung up on a reef toward the south, and as the men scrambled out to start wading ashore, the Japanese opened up with enfilading mortar fire from an unnamed, rocky islet near by. At about the same time, fire from heavier weapons was opened from the ridge which rose slightly north of the airfield and formed the backbone of the island. The enemy emplacements were taken under fire by warships and attacked by fighter-bombers.

The Japanese had been compelled by the bombardment to withdraw from the beach defenses. The assault waves were landed with only a fraction of the casualties suffered in a similar period at Tarawa. The marines were not using their usual rushing tactics; they advanced steadily and methodically, waiting for a tank or flamethrower to make sure that each pillbox had been rendered harmless before it was bypassed. Progress was good; by late afternoon the beachhead was a mile and a half wide, and at one point, where it bulged clear across the island, it was a full thousand yards deep.

The Japanese fought with somewhat more imagination than usual. They launched two counter-attacks with tanks, one in the American center and one on the left flank, which had to be broken up by a combination of naval gunfire and aerial attack. Fortunately, the enemy was not able to get a single plane into the air over Palau; the islands' own fields had been bomb-pocked and littered with wrecked aircraft, and squadrons on other islands to the east (in the Carolines) or to the west (in the Philippines) were evidently not in much better shape.

On the second day also, progress was good, and before night-fall the entire airfield was captured. But the enemy was far from having been disorganized by the tremendous weight of explosives which had been loosed upon the island. He had burrowed so deeply and extensively into the sides of the lime-stone ridges that he still had an abundance of combat effectives who were thrown into action in a succession of well co-ordinated counter-attacks. By the end of this day, more than 1,400 enemy dead were said to have been counted. The number of fatalities among the attackers was far smaller, but the number of casu-alties of all types was increasing rapidly and giving the com-mand cause for concern. Most of the wounds were caused by fragments of Japanese mortar shells, and some of these were reported to be of 8-inch caliber.

On the morning of September 17, the second half of the Palau play was revealed: two regiments of the Army's 81st Division went ashore on the northern beaches of Angaur, an irregular-shaped island 1½ by 2½ miles, lying seven miles south of Peleliu. Angaur, where the Japanese had had an im-portant phosphate plant but had neglected to build an airfield, had been subjected to the same treatment as Peleliu, and in the last hours before the troops went ashore it was the target for 12,000 rounds of naval ammunition of 5-inch caliber or bigger, including a large quota from old battleships with 14-inch guns. The enemy garrison here had been estimated at 2,500 to 3,500, but evidently it had been reduced to reinforce Peleliu, and the remnant withdrawn to the southern end of the island. Again there were casualties among men who had to gain the beach under mortar fire, but the invasion was run off smoothly and was not seriously contested. In one day, the men of the "Wildcat" Division, in their first combat, seized the northern third of the island. In a few days, it was overrun, and military government was established at the end of the month. The Japanese killed on the island numbered about 1,200.

On Peleliu, meanwhile, the fighting had increased in bitter-ness, if that were possible. All three regiments of the 1st Marine Division were now committed: the 1st, under Colonel Lewis B. Puller; the 5th, under Colonel Harold Harris, and the 7th,

under Colonel Herman Hanneken. Still, the casualty rate was
too high to be endured—the 1st Marines had had 60% casualties from one cause or another. The eastern side of Peleliu
was mostly mangrove swamp; the spine of the island consisted
of limestone ridges from which rose five dominating heights,
and the road up the west coast was made almost impassable by
fire from these ridges and heights. The most southerly eminence, near the town of Asias, was Umurbrogol, which the
marines, because of some fancied resemblance to the battered
proboscis of a prize-fighter, renamed Bloody Nose. This position earned its new name a thousand times in the weeks that
followed.

The 321st Infantry, the one regiment of Major General Paul
J. Mueller's 81st Division which had not been committed on
Angaur, was landed on Peleliu to support the marines. The
fighting was stalemated, and only after some days of intensive
preparation was the deadlock broken. This enabled the attackers to push through to the north on both sides of the spinal
column, and the number of Japanese killed by this time was
said to be about 8,000, but the ridge positions proved all but
impregnable. The Japanese had countless deep, interlocking
caves, many of them with steel doors, all with well-sited firing
slits which gave them interlocking fields of fire in which attacking forces were repeatedly made to pay heavily for their rash-
ness. Every type of aerial attack was tried; both skip-bombing
and fire-bombing proved helpful, but there was no single,
simple answer to a complex problem.

A serious feature was the manpower shortage. Two and a
half weeks after the landing, a battery of the 11th Marines
(Artillery), which had landed on D-plus-one and had been in
action continuously, was ordered to furnish five companies
(about half-strength) to man a defensive sector. It was only a
temporary expedient, but the "infantillery," as the men styled
themselves, stayed in the line eight days. And this lasted until
almost two weeks after the island had been declared "secure."
Actually, it was not until the middle of October that the "assault phase" on Peleliu could be considered ended, and not
until November 27 that the last Japanese holding out in the
caves was killed. By this time the enemy dead totaled about
12,500.

With the landings on Morotai and Palau, and the securing of perimeters there, a two-lane highway leading to the Philippines had been paved. But there was still considerable preparation to be undertaken before this way could be used by armies of liberation. The Navy had urgent need of fleet anchorages: during the landings in the southern Palaus, minesweepers were busy at the north end of the group, clearing Kossol Pass and the roadstead beyond it, and this emergency haven was used by seaplane tenders as early as September 16. However, an anchorage to which the fleet could return without having its security compromised was also needed. The best available, without incurring an expensive campaign, appeared to be Ulithi, an atoll also known as Mackenzie, which lies about 350 nautical miles northeast of Palau. On September 21 it was found to have been abandoned by the enemy; minesweepers cleared the lagoon, and on the 23rd it was occupied by elements of the 81st Division withdrawn from Angaur. It was quickly developed and became the chief forward base and refueling station for the fast carrier task forces.

As soon as these fast carrier task forces had insured the establishment of the beachheads on Peleliu and Angaur, they set off for the west to hammer again at Japanese air and sea power in the Philippines. Weak though the enemy had been in the southern and central Philippines earlier in the month, it was expected that the island of Luzon would be well defended. But it developed otherwise.

On the blustery, overcast morning of September 21, the carriers were almost within sight of central Luzon before they launched their planes. The fighter sweep was divided into two groups, one of which headed for the complex of a dozen runways known collectively as Clark Field, 70 miles north of Manila, while the other headed for the airfields in Manila's suburbs. The Japanese warning system failed, and many of the enemy's Luzon-based aircraft were caught on the ground. Those which got into the air were flown by pilots who showed more respect for the Hellcats than desire to tangle with them. Nevertheless, before the day was ended slightly more planes had been shot down than were destroyed on the ground: 110 as against 95.

The air having been made safe for the dive-bombers and

torpedo bombers, devastating attacks were made against the shipping which had used Manila Bay and Subic Bay with impunity for 28 months—for this was the first American air assault on the area since May, 1942. The operation was repeated the second day, and the preliminary tally, based on pilots' reports, then showed: 169 planes shot down, 188 destroyed on the ground; 40 ships and six small craft sunk; eleven ships probably sunk; 35 ships, eleven small craft and two floating drydocks damaged. American losses in this "daring and highly successful strike" were eleven planes in combat, ten pilots and five crewmen (in addition to operational losses). No American ship was damaged; the only Japanese air strike against Task Force 38 resulted in the killing of two seamen by machine gun bullets and damage to planes parked on a carrier's deck.

It was with good reason that Admiral Nimitz, who was not given to making sweeping claims in his communiqués, proclaimed: "The operations of the Third Fleet have broken [the Japanese] air force in the Philippines just as operations of the Fifth Fleet broke the enemy's carrier-based air force in the Battle of the Philippine Sea."

The fleet turned south, and to be sure that there could have been no mistake, attacked the Visayas again on September 24. Airfields on Cebu, Negros and Mactan, as well as southern Luzon, were the targets, as well as shipping in the inner island seas. A particularly heavy strike was made on Coron Bay, in the Calamian group just south of Mindoro Strait, where several ships sunk included two fleet tankers. The tally of shipping destroyed read: one destroyer, one troop transport, three large cargo ships, three tankers (including those at Coron), six medium and five small cargo ships, and three vessels loosely classified as destroyer escorts. More than 40 vessels were listed as damaged, and some of these as probably sunk. Only seven Japanese planes had to be shot out of the air; 29 were destroyed aground. American losses in combat were ten planes, five pilots and three crewmen.

It was plain that the Japanese throughout the Philippines were far weaker in the air than any Allied strategist had dared to hope; the fact that their fleet was far weaker than the reborn American fleet was well known; it was reasonable to assume that if they were given time they would build up the air and ground defenses of the Philippines against the invasion which they knew was inevitable, but which they did not expect in the near future. As soon as the fleet got back to friendly waters, Halsey had himself transferred by destroyer and breeches buoy (or a comfortable modification of it known as a "Halsey chair") to Mitscher's flagship. After conferences there, he went ashore to see Nimitz. Soon, he boarded a plane and followed Rear Admiral Forrest Sherman on a trip south to see MacArthur. Halsey had something to sell.

XIX. Return to the Philippines

THE IDEA WHICH Admiral Halsey wished to sell to General MacArthur was that he should speed up his campaign to fulfill his pledge, "I shall return," to the Philippines. As of mid-September, the plan at Southwest Pacific GHQ was to continue the leapfrog approach. Landings were scheduled to be made in the Talaud Islands, between Morotai and Mindanao, in mid-October; with the air cover thus extended, a move was planned for a month later, into the southern peninsula of Mindanao; eventually the leapfrogging was to carry by way of Leyte and other Visayan islands to Luzon and the great goal of Manila.

The strikes by Task Force 38, operating under Halsey, had shown that the Japanese in the Philippines were brittle, especially in the air, and a comparatively weak spot had been found in their ground defenses. A carrier pilot whose plane was disabled in one of these strikes bailed out off Leyte and was rescued by guerrillas; when the Navy picked him up he reported that the enemy was weak, and spread thin, on Leyte and the adjoining island of Sámar, between which the great anchorage of Leyte Gulf was enclosed. A further check with Colonel Ruperto Kangleon, leader of the guerrillas in the Leyte-Sámar area, showed that the Japanese had on the two islands only a reinforced division, totaling about 24,000 men. (It has been identified as the 16th Infantry Division, one of the many outfits which have been described as the "Butchers of Bataan.")

There could be no doubt that the Japanese, expecting an invasion of the Philippines within a few months, would reinforce the islands. There could be no doubt that it would be immensely to the Americans' advantage to return to the Philippines sooner rather than later, and to return to Leyte rather than to Mindanao, both because the enemy was weaker on the former island, and because a landing there would bypass tens of thousands of his troops on the latter. The great question was, could it be done in such a hurry as Halsey suggested, and could it be done without too great risk of failure?

The answer seemed to be that the risk could be cut below the danger point if MacArthur threw in everything available under his command, and also received everything that was available from Nimitz's command. Halsey had authority to offer this, and the plan was drawn with the utmost speed. Nimitz would lend MacArthur the support of the Third Fleet (in effect, the full striking force of the United States Navy's battle fleet); he would lend him half a dozen old battleships to incorporate temporarily into his Seventh Fleet (commanded by Vice Admiral Thomas C. Kinkaid), along with dozens of smaller gunnery ships; he would lend 16 escort carriers to supply tactical air support during the landings and the embyronic stage of beachhead development; he would lend the entire Twenty-Fourth Corps, which had been ready for the invasion of Yap (now called off), together with all the transports, landing craft and supply ships needed to put them ashore and sustain them, with Vice Admiral Theodore S. Wilkinson to command the amphibious phase of their operation.

MacArthur's operations up to this time had been, for the most part, on a small scale, and executed by Lieut. General Walter Krueger's Alamo Force—an operational *alter ego* for the Sixth Army, which existed only as an administrative unit during the early stages of the advance from Port Moresby, because of the technicality of joint American-Australian command. Now, the time had come for the United States Army forces in the theater to take the field as the Sixth Army under Krueger, with two corps commands under it (one of them being the borrowed Twenty-Fourth). The forces employed would still be much smaller than those committed in Europe, but the war in the Southwest Pacific was emerging onto a wider stage.

The first episode in the drama of the return to the Philippines was, of course, the isolation of the stage on which the battle was to be joined. This task could be carried out only by the fleet. After a few days of respite, the Halsey-Mitscher Third Fleet put to sea and by October 10 was bearing down on the chain of islands lying between Japan and Formosa, variously

known as the Nansei Shoto or Ryukyu Islands (or Loo Choo
or Lew Chew—there are more than a dozen recognized spellings). Admiral King has disclosed an interesting detail of this
operation, involving the use of a new technique which later
was to be greatly developed and improved for fleet operations
in the enemy's coastal waters. The tactic was to send search
planes (flying boats) and submarines ahead of the fleet to run
interference for it by attacking and destroying enemy search
planes and picket boats. (The Japanese dependence upon fish
as a staple of diet has always enabled them to operate a large
number of picket boats economically.) When the carriers' air
groups swooped down upon their targets on the island of Okinawa (where Commodore Perry had advocated the establishment of an American coaling station 90 years earlier), they enjoyed the great advantage of tactical surprise. The benefit was
apparent in the results of the strikes: scores of ships were sunk
or damaged; 82 planes were destroyed, for a loss of eight.

The Japanese had not had time to organize their air forces to
offer effective opposition, or to re-route their shipping.

The carrier planes' second operation was a by-blow fighter
sweep against Japanese airfields at Aparri, on northern Luzon.
Again, the Japanese seemed weak and unready. But this was
not the case on October 12 when Task Force 38 sent its full
striking force against the enemy stronghold of Formosa and
the Pescadores Islands lying in Formosa Strait between the big
island and the China coast. The Japanese were ready with a
numerous air force to defend the bases, hangars, docks and shipping. No less than 193 enemy aircraft were shot down in this
one day, and 123 were destroyed on the ground—"sitting
ducks," in the language of the aviators.

On October 13, the enemy did better: at dusk, one of the
American task groups was "skillfully attacked," as Admiral
King puts it, and the new heavy cruiser *Canberra* took an
aerial torpedo. Part of the task group was detached to escort
her to an advanced base, but their taste of blood seemed to
have whetted the Japanese appetite. They returned again and
again to the attack, and succeeded in putting a torpedo into
the new light cruiser *Houston*. In the three days beginning
October 13, no less than 95 enemy aircraft were shot down in

day and night attacks on the task force—for a loss of only five American planes in combat.

The Japanese high command was in urgent need of a victory, and the loss of many of these planes, by an ironic twist, supplied some of the synthetic material from which they tried to manufacture a triumph. So many aircraft crashed into the sea in flames that fellow Japanese pilots believed hits had been scored on American ships; in night actions, the explosion of a bomber on the water was likely to be mistaken by an eager Japanese observer, with poor night vision, for the explosion of an *Essex*-class carrier. The enemy started to trumpet loud claims of great successes, and proclaimed that the Japanese fleet was steaming out to administer the knock-out blow to Halsey's fleeing fleet. Some heavy Japanese surface units did in fact poke their prows through the protective chain of islands (the Ryukyus), but their scout planes hastily reported that it was all a mistake. Halsey had his little joke, reporting to Nimitz that he was "retiring at full speed toward the enemy." But the enemy retired faster.

On October 15, planes from the two carriers which were covering the cruisers' withdrawal shot down no less than 50 of approximately 60 Japanese aircraft which attacked the group around the *Canberra* and *Houston* (this figure is in addition to the 95 mentioned above). On this day, as on the preceding day, the rest of Task Force 38 was engaged principally in sending air strikes against Formosa and northern Luzon to lessen the weight of Japanese blows against the damaged ships. It seems likely that this was a departure from the original plan, and unwise because it delayed the projection of the fleet's full strength against the rest of Luzon and the Visayas.

This period, which produced the first carrier-borne air attacks upon the Ryukyu-Formosa chain which stands like a fence off the east coast of Asia, was notable also for the first coordination of fleet operations with those of the B-29 Superfortresses. The big bombers, flying from hand-carved bases around Chengtu in western China, flew long missions on October 14 and 16, carrying "the heaviest bomb loads so far employed by the Superfortresses" (probably three to four tons) to attack air force installations at Okayama and Heito, on the island of Formosa.

After a two-day lull, Task Force 38 resumed combat operations on October 18. But in the meantime, the return to the Philippines by American ground forces had begun.

The amphibious forces had been assembled at various bases along the recently captured New Guinea coast and in the Admiralty Islands. On October 17, the first elements appeared in the mouth of Leyte Gulf: an advance guard commanded by Rear Admiral Arthur D. Struble, its air cover furnished by escort carriers, its assault troops consisting of the 6th Ranger Battalion, normally commanded by Lieut. Colonel Henry A. Mucci.

The arrival in Leyte Gulf was a portent of what was to happen throughout the campaign. The northeast monsoon season, which gives the eastern slopes of the Philippine Islands a perpetual drenching from November on, had begun early. The weather was so bad that Struble did not wish to put the Rangers ashore, but Major Robert W. Garrett, executive officer and acting commander of the battalion, said his men would try it anyhow. He stepped out of a landing craft, into water up to his neck, and waded ashore on the island of Dinagat. His patrol found an abandoned Japanese position near Desolation Point, and in an officer's trunk was an American flag taken, no doubt, from Bataan. The flag was promptly liberated and raised over the miniature beachhead—the first to mark the return of American forces to the Philippines. Other patrols went ashore on Suluan and Homonhon (respectively the first islands in the Philippines sighted by Magellan and the first on which he landed when the islands were discovered in 1521). There were no Japanese on Homonhon; on Suluan about 60 were killed in two encounters, and a lighthouse and signal station were knocked out; on Dinagat, 30 to 40 were killed within a few days.

Of equal importance with the Rangers' operations were those of the underwater demolition and minesweeping units which went in under Struble's command. For three days, while enemy shore batteries and other positions were pounded by shells and bombs, these units worked to remove static defenses installed by the Japanese, and thus to make the gulf safe for the great amphibious fleets which were to follow.

These arrived on the morning of October 20. Collectively,

they were known as the Central Philippine Attack Force, under Admiral Kinkaid. The Northern Attack Force, which was to put Major General Franklin C. Sibert's Tenth Corps ashore, was really the Seventh Amphibious Force, with Rear Admiral Daniel E. Barbey commanding, as he had in so many Southwest Pacific invasions. The Southern Attack Force was really the Third Amphibious Force which had served under Nimitz and Halsey in the Solomons; commanded by Vice Admiral Wilkinson, its task was to put Major General John R. Hodge's Twenty-Fourth Corps on the beaches.

The two beachheads selected were both about three and a half miles wide, and were eleven miles apart. In the Tenth Corps sector, the 1st Cavalry Division was assigned to the northernmost beach and was to strike out for the provincial capital of Taclóban and its airfield on Calaisan Point, while the 24th Division (less one regiment) was to land a little farther south and push into the Leyte Valley. Beyond (south of) the gap in which no landings were planned, the Twenty-Fourth Corps was to put the 96th Division ashore near Dulag, and the 7th Division to the south of it, both with orders to drive inland for the area around Burauen in which the Japanese had several airfields. The order of battle placed the more experienced divisions on the flanks; the 7th and 24th, of course, had orders to close the gap between the two corps as fast as possible. The 21st Infantry, detached from the 24th Division and fleshed out as a regimental combat team, was assigned to an area far south of the main landings—the island of Panaon, off the southern tip of Leyte, and facing Dinagat across Surigao Strait.

Although the invasion fleets had traveled for days along routes from a thousand to 1,500 miles long, they had not been attacked by Japanese aircraft. On the morning of October 20, when the 600-ship armada steamed into Leyte Gulf, only one enemy aircraft appeared. The range was too great for General Kenney's land-based fighters to give the assault troops tactical support, so this became the duty of the pilots from the Third Fleet's big carriers and the Seventh Fleet's escort carriers.

At dawn, as for two days previously, the fire support ships began to lay down a withering fire on the target areas. Among the ships were such veterans as the *California, Pennsylvania* and *West Virginia,* all damaged at Pearl Harbor; the cruisers

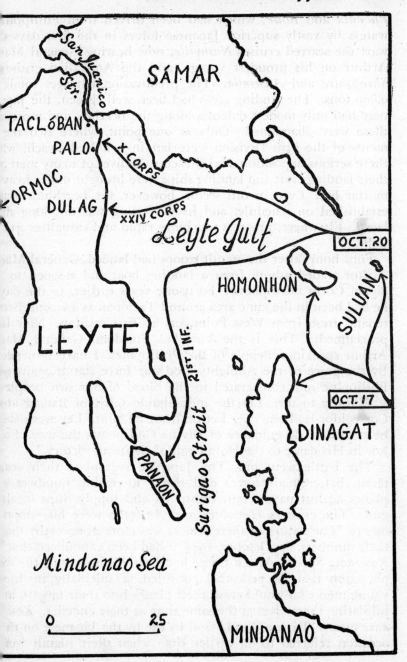

SÁMAR

San Juanico Str.

TACLÓBAN
PALO
X CORPS

ORMOC

DULAG
XXIV CORPS

Leyte Gulf

OCT. 20

HOMONHON

SULUAN

LEYTE

21ST INF.

DINAGAT

OCT. 17

PANAON

Surigao Strait

Mindanao Sea

0   25

MINDANAO

Phoenix and *Boise,* which had been driven from Philippin
waters by vastly superior Japanese forces in the first days o
war; the scarred cruiser *Nashville,* now bearing General Mac
Arthur on his proudest voyage, and the Australian cruiser
Shropshire and *Australia.* The pre-invasion barrages totale
9,600 tons. The landing areas had been well chosen; the Japa
nese had only modest defenses along the beaches, and most o
these were abandoned. Only at one point, where two regi
ments of the 24th Division were landing on Red Beach, wa
there serious opposition, and this cost the lives of many men a
their landing craft and landing ships were brought under heav
mortar fire. Even in this sector, however, the beachhead wa
established on schedule, and its deepening was not long de
layed. Elsewhere, progress was more rapid and casualties wer
light.

Four hours after the assault troops had landed, General Mac
Arthur waded ashore from a landing boat and stepped to
Signal Corps microphone. Forty-one years earlier, to the day
he had been in the same area around Taclóban as a second lieu
tenant, fresh from West Point, on his first mission. Now h
proclaimed: "This is the Voice of Freedom, General Mac
Arthur speaking. People of the Philippines: I have returnec
By the grace of the Almighty God our force stands again o
Philippine soil, consecrated in the blood of our two people
. . . Rally to me. Let the indomitable spirit of Bataan an
Corregidor lead on. . . . Let no heart be faint. Let every arn
be steeled. The guidance of Divine God points the way. Fo
low in His name to the Holy Grail of righteous victory."

The battle went on. The Japanese regrouped their scat
tered, battered air forces and threw increasing numbers o
planes against naval craft, transports and supply ships in th
gulf. The cruisers *Honolulu* and *Australia* were hit, amon
others. The nature of these attacks was more noteworthy tha
their numbers. In October, 1943, it had been announced that
Kamikaze Special Attack Corps had been formed, with the ex
planation that its personnel consisted of suicidally incline
young men who would crash their planes into their targets, ar
nihilating themselves at the same time as their enemies. *Kam
kaze* means "Divine Wind," and its use by the Japanese on thi
occasion referred to an earlier time when their islands wer

threatened with invasion, only to be saved by a "divine wind" which scattered Kublai Khan's invasion fleet.

Kamikaze planes were first used on a large scale off Leyte. Their initial successes were properly concealed by censorship, because in most cases the enemy had no idea what results these planes had achieved, unless there happened to be a snooper in the area who was able to send back a report of what the *kamikaze* had done.

The "divine wind" blew strong from the west against the American beachhead on Leyte and its ship-borne supplies in the gulf, while the monsoon beat upon them from the northeast, hampering beach operations and turning the first captured airfields, such as Dulag and Taclóban, into ribbons of mud from which American Army fighters could not operate. From their own fields on the drier western side of the Visayas the Japanese could fly all the planes they could muster. Four days after MacArthur's triumphant return to the Philippines, his forces there were vulnerable, and the Japanese knew it.

xx. The Battle of Bull's Run

By the middle of 1944, the Japanese Naval General Staff had evidently come to the conclusion that it was futile to send in its surface forces in driblets, two battleships at a time, two or three carriers at a time, as it had done in the campaign for Guadalcanal. To achieve decisive results, a decisive force was needed: something which could be dignified by the name of a battle fleet. For the First Battle of the Philippine Sea, the Japanese still had not screwed up their courage to the point where they were willing to risk all on a single throw of the dice. They sent out only a portion of their carriers and battleships, and they tried to buy a bargain victory with the device of refueling their planes in the southern Marianas. The failure of that attempt has already been described.

One salutary effect of that battle, so far as the enemy was concerned, was to make it crystal-clear that henceforth it was all or nothing. The United States Navy was advancing relentlessly across the Pacific, and it had to be stopped somewhere if the Japanese homeland was to be saved. The loss of the southern Marianas was, of course, critical; but by themselves, those islands did not constitute a large enough base for mounting an invasion of Japan. The Philippines, although farther from Tokyo than Guam, were no farther from Kyushu, and they provided the great land mass which Admiral Nimitz and General MacArthur would have needed for basing the most daring amphibious operation in history. The Japanese must have decided that the time to risk their entire remaining navy was in defense of the Philippines.

It is certain that they expected MacArthur to reinvade by way of Mindanao; perhaps they had guessed the intended date with reasonable accuracy. They were thrown off balance when MacArthur struck at Leyte two months early, but they could soon recover their balance, because the bulk of their fleet was in southern waters, based at Singapore.

When MacArthur's Rangers landed on the small islands guarding the entrance to Leyte Gulf, the Japanese naval commanders waited for the landing in force on Leyte, to be sure that this was the real thing, and no diversion. Then they calculated at what point in its development the bridgehead on Leyte would be most vulnerable. If the invading Americans were subjected to a determined attack in the first day or two, it was conceivable that they might cut their losses and pull out. But if the attack came four or five days after the landing, the bulk of the American troops would be committed ashore, and could not be hastily withdrawn. Most of their supplies would be on the beaches, but they would not yet be properly dispersed in safe storage areas. At the end of four or five days, Leyte Gulf would be crowded with the maximum number of supply ships, in the process of unloading, and in no shape to weigh anchor for a quick dash to sea. If, as the enemy expected, the escort carriers left the beachhead about October 24, and the air defense was taken over by Army squadrons struggling for a toehold in the mud of Tacloban, the scene would be perfectly set for a major naval counter-offensive at that time. In its broad outlines, then, the enemy strategy was excellent.

The enemy's tactics were as complex as the geography. The objective was to bring heavily armored, heavily gunned naval craft within range of the soft-shelled Allied transports in Leyte Gulf at a time when the American battle force was engaged elsewhere. The Japanese knew that they could not engage the United States Pacific Fleet with any hope of success. This point is of the utmost importance: the enemy was not seeking a fleet engagement in the old-fashioned sense, and any idea that the resulting conflict resembled Tsushima or Jutland is merely misleading. The Japanese were planning to stop the American advance upon their homeland by destroying the Leyte beachhead and the ships supporting it. If they had succeeded in this, they would have won an invaluable respite.

Meanwhile, to draw off the American battle fleet from its cruising area east of the central Philippines, the enemy decided to send a force of carriers and carrier-battleships down from the north. This force was not to seek direct engagement; the carriers' planes were to engage the Third Fleet on the afternoon of October 24, and draw it northward to a position where Mitscher's fliers and Vice Admiral Lee's gunnery ships would be too far away to help in defending Leyte Gulf and the Leyte beachhead.

Thus, the Japanese reasoned, there would be created the opportunity for their own gunnery ships to break through the screen of islands before dawn on October 25, and collect a huge bag of sitting ducks. They had seven battleships, seventeen cruisers and 26 destroyers in the Singapore area. American land-based aviation, at Morotai, could make the passage south of Mindanao too hot for comfort, so there remained only two main channels through the central Philippines: * Surigao Strait, between Mindanao and Leyte, and San Bernardino Strait, between Sámar and Luzon.

Neither Surigao nor San Bernardino was wide enough to leave maneuvering room for 50 warships, half of them large and all of them fast; besides, the chances of success against the targets in Leyte Gulf would be greatly increased if they could be trapped between two powerful forces and denied an opportunity to flee either north or south. These reasons were sufficient to induce the Japanese to divide their battle fleet.

On the morning of October 23, little more than 72 hours after the assault troops had gone ashore on Leyte, an American submarine (either the *Darter* or the *Dace)* on offensive patrol in the South China Sea was running on the surface, recharging her batteries. The pagoda masts of a great force of Japanese warships appeared over the southwestern horizon. While details of this first contact with the enemy are still meager, it appears that the Japanese fleet had already divided and that this was the central task force heading up the west coast of Palawan. The sub radioed the position, course and approximate number and classes of vessels sighted, and added: "We are moving in to attack." The second submarine was also within sight of the enemy, and also moving in to attack. It is reported that four torpedoes hit each of three heavy cruisers —surely the most amazing accuracy in the history of torpedo warfare!—and if this is true, there can be small wonder that

* A third channel, San Juanico Strait, between Leyte and Sámar, is not passable for anything much bigger than a rowboat.

two of the cruisers soon lay dead in the water, in a sinking condition: the *Atago*, hit by the *Darter*, and the *Maya*, hit by the *Dace*. The third was limping away.

The submarines trailed the enemy as long as their low underwater speed and the endurance of their batteries would permit. One, the *Darter*, ran aground on a reef and had to be destroyed to prevent capture, but her entire complement was saved by Palawan guerrillas.

It was in this general vicinity also that the Japanese fleet had divided. As the submarine *Guitarro* reported at this time, the southern task force had turned to the right, through Balabac Strait into the Sulu Sea, heading for Surigao. It consisted of the battleships *Huso* and *Yamasiro* (the names are sometimes rendered *Fuso* and *Yamashiro*), two heavy cruisers, two light cruisers and thirteen destroyers. It was logical that this task force should be assigned to the shorter route, since it contained old, slow ships.

Since the central task force, headed for San Bernardino Strait, had the greater distance to travel, it was logical that it should comprise the faster ships: two new dreadnaughts, later identified as the *Yamato* and *Musashi*, which must have been capable of more than 30 knots; the ancient and durable *Kongo* and *Haruna*, which could make a respectable 26 knots or better, and the *Nagato*, whose speed is variously given as 23 to 26 knots.

At this point in describing the development of the three-ring battle, it is best to break it up into its component parts. The entire series of engagements was at first given the cumbersome name of "Second Battle of the Philippine Sea"; later an attempt was made to change this to the equally impossible "Battle for Leyte Gulf." Future historians may be able to devise something which will be both more apt and easier on the tongue. Be that as it may, each engagement was on a sufficient scale to justify its being called a battle.

Battle of Surigao Strait

The Japanese southern task force, built around the *Huso* and *Yamasiro*, appears to have escaped attack until early in the morning of October 24. At this time, three task groups of the Halsey-Mitscher fast carrier task force were east of the Philippines: the most northerly, commanded by Rear Admiral Frederick C. Sherman, was off Luzon, and soon became preoccupied with the Japanese central force; the next, under Rear Admiral Gerald F. Bogan, was off San Bernardino Strait, and its air groups became involved in action against both the Japanese forces; the most southerly was off Leyte Gulf, under Rear Admiral Ralph Davison, and its air groups also contributed to the attacks on the Japanese southern force.

Commander Frederick E. Bakutis and Commander Emmet Riera were leading a search mission south of Negros Island, and Lieutenant Ray Moore was leading a similar mission in the adjoining area to the west, when both elements sighted the Japanese southern task force at about the same time—8:30 A.M. The contact was made near the extreme outer limit of the search area. While the American aircraft were still 12 miles away, the Japanese opened fire—with the main 14-inch batteries of their battleships. This is the first reported instance of the Japanese using main-battery fire against aircraft, although the United States Navy had been experimenting with the idea for two years. It does not appear that the Japanese scored any hits with this type of fire.

The attack was made at 9:05, out of the sun. Bakutis's fighters went in, firing rockets, ahead of Riera's dive-bombers, making the lead battleship their principal target. At least one rocket or bomb must have found its mark on the fantail of the *Huso,* for a brisk fire was burning there as the planes completed their strafing runs and turned away to the northeast. A cruiser and two destroyers also were reported hit. Riera was realistic enough to believe that negligible damage had been done, because the bombs were too small and too few. If any further attention was paid to the Japanese southern task force by the Halsey-Mitscher air groups that day, there is no record of it—a remarkable omission in either case.

The explanation may lie in the complicated and unsatisfactory command set-up for the liberation of the Philippines. Since Vice Admiral Kinkaid was subordinate to General Mac-Arthur, the usual practise of having the senior naval officer as over-all commander until the ground forces were securely established was a mere fiction. MacArthur had required the services of the fleet, under Halsey, without which he would have been unable to move into the Philippines for several months longer. But he had drawn a sharp line, down the east coast of the Visayas, beyond which the carrier planes could not operate westward without his specific permission. The result was that when Halsey's fliers located naval targets in the Sulu or Sibuyan seas, Halsey had to break radio silence to get permission to launch attacks.

While other and perhaps greater events were brought to an issue in the north, dispositions were made to meet the Japanese southern task force in the narrow waters of Surigao Strait. The defense was entrusted to the Seventh Fleet, under Kinkaid, which included a large number of battleships and cruisers. Admittedly the battleships were of the World War I vintage now referred to in the Navy as "OBBs"—old battleships—and admittedly they had expended much of their ammunition in the bombardment of shore targets in the preceding few days. But two of them, the *Maryland* and *West Virginia,* had eight 16-inch guns; four others, the *California, Tennessee, Mississippi* and *Pennsylvania* each had twelve 14-inch guns. All but the *Mississippi* had been damaged in varying degrees at Pearl Harbor and if any ships can be considered as thirsting for revenge, these were they.

The commander of this task force, which contained all the punching power of the Seventh Fleet, was Rear Admiral Jesse B. Oldendorf. Under him, in immediate command of the two battleship divisions, was Rear Admiral George L. Weyler. Among Oldendorf's nine cruisers was the Australian Squadron, with Rear Admiral V. A. C. Crutchley. Oldendorf flew his own flag in an American cruiser. He had about a dozen destroyers and some squadrons of PT boats.

Oldendorf adapted his strategy to the geography, which greatly favored him. Surigao Strait, through which the Japanese task force must pass to reach Leyte Gulf, is an irregular-shaped piece of water, with its narrowest pass at the southern end, between Mindanao and Panaon. Here it is only ten nautical miles wide. Northward to Leyte Gulf it broadens out considerably, but the effective width of the debouchement, between Hibuson Island and Cabugan Grande Island, is a scant 20 nautical miles.

Oldendorf posted his PT squadrons just outside the southern extremity of the strait, where the Japanese force would have to leave the open waters of Mindanao Sea and form into column to enter the bottleneck. It was unlikely that the Japanese could be driven off, but there was a chance that the force could be disorganized and some of its units crippled. As his second line of defense, Oldendorf disposed two squadrons of destroyers, one on each side of the strait, in the middle narrows. North of these again were his cruisers, five on the left (east) flank and four on the right. North of these, finally, were the six battleships, in column, strung out east to west across the exit from the strait to the gulf. This layout was a strategic dream: no matter what the Japanese did, they had to come up from the south, forming the vertical bar of a letter T, while the American battleships formed the cross-bar. According to the text books, nothing could be better. And, as occasionally happens, the text-book formula worked out perfectly in practise.

It was just after midnight, in the first few minutes of a fateful October 25, that Ensign Dudley J. Johnson sighted the enemy task force from the bridge of *PT 127* and alerted the other boats and the task force to the north by radio. After that, it was like a scene in the movies. There was, for example, the enthusiastic PT skipper who thought he saw battleships, and began to announce confidently over the TBS: "Jeez, here come two big ones. . . ." The voice trailed away, then resumed in a crestfallen tone: ". . . Two big destroyers." The sea was quickly illumined with searchlights and pocked with shell splashes as the Jap gunners let loose with everything they had. The enemy scored a negligible number of hits, but near misses were enough. In the end, one PT boat was lost, and the squadrons were credited with two hits on enemy ships.

Still the Japanese bored into the strait. Oldendorf let them come. He had the best of reasons for patience, although the men of his ships had been at battle stations for hours, and were pardonably trigger-happy. In his own words, Oldendorf had "operated on the gambler's theory of 'Never give a sucker a chance.'" As the Japanese were reported drawing within range of successive American formations, Oldendorf held his fire until the enemy was squarely between the two flanking squadrons of destroyers. When he gave the order, "Let 'em

have it—commence firing!", it was almost exactly 3 A.M. The moon had set; no stars cast any faintest light through the heavy overcast; Surigao Strait was as dark, appropriately, as the tomb. The destroyers launched torpedoes first. They ran silent and unseen until they found their targets, and then the gloom of night was rent by great white flashes, illuminating columns of water thrown up against the enemy ships' sides. This was the prearranged signal for the cruisers to open a crossfire, those on the left under Oldendorf's direct command, and those on the right flank under Rear Admiral Russell S. Berkey. The range was 16,000 yards. The Japanese had elected to advance in two parallel columns, and when the cruisers' fire fell upon them, the enemy commanders in each column thought they were being shelled in error by friendly ships in the other column. They began to flash their recognition signals, which conveniently pinpointed the targets for the American gunners.

When the Japanese commander gathered his wits, his destroyers began to lay smoke around the heavier units, but he continued to advance, although the speed of his ships was gradually cut from 18 or 20 knots down to 12 knots. The Japanese gunnery was poor: only one American destroyer, the *Albert W. Grant,* was hit in this phase of the engagement. The enemy ships wobbled around uncertainly until the range for the American cruisers was down to 11,000 yards. It was at this point that the Japanese commander was convinced he was licked. His star shells, designed to illuminate targets by silhouetting them, had been falling in all the wrong places, but by now he became aware of the presence of a still more formidable foe: Weyler's battle force. Whether the Japs saw them with the aid of a chancely-placed star shell, or whether their radar finally detected them, is not known.

Whatever the cause, the result was decisive. The Jap commander ordered a 180-degree turn, in column, for each of his two columns. In other words, the lead ship in one column would turn at a given point; the next ship would not turn simultaneously, but would turn at the same point where the lead ship had turned, and so on. The fascinating thing about this operation was that the turning points chosen by the Japanese commander were within 20,000 yards of Weyler's battleships, which is considered virtually point-blank range for

16-inch guns, and close for 14s. As each enemy ship came up to the turn, it presented a perfect, broadside target to hundreds of American gunners. "We gave 'em hell on the turn," says Oldendorf. Two ships were set afire almost at once; a battleship next burst into flames; a cruiser and a destroyer began to sink. Within 15 minutes, the American battle line ceased fire. The targets were getting out of range, and there was danger of hitting the damaged *Albert W. Grant.* It was about 3:45 A.M. when the American screening squadrons resumed the chase which had been interrupted while the heavyweights had their revenge for Pearl Harbor.

The *Grant,* a 2,100-ton *Fletcher*-class destroyer, had just fired her first spread of five torpedoes at the beginning of the action when she was raked by a salvo from a Japanese cruiser. One of the engine rooms received a direct hit which released super-heated steam, killing some men and terribly burning others. Ready-service ammunition began to explode all over the ship. The medical officer, Lieut. (j.g.) Charles A. Mathieu, was killed, as were all the corpsmen but one. W. H. Swain, Jr., the only pharmacist's mate left alive, had to minister, with volunteer help, to dozens of wounded. Neither the squadron commander, Captain Kenmore M. McManes, nor the task group commander expected the *Grant* to survive, and her commanding officer, Commander T. A. Nisewaner, received an order to surrender a radio transmitter to one of the other destroyers which had burned one out. Nisewaner protested in the most vigorous terms permissible against this attempt to cannibalize his ship while she was still afloat, and added that he intended to keep her that way. At dawn his confidence was justified; another destroyer went alongside to give aid, and the *Grant* was brought out to fight another day.

As usual, there is the utmost confusion as to how many Japanese vessels were engaged in the gunnery action in Surigao Strait, and how many were sunk.

This much is certain: two identified battleships were sunk, the *Huso* and *Yamasiro,** along with the heavy cruiser *Mogami,* and the balance of the task force was effectively destroyed. (The damaged light cruiser *Abukuma* was finished off next day south-

---

* Previously, when Japanese capital ships had been sunk or reported sunk, their identity had always been in doubt.

west of Negros by Army B-24 bombers.) It had fired not a single shot at the transports in Leyte Gulf. The Battle of Surigao Strait was an unqualified victory for a greatly superior American force. Or as Oldendorf put it: "A dream of an action!"

Battle of Sámar

After being attacked by the *Darter* and *Dace*, during the morning of October 23, the Japanese central task force maintained its northeasterly course through Palawan Passage, the main seaway west of the southern Philippines. Later in the day, when the force had turned south of Mindoro to run through Tablas Strait into the Sibuyan Sea, it was attacked by a third American submarine. Once again a heavy cruiser was hit, and this one was forced to retire to Manila Bay. If the original count of eleven cruisers in the force was correct, the number should by now have been reduced to seven, but all official accounts speak of eight as continuing eastward with the battleships and destroyers. It was too late in the afternoon for an air strike to be flown from the Third Fleet carriers at extreme range, and night closed with the Japanese still advancing.

Word spread through the Third Fleet, with its great new battleships and carriers, of the submarines' contacts. The news generated an air of hopeful expectancy even among men who had been at sea for two months; they knew that their fleet was far more than a match for the enemy's. The word spread also through the Seventh Fleet, with its old battleships and tin-plated escort carriers. There it generated an air of expectancy that was more anxious than hopeful. But there was not too much anxiety; the men in the more vulnerable ships knew that the whole might of the Third Fleet was there to cover them in just such an emergency.

It was about 8 A.M. on the 24th when contact was renewed with the Japanese central task force. It had not advanced far through the Sibuyan Sea, and was near the limit of the range of Third Fleet carrier planes. However, air strikes from both Admiral Sherman's group and Admiral Bogan's group, off Luzon and Sámar respectively, were flown off and made highly effective contact with the enemy.

Perhaps the best record is that claimed for Air Group 15, flying from the *Essex.* Commander James H. Mini, commanding the Helldiver squadron, is credited with having laid the first 1,000-pound bomb on the *Musashi.* In this strike and another made during the afternoon, Mini's squadron is reported to have scored no less than ten hits on the *Musashi,* besides three on another battleship and one on a heavy cruiser. Lieut. Commander V. G. Lambert's Avengers (carrying both bombs and torpedoes) reported three hits on one battleship, two on another, and two on each of two heavy cruisers. The *Musashi* is supposed to have absorbed three torpedoes, and in the light of her subsequent fate, this claim seems reasonable, but the many reports of bomb hits on the *Yamato* and the claim of four torpedo hits on the *Nagato* evidently were over-optimistic. It is noteworthy that although Sherman's task group was preoccupied during much of the morning by the Japanese air attack on its ships, especially the *Princeton,* it was nevertheless possible to make two strikes against the enemy battle force.

When the air groups had returned to Sherman's ships, the Japanese heavy units were struck from another quarter. The air group from the *Enterprise,* in Davison's group, led by Commander Dan E. Smith, Jr., flew up from the southeast. Beneath a virtually solid overcast at about 6,000 feet, the enemy force was divided into two groups, with three battleships in one and two in the other. The last battleship in the larger column evidently had been damaged, for it turned away to the north in an attempt to escape, while the rest of the group remained on an easterly course. Smith selected as his target the ship which had been most heavily damaged previously—the *Musashi.* This enabled him to avoid the worst concentration of anti-aircraft fire, but it also meant that even if he should succeed in inflicting further damage, it would have little effect on the fighting strength of the Japanese force as a whole. The big ship, listed by the United States Navy as of 42,000 tons, was strafed, rocketed and dive-bombed, and then was made the target of torpedoes. Two were seen to explode against her port side, and four others were seen heading for her starboard side although these were not actually seen to hit. When the *Enterprise* fliers left, the *Musashi* was down by the bow, circling slowly and spewing oil in her wake—as was only natural considering the treatment to which she had been subjected. She sank a few hours later between Mindoro and Marinduque islands.

Unfortunately, it was not realized how much effort had been concentrated on the *Musashi* which might better have been spread over a greater number of enemy units. As a result, it was believed that all four of the other battleships (*Yamato*, *Kongo*, *Haruna* and *Nagato*) had been heavily hit, that nearly every other ship in the force had been damaged to some extent, and that a cruiser and a destroyer had been sunk.

The picture was immensely encouraging to air combat intelligence officers aboard the carrier flagships, and encouragement was most welcome as the sun sank behind the hills of Luzon that evening, because information had been received that a third Japanese task force, built around four aircraft carriers, was on its way down from the north. If the central enemy task force could be considered so crippled as to be incapable of further offensive action, then Halsey and Mitscher would be free to leave the waters around San Bernardino Strait, and advance northward to meet the newly reported foe. At twilight the last reconnaissance planes over the central Japanese force reported that the enemy had turned back to the northwest in disorder.

Heavy as was the damage inflicted on the Japanese central force, it would have been heavier still but for the attacks made by the Japanese themselves against Rear Admiral Sherman's task group. Since these ships were lying off Luzon only 125 to 150 miles east of Manila and the great network of runways at Clark Field, the enemy had plenty of strips from which to fly the attacking planes. Not until the next day was it apparent that these aircraft had come from the Japanese carrier force, advancing from the north, and that many had staged at fields on Luzon.

The Japanese attacked Sherman's carriers at 8 A.M., just as Air Group 15 from the *Essex*, under Commander David McCampbell, was about to scramble for a strike against the Japanese task force in the Sibuyan Sea. Instead, McCampbell's fighters took to the air to defend their own floating base. Including the commander's, eight Hellcats took off, but one had to return because of a malfunction, leaving seven in the first flight. About 30 miles out they met the Japanese: 40 fighters, most of them carrying bombs, and about 20 bombers. Eight more fighters were flown off to support McCampbell, but they had to be diverted to intercept another enemy formation. McCampbell sent five of his fighters after the Japanese bombers, and he stayed with his wing man, Lieut. (j.g.) Roy Rushing, to tackle the enemy fighters who outnumbered them 20 to one. The Japanese fighters formed themselves into a protective circle, and maneuvered in that fashion for about ten minutes. Then, evidently being at the limit of their range and afraid of running short of gasoline, they resumed a cruising formation and headed toward Manila. This was McCampbell's chance. He and Rushing hung on to the edges, waiting for one or two of the Japanese to drop slightly out of place, and then attacked these stragglers. In all, each made 16 passes. Rushing was credited with four kills, McCampbell with nine—five Zekes, two Oscars and two Hamps—the greatest score ever run up by a fighter pilot in a single day, let alone in a single sortie. Besides the nine confirmed kills, he had two probables, and gave up the murderous pastime only when he was out of ammunition, and running short of fuel. As it turned out, Rushing was able to reach the *Essex,* but McCampbell had to land on another and nearer carrier.

There was a great slaughter among the 200 Japanese aircraft which had sortied against Sherman's group, but it was impossible to prevent every enemy plane from breaking through the combat air patrol and launching an attack. At 9:38 A.M., one of them made for the light carrier *Princeton.* No explanation has been permitted as to why the plane was unmolested, but naval authorities have passed the statement that the plane was not even "disturbed by gunfire," and the bombardier's aim was perfect. The *Princeton* was squarely hit amidships. As usual in such cases, the bomb itself did comparatively slight damage, but the airedales were fueling planes, there were open gasoline lines around, besides bombs, torpedoes and rockets, machine-gun ammunition for the fighters and ready-service ammunition for the anti-aircraft batteries. Amidst all these explosives and combustibles, fire began to wreak havoc. Twenty minutes after the bomb hit, there was the first major explosion: the fire had reached the loaded torpedo planes. At this time Captain William H. Buracker of the *Princeton* was asking for destroyers to come alongside and play hoses on her fires. As the *Morrison* and *Irwin* prepared to go alongside to give this assistance, there was a second major explosion aboard the *Princeton,* the force of which traveled downward from the steel deck and wrecked the fire rooms. With the steam supply cut off, the turbines slowed and eventually stopped; the *Princeton* lost way and swung broadside on to the wind and began to wallow in the long Pacific swell.

The *Irwin* took the position on the port side, to windward of the carrier. Although they were soon secured bow to bow, the *Irwin* found it almost impossible to keep station because the carrier, with a side far bigger than any barn, drifted to leeward much more rapidly than the low-slung destroyer. Belts of machine-gun ammunition were going off in the *Princeton's* planes, spraying the rescue ship with .50-caliber slugs. But at least the windward station was bearable, because the smoke from fires extending through the after half of the carrier was blown away, and so were the most scorching blasts of hot air. For the *Morrison,* on the starboard side, there was no consolation. The smoke and heat drove down relentlessly upon her men. The *Princeton* listed in yielding to the pressure of the wind, forcing the overhang of her flight deck and her outboard gun positions into the upper works of the *Morrison.*

The rescue mission could hardly have been more difficult. Hundreds of men jumped from the bow of the *Princeton* to that of the *Irwin* or to the deck of the *Morrison.* Thousands of gallons of water were poured from the destroyers' hoses into the burning carrier. Wounded men were being moved across by breeches buoy, and it seemed that there was at least an even chance of saving the tortured ship when a renewal of the Japanese air attack made it necessary to interrupt the operation. The destroyers pulled clear while the new assault was fought off. When they returned to their stations, the fires were out of hand. The battle to save the men and, if possible, to save the ship, went on for hours. By afternoon, only the captain and damage control parties remained aboard; all other surviving personnel had been removed. The destroyers were ordered away.

The *Irwin* pulled clear almost immediately, but the *Morrison* was trapped. The *Princeton* had borne down upon her so heavily that gun positions and other projecting equipment were tightly interlocked. The *Irwin* gave the *Morrison* a tow-line and was beginning to pull her away when a freak accident deprived the *Irwin* temporarily of all power in her port engine. The tow-line had to be slipped, and the operation begun all over again. Meanwhile, the light cruiser *Birmingham* had moved in on the carrier's port side, and was using her more powerful pumps in a final, all-out effort to quench the fires. The light cruiser *Reno* and the destroyers *Gatling* and *Cassin Young* also were giving assistance.

The *Irwin* succeeded in breaking the carrier's death-lock on the *Morrison,* and the latter began to pull away under her own power. But as she did so, her whole superstructure was raked by the overhang of the *Princeton,* smashing her bridge, her stacks, her masts and her exposed gun positions on the port side. It was, however, a small price to pay for deliverance from what followed. The *Morrison* miraculously escaped without personnel casualties, but five minutes after she drew clear, the *Princeton's* magazines went up. The *Birmingham,* only 50 feet away, took the full force of the blast, and had no less than 229 men killed and 420 injured.

Meanwhile, information of the greatest importance had been received: a search plane had encountered a third Japanese naval force containing carriers and two carrier-battleships, northeast of Luzon. It seemed likely that this force was intending to launch its aircraft for a coordinated attack at dawn on the transports in Leyte Gulf—at the very time when both the Surigao and San Bernardino task forces should be engaged in a slaughter of sitting ducks. It was impossible, in the face of this threat, to leave the *Princeton* afloat, because she would have had to be attended by destroyers and perhaps protected by aircraft. Admiral Mitscher ordered her sent to the bottom by torpedoes.

The question at once arose as to what Admiral Halsey should do about the third Japanese task force now bearing down upon Leyte Gulf. His directive was clear enough: he was to protect the infant bridgehead on Leyte against any Japanese attack delivered on or over the sea. But it was by no means clear what was the best way to meet the triple threat which the Japanese now offered. The enemy's southern task force was to be met by the bombardment force under Rear Admiral Oldendorf. That could be dismissed from further consideration, as it included only gunnery ships—no aircraft carriers. The enemy's central force was reported by this time to have turned back in confusion toward the South China Sea. On the face of it, the newly-reported northern force, containing the enemy carriers, was the most immediate and by far the greatest threat. However, there was the possibility that the turnabout by the central force was only a temporary, deceptive maneuver, and that the apparent advance of the northern force (which must have known that its position had been reported by the American reconnaissance plane) was only a feint designed to draw off the fast carrier task forces in pursuit. Surely this possibility must have been considered by Halsey's staff. Yet, when a second fix on the enemy carrier force was provided by one of the American carriers' scout planes, "Bull" Halsey decided to run north in the night and try to destroy the Japanese carrier force at dawn. (The planes from Sherman's group had not yet returned from the Sibuyan Sea. When they got back, it was too late to hit the Jap carriers that afternoon.)

Halsey was not limited to the choice between taking his entire force north and leaving it off the mouth of San Bernardino. True, the force was below its full strength temporarily, because several carriers had retired to the east to take on fuel. But it still contained about eight fast battleships, each mounting nine 16-inch guns, and a slightly greater number of carriers. The Japanese central force contained at least two battleships with 16-inch guns, besides two with 14s, and it would be standard practice to leave battleships to oppose battleships. Halsey had battleships and to spare, because the enemy's northern task force contained only carriers and two hybrid ships— the *Ise* and *Hyuga,* former battleships which now had short flight decks aft, and eight 14-inch guns forward. Two modern American battleships would have been ample to deal with these, and the American carriers were plainly a match for the enemy carriers. Nevertheless, the fast carrier task forces, guarded as usual by their full quota of fast battleships, steamed north as a unit.

Through the night, there was no reconnaissance report to show Seventh Fleet commanders the whereabouts of the Japanese central force. Officers of the jeep carriers patrolling east of Leyte Gulf did not even know that their northern flank had been laid open by Halsey's run north. These officers had been far less confident than Halsey's staff about the retirement westward of the enemy's central force. They reasoned, plausibly, that since the southern force was still heading in toward Surigao Strait, the central force would probably come through also: it was unlikely that the weaker southern force would be committed alone.

It was about 3 A.M., October 25, when the commanders of the escort carrier groups heard that action had been joined in Surigao Strait. They had no occasion to fear the result: Admiral Oldendorf had plenty of power. But after a surface ship engagement, and especially one in which the victor would hesitate to pursue a defeated foe, there were likely to be crippled enemy ships requiring attention at dawn. Therefore, most of the escort carriers' Avengers (Grumman planes which can carry either torpedoes or bombs) were loaded with torpedoes, which would be most effective in polishing off cripples or stragglers. However, by no means all of the jeep carriers' planes could be assigned to this interesting work; their primary mission was to give tactical air support to the Leyte beachhead, as it had been ever since the landings of October 20. At 5 A.M., the northern group flew off Wildcat fighters to establish a combat air patrol over Leyte. At 5:45 (half an hour before sunrise), more Wildcats were flown off, to set up the local combat air patrol around the carriers themselves. These were followed quickly by Avengers on anti-submarine patrol, and more Avengers, carrying bombs, for the first of the day's strikes against enemy positions on Leyte.

The sixteen escort carriers, under Rear Admiral Thomas L. Sprague, were divided into three groups:

1) Northern group, under Rear Admiral C.A.F. Sprague (no relation of Thomas Sprague): six carriers with a screen comprising three destroyers and four destroyer-escorts. The carriers were the *Fanshaw Bay* (Captain Douglas P. Johnson), serving as C.A.F. ("Ziggy") Sprague's flagship; *Gambier Bay* (Captain Walter V. R. Vieweg); *Kalinin Bay* (Captain Thomas B. Williamson); *Kitkun Bay* (Captain John P. Whitney), serving as the division flagship of Rear Admiral Ralph A. Ofstie;

Saint-Lô (formerly the *Midway*) (Captain Francis J. McKenna), and *White Plains* (Captain Dennis J. Sullivan). The screening craft were under the command of Commander William D. Thomas. This force was about 25 miles east of the southern peninsula of Sámar.

2) Center group, under Rear Admiral Felix B. Stump, six carriers and screen: *Kadashan Bay* (Captain Robert N. Hunter), *Manila Bay* (Captain Fitzhugh Lee), *Marcus Island* (Captain Charles F. Greber), *Natoma Bay* (Captain Albert K. Morehouse), *Ommaney Bay* (Captain Howard L. Young) and *Savo Island* (Captain Clarence E. Ekstrom). This force was somewhat farther offshore than the northern or southern groups, and while the relative positions naturally changed during operations, it was usually about 25 miles southeast of C.A.F. Sprague's group.

3) Southern group, under Rear Admiral Thomas Sprague himself: four carriers and screen, comprising the *Petrof Bay* (Captain Joseph L. Kane), *Sangamon* (Captain Maurice E. Browder), *Santee* (Captain Robert E. Blick) and *Suwanee* (Captain William D. Johnson, Jr.). This group was directly south of C.A.F. Sprague's, and usually about 70 miles away.

It must again be emphasized that during the night there had been no report of the Japanese central task force's second reversal of course, toward San Bernardino Strait. At 6:45 A.M., one of the pilots in the local anti-submarine patrol from Ziggy Sprague's carriers reported by radio that he had sighted an enemy force, containing battleships, cruisers and destroyers, steaming southward off the coast of Sámar, toward the jeep carriers and Leyte Gulf. It is easy to understand that Sprague was, as he puts it, "surprised" to learn that a force which was supposed to have been heading back to the South China Sea had in fact negotiated the narrow and treacherous strait during the night—a feat for which the Japanese commander deserves congratulation—and had emerged undetected into the Philippine Sea. Sprague, a short, dark man with a puckish, wrinkled face and a slight list to port, seemed calmer than usual after the receipt of this disquieting news. He ordered the other aircraft in the vicinity to verify the report.

Sprague's own account of what followed is the best connected story of a strange and strangely unequal contest.

"The report came back: four battleships, seven heavy and light cruisers and about nine destroyers—with pagoda masts," says Sprague. (It appears to have been determined later that only five were cruisers, and that two were large flotilla leaders or "torpedo cruisers" which are classed as oversize destroyers.) "Simultaneous with the pilot's verifying report, we sighted anti-aircraft fire. The whole Japanese force had opened up on him. I knew we were in a tough spot. I didn't think anything could save me, since the Japs were reportedly making 30 knots my way." It was 6:55 A.M.—only ten minutes after the first contact report—when salvoes of Japanese heavy shells began to fall among the unarmored carriers. Ziggy Sprague called Thomas Sprague over the short-range voice radio: "We have enemy fleet consisting of battleships and cruisers fifteen miles astern of us, and closing. We are being fired on." This far-from-reasurring report was heard throughout the jeep carrier force, and one wit wisecracked: "Tell Halsey we've got the Jap fleet cornered."

"The only thing to do," says Sprague, "was to *think* of something to do. I ordered my screen to drop back astern of the carriers and make smoke. We made smoke, too, and immediately launched all our planes. Fortunately, the wind was right. My course was 90 degrees [due east] and the wind was from 70 degrees [east-northeast], so I could run and launch at the same time. To the north of us there was a rain squall which extended out of sight. It wasn't thick, but the squall, combined with our course change, gave us a few minutes' breather.

"I didn't like our 90-degrees course, for the Japs could have stayed on it forever. I asked for all possible aid and assistance from our forces to the south, and also ordered the Leyte strike to return immediately. Then I ordered a course change to the south. I figured we'd be blown out of the water the instant we came out of the rain squall. But for some reason the Jap fleet failed to cut across the triangle to cut us off."

It seems certain that the explanation lay in the confusion created by the American destroyers' operations. When these were ordered to place themselves between the carriers and the enemy, and to lay smoke, the Japanese were on a southerly course in direct pursuit of the jeep carriers. Then the carriers turned east to launch their planes. This created the first opportunity for the Japs to cut across the triangle, but it was made too dangerous for them by the American flotilla: they would have exposed themselves broadside on to the American torpedo craft.

At this stage, the destroyers and DEs had no orders from the admiral except to lay smoke. However, this was not understood aboard the destroyer *Johnston*, which was far in the lead and drawing the heaviest fire from both battleships and cruisers. The enemy's shells contained different colored dyes, so that gunnery officers aboard individual ships could identify their bursts and correct their aim. As the geysers rose in livid shades of orange, purple, red and green, perilously close to the target, a man whose name should have been recorded was heard to exclaim: "My God, they're shooting at us in technicolor!" At 7:15 the *Johnston* was within range of the nearest enemy cruisers, and opened with her 5-inch guns. The Japanese aim was bad. At 7:20 the commanding officer of the *Johnston*, Commander Ernest E. Evans, gave the order to fire torpedoes. By this time the destroyer was dueling with the *Tone*, a heavy cruiser with eight 8-inch guns, or her sister ship, the *Tikuma*. Two torpedo hits are claimed to have been made on the cruiser. But at 7:30 the Japs got the range on the temerarious destroyer: a salvo of three 14-inch shells struck her, and a moment later a light cruiser was on with three 6-inch shells. The devastation aboard the 2,100-ton *Johnston* can be imagined. Her steering engine was gone. There was no power to the three after gun mounts; there was no communication with No. 2 gun forward; the captain was wounded; scores of officers and men were killed and injured. Despite the disruption of fire control, and with the three after guns manually operated, the *Johnston* kept firing. If the reports of her gunnery officer, Lieutenant Robert C. Hagen, are not over-optimistic, she had by this time rolled up an impressive total of dozens of hits on battleships, cruisers and destroyers.

About 7:45 the jeep carriers and their screening craft emerged from the rain squall which had protected them for 15 minutes. Because the Japanese force had followed his carriers in their easterly and southerly turns instead of cutting the corner, "when we came out of the rain squall their ships were no closer to us than they had been when we entered it," says Ziggy Sprague. "I figured we might as well try to do some

damage, since it seemed certain we were in for it, so I ordered
the escorts to launch a torpedo attack. It was a very gallant
attack."

The *Johnston* had fired her torpedoes, and as the *Hoel* and
Heerman, with eight tubes each, and the *Samuel B. Roberts*
with three tubes, raced past her on their way to attack, it
seemed that the *Johnston* could be of no help. But Commander
Evans ordered her in any way, limping as she was on one
engine, to give fire support with her guns. During this operation the *Heerman* closed to within 2,000 yards of the *Kongo*
and drew no fire: evidently the old ark had lost all automatic
fire control because of damage in two days of attacks, and was
virtually incapable of defending herself. One confirmed torpedo hit on the battleship was reported.

Simultaneously, the two escort carrier groups to the south
were contriving to add to the enemy's discomfort. Permission
had been obtained from the commander, support aircraft,
aboard Vice Admiral Kinkaid's flagship, to throw every available torpedo plane into the attack against the onrushing
Japanese task force.

The Japanese commander realized that even with the superior speed of his battleships, a stern chase after the American carriers was going to be a long chase, and thoroughly
uncomfortable. So he detached two heavy cruisers, which were
several knots faster than his battle force, and sent them on a
flanking movement to the east. There, they would be on the
port side of the retreating American carriers. His battleships
were now directly astern of the quarry, and closing. His destroyers were on the starboard side, and also closing. It looked
as though the jeep carriers would soon be boxed in. Fortunately—and miraculously—the destroyers and destroyer escorts
had escaped damage during their first torpedo attack. Except
for the limping *Johnston,* they were still in good shape and
available for another supreme effort when the crisis should
come.

The crisis began to develop after 8 o'clock. At 8:10 the
enemy scored his first clean hit on one of the jeep carriers:
a 16-inch shell (from either the *Yamato* or the *Nagato*) struck
the *Gambier Bay* below the water line, flooded the engine
room and put one engine out of commission. With her speed

cut in half (to 10 knots or less) and her maneuverability reduced as she was forced to rely on the one surviving engine, the *Gambier Bay* fell astern of the formation and came under the fire of the Japanese heavy cruisers advancing on the port flank. At 8:30 the *Johnston,* also trailing, came upon the scene where the *Gambier Bay* was being mercilessly shelled, and repeatedly hit, by one of the enemy cruisers. Commander Evans gallantly engaged the cruiser with his stuttering, hand-loaded guns, but the enemy refused to have his attention diverted. He concentrated on the carrier, which could answer with nothing more effective than the single 5-inch gun mounted on her stern. As Captain Vieweg put it, the shells fired by the *Gambier Bay's* gunners "didn't have the chance of a spitball." But the men stayed at their stations until, toward 9 o'clock, Vieweg ordered the ship abandoned. There were repeated shell hits on the bridge as the captain himself left the ship. She keeled over and sank at 9 A.M.

It was during the *Gambier Bay's* agony that the screening destroyers and DEs were ordered by Ziggy Sprague to interpose themselves between the five carriers, now under incessant fire, and the enemy force. The operation has been described as a torpedo attack, but it is not certain how many tubes had been reloaded. What is certain is that Commander Thomas's flotilla again charged the Japanese battle line. The enemy battleships turned out of column to avoid such torpedoes as were launched, but then quickly re-formed, on a course directly opposite to that of the torpedoes (thus presenting the narrowest possible target), and bore down upon the American flotilla. The range was short to begin with; it was soon point-blank, and the American flotilla paid the price. Hit by 16- and 14-inch shells, the destroyer *Hoel* (Commander Leon S. Kintberger, commanding) and the destroyer escort *Samuel B. Roberts* (Lieut. Commander Robert W. Copeland) were quickly reduced to masses of burning and exploding wreckage, and lost with heavy casualties. One destroyer (unidentified) which had launched three torpedoes is credited with a hit at 4,000 yards on one of the old Japanese battleships.

Out of the smoke, to rejoin the battered carriers, came the destroyer *Heerman* and the destroyer escorts *Dennis, Raymond* and *John C. Butler.* The *Johnston* had not yet sunk, but she was not seen again by the carrier group. She was engaged in a private war with seven Japanese destroyers which appeared to be getting into position for a torpedo attack on the American carriers. The enemy's lead destroyer was taken under fire and the *Johnston's* gunnery officer claims twelve hits which turned her away. Then five hits on the second ship in the Japanese column are reported. The *Johnston* was taking hits, but not so many, when the Japanese destroyers changed course. On the turn, they fired their torpedoes at the carriers—but at extreme range of 10,000 yards or more, so all the torpedoes ran wild. Then the Japanese destroyers headed back toward the north. It was 9:20 A.M.

Within five minutes, the Japanese cruisers also turned and laid a course for San Bernardino Strait. They had sunk the *Gambier Bay,* the *Hoel* and the *Samuel B. Roberts;* the *Johnston* was blowing up piecemeal and would sink in a few minutes. They had scored several hits on the *Kalinin Bay* and *Fanshaw Bay,* but failed to cripple them. They are reported to have obtained several hits with 14-inch armor-piercing shells (all of which failed to explode) on the *Kitkun Bay.* They had laid one salvo so close under the overhanging stern of the *White Plains* that her frame was weakened. The little carrier's stern was lifted out of the water, but she continued to fly off her aircraft.

"During the surface engagement we made frequent course changes to throw the Japs off their gunnery problem," says Ziggy Sprague. "Each individual ship captain *chased* the splashes from Jap salvoes. It was miraculous that we emerged as we did. During the two and a half hours of the attack, I estimate that 300 salvoes were fired, of which only one scored a vital hit on any of the carriers" [the 16-inch hit on the *Gambier Bay*]. Some hits were scored by the carriers' own 5-inch guns, says the admiral, and he quotes a battery officer as having said, during this phase of the engagement: "Just hold on a little longer, boys—we're getting 'em into 40-millimeter range." When the Japs turned away, a signalman on the bridge of the *Fanshaw Bay* protested to the admiral: "Damn it, they're getting away." The mood was far different from that of an hour or so earlier, when the refrain had been: "Where the hell's

Halsey?" However, the jeep carriers were not yet out of the woods.

The Japanese withdrawal at this time has been represented as something of a mystery. But it must be remembered that the Japanese commander's final objective was not the carrier group, but the transports and supply ships lying off the beachhead in the Gulf of Leyte. And by this time it was clear to him that he could not hope to attain this final objective without sacrificing his entire task force. His ships were being damaged by aircraft at a rate which foreboded ultimate disaster; he must have been advised by this time that the *Huso* and *Yamasiro* had been destroyed in Surigao Strait, and he therefore could expect no support from that direction. He must have feared that Oldendorf's OBBs would be steaming north;* and he undoubtedly expected to be attacked shortly by carrier aircraft of the Third Fleet returning from the north. There were sufficient reasons for withdrawal.

The only support which the Japanese commander could count upon was that provided by aircraft flying from Luzon. Yet it was only when he had turned tail that these planes arrived over the scene and attacked the American escort carriers. Of eight enemy aircraft (variously described as dive-bombers, fighter-bombers and assorted suicide planes), three were shot down before they could reach their targets. The rest went for the jeep carriers—one apiece. The *Kitkun Bay* and *Kalinin Bay* were hit directly by these planes, but were not severely damaged. The *Saint-Lô* was hit near the center line of the flight deck by a plane which may have been damaged and therefore deliberately crashed by a despairing pilot, or which may have been one of the *Kamikaze* Corps. Whichever may have been the case, the result was the same. A bomb penetrated the flight deck and set off a series of secondary explosions in the hangar deck. Fire-fighting was hindered by the fact that hose parties were driven away from the burning planes by showers of machine-gun bullets exploded by the heat. The third explosion blew huge pieces of the flight deck high into the air, and debris rained upon the hundreds of men who

---

* The Japanese commander probably had no way of knowing that Oldendorf's battleships had almost exhausted their ammunition in days of shore bombardment and in the night action, and therefore were unlikely to be committed.

had abandoned her and were seeking safety in the water. Captain McKenna timed the abandonment perfectly: he left after the seventh major explosion, and the ship sank after the eighth, rolling over on her side and going down rapidly, stern first. It was just 32 minutes after she was hit.

Of the *Saint-Lô's* complement, 114 were killed or missing, while 784 were rescued—about half of them wounded. Since she was sunk late in the morning, when the force had withdrawn well to the south, the *Saint-Lô's* men were in waters filled with friendly ships, and virtually all were picked up that day. The 750 survivors of the *Gambier Bay,* and those from the lost destroyers and the destroyer escort, were less fortunate. No adequate explanation has been offered as to why it took almost 48 hours to rescue these men after Japanese surface ships had withdrawn. The rescue of the *Saint-Lô* survivors was greatly speeded by the fact that Ziggy Sprague detached all four of the screening craft which remained to him *(Heerman, Dennis, Raymond* and *John C. Butler)* and ordered them to stand by the stricken carrier. As he put it, "We had been through so much by then that it didn't seem to matter whether we had escorts with us or not."

One Japanese cruiser and one destroyer are considered to have been sunk during the running fight. A damaged cruiser was sunk later by planes from Thomas Sprague and Felix Stump's groups. The two cruisers are officially reported to have been the *Suzuya,* of the *Mogami* class, and the *Tikuma* (also spelled *Chikuma*) of the *Tone* class. No identification of the destroyer is available. Other damage which may have been inflicted subsequently upon this central Japanese task force will be considered later, in connection with the return of elements of the Third Fleet to the vicinity of San Bernardino Strait.

As a talker on the bridge of Admiral Kinkaid's flagship said when he heard of the jeep carriers, with negligible armament and no armor, taking on the Japanese battle force, "This, sir, is a hell of a way to run a war." If it was true that the Battle of Surigao Strait had been "a dream of an action," the Battle of Sámar was a nightmare.

Battle of Cape Engaño

During the October 24 strikes against Japanese task forces in the Sulu and Sibuyan Seas, the fast carriers of the Third Fleet had been divided into three rather widely separated groups, strung out along 350 nautical miles off the eastern Philippines. Still another group was off to the east, refueling. While Admirals Halsey and Mitscher were taking the difficult decision on how to dispose their greatest strength to meet three possible enemy attacks, it was necessary to bring the groups somewhat closer together, and it may be that the time consumed in this operation had a bearing on the course of events. The final decision to proceed northward with the Third Fleet was not taken until a second and possibly a third reconnaissance report had been received as to the strength of the Japanese carrier force. Originally, it had been assumed that it included all the Japanese fleet-type carriers not known to have been sunk. This could have been a truly formidable force, which might have been almost a match even for T.F. 38. But reconnaissance reports received by Halsey and Mitscher during the afternoon or evening of the 24th surely showed that there were in fact only four carriers in the Japanese northern force, one heavy and three light, accompanied by the two hybrid carrier-battleships. This was a force which a single one of the American groups could have tackled, since a typical task group contains four fast carriers and two or more battleships.

At least one of the American fast carriers had planes equipped for night reconnaissance work, and these tried to locate the Japanese central task force west of San Bernardino while the fleet steamed north. There are conflicting reports as to the results of this reconnaissance. From the subsequent disposition of the Third Fleet, it would appear that the results must have been negative. However, if the enemy force was, as some say, detected steaming eastward at reduced speed, then the continued northerly course of the Third Fleet is much harder to justify.

There was no doubt that it would be most desirable for the air groups from the Third Fleet's fast carriers to hit the Japanese without delay at dawn of the 25th—before the enemy had time to fly off his own planes. Admiral Halsey took the advice of staff officers who urged that reconnaissance planes be sent out shortly after midnight, to have maximum time for searching. Within a couple of hours one plane obtained a fix on the Japanese force, which was heading south on a collision course toward the American force. But then, as wiser staff officers had anticipated, the Japanese commander knew that he had been detected, and promptly changed course. He succeeded in shaking off the American fleet's flying scouts for several hours.

So great was the determination to strike the Japanese at the earliest possible moment that several of the American carriers' air groups were flown off before dawn. These groups failed to find the enemy, for they were searching to the north of Task Force 38. However, Sherman had suspected that the Japanese might work eastward, and sent scouts in that direction. This foresight paid off: at 7:10 A.M. one of these scouts found the enemy steaming away on a north-northeast course. The American striking groups were beginning to run low on gasoline, and the Japanese were going away at good speed, but Mitscher increased the speed of his own force so that his planes would not have so far to fly on the return trip, and ordered an immediate attack. It began at 8 A.M.

Direction of this assault was entrusted to Commander David McCampbell, of the *Essex's* Air Group 15, who had distinguished himself so greatly the day before. This time, however, he was to be the brains rather than the trigger man in a carefully calculated mass murder. The weather was good; the enemy force was visible 30 miles away, and the first stages of the attack went exactly as planned. McCampbell counted only about a dozen Zekes leaving the carriers, and decided not to bother with them at first.

His principal targets were the enemy's heavy units, carriers and battleships. His task was to inflict the maximum damage on them with bombs and torpedoes, but before his fliers could deliver their cargoes they had to penetrate the anti-aircraft fire from the screen of cruisers and destroyers. McCampbell sent fighters in first, to strafe the exposed automatic-weapons positions of the screening ships. The Japanese had few defensive aircraft, but they had plenty of artillery, and the dense curtain of multi-colored bursts greatly impressed the attacking pilots.

However, they bored through it, and created enough diversion so that the dive-bombers could slip over the screen at medium altitude and swoop down upon their prey.

Aircraft from all three components of Task Force 38 were soon engaged. They had a wide choice of targets: the *Zuikaku* (29,800 tons—larger than an *Essex*); the light carriers *Zuiho, Titose (Chitose)* and *Tiyoda (Chiyoda);* the experimental carrier-battleships *Ise* and *Hyuga;* a heavy cruiser, four light cruisers and six destroyers. Dive-bomber pilots from McCampbell's own air group reported that they had stitched seven 1,000-pound bombs along the flight deck of one Japanese carrier which appears to have been a Titose.* She was left dead in the water, for a time at least. The other Titose was hit by three torpedoes from the *Lexington's* air group, and also took several bomb hits. Within a few minutes she was not only dead in the water, but burning furiously. McCampbell sent the *Essex's* torpedo squadron against one of the battleships, on which one hit was scored, and others from one of these carriers or from the *Langley* obtained one hit on a light cruiser—a Natori. Other carriers whose air groups were attacking at this time, or shortly afterward, included the *Hornet, Wasp, Enterprise* and *Belleau Wood.*

None of the Japanese carriers did anything spectacular such as blowing up or turning turtle within a few minutes of being hit, as has been fancifully reported. When the first strike ended, at 9:25, all the targets were still afloat, although several were in urgent need of drydocking. The first major success of the day became an accomplished fact about 10 o'clock, when McCampbell had the satisfaction of seeing the more seriously damaged Titose capsize and sink. At 10:15, the second strike began, with planes from the *Enterprise, Belleau Wood* and other ships. During this attack, at least two torpedoes were put into the *Zuikaku,* which probably had been damaged earlier. The fliers by this time were operating under a new order from Admiral Halsey, issued after he received word of Ziggy Sprague's plight far to the south: "Instruct all pilots to strike at undamaged ships. Leave cripples until later." Halsey was preparing to break off, or at least curtail, the action; several

---

* The name appears in Roman type when it indicates merely a ship of the *Titose* class.

hours earlier he had culled the battleships out from among the carrier groups, and had formed them into a separate force, ready for use in a line-of-battle action if opportunity offered.

At 11 A.M., Halsey announced his decision on the problem presented by the Japanese breakthrough from San Bernardino Strait. (Apparently he did not yet know that the Japanese already had begun to retire.) He ordered Rear Admiral Bogan's carriers and Vice Admiral Lee's battleships to turn south at 11:15, leaving Vice Admiral Mitscher with Rear Admirals Sherman and Davison's groups to finish off the Japanese carrier task force. Although the enemy had 14-inch-gun hybrid battleships present, Halsey refused to leave a small number of American battleships (two would have sufficed) to sink the Japanese heavy ships in case they survived the air attacks.

At noon, the officer exercising air control reported that the Japanese ships were in two groups: (1), those already hit, which had fallen behind and were therefore to the south of the others; these comprised an Ise, a light cruiser and two destroyers, all circling the second Titose which was dead in the water and being abandoned; and (2), the *Zuikaku, Zuiho,* the second Ise, and two or three destroyers, all heading north at 15 to 20 knots and already about 25 miles away from the cripples. In conformance with Halsey's order, the air groups from Sherman's carriers were ordered to concentrate on the second group of enemy ships.

In an attack beginning at 1:10 P.M., these fliers scored no less than nine direct hits on the *Zuikaku* with 1,000- and 2,000-pound bombs. Japanese damage control has been excellent throughout the war, and their ships have shown great tenacity of life, thanks largely to their minute compartmentation. But the *Zuikaku* by now had taken more punishment than even her honeycomb construction could absorb; she was reduced to a burning, exploding hulk. In this phase of the attack, one torpedo was put into the fleeing Ise, and fliers from Davison's group scored several hits on the *Zuiho,* which dropped out of the formation, burning badly, and was soon dead in the water.

It was 2 o'clock before the commander of the *Lexington's* air group saw the *Zuikaku,* most formidable of all the Japanese ships engaged in this action east of Cape Engaño, settle beneath the waves. By this time, a squadron of torpedo bombers from one of Davison's carriers had scored no less than three torpedo hits on the more northerly Ise. She slowed down for only a few minutes. The hybrid ships may have been monstrosities of design, but they were tough. By this time the newer and more brittle *Zuiho* had burned almost to the water line; in mid-afternoon, a *Langley* flier saw her sink.

That left only one Japanese carrier afloat, the Titose which had been damaged shortly after 8 A.M. The two Ises were still capable of fight or flight, as their commanders chose; so were a heavy cruiser, three light cruisers and three destroyers. In an attack which began at 5 P.M., both the Ises were hit with both torpedoes and bombs, but soon picked up to 20 knots again. A fourth destroyer was believed to have been sent to the bottom at this time.

This was the last air strike of the day. Meanwhile, Mitscher had pulled out cruisers and destroyers from the carrier task groups and sent them under a cruiser division commander to finish off the cripples after dark, when the carrier planes would have to suspend operations. The task force of gunnery ships, including rebuilt veterans of Guadalcanal such as the *New Orleans* and new vessels like the *Mobile,* turned their guns first on the foundering Titose, which capsized and sank as the carrier planes were completing their strike farther north. This marked the end of the Japanese carrier fleet as a sea-going force.

Pursuing the Japanese gunnery ships, the American cruisers and destroyers had to keep out of range of the Ises' 14-inch guns, and these enemy vessels escaped. The two Japanese destroyers got away by virtue of their speed; one of the light cruisers was brought to bay and put up a good fight against overwhelming odds, but shortly before 9 P.M. it was hit in a magazine, and blew up. Of the two light cruisers which at first appeared to have escaped, one (the *Tama*) was picked off later by an American submarine, the *Jallao.*

Meanwhile, Halsey had run south at high speed. He had not gone far when he literally ran into the explanation for the shortage of Japanese aircraft around their carrier force. The enemy planes were returning from Luzon, where they had landed to refuel and rearm after the previous day's attacks in which the *Princeton* was fatally damaged. They had received poor service from the maintenance crews on Luzon, for many of them had no ammunition. Twenty-one were shot down—two of them by the destroyer *The Sullivans,* named for the five brothers lost in the *Juneau* south of Guadalcanal in November, 1942. The only one which succeeded in hitting an American carrier, killing a gun crew, had been crippled beforehand.

As the relief force continued its belated run southward, retracing its wake of the previous night, it had to turn repeatedly into the northeast wind to launch and recover aircraft. This meant turning almost directly away from the objective, and delayed the return to the neighborhood of San Bernardino. Air groups from McCain's carriers, which had been off to the east refueling, and those from the carriers in Bogan's group with Halsey, succeeded in joining up with the squadrons from the Seventh Fleet's escort carriers in harrying the fleeing Japanese. However, the enemy slipped into San Bernardino Strait under cover of dusk, and the American gunnery ships did not arrive until after dark. It was too late to attempt a pursuit. Halsey had the small consolation of using his flagship, the 45,000-ton *New Jersey,* to sink a small Japanese ship (apparently a flotilla leader) which was found outside the strait in damaged condition.

The next morning, October 26, Mitscher was back on the scene with the rest of the carriers; his air groups, together with Seventh Fleet squadrons, sallied out again over the Sibuyan Sea to pick off cripples. Through their efforts, two cruisers were sunk off Mindoro: the *Kino* and *Nosiro (Noshiro).*

The air groups also renewed the attack on the battleships, evidently with indifferent success as a result of the lengthening range, because all of the four surviving heavyweights were able to get away. However, the *Yamato* was so severely mauled by the carrier fliers and the Liberator bombers of the Thirteenth Air Force that she went only as far as Brunei Bay, in northwest Borneo, where she holed up for emergency repairs.

The Army bombers of the 5th and 307th Groups ("Bomber Barons" and "Long Rangers") flew from Morotai, and reached the area where the Japanese ships were retreating shortly before 11 A.M. on October 26. Led by 1st Lieutenant Warren McMillan and 2nd Lieutenant Howard B. Johnson, two elements of the 307th Group attacked the *Yamato;* two direct hits on the dreadnaught were reported, but the anti-aircraft fire was so heavy and accurate that three of the Liberators were shot down in flames from 10,000 feet. Excellent photographs of the ship were obtained, and were the first to be published showing the characteristics of a class of ships which had been a mystery for five years. Other elements of the 307th, led by Major Russell W. Neely, attacked the *Kongo,* and they also reported two hits. Planes of the 5th Group took as their target a *Kuma*-class cruiser which was at first believed to have been sunk.*

With these scattered operations, the three-ring battle ended. There is not the slightest question that it was a victory for American forces: the Leyte beachhead and the shipping in Leyte Gulf had been saved at what was, relatively, a negligible cost in American warships, and the number of lives lost was small in proportion to the enemy's casualties. Superficially, the Japanese material losses were heavy indeed by the estimates then accepted: two or three battleships, four carriers, nine cruisers, nine destroyers, and twice as many ships damaged.

But the factor which sets the battle apart is the opportunity it provides for endless debate on the merits of Bull Halsey's decisions to run north one evening and south the next morning, in each case leaving behind him a force which was inadequate for the task which it eventually was called upon to perform. No doubt the Navy wit who dubbed the whole operation "The Battle of Bull's run" would prefer not to be identified while still in uniform.

Every effort has been made in the above account to state, as fully and fairly as possible, the factors which prompted Halsey to make the decisions he did. But to the writer, at least, the conclusion is inescapable that whereas Halsey, by bolder tactics, might have done better in the First Battle of the Philippine Sea, Spruance with his finer calculations would have sunk six more Japanese battleships in the second battle.

---

* The *Yamato* was hit again in Brunei Bay on November 16 by the Thirteenth Air Force heavies, but succeeded in getting back to Japan for major repairs. The *Kongo* was less fortunate. This ubiquitous vessel, which had figured in so many Japanese fleet operations and had often been reported crippled or possibly sunk, was sunk with finality off the China coast, near Foochow, on November 21, by the submarine *Sealion* (II), in one of the most daring attacks of its kind ever executed.

XXI. On to Manila

THE PRIZE for which American forces were struggling against the enemy and the elements in the first few days of the Leyte campaign was a set of air strips from which land-based planes could operate in tactical support of the ground troops. It had been estimated in advance that the first and most important of these, on Calaisan Peninsula at Taclóban, would be ready for service by October 25. This left no margin of safety: the escort carriers under Rear Admiral Thomas L. Sprague were scheduled to leave the area on October 26, for they could not stay in combat operations of this kind (involving heavy daily expenditures of bombs, torpedoes and ammunition) more than a few days. Task Force 38, with its bigger carriers, could stay in action longer, but it could not be used primarily for close tactical support: its mission was to cut down Japanese air power on Luzon and the neighboring islands, to guard against the Japanese fleet, and to give tactical support to the ground troops only during the period of greatest urgency—when the landings were being made on October 20. It had been estimated that Task Force 38 would be able to leave the eastern Philippines a couple of days after the jeep carriers, and Admiral Halsey was anxious to get away because he had an appointment in the neighborhood of Tokyo for the latter part of November.

The Engineer Construction Battalion assigned to rebuild the Japanese strip at Taclóban into an operating American air base was landed late on October 20, and early the next morning it began work, under the command of Major Richard P. Davidson. Despite Japanese raids and the monsoon rains, the battalion would have had the first strip completed during the night of October 24-25 if it had not been for an unwise change of plan.

The Japanese had had a single strip: this was to be lengthened a little, and improved a great deal, by the 25th; as soon as this task was finished, the engineers were to set about building a second strip parallel with the first, and a thousand feet longer. During the afternoon of October 23 Davidson was ordered to suspend work on the short strip and begin at once on the longer one. It was impossible to incorporate the first strip into the desired longer runway, because it had one end in the water and the other in a swamp. The command's sudden change of plan meant that nearly all the work already done was wasted; it would probably take five days from the fresh start before a long strip could be finished—October 28. Lieut. General Kenney was present at this time, and although the decision may have been made by a subordinate, Kenney must be held responsible for having permitted it. Doubtless he bitterly regretted it later.

When the battle-torn dawn broke on October 25, about 3,000 feet of the new runway had been packed down; the rest was still soft. Planes from Rear Admiral Thomas Sprague's escort carriers could not land on their own decks when the sea and air battles were in progress. Their pilots decided to try the unfinished Taclóban strip. About 8:30 A.M., an Avenger torpedo bomber came in, ran off the packed runway onto the soft, unrolled fill and turned a somersault. The landings had not been foreseen, and naturally there was no proper organization to take care of them. By accident, Lieutenant Edward Worrad, of Fifth Air Force fighter control, was looking over the progress that had been made on the strip when the Grummans appeared. Also by accident, Lieutenant Russell Forrester, a Navy radio liaison officer who was to be attached to the field communications center, was present in a radio jeep. Worrad and Forrester, with Sergeant Sam Halpern, improvised the control system which brought about 70 Navy planes into the Army's unfinished field within two hours. There were many casualties among the planes, but fortunately there were few among the pilots and crews; most of the aircraft were refueled, remunitioned (some were even bombed up by emergency methods) and were able to take off again within a short time.

When it was clear that the emergency operation of the unfinished strip was a great success, higher ranking officers tried to supersede Worrad and Forrester; however, the attempt failed because the planes were under naval jurisdiction. By midnight, the young officers had handled more than 200 landings. The next day, the field had been cleared of wrecks and somewhat improved. Planes from Ziggy Sprague's carriers used the strip during operations against fleeing remnants of the Japanese battle force.

There had been 17 enemy air raids on Taclóban on October 25; it was clear that a large force of interceptors should be based there. But on the 27th, when the steel mat for the runway was finished and the 308th Bombardment Wing took over, only two squadrons of P-38 Lightnings from the 49th Fighter Group appeared; there were 34 planes to defend the northern sector of the Leyte beachhead. General Kenney reported that the Army Air Forces were able to take over the air command, and Admiral Halsey was notified that air support from Task Force 38 would no longer be needed. The jeep carriers had left or were leaving.

Within a few hours, it was shown that air control could not be exercised by the pitiful token force of land-based planes available. The P-38s were primarily interceptors, and not suitable for use as fighter-bombers; there was a period when the only effective ground support the Sixth Army could have was supplied by eight Curtiss P-40 Warhawks. Early one morning, a sneak raid by one or two Japanese planes landed bombs in a mass of P-38s parked on the runway (hard stands could not be built in the mud), and destroyed 27 of them. General MacArthur had to ask Admiral Nimitz to send Admiral Halsey and the Third Fleet back to protect the beachhead.

When the fleet returned, Vice Admiral John S. McCain had relieved Vice Admiral Mitscher as Commander, Task Force 38; Mitscher was badly in need of a rest after many months of continuous duty at sea with both Admiral Spruance and Admiral Halsey. It was thought at first that a single heavy blow, such as might be delivered in two days by all the available carrier air groups against the enemy air force in central Luzon, would suffice to tip the scales in MacArthur's favor so that Kenney's fliers could handle the situation—and so that Halsey and McCain could go north to attack Tokyo at the same time as the first B-29s flying from the Marianas struck the city.

It was not to be. On November 5 and 6, with the fleet standing in to Lamon Bay on the east coast of Luzon, the air groups wrought great destruction around Manila: 113 planes shot down, 327 destroyed on the ground, almost 300 more probably destroyed or damaged; a heavy cruiser, a destroyer and a destroyer escort sunk; a light cruiser and four destroyers damaged; a score of freighters sunk or damaged and effective blows against many small combat vessels such as escort craft. McCain thought on the evening of the 6th that he was on his way to Tokyo, but once again the fleet was ordered held in the Philippines—this time, for as long as MacArthur might need it. The coordinated attack on Tokyo by carrier planes and B-29s was scratched from the schedule.

The Japanese evidently had come to the conclusion that the best place to fight the battle for the Philippines was on Leyte. MacArthur poured troops ashore from the east—the northern beachhead alone absorbed 84,121 men and 86,440 tons of supplies from Admiral Barbey's Seventh Amphibious Force transports—while Field Marshal Terauchi, commander of all Japanese in southern areas, tried to pour them in from the west. Terauchi got off to a head start. On November 1, he got reinforcements from four large transports which were shepherded into Ormoc Bay (on the west coast of Leyte) by four destroyers and two torpedo boats. After they had unloaded, one of the transports is believed to have been sunk. Two days later, three more transports got through; on November 7, there were seven; on the 9th, four more—which had unloaded and were withdrawing before B-25 Mitchell bombers got to them.

The next Japanese attempt was less successful. On November 11, four large transports headed into Ormoc Bay with an escort of five destroyers and a torpedo boat. McCain's fliers caught this convoy before it could discharge its human cargo, and all four transports were sunk; four destroyers and the torpedo boat were seen to sink, and the odd destroyer was ascertained to have gone down later.

Covered by carrier plane strikes against the Manila Bay region and its airfields, which prevented enemy interference, MacArthur began to land great bodies of reinforcements on November 14. (Of the men already ashore on Leyte, more than half were engineers.) The first units to arrive were the 32nd ("Red Arrow") Division and the 112th Regimental Combat

Team; these were followed within a few days by the 11th Air-
borne Division and the 77th Division. Unlike the earlier leapfrogging operations, the Leyte campaign had been planned by
Lieut. General Krueger as a full army operation: a war of
maneuver, with two double envelopments. The tactical execution of the plan was interfered with by the weather; the
rains cut down the speed of maneuver to the vanishing point.
But the strategic plan remained, and was executed (although
not as quickly as the rosy statements issued by the command
would indicate *).

This is not the place for a detailed account of the land fighting on Leyte; the campaign was as complex as it was protracted,
and to describe it adequately would require far more space
than it can be given here. The outstanding feature was the fact
that although progress was painfully slow in November, the
Japanese wore themselves out so that they were incapable of
further major counter-attacks and had to content themselves
with the fight-to-the-death in their prepared positions which
has been so characteristic of their campaigns in smaller spaces.
Even this could have left the situation hopelessly deadlocked,
and a daring amphibious movement was needed to break the
jam.

The Third Fleet had at last been withdrawn, after a final
and highly rewarding strike against shipping in the Manila
Bay area on November 25. Japanese air power, although
drastically cut down, was not much inferior to the slender
forces which Kenney had been able to operate from the gumbo
fields of Leyte. Most important, the Japanese still dominated
the sea approaches to Ormoc, despite their losses. Their destroyers, which they seemed willing to expend recklessly, could
be used against American troop convoys if any should venture
into the Camotes Sea between Leyte, Bohol and Cebu.

An American destroyer squadron which included the *Cooper*
was sent through Surigao Strait after dark on December 2, to
conduct a sweep against Japanese shipping and to test out
enemy naval strength in the Camotes Sea. After midnight, in

* On October 30 it was officially stated that two-thirds of Leyte had been
brought under American control; the communiqué declared that "the liberation
of . . . Leyte and Sámar virtually is completed." These statements became true
much later, as the result of bitter fighting.

Ormoc Bay, the destroyers were involved in a triple engagement, against Japanese ships (including destroyers) caught in the harbor, against shore batteries and against bombers and torpedo planes. At about 3 A.M., when at least one Japanese destroyer in the harbor had been hit several times and was "helpless and burning," the American ships had been fighting off enemy air attacks for an hour. Suddenly the *Cooper* was hit amidships: some of her men thought she had struck a mine, others reported having sighted an exceptionally large aerial torpedo. Whatever the cause, the new 2,200-ton destroyer's back was broken, and she sank in 55 seconds. It is probable that more than 300 men survived the explosion, and they were thrown into the water within three miles of the coast. During the afternoon, four Catalina flying boats executed "Dumbo" (rescue) missions and picked up 140 officers and men—one of the planes carrying the incredible load of 56 survivors besides its crew of seven.

Four nights after the destroyer sweep, another American naval force threaded its way through Surigao Strait and into Camotes Sea. But this was vastly different: it numbered about 80 ships, including several destroyer transports on which assault troops drawn from the 77th Division had been embarked. The entire force was under the command of Rear Admiral Arthur D. Struble. Its passage was uncontested. Shortly after 7 A.M. the destroyers covering the American landing force began their bombardment runs off a stretch of beach three miles south of the town of Ormoc. Not a shot was fired in answer, although the barrage lasted 20 minutes and was topped off by a still more intensive five-minute attack by rocket-firing LCIs. The troops went ashore in Higgins boats from the APDs and waded onto the beach without a casualty; indeed, they were well inland before the enemy reacted.

Struble had planned to unload the men in the shortest time possible. Actually, about half the soldiers were put ashore within the first hour, and then the Japanese planes arrived, proving the wisdom of the fast schedule which had been adopted. Fortunately, the *Ward* was one of the APDs which had completed unloading when five Japanese dive-bombers attacked a few minutes after 8 A.M. The first plane missed, but the second struck the 26-year-old converted destroyer amidships. One of her two funnels was demolished and a large fire broke out. Within 20 minutes, Lieutenant Richard F. Farwell, her commanding officer, had to give the order to abandon ship. A minesweeper stood by to pick up the crew, none of whom was lost.

Meanwhile, another bomber had struck the forecastle of the destroyer *Mahan,* which was to the north of the invasion fleet, on picket duty. Fire began to spread aft, toward the magazines for the forward 5-inch gun mounts, and it was not long before Commander Ernest G. Campbell had to give the order, "Abandon ship." There were only nine fatal casualties. Both the *Ward* and *Mahan* had to be sunk by gunfire from an American destroyer. The process of unloading the rest of the assault force and their heavy equipment was completed in the face of persistent Japanese air attacks—which lasted more than nine hours, until the support force was lost to the enemy in the dusk off the southern tip of Leyte.

The P-38 fighters from Leyte had been as busy as the warships. Theoretically, they should not have been flying in any numbers, for the Japanese had made an effort during the night to eliminate air opposition by dropping parachute troops around the air bases on the embattled island. This was by no means the comic event it was first represented to be: about 300 men were landed, did some damage, killed some Americans, and caused great confusion. Fortunately, they had landed at small fields around Burauen, used principally by liaison planes, and failed to interfere with the operation of American fighter squadrons. The latter were in the air all day in substantial numbers, led by Major Richard Bong, who had just taken a course in new gunnery methods in the United States and was serving as a fighting instructor. Large numbers of enemy aircraft were shot down by fighters maintaining a patrol over Struble's invasion force, but the most spectacular score of the day was made against a Japanese reinforcement group which headed into Ormoc Bay during the morning, its commander evidently unaware that berthing space in the bay had been pre-empted by scores of American ships. His six transports and seven escort craft, supposedly carrying about 4,000 troops, were all listed as sunk in attacks by American fighters and fighter-bombers.

The amphibious "end run" around southern Leyte decided the campaign for the entire island. Ormoc fell to the 77th on December 10; the next day there was a repetition of the events of the 7th, when a Japanese convoy seeking to land troops north of Ormoc was brought under American air attack, and an American convoy was brought under Japanese air attack. In this action, the destroyer *Reid* was sunk. Penned into the northwest corner of the island, the Japanese had lost all initiative, but fought until they were killed. It was December 26 when General MacArthur asserted in his communiqué that "The Leyte-Sámar campaign can now be regarded as closed except for minor mopping-up operations." It was reported that 54,338 Japanese had been "counted dead," while numbers estimated to have died in various ways, including those on transports, were said to bring the total enemy casualties to 113,221. The campaign on Leyte was turned over to the Eighth Army of Lieut. General Robert L. Eichelberger; while it consisted technically of "mopping-up operations," they were far from minor if the figure given for Japanese killed in the next six months is even approximately accurate, for it was more than 26,000.

The focus of war in the Philippines had shifted almost two weeks before MacArthur proclaimed the end of the campaign for Leyte. That island, with its monsoon rains, was useless for the extension of American air domination northwest toward Luzon; another base on the drier, western side of the archipelago was needed. The choice was Mindoro. But to get to Mindoro, an Allied invasion force would have to pass through the narrow, inner seas of the Visayas, between islands on which the enemy had half a hundred airfields. Fighter cover from Leyte could be extended only part of the distance and part of the time. The Third Fleet's planes might operate over Luzon, which alone had about 50 airfields, but there was no conceivable way of eliminating Japanese air power entirely—particularly the *Kamikaze* attacks which were becoming more frequent. It was clear that heavy losses among ships would have to be anticipated: if not in the first thrust, then in re-supply operations. Naval strategists, therefore, were opposed to the plan for an invasion of Mindoro at this stage.

But the Army strategists, and especially MacArthur himself,

were convinced that the cost of invasion must be paid; after that, American planes would be able to operate freely on the drier side of the islands, and the enemy's advantage would be canceled. Moreover, they thought that with adequate naval air support, and if Vice Admiral McCain's Task Force 38 was used to neutralize Luzon, even the initial cost might not be great. They won the argument, and the campaign was laid on.

As it developed, both the Army and Navy points of view had been largely justified: the opening phases were not costly, but the price had to be paid later, when supply convoys were running on a fairly regular schedule through the narrow seas. However, by this time the objective had been gained, and the cost, although heavy, was not unbearable.

McCain's carriers opened the campaign on December 14, with strikes against Luzon. The air groups were not the same as those which had taken part in previous operations. McCain had had to fight off a bitter *Kamikaze* attack on November 25, the last day of the earlier strikes, in which the carrier *Intrepid* was severely damaged. He had then made up his mind to increase the number of fighter planes borne by each carrier, so that a larger "cap" (combat air patrol) could be maintained over the force to fight off *kamikaze*. Most of the dive-bombers had been discarded in favor of additional fighter squadrons—many of them Marine Corps squadrons flying Vought-Chance F4U Corsairs. In its first application, the revised set-up of the air groups proved very successful.

The operations plan called for maintaining a "constant cap" over all known Japanese airfields on Luzon by day, and to keep up the harassment by night. On the first day, only 14 Japanese planes were found in the air to be shot down; on the second day, 133; on the third day, 88; many were destroyed or damaged on the ground, bringing the three-day total to 373 enemy aircraft put out of action. Most remarkable of all, not a single enemy plane broke through the cap to get at Task Force 38: only eight tried it, and all were shot down.

The amphibious force and its supporting elements, under the command of Rear Admiral Theodore D. Ruddock, had to leave Leyte Gulf during the afternoon of December 12. Again, the weather had been bad on Leyte, and several Japanese airfields on Mindanao and in the Visayas had escaped neutralizing

324 The Great Pacific Victory

raids. Air attacks from these sources were to be expected. During the late afternoon, the force made a sortie into the open sea on an easterly course, in the hope of throwing the Japanese off the trail, and at dusk it turned back into Surigao Strait. During the afternoon of the 13th the American force was steaming on a glassy sea under a brassy sky, with no hope of escaping detection, through the Mindanao Sea. Just when dirty weather would have been appreciated, the sun shone brilliantly.

The first attack came at 3 P.M. The targets were the jeep carriers in Rear Admiral Felix Stump's air support group, whose mission was regarded as little better than suicidal. Fortunately, the prevailing calm had been broken by light airs which had permitted the slow carriers to fly off their small complement of Corsair and Wildcat fighters: the attack was beaten off without any damage having been done to the jeeps. The assault was renewed later in the afternoon and at sunset; the damage suffered by the plodding ships has not been detailed. There was a minor attack by the first daylight of December 14, and then a lull until nightfall. The last few hours of the run through Cuyo Pass and into Mindoro Strait were made hideous by continuous, desperate assaults, carried out regardless of darkness: damage was suffered—though it was less than might have been feared or expected.

At dawn on the 15th, the invasion force was off San José, on the southwest coast of Mindoro. During the voyage, Brigadier General William C. Dunckel, commander of the Western Visayan Task Force (comprising elements of the 24th Division and the 503rd Parachute Infantry Regiment), had been wounded in the head and arm by a Japanese bomb which went through his cabin, but he insisted on directing the establishment of the beachhead, 155 air miles south of Manila. There was the usual preliminary bombardment by destroyers and rocket-firing LCIs, but it had to be interrupted because the Filipinos were trooping down to the beach carrying American flags. There were no Japanese in the area—a fact which G-2 had not been able to discover. There were some casualties among the Filipinos, but none among the Americans. The three Japanese airfields in the neighborhood could not be extended, so American and Australian aviation engineer battalions at once set to work building new and larger strips.

Although the beachhead had been won without cost, the battle was not yet over, either on the ground, on the sea or in the air. The Japanese made persistent, if scattered, air attacks on the invasion fleet even on D-day and D-plus-one, when Halsey and McCain's planes were still neutralizing Luzon. On the 17th (D-plus-two) a typhoon began to make up east of Luzon, and the Third Fleet had to pull out of Lamon Bay and abandon its close support operations. Accounts which have been passed by censorship make it clear that insufficient attention was paid to the storm warnings, and the fleet was kept on a course which made it inevitable that part of it, at least, would receive the full fury of the typhoon's center. As a result, the destroyers *Hull*, *Spence* and *Monaghan* were lost with heavy casualties, and other ships were damaged.

Relieved from harassment by Third Fleet planes, Japanese air forces on Luzon resumed operations and intensified attacks against the Mindoro beachhead and the supply ships offshore. Many LSTs were sunk. One of the few ships identified as damaged was the PT tender *Orestes*: an enemy plane already hit by anti-aircraft fire ricocheted from the sea and crashed into the anchored ship; no less than 60 men were killed or fatally wounded, and 80 others were injured. This was no isolated instance: the enemy's toll of the Mindoro supply fleet was, as the Navy had anticipated, heavy indeed.

The action on the ground was swift and satisfactory: the Japanese made no determined stand with large forces, and launched no major counter-attack. Six days after the landings, the first Allied-built air strip was in operation: as fast as planes could be brought in (and supplies sent in for them by ship), Allied air cover could be extended to Manila and beyond—as far as Lingayen Gulf. A partial blockade could be maintained in the South China Sea, constricting the Japanese lifeline to their southern conquests.

The enemy's reaction on the surface of the sea was belated and somewhat ineffectual. The Japanese waited until the old battleships and jeep carriers, and the light screening force of cruisers and destroyers under Rear Admiral Russell S. Berkey, had been withdrawn. When the beachhead had been left to defend itself with its own resources, the Japanese sent a task force to attack it. This was on December 26. The force was sighted by a Navy search Liberator piloted by Lieutenant Paul F. Stevens, Jr., and was described as consisting of a battleship, a heavy cruiser and six destroyers. (The identification of the battleship has not been confirmed.) Stevens landed his heavy plane on the new Mindoro strip, which was not considered ready for four-engined craft, bombed up and went out to attack. Army Mitchells meanwhile had taken off with bombs, and Thunderbolts accompanied them although they were not well suited for night strafing. The enemy ships were within 50 miles of the beachhead, steaming south, when they were attacked. Stevens is credited with two hits on the biggest ship, and an Army flier with two hits on the cruiser, while a destroyer is said to have been sunk. The enemy was forced to abandon his plan to bombard the beachhead.

Meanwhile, General MacArthur had issued a directive to Lieut. General Krueger, as commander of the Sixth Army, to invade Luzon. The precise point at which the landing should be made was left to Krueger. He decided that the Japanese would expect an attack in southern Luzon, within easy flying distance of the Mindoro air base. The nature of the terrain was a factor just as important as the enemy's dispositions: there was rugged ground between Batangas and Manila; the mouth of the bay was closed by Corregidor's guns; the road from Subic across the base of Bataan Peninsula could be easily blocked and enfiladed. There was only one inviting military highway to Manila, running through relatively flat ground where a modern, mechanized army would have room to maneuver, and that was from Lingayen Gulf, south through the great Central Plain.

But the mouth of Lingayen Gulf was 300 miles from Mindoro, so fighter planes would have little endurance over the target area. And to reach Lingayen, the invasion fleet would have to steam almost 300 miles through the South China Sea, which had been a Japanese lake for three years. Moreover, the Japanese themselves had landed at Lingayen in 1941; they knew the possibilities of the shoreline, and might be expected to have prepared especially strong defenses. Nevertheless, Krueger decided that Lingayen was the place to land. The advantages it offered were greater than its drawbacks.

The Japanese knew perfectly well that the next goal of the forces engaged in liberating the Philippines must be Luzon,

so the claim by the Southwest Pacific Command that strategic
surprise was achieved in landing at Lingayen is utter nonsense.
There was a certain amount of tactical surprise: the Japanese
could not know, until the fleet steamed past Manila Bay, that
Lingayen was the chosen beachhead. To keep the Japanese
ground commander, General Tomoyuki Yamashita (the con-
queror of Malaya) off balance, various feints were made toward
Batangas by minesweepers and even transports; guerrillas were
ordered to emerge from the hills as though to welcome a liberating army in the south. There is some evidence that Yamashita
altered his dispositions as a result of these moves, and had few
divisions in place to repel an assault in the north.

Meanwhile, there had been action aplenty, of a preparatory
kind, in the skies over Luzon and around the islands to the
north. The Japanese had had three months in which to rebuild
their air force on Formosa. On January 3, before dawn, Mc-
Cain's air groups flew off the carriers, and while the fighters
maintained a "constant cap" over enemy airfields, the bombers
worked over military storage areas aground and anything they
could find afloat. The weather was bad during the two-day
strike, and did more to protect the Japanese installations than
their own air force could do. Of 25 vessels sunk, half were small
craft; 51 more were listed as probably sunk or damaged. The
most remarkable feature of the operation was the unwilling-
ness of the Japanese pilots to give battle: on January 3, no less
than 204 sitting ducks were destroyed, while only 27 were shot
down; on the 4th, the figures were 82 to three. Admiral Mc-
Cain believed that the Japanese at this time were short of
skilled pilots. No Japanese aircraft got close enough to attack
the ships.

On January 6, the carrier aircraft turned their attentions to
Luzon. Again, the weather was bad, and many fields were
"socked in" so the strikes had to be extended through a second
day. The disproportion between airborne and grounded planes
remained; 207 sitting ducks, as against 18 in flight. Task Force
38 swung north while the invasion convoys were on their way
to Lingayen: on January 9, simultaneously with the landings
on Luzon, fleet planes worked over Formosa again, and some
groups went as far north as Okinawa. Fifty sizable ships were
sunk, and 60 small craft; 103 Japanese planes were caught on

the ground, and only five were caught in the air. The importance of these operations in cutting the enemy's aerial reinforcement line to Luzon cannot be over-estimated.

Promptly, the fleet reversed course and headed south, then southwest through Bashi Channel (part of Luzon Strait) into the South China Sea. The Third Fleet was making the first offensive sweep into what had been a Japanese pond since the *Prince of Wales* and *Repulse* were sunk. For a thousand miles, its passage was undetected by enemy reconnaissance planes, and on January 12 its air groups flew off to attack shipping and airfields at Saigon, Cam-Ranh and Quinhon. The Japanese were taken by surprise, and suffered heavily in ships and aircraft; on the 15th and 16th, when the element of surprise had been lost, they suffered no less heavily at Canton, Hong Kong, Hainan, Swatow and Mako (a navel base in the Pescadores Islands, in Formosa Strait).

The support given to the Lingayen landings by these last operations was somewhat indirect, although the damage to the enemy's lifeline between the Empire and the southern islands was no less great on that account. The Japanese fleet remnants did not choose to fight, so Halsey was denied an opportunity to polish off the vessels which had escaped him in October.

The Luzon Attack Force, commanded by Vice Admiral Kinkaid, was built around Seventh Fleet units, reinforced even more heavily from the Pacific Fleet than had been the case in the Leyte operation. After the minesweepers, the first element to push through Mindoro Strait and into the South China Sea was the fire support and bombardment group, under Vice Admiral Jesse B. Oldendorf, who had been promoted for his victory at Surigao. The old battleships and their surface screen were placed under an umbrella of aircraft supplied by a group of escort carriers (all of which, for this operation, had been placed under the command of Rear Admiral Calvin T. Durgin). They needed all the air cover they could get. Despite heavy and widespread attacks by Lieut. General Kenney's air forces, Japanese air bases in the Visayas and Mindanao had not been flattened. Enemy aircraft dogged the American task force from the moment of its entry into the narrow seas on January 2; late that night, they began sporadic attacks which grew in frequency and intensity during the passage to the South China

Sea, which was entered at dawn on January 5. Among the attacking planes were many *kamikaze;* others turned themselves into *kamikaze* when they had been hit by anti-aircraft fire.

At noon the bombardment force steamed past the entrance to Manila Bay; by evening it reached Lingayen Gulf, and stood offshore while the minesweepers worked. On the morning of January 6, the big guns heralded the coming of a liberating army to northern Luzon. They swept the entire shoreline of the gulf in an arc extending counter-clockwise from the port of Lingayen, through San Fabian and Damortis toward Bauang and San Fernando. When the Japanese effected their landings in 1941, they chose the last-named and more northerly beaches; evidently they expected that an American force would make the same choice, for that was where their defenses were strongest, and when the bombardment became too hot around Lingayen they withdrew troops from there and sent them by road up to San Fernando. On the second day of the barrage from the sea, an American who had married and settled near Lingayen tried to row out to the warships with information that the Japanese had withdrawn, but he was driven back by the shellfire, and the destruction of the town continued. Not all the shells were wasted, however, because seaplanes catapulted from the battleships reported the flight of the Japanese troops, and their truck convoys were brought under fire.

By January 9, the gulf had been swept of mines and the beach defenses had been pounded into uselessness. Even so, it must have seemed to the Japanese that the Americans could not land much to the south of Bauang, because the shore was flat and marshy, and lined with a patchwork of interconnected, artificial ponds for fish culture. They learned better when the 850 ships of the Luzon Attack Force arrived in the gulf. (The groups following Oldendorf's battleships also had been subjected to incessant attacks from the air, and had been the target of a midget submarine and a destroyer as they passed Manila Bay. Both the enemy craft were sunk—the submarine by ramming.)

The landing force was divided into two parts: the San Fabian Attack Force under Vice Admiral Daniel E. Barbey (recently promoted), charged with the task of putting two divisions ashore on the more northerly beachhead, and the Lingayen

Attack Force under Vice Admiral Theodore S. Wilkinson, which was to put two divisions ashore at the southernmost part of the gulf. A reinforcement group was on its way, Rear Admiral Richard L. Conolly commanding.

The 6th and 43rd Divisions, constituting the assault formations of Major General Innis P. Swift's First Corps, were landed by Barbey's northern force. The beaches were favorable for the operation, but only a fraction of the Japanese mortar and artillery positions to the north had been eliminated in the early bombardment, and Barbey's landing craft had to be unloaded under enemy fire, with consequent casualties. The beaches on which Wilkinson landed the 37th and 40th Divisions of Major General Oscar W. Griswold's Fourteenth Corps were not under enemy fire, but they were shallow, and the landing craft grounded far out on a shelf where a heavy surf was breaking.

In spite of the obstacles at the respective beaches, and in spite of incessant enemy air attacks, great numbers of men and great bodies of supplies and mechanical equipment were landed in the first hours of the invasion of Luzon. This phase of the operation was not without cost: the *New Mexico* had been hit by two *kamikaze* while approaching the area, resulting in the death of a distinguished Allied observer, Lieut. General Herbert Lumsden, an able war correspondent, William H. Chickering, and many of the ship's officers and men; the *California* had been hit by a damaged Zero which caused the death of 48 and injured 155 of her complement; the *Mississippi* had been hit, with 22 killed and 18 injured; the *Columbia* had been hit early in the bombardment by a Zero and a Val dive-bomber (whether they were *kamikaze* is not clear), which killed 60 and wounded 124, although she stayed in the engagement until the beachhead was secured. In support operations, the escort carrier *Ommaney Bay* was lost. Many other ships, big and little, were damaged in varying degree and, like those named, stayed in the fight while effecting emergency repairs and tending their wounded.

Another source of damage to ships, especially the slower transports and cargo craft, appeared the next morning—small power boats rigged for suicide missions. Several of them met with some success, until their hideaways were located and attacked by aircraft which destroyed the menace at its source.

There were also several cases of individual Japanese swimming out to the ships with explosives strapped to them.

Twenty-four hours after the landings, the four American divisions had pushed inland an average of four miles; a few isolated Japanese positions had to be knocked out, but generally speaking the enemy failed to contest with his ground troops either the establishment of the beachhead or its immediate expansion. The network of fish ponds, lying in boggy ground and with sponge-like dikes between them, proved to be the greatest obstacle to the inland movement of heavy equipment. Nevertheless, the two beachheads were joined and widened to about 20 miles the second day.

The First Corps' assignment was to hold and extend the left flank, while the Fourteenth Corps and other units landed in support were to push southward as rapidly as possible through the Central Plain of Luzon, on to Manila. The terrain facing the First Corps rose swiftly toward the mountain stronghold (and former summer capital) of Baguio; in the foothills the Japanese had innumerable artillery positions, and they had their guns zeroed in on the roads which the Americans must use from the greater part of the beachhead. How well the First Corps did its work—although for several weeks it gained but little ground, expressed in mileage—is shown by the fact that the San Fabian beachhead alone handled 134,000 men and 151,850 tons of supplies during the early stages of the campaign. The Lingayen beachhead, less exposed to enemy fire, handled as much or more.

There were several positions on the route to Manila where the terrain favored the defenders, and where the Japanese might have been expected to make a determined stand. But Yamashita had been caught with his guard down; most of his divisions were in motion, and could not be deployed to take up defensive positions. It was characteristic of the operation that the stiffer fighting occurred on the eastern (left) flank of the American advance, because the Japanese had intended to use the more easterly of the two highways between Manila and Lingayen as an escape route.

There was particularly bitter resistance around Pozorrubio, where the 43rd Division, now commanded by Major General Leonard F. Wing, was engaged. In an eerie night action when the Japanese infiltrated a position of the 103rd Infantry, Captain Pincus Pesso (who had led the first patrol to Munda 18 months earlier) again distinguished himself. Farther to the southeast, the 25th ("Tropic Lightning") Division had a house to house, cellar to cellar fight in San Manuel, where the Japanese were using dug-in tanks as artillery.

But such occasions as this were the exception. Fresh troops were poured ashore: the 32nd and 33rd Divisions, the 158th Regimental Combat Team, the 6th Ranger Battalion (which liberated Allied prisoners by a bold strike at the Cabanatuan camp), the 112th Cavalry Regiment and the 1st Cavalry Division. They maintained the momentum of the advance so well that by January 21 it had carried 58 miles to Tarlac; three days later, the Japanese sacrificed another natural defensive position, and patrols reached Clark Field. The Japanese reacted too late: their artillery and mortars were well sited in hills southwest of the field, and kept up a harassing—but in the long run, ineffective—fire until they were rooted out with satchel charges and flamethrowers.

The race to Manila was thrown wide open by the landing of the 1st Cavalry, dismounted from its horses but mounted on trucks, to compete with the fast-marching, hard-fighting infantrymen of the 37th ("Buckeye") Division, still, as at Munda, under its National Guard commander, Major General Robert S. Beightler. To insure against a Japanese withdrawal into Bataan, the 24th and 38th Divisions of the Eleventh Corps were landed near San Narciso, north of Subic Bay, on January 29. The amphibious operation was commanded by Rear Admiral Struble. The lesson of Mindoro and Lingayen had been learned: when it was clear that there were no Japanese defenses, the scheduled bombardment was canceled. The Eleventh Corps had been prepared for this operation by Eichelberger's Eighth Army, but passed under Krueger's Sixth Army on landing. A triple envelopment was achieved by what had been planned as a sacrifice diversion: elements of the 11th Airborne Division were landed from boats at Nasugbu, southwest of Manila, and the 511th Parachute Infantry Regiment later flew over them and dropped on Tagaytay Ridge, between Nasugbu and the capital.

On February 3 it was clear that the romp was over. The

Japanese had determined to hold that half of Manila which lies south of the Pasig River and, in default of being able to hold it, they were bent upon destroying it. Ships were sunk alongside the piers for ocean steamers, near the river mouth; the Escolta and other principal streets on the northern approaches to the river were prepared for demolition by the planting of explosive charges and gasoline drums in the large warehouses and stores with which they were lined.

The 37th Division had been held up by a short but stubborn stand made by the Japanese at Calumpit on the Pampanga River; the 1st Cavalrymen swooped around to the east and two squadrons raced into northern Manila, slicing through token resistance to enter the city at 7 P.M. on February 4—26 days after the landings at Lingayen. When the infantry arrived and tried to cross the Pasig, the Japanese set off their incendiary and explosive charges along the Escolta, and drove the Americans back. The devastated area had to be fought over; the river bridges were shattered and had to be replaced with pontoon crossings built under fire. When the river had been forced, the real battle for Manila began. General MacArthur proclaimed the city "liberated" on February 6, but this was tragically premature. For three weeks, Manila was in torment. The old walled city of the Spaniards, the Intramuros, was a natural fortress even against modern artillery fire power. The Japanese made its capture more difficult by holding Filipino civilians as hostages and using them as human shields. In large buildings such as the Manila Hotel, the Army and Navy Club and those of government departments, the fighting raged from floor to floor and room to room.

By the end of February, when Manila was cleared of the enemy, the entire southern half of the city had been destroyed, as had much of the northern half which came under Japanese counter-battery fire. But the work of clearing the bay could begin: Corregidor had been taken in a combined paratroop and amphibious operation beginning February 16, and the mouth of the bay was open. Manila became General MacArthur's headquarters for the rest of the campaign on Luzon, which produced no major engagement although it went on for months. By late July, when MacArthur declared that it had ended except for "minor mopping-up," it was estimated that as many as 450,000 Japanese had died in the campaign for the Philippines, which by now had extended to all the southern islands, including Mindanao, second largest in the archipelago.

Just as important as the liberation of the Philippines from enemy rule was the opportunity afforded the Allies to build a great base where amphibious operations could be mounted on a great scale. Luzon was intended to be to Japan what Britain had been to Normandy.

XXII. Hell's Acre

WITH THE SEIZURE of the southern Marianas in the summer of 1944, Admiral Nimitz's forces had completed the demolition of the outer defenses of Japan. From Saipan, the smaller islands of the northern Marianas could be, and were, effectively neutralized. By December, a similar situation had been brought about in the Southwest Pacific by the occupation of the strategic area around Leyte Gulf, and plans could be made on the assumption that within a few months the rest of the Philippines would be under effective American control, no matter how much mopping-up might still have to be done. For the war plans officers, who must always be months ahead of the assault troops, this meant that Japan's empire on the ocean side had been reduced to the inner fortress, in which the four main islands of the homeland were protected by three chains of defensive positions radiating to the northeast, south and southwest—respectively the Kuril Islands, the Izu-Bonin-Volcano series and the Ryukyu Islands leading to Formosa. Although some of these islands were 750 miles from Japan proper, they were part of the inner fortress because they could be reached by tactical aircraft flying from home bases, and the defense of the island chains had been integrated with the defense of the homeland.

By the last days of November, 1944, the Army Air Forces had built up bases in the southern Marianas so that B-29 Superfortresses were able to attack the Tokyo area. This operation was vastly more promising than the earlier ones from Chengtu, in western China, because all the thousands of tons of supplies, bombs, ammunition and gasoline needed by a strategic bombing force could be shipped economically to Guam, Tinian and Saipan, whereas there was only a tenuous, uneconomic and over-burdened air supply route from India to Chengtu. But even so, there were great difficulties in operating B-29s from the southern Marianas. Distance was one: 1,500 miles to Tokyo. This meant a minimum round trip of 3,000 miles, and in practise it usually was nearer 4,000, so the bomb-load was cut down to about three tons although the planes were capable of carrying ten tons. There could be no fighter cover,* so the giant bombers had to fly at great heights, consuming extra gasoline in the climb to 25,000 or 30,000 feet. At these altitudes, "precision bombing" was a mockery. Weather forecasting was impossible, because weather formations usually approach Japan from the west, and no Allied planes could reach beyond the islands. Surprise was almost impossible, because the Japanese had radar stations on the Bonin and Volcano Islands and search planes based there; one or the other would tattle to Tokyo when the big bombers passed. Finally, the B-29s were exposed to air attack, going and coming, from interceptors at these same island bases.

It was clear that neither the strategic bombing of Japan, nor an invasion of Japan, could be successful unless an opening was made in the walls of the inner fortress. An opening in the Kurils would not help the big bombers; it was too early to open the Ryukyus. There was one approcah left—through the chain of islands extending south from Tokyo Bay toward the Marianas, and the seizure of one of these islands would serve a multiple purpose. In December, the Joint Chiefs of Staff directed Admiral Nimitz to take Iwo Jima. They had only a narrow choice, because most of the islands in the chain were too small for effective bases; of two other possibilities, Hachijo was only 150 miles from Tokyo, so that the enemy defending it would have an immense advantage over attackers whose nearest base was at Saipan, 1,200 miles away, and Peel Island † in the Bonins

---

* As previously noted, it had been intended to send Task Force 38 to Japanese waters to fly fighter sweeps in coordination with the first B-29 operations against the Tokyo area, but the fleet was held in Philippine waters.

† All these islands have many names, and it is unfortunate that the Navy has perpetuated those conferred by the Japanese. The Bonins, also known as the Ogasawara Shoto and Arzobispo Islands, were uninhabited until 1823 when they were claimed by Great Britain and colonized by a group of many nationalities. The settlers used names given by early British and American navigators: Peel Island for the largest island in the central group, and Hillsborough for the largest in the southern group. These names were accepted by Commodore Perry when he surveyed the islands in 1853 and bought land at Port Lloyd, on

was almost unassailable behind steep cliffs, while its rugged, forested terrain offered room for only one airfield.

The decision to invade and capture Iwo was inescapable, but it came too late to be carried out except at terrific cost. Although the Japanese had occupied Iwo since 1891, and had begun fortifying it at least as far back as 1937, they were far from having made it an impregnable fortress at the time the southern Marianas were invaded in June, 1944. If Iwo could have been invaded promptly after the securing of Guam, it could have been taken at far less cost than was the case in 1945. It is useless, however, to criticize the Joint Chiefs of Staff for having delayed the decision: even if the decision had been taken earlier, the island could not have been taken earlier because the Pacific Fleet and all the fresh divisions of troops (both Army and Marine Corps) were earmarked for other operations —such as the western Carolines and the Philippines. The high command had to view the strategic picture as a whole, and Iwo had to wait.

The Japanese made good use of the respite. In June, 1944 —immediately after the invasion of Saipan—they sent to Iwo a highly experienced and skillful officer, Lieut. General Tadamichi Kuribayashi, as commander of the Bonin-Volcano Islands sector. Kuribayashi had a genius for thoroughness, and for getting work done. A glance at the island's topography was enough to tell him what the broad outlines of his defenses must be.

Iwo is five miles long, a fraction under three miles across at its widest point, and embraces eight square miles. For so small a flyspeck it has been compared with an extraordinary catalogue of shapes: a pear, an otter, a mutton chop, a sea monster, a

---

Peel Island, for an American coaling station—which never materialized. After the Japanese seized the Bonins in 1876, Peel was renamed Chichi Jima and Hillsborough became Haha Jima. Perry used the descriptive Sulphur Island for the largest in the Volcano group, which the Japanese settled in 1891 and called Iwo Jima, a literal translation of Sulphur Island.

Admiral Nimitz and his staff intended to revert to the English form for Iwo after it was secured, but the long and sensational battle for the island made "Iwo Jima" a household word, and it was then too late to change it. However, there is still time to change back to the original names for the islands in the Bonin group: if the Japanese are to be ejected from all the territories seized since they began their overseas expansion in 1875, their nomenclature should be ejected with them.

gourd, a leg of mutton, a miniature South America and a mis-shapen dumbbell. Militarily, these fanciful figures were un-important. What was important was that the island offered only two possible landing areas, both along the slim, south-west projection: Futatsune Beach, facing southeast, and the unnamed beach on the opposite side facing northwest. The latter was more obstructed by rocks than the former, but there were no reefs (Iwo is beyond the northern limit of coral growth), and either might be used, depending on the direction of the wind. For there was no harbor of any kind; ships must lie in the open ocean and discharge their cargoes, human and material, on a completely exposed shore.

Kuribayashi did not expose himself to surprise by trying to guess in advance which beach the Americans would try to land on. He took out full insurance by constructing defenses for both. The narrow part of the island between the beaches con-sisted of a bare, low ridge of black, volcanic ash; into its two faces the Japanese built scores of blockhouses, each protected by a group of outlying pillboxes, all interconnected by a spider-web system of trenches. For the most part, these were equipped with light, rapid-fire automatic weapons such as machine guns and 25-mm. guns.

At the southwest extremity of the island, the 556-foot cone of the dormant (but by no means extinct) volcano known as Mount Suribachi provided Kuribayashi with a superb position for observation and for siting larger guns and mortars. To the northeast, beyond the low ridge between the beaches, rose a broken tableland, of jagged, upthrust rocks and intervening gullies. Rising to a maximum of 382 feet, this area provided Kuribayashi with observation almost as good as that from Suri-bachi, and with a far greater area in which to conceal artillery and mortars. This was the region, incidentally, in which the Japanese had two airfields completed and a third under con-struction. Taken together, the two highland areas afforded near-perfect positions for enfilading an attacking force on the beaches and in the early stages of an advance along the saddle; separately, either Suribachi or the Motoyama tableland was a fortress in itself, and the latter particularly was suited for a last-ditch defense, not at one point or along a single line, but along a series of lines where mutually supporting blockhouses were cut into the rock.

The plateau area, comprising most of the area of Iwo, consists like Suribachi of consolidated ash which makes a soft, friable rock of varying shades of grey and brown. When broken down, this is remarkably fertile, and before the island was subjected to heavy bombardment, much of its area was covered with greenery—sugar cane and sisal, which supported a civilian population of 1,100, a few coconut and banana palms, banyan and *hala* trees, and abundant ground vines, grasses and wild flowers. The island's reputation as a barren rock results largely from the fact that the first recent American descriptions of it were written after a series of devastating bombardments without precedent even in World War II.

This campaign began at the time of the Saipan landings; on June 15 and 16, 1944, aircraft from carriers of the Fifth Fleet struck at Iwo and the Bonins, but these were raids designed to neutralize the airfields temporarily, during the campaign in the southern Marianas. They had to be repeated as that campaign progressed and was extended to Tinian and Guam; Iwo was bombed on June 24, bombed (and also bombarded by warships) on July 4, bombed again on three days in August and the first two days of September. After that, the carriers were busy in southern waters, and when the attack was resumed on November 11 and 12, it was by cruisers and destroyers under Rear Admiral Allan E. Smith. By December 8, when Iwo was marked for invasion, Kuribayashi had shipped the civilians back to Japan and was building fortifications in a race against time. Three times that month, and again in January, Smith's cruisers lashed at Iwo in coordinated strikes with B-29 Superfortresses and P-38 Lightning fighters. After the first week of December, the island was a daily target for B-24 Liberators of the Seventh Air Force flying from the Marianas.

The remarkable feature of this campaign of reduction was that although it undoubtedly did substantial damage, it did not reduce the island's defenses; Kuribayashi was able to repair the damage and build new fortifications faster than the attackers could tear them down. Aviators noted a persistent increase in the anti-aircraft fire from the islet; very few coast defense guns answered the warships, but this did not indicate any scarcity of these weapons—it was simply that they were being saved for the day of greatest need. Despite the efforts of Marine Corps medium bombers (fitted with radar) to maintain a blockade of Iwo, many ships carrying guns and ammunition continued to reach the island.

By the third week of February, 1945, when the invasion of Iwo was to begin, the Seventh and Twentieth Air Forces had aimed 5,800 tons of bombs at the island. The surface ships must have fired a couple of thousand tons of shells at it. But this was only a small sample of what was to come. While Admirals Spruance and Mitscher took Task Force 58 to the coast of Japan to isolate the battlefield (see Chapter XXIV), the amphibious and support forces of the Fifth Fleet began to close in on Iwo. The first to arrive, on February 16, were escort carriers and a bombardment force of six OBBs under Rear Admiral W. H. P. Blandy: the *Idaho, Tennessee, Nevada, Texas, New York* and *Arkansas*—this last the oldest American battleship remaining in combat service. The weather was bad, with low clouds hampering the efforts of spotting planes, and thus the effectiveness of the bombardment was lessened. Air strikes were canceled, and the only work which could be done satisfactorily was minesweeping. On the 17th, clear weather enabled air strikes to be carried out in force; the bombardment was better, and LCI gunboats fitted with rocket-launching racks stood in close to the beach. Other LCIs carried reconnaissance parties to the shore, to survey landing areas, and when these retired—several having been damaged—the Japanese thought that an attempted landing had been driven off.

Although the OBBs, with their attendant cruisers and destroyers, were within rifle shot of the beach on the 18th, few Japanese coastal guns fired on them and it was believed that these few were knocked out. During the night the occupation force arrived, with Vice Admiral Turner as amphibious commander, and the number of ships assembled around Iwo grew to 800. D-day, the 19th, dawned with a tremendous bombardment by every seaborne gun available, and climactic air strikes. The words which have recurred like a mocking chorus throughout the central Pacific war were again on the lips of the Marines: "It doesn't look as though there could be a Jap left alive on the island."

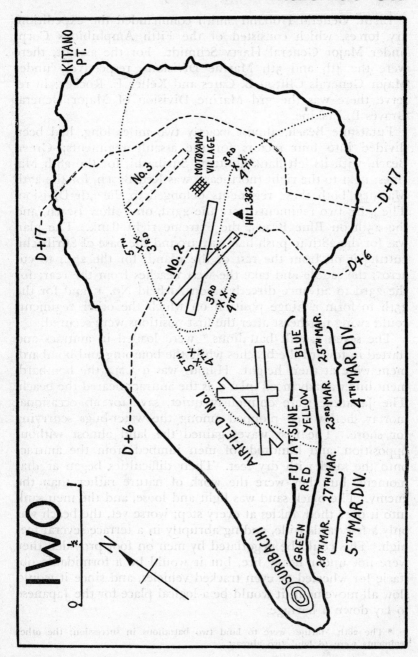

IWO

N

0   ½

KITANO PT.

No.3

MOTOYAMA VILLAGE

3RD
X X
4TH

HILL 382

5TH
X X
3RD

No.2

D+17

D+17

3RD
X X
4TH

D+6

5TH
X X
4TH

AIRFIELD No.1

D+6

BLUE
25TH MAR.

YELLOW
23RD MAR.

RED
27TH MAR.

GREEN
28TH MAR.

4TH MAR. DIV.

5TH MAR. DIV.

FUTATSUNE

SURIBACHI

Lieut. General Holland Smith commanded the expeditionary forces, which consisted of the Fifth Amphibious Corps under Major General Harry Schmidt. For the assault, there were the 4th and 5th Marine Divisions, respectively under Major Generals Clifton B. Cates and Keller E. Rockey; in reserve there was the 3rd Marine Division of Major General Graves B. Erskine.

Futatsune Beach, almost exactly two miles long, had been divided into four sectors for the assault regiments: Green Beach, with its left flank abutting Suribachi, for the 28th Marines; next to the right (northeast) was Red Beach, for the 27th Marines; both these regiments belonged to the 5th Division. The 4th's two regiments were the 23rd, on Yellow Beach, and the 25th on Blue Beach, the extreme right flank. The plan was for the 28th to push half-way around the base of Suribachi, cutting it off from the rest of the island; for the 27th to cut across the saddle and take the west beaches from the rear; for the 23rd to advance directly upon Airfield No. 1, and for the 25th to form a hinge position on which the other regiments could swing northeast after the first positions were secured.

The seven assault battalions * were loaded in amtracs and started in toward the beaches while the bombing and bombardment were at their height. H-hour was 9 A.M.; the bombardment line was advanced inland as the amtracs neared the beach. The Japanese were ominously quiet, save for an occasional mortar shell which plopped among the water-bugs scurrying for shore. The first waves gained the land almost without opposition, and hundreds of men jumped from the amtracs onto the sand with dry feet. Their difficulties began at that moment, but they were the work of nature rather than the enemy. The black sand was light and loose, and the men sank into it over their ankles at every step; worse yet, the beach was only a few yards wide, ending abruptly in a terrace several feet high. This could be negotiated by men on foot provided they were not under heavy fire, but it would be a formidable obstacle for wheeled or even tracked vehicles, and since it would slow all movement, it would be a logical place for the Japanese to lay down a barrage.

* The 28th Marines were to land two battalions in succession; the other regiments were to land two abreast.

The enemy continued to withhold his fire, except for sporadic shooting with small arms and an occasional shell, while the invading platoons formed up and crawled over the first terrace. There was a gentle slope ahead of them, and then another terrace. The landscape had been so churned by bombs and shells that it was impossible to tell whether a mound of black sand covered an enemy pillbox, and many of these positions were by-passed during the first hour. No doubt the Japanese had been stunned to some extent by the rain of explosives, but their inertia at this time was largely deliberate: it was to their advantage to let the Marines filter through, so that they could be fired on from the rear, and to wait until the beaches were choked with equipment and supplies, offering a concentrated target, before they expended ammunition on them.

At 10 A.M. the Japs opened up with everything they had. Innocent-looking mounds of sand began to spit rifle and machine-gun bullets, for most of the pillboxes concealed under them had not been touched in the preliminary bombardment. Most of the larger blockhouses had been damaged, but were far from having been demolished, and there were enough Japanese available to man them effectively. Worst of all was the mortar and howitzer fire. Every square foot of Futatsune Beach and the saddle behind it had been carefully plotted by Kuribayashi's artillerymen, and all their weapons were zeroed in on the area where the Marines, of necessity, were jammed together. Rifled guns up to 6-inch caliber fired on the landing ships bringing in heavy equipment.

Fortunately, during the last few minutes before the enemy fire became so murderous, LSMs had gone in ahead of schedule and landed tanks and armored bulldozers. Later, these comparatively large vessels were unable to reach the beach, and the lighter mechanized equipment landed from Higgins boats would have been helpless to move if it had not been for the efforts of the armored bulldozers which tore down part of the terrace and enabled jeeps, half-tracks, trucks and gun trailers to deploy on the first slopes above. This modest dispersal was not sufficient to save either men or equipment from frightful losses, but it was enough to turn the decision in the invaders' favor. Without it, Kuribayashi might have succeeded in his plan to destroy the bulk of the assailants' equipment on the beaches and then drive the assault waves back into the sea from lack of ammunition and other front-line supplies.

The weight of the Japanese fire power had not been anticipated by the American command; it moved Admiral Turner to remark: "Iwo Jima is the most heavily fortified and capably defended island in the world." Such a sweeping superlative can never be proved, but fortunately the Allies have encountered nothing to disprove it.

While the battle of supply was being fought on and near the beaches, the combat battalions were pressing inland. Resistance on the right flank facing the 4th Marine Division was much more concentrated than that on the left, facing the 5th, for the sector at the extreme northeast where the 25th Marines had landed was directly against the outposts of the plateau, across the end of which the Japanese had built their main line of fixed positions, while the 23rd Marines, only slightly to the left, faced the escarpments below Airfield No. 1. The center of the outer runway proved unassailable on D-day; however, elements of the division got across the northeastern extremity of the strip before nightfall.

The 27th Marines overran the southwestern tip of the same runway in a surge which carried 1,400 yards, clear across the island, before 4 p.m. On the far left, the 28th Marines of Colonel Harry B. Liversedge swept over the lowest part of the saddle, where the island is at its narrowest, and thus cut off Suribachi completely. Then they reorganized for a left wheel against the cone itself, and launched an attack to the south at 4:45, but were pinned down after gains of only a hundred yards, and dug in for the night.

The reserve battalions of the assault regiments had been scheduled to begin landing at 2 p.m., but by this time the hail of enemy fire on the beach and its water approaches was so heavy that many units were turned back; indeed, the weight of Japanese fire was officially reported to be increasing. Moreover, even when isolated companies were able to disembark, they found that supposedly "secure" beach areas had to be fought over again, because a high proportion of the Japanese in the outer defenses had not disclosed themselves when the first assault waves passed through. Each of these positions—most of them minute, and manned by only two or three defenders with an abundance of light weapons and grenades—had to be covered with rifle or machine-gun fire, stalked by grenadiers or men with satchel charges, and blown up. Often, point-blank fire from a tank's 75-mm. gun was ineffective, and a high percentage of the pillboxes had to be treated by flamethrowers.

Even while the reserve regiments (the 24th Marines of the 4th Division and the 26th Marines of the 5th Division) were being landed in the last hours before dark, fire was being laid down by Japanese guns whose positions were so skillfully concealed that their existence had not been suspected. "Howlin' Mad" Smith said: "Our men are spread all over hell's acre out there, and they're going after those hidden Jap guns." The high command had laid out a schedule for Iwo to be taken in five days; at the end of the first day, the schedule was as badly shot as many of the units engaged; except for one or two points, they were far from their objective lines. Casualties, which had been so much lighter than expected in the first landings, were running much heavier than expected as the day closed: many had been killed, almost as many were missing, and no less than 1,700 wounded had been evacuated. There were comparatively few simple wounds, such as a rifle or machine-gun bullet would make; the great majority were tears and gashes from fragments of mortar shells. The Japanese were using these in a great variety of calibers, from 90 mms. up to a monster of 320 mms. (12½ inches) which had never before been encountered. There was also a new 8-inch rocket.

About 40,000 men had been landed by sunset, and were crowded into an area of about one and a half square miles. During the night they were "protected" to some extent by harassing fire directed from American warships into the enemy areas, but the Japanese enjoyed the protection of their underground positions, and directed a far more harassing fire into the Futatsune area. Aid stations and ammunition dumps were hit by this haphazard but effective fire; some of the enemy shells were fitted with "proximity fuses" so that they exploded a few yards above the ground—insuring maximum spread of both fragments and blast effect. There was a picayune attempt at infiltration behind the 28th Marines, apparently by a single barge-load of Japanese, and a somewhat stronger effort to counter-attack at the end of the airfield, but both were beaten off with a heavy expenditure of ammunition.

Every visible Japanese position was subjected to intensive bombing beginning at dawn on February 20, and the gunfire barrage from warships was supplemented by the exertions of two artillery regiments ashore—the 14th Marines, attached to the 4th Division, and the 13th Marines, with the 5th Division. The four regiments in the line pushed off to launch their attacks on schedule, but progress was spotty and followed the pattern of the previous day. On the extreme right, the 25th Marines were able to gain only about 200 yards. Inland, both the 23rd Marines and the 27th on their left (the west shore of the island) won as much as 800 yards, and the whole of Airfield No. 1 was overrun. Work was begun at once to prepare it for use by American aircraft, although it remained under heavy fire. On the extreme left, the 28th Marines made gains which were less impressive in yardage than in tactical importance.

Liversedge's men, with the 2nd and 3rd Battalions in line and the 1st in reserve, found comparatively few Japanese manning the positions directly in front of them, but there was heavy and accurate fire from Suribachi, on whose summit the enemy artillery observers were looking down the attackers' throats. Moreover, the blockhouses and pillboxes protecting the base of the cone were so stoutly built that in many cases they could not be reduced by infantrymen unless aided by tanks and flamethrowers. The gain for the day was only 150 to 200 yards.

The attack was resumed under similar conditions on February 21, and again progress was negligible until tanks were brought up, although by this time all three battalions were in the line. Toward noon, the pace accelerated, and the 2nd Battalion (Lieut. Colonel Chandler W. Johnson) began to creep up the base of the cone of Suribachi, along a ledge overhanging the southeast shore. Visibility was so poor the next day that air strikes were canceled and even artillery fire could not be used in the confined arena. The 2nd Battalion sent a patrol around to the southern tip of the island, and the 3rd (Lieut. Colonel Charles E. Shepard) sent one to almost the same point by the opposite (western) route. Most of the day was spent in cleaning out by-passed positions and in attacking one especially strong concentration in a depression to the west of the cone.

One difficulty about attacking the steeper western face was that the Japanese developed the habit of rolling hand grenades down it.

The decisive day was the 23rd (D plus four). The 3rd Battalion was still busy with the Japs in the depression; the 1st had orders to attack on the west side to keep the enemy engaged there although that face could not be scaled; the 2nd was to go to the top. The achievement of this objective proved anticlimactic, because the Japanese had concentrated their manpower near the base of the cone—about 1,200 men in more than 200 blockhouses, pillboxes and covered emplacements which the regiment had already reduced, and upward of 180 caves which the engineers sealed. With these men dead or immured, Suribachi had lost its sting.

Early in the morning, a four-man patrol from Company F, led by Sergeant Sherman Watson, got well up the cone, close to the crater; this unit found prepared enemy positions, but no enemy manning them. Johnson then sent out a 40-man patrol led by 1st Lieutenant Harold G. Schrier, of Company E, equipped with a small flag. This unit had to fight its way through scattered opposition, but gained the highest point on Suribachi at 10:20 A.M.; Sergeants Ernest I. Thomas and Henry O. Hansen helped Schrier to raise the flag, secured to a piece of Japanese iron pipe. The occasion was marked by a number of Japanese who emerged from caves throwing hand grenades; Technical Sergeant Louis R. Lowery took pictures of the event, but fell and broke his camera while dodging grenades. Three hours later, another unit walked to the top of the mountain with a larger flag, which was raised with skillfully posed ceremony for the benefit of a press association photographer, whose artistry has received great acclaim.

Mopping up on Suribachi lasted several days, as always where the Japanese used underground defenses. However, the capture of the peak deprived the enemy of an invaluable observation post and presented it to the American artillerists. This achievement had cost the 28th Marines a thousand casualties in all categories, or one-third of the regiment's strength.

Meanwhile, other regiments had been as desperately engaged and had suffered similarly. Over-all casualties for the first three days were approximately 5,400, and the third day's battle on the northern front had produced only limited gains. The 23rd, in the center, was meeting even stiffer resistance than the units on the flanks, and could not be relieved by elements of its parent 4th Division, so it was decided that the 21st Marines of the 3rd Division should be landed and brigaded with the 4th. (The decision to put the 21st ashore as reserve had been taken as early as February 20, but high winds and choppy seas made a landing under fire impossible, and the regiment did not assemble on Iwo until late afternoon of February 21.)

The 21st was under the command of Colonel Hartnoll J. Withers. During the night of February 21-22 it relieved the 23rd in the center, where the American line sagged dangerously, and it pushed off at 8:30 in the morning, with the 2nd Battalion on the left and the 1st on the right. A few yards were gained, and then platoon after platoon was pinned down. No sooner was a pillbox reduced than the men were taken under fire from another at the side, or even in the rear. At the end of a day of bitter combat and heavy casualties, the best that the 21st could show was a gain of about 25 yards. Neither regiment on the flanks—the 26th Marines had relieved the 27th on the left—could advance safely as long as the center sagged. Next day, while the 24th Marines relieved the 25th on the right, the 21st jumped off with the same determination to break through, but it met the same kind of opposition and the result was the same, except that the yardage gained was somewhat more impressive (a hundred yards on the right, 50 on the left); there was still no breakthrough.

On February 24 the 3rd Battalion (Lieut. Colonel Wendell Duplantis), which had been passed through the 1st on the right sector, took up the assault. Progress was bought at murderous cost (Company I lost all its officers), but it was bought, and two companies surged across the center of Airfield No. 2, where the runways intersected, at 1 P.M., after two unsuccessful attempts in which men rushing across the bare strip were mowed down by concealed Japanese machine guns. During this phase of the assault, American tanks were more and more impeded by enemy mines. As evidence of Kuribayashi's thoroughness, it was discovered that there had been no less than 800 mutually supporting positions (blockhouses and pillboxes) on a sector only a thousand yards wide before the airfield. It was decided to commit the 3rd Division (less one regiment), and to assign it to the center of the island between the 4th and 5th. Major General Erskine landed during the afternoon of the 24th, with the 9th Marines, and took back command of the 21st Marines. The latter regiment was depleted and exhausted after its three days of exceptionally savage action, and was promptly relieved by the 9th (Colonel Howard N. Kenyon).

Although Airfield No. 2 stood on comparatively high ground, its capture did not make any material change in the conditions of the fighting, for there was still higher ground beyond it (notably two hills known as 199-O and 200-P, about 350 feet high), from which the Japanese looked down on the attackers. On one of the hills there was a battery of 120-mm. dual-purpose guns, long since put out of action by bombing; even after their weapons were made useless, the enemy gun crews remained in their underground shelters and fended off the attack with small arms. The same was true of the other knob, where a twin 25-mm. mount had been put out of action. The whole area was criss-crossed with gullies in which jumbled rocks gave perfect concealment to the entrances of countless inter-connected caves: when American artillery fired a smoke shell into a cave mouth, it was not unusual to see the smoke emerge from other outlets 50 or a hundred yards away. Some cave-and-tunnel systems are said to have extended several hundred yards. Whatever the precise dimensions, it is certain that the Japanese were living underground, where it seemed that no weight of explosive could reach more than a small fraction of them, and from their rat holes they waged an amazingly effective and deadly kind of warfare.

It took Kenyon's 9th Marines two days to secure the twin hills north of the airfield, even with the aid of extraordinary artillery preparation; then the regiment was spent and the 21st had to go into the line again, on February 28. For this day's attack, a still heavier barrage was ordered by General Erskine: a 49-minute rolling fire by all the 105- and 155-mm. pieces ashore, and 5-, 6- and 8-inch rifles of cruisers and destroyers. In the no man's land between the waiting infantrymen and the artillery bombardment line, the regiment's own heavy weapons company laid down interdictory fire with mortars and machine guns. On the left, the 1st Battalion (Lieut. Colonel Marlowe

C. Williams) made a rush of 200 yards before the Japanese recovered sufficiently to interpose a curtain of fire; on the right the 3rd Battalion (Duplantis) reached high ground at the northeast extremity of the airfield. Shortly after noon, an attempt to capitalize on these gains and score a complete breakthrough was made, but only the 3rd Battalion was able to break loose and overrun the so-called village of Motoyama (actually a collection of pillboxes) and the sulphur mine near by. At nightfall the front line was ragged; however, the day's gains had deprived the Japanese of more commanding ground and reduced their powers of observation.

The amazing feature of this stage (and of later stages) of the campaign is that the Japanese were still able to deliver a murderous volume of fire on any part of the island. Even the Marine artillery regiments, emplaced far back toward Suribachi, were never out of range until the battle ended. It was obvious, early in the campaign, that aerial reconnaissance had failed to disclose at least half of the enemy's guns; it seems likely that the proportion which escaped detection was actually much greater. Some of the guns were on tracks so that they could be advanced to a cave mouth, fire a few rounds, and then be withdrawn before counter-battery fire could be effective. A few are said to have been in caves equipped with heavy steel doors. Mortars and rocket-launchers were everywhere, and even when the Marines captured the top of a ridge, so that they could cover the entire face of the next ridge opposite, the enemy would fire resolutely from positions on the reverse slopes.

There seemed to be no end to the process. Even after the village of Motoyama had been seized, the 3rd Division was unable to advance for four days, although every attack was prefaced by a thunderous barrage. To the east, the 4th Division went through a similar series of experiences. Its main objective during this phase of the campaign was Hill 382, lying a short distance due east of Airfield No. 2. After Suribachi, it was the highest point on the island, and it proved to have been even better equipped for defense. The attack was started on February 25 by the 23rd Marines of Colonel Walter W. Wensinger; during the first few hours the 1st and 3rd Battalions made good progress, but then it developed that whole platoons were cut off because they had passed concealed caves from which the Japanese had not been rooted out. These advanced platoons had to be withdrawn under cover of smoke, after suffering heavy casualties.

It went on that way for a week; besides a formidable array of artillery, the enemy had a number of dug-in tanks which increased his fire power. American tanks and mobile guns took severe losses. In the end, the job had to be done by infantry, with as much support as possible from aircraft, warships, artillery, mechanized weapons and such ultra-modern infantry weapons as the flame-thrower and bazooka. On March 1, the 24th Marines' 2nd Battalion (Lieut. Colonel Richard Rothwell) went into the line. The nature of the fighting can be judged from the fact that within 24 hours Company G had to be relieved by Company E, and also from the latter company's officer casualties. Before 10 A.M., the company commander was wounded; shortly after 2 P.M. his executive officer who had assumed the command was wounded; within 15 minutes the ranking platoon commander who had succeeded to the command was killed and two other officers were gravely wounded. A second lieutenant took over temporarily; before the day was out he was relieved by a first lieutenant from battalion headquarters—who was wounded early the next morning. The captain who replaced him was incapacitated. Captain Robert M. O'Melia, band officer, commanded the company during the last day. When the ghastly process of attrition had run its course, the Japanese were gone from Hill 382, but Company E was gone also, and its few survivors were merged with Company F.

No offensive was scheduled for the next day (March 5); while artillery and the gunnery ships and support aircraft had a field day, the infantrymen were supposed to rest and reorganize. But the Japanese did not rest; during the first hours, Captain O'Melia was killed, and casualties all along the stalled front were found to be almost as heavy as they would have been during offensive operations. There was nothing to do but keep grinding ahead, paying with casualties for each little piece of uninviting ground, but gradually reducing the area from which the Japanese could fire the weapons with which they were so plentifully supplied. Before the jump-off on

March 6, the greatest massed artillery fire yet seen, even on Iwo, was laid down: 45,000 rounds. Yet the best that the 3rd Marine Division in the center could do was to hack out a gain of a hundred yards.

General Erskine decided to try a night attack—almost without precedent for Allied forces in the Pacific. It got off at 5 A.M. on March 7, and was not an unqualified success because of confusion as to lines of departure, and some stranded units were decimated, but it gained enough of the invaluable high ground to put the 21st Marines astride the last ridge, looking down upon the northern cliffs of the island.

Meanwhile, the 5th Division on the western sector had been ground down by forbidding casualties. The 27th Marines (Colonel Thomas A. Wornham) had beaten off the first Japanese counter-attack before dawn on February 20; the 26th Marines (Colonel Chester B. Graham) had to meet a daylight attack on February 21, in which the enemy gained 200 yards before he was stopped. The 28th Marines were gravely reduced in numbers around Suribachi before they could join the rest of the division for the advance northward. They were still further reduced as the regiment threw its weight against the western end of the enemy's ridge line: both Sergeants Thomas and Hansen, who had helped to raise the original flag on Suribachi, were killed; men who had raised the second flag were killed or wounded. The nexus of the enemy's positions in this sector was an eminence known from its height as Hill 362 (and therefore subject to confusion with two other hills of the same height and designation on the 3rd Division front). General Rockey's men captured their Hill 362 on March 1 but, as on other sectors, the taking of what had seemed to be a key point failed to unlock the portals to the northern shore.

That shore was first reached 18 days after the landing when, on March 9, a patrol from Company A of the 21st Marines scrambled down the cliffs and filled a canteen with sea water which they sent back to Generals Erskine and Schmidt—"for inspection and approval, not for consumption." In those 18 days, the Marines had traveled four miles, of the island's five-mile length. In the next seven days, the 4th Division turned east and cut the defenders into ever smaller pockets; the 3rd Division spread out along the northeast coast, and the 5th

Division wiped out the last "organized resistance" in an enemy pocket at the northern tip of the island, near Kitano Point. Officially, the end came after 26 days, but the wretched job of cleaning out the last rat holes went on for weeks, long after Iwo had begun to take shape as an advanced base and to repay the heavy cost of its capture.

And that cost was heavy indeed: offshore, the escort carrier *Bismarck Sea* (sunk on February 21 by Japanese aircraft, with approximately 300 casualties), and damage to many other ships of all sizes; in material, no less than 40,000 tons of ammunition of all types, expended against a garrison of scarcely more than 20,000 Japanese (a rate of two tons of high explosive per man); 4,630 Marines dead or missing, and 19,938 wounded. Quite properly, the high cost in human life and limb was widely questioned in the United States: had it been necessary to take Iwo, and had the islet been taken as cheaply as possible?

The military necessity for eliminating Japanese radar installations and airfields at Iwo, and the corresponding necessity for installing American radar and basing American aircraft there, have already been discussed.

As for the cost, there can be no doubt that there were the usual errors of omission and commission by commanders on the spot, and that some of these resulted in loss of life. But both the errors and avoidable casualties appear to have been few. Most of the lay critics of the campaign were reduced to hysterical outbursts, saying in effect, "This is so terrible that there must be some other and cheaper way to do it." None of them could suggest any—except poison gas. On the effectiveness of that outlawed weapon, even the exponents of chemical warfare were divided when its application to Iwo was discussed. There is no doubt that a heavy gas fired into the mouths of caves would have killed the enemy within, and the caves could then have been sealed so that Allied forces need not have been exposed to the gas. But the difficulty on Iwo was to get any kind of shell into the enemy caves, even after the almost invisible entrances had been located; there would have been just as high a proportion of misses with gas shells, and all those which exploded in the open would have left dangerous pockets in which American forces could have operated only with the greatest difficulty, burdened with masks and protective clothing. There is no assurance that the use of gas would have appreciably lessened the cost of capturing Iwo.

In any case, the decision not to use gas was taken on a higher level than the military, and was based upon non-military considerations. There were two principal factors: the likelihood that the Japanese would take horrible reprisals against Allied prisoners of war and civilian populations, and the certainty that there would be a strong reaction in the United States and among the United Nations against the use of gas, on moral grounds. The argument as to whether such scruples are justified is endless; the fact that it would have broken out in virulent form, dividing the country and the Allies at a time when unity was most to be desired, is incontrovertible. The decision not to use gas was proper, having regard to the state of public opinion on the subject.

There is no question that Iwo was bombed and bombarded as heavily as it could have been, even if the number of defensive positions had been more accuratly known. Even after their number became apparent, most of them still could not be hit, because of their nature and the skill with which they had been concealed. To Americans, Kuribayashi (who died in the obscurity of an unknown cave) must always remain an evil genius, but the fact of his genius should not be overlooked. It was that genius, more than any other single factor, which filled the Marine Corps cemeteries which stretch in harrowing whiteness on the black ash of the saddle, and on the first bluff overlooking the northeast end of Futatsune Beach.

Even after the general was dead, his orders continued to be executed by survivors of the garrison who remained in undetected caves. Ten days after the island was declared secure, a major succeeded in organizing no less than 200 stragglers (with whom he must have had underground communication) and in launching a night attack which carried almost two miles through the bivouac areas of unsuspecting engineers, construction battalions, and other service forces, to the camp of the Seventh Fighter Command, where scores of pilots and ground crew men were slain in their cots. The attack was no banzai charge, sparked with Dutch courage; it was purposeful, skillful and deadly. It was of a piece with the entire battle for Iwo.

XXIII. To the Last Line

THE CAPTURE of Iwo gave assurance that the strategic bombing of Japan could be continued and greatly intensified. Indeed, with the war in Europe expected to end within a few weeks after Iwo was secured, it was certain that all the heavy bombers of the Allied air forces could be thrown against Japan as soon as the necessary bases were available, and the island empire would have to absorb aerial punishment the like of which had never been visited upon any belligerent. But there was still one prerequisite to be met: the necessary bases were not yet available, and for these a large land area within about 500 miles of Kyushu was essential. Furthermore, there was no assurance that any foreseeable weight of bombing would induce Japan to surrender without invasion. In the short history of aerial warfare, only the wretched little island of Pantelleria had ever surrendered in the face of air attack alone. In none of their continental positions had the Germans been bombed out of the war, and since the Japanese had shown a far greater tenacity in fighting, literally, to the death than the Germans ever had, it seemed most unlikely that Japan could be bombed out of the war. Certainly, Allied war planners could not afford to count upon any such fortunate chance; they must be prepared to follow up their aerial assault with an amphibious assault by infantrymen, and for this purpose it was desirable to have a staging area closer to Japan than the Marianas or the Philippines.

Okinawa, in the Ryukyu Islands (or Nansei Shoto), was perfectly adapted to supply both the bomber bases needed in the first phase of the decisive assault upon Japan, and the staging areas for ground forces needed in the second phase. The island is 70 miles long, and consists of a series of loose-jointed peninsulas so that its width varies from three to 15 miles. Its area of 485 square miles is slightly more than double that of Guam; it has sufficient level areas to permit the construction of a score or more of airfields, although the Japanese had only half a dozen. Measuring from Kadena, in the region where airfields can be built most readily, the airline distances in statute miles are: 365 miles to the southern tip of Kyushu, 460 to Nagasaki and 950 to Tokyo. The former were well within the range of older four-engined bombers, such as B-24 Liberators, carrying a reasonably full load; Tokyo would have been within handy range for B-29 Superfortresses and the new planes in that classification, such as B-32s.

Allied intelligence regarding Okinawa, its defenses and its garrison was pitifully inadequate and largely inaccurate. The 435,000 civilians were pictured as little better than animals; the island was supposed to be overrun with venomous snakes; the defenses were believed to have been designed to protect the eastern and southern beaches; the garrison was estimated at anything from 50,000 to 75,000. Even the number of airfields was not precisely known. To a great extent, these deficiencies were inevitable in war against a police state which had kept its colonies closed to foreigners, and especially in a campaign directed at an island where there was no pro-Allied native population. Nevertheless, some of the extremes of misinformation are hard to understand.

To isolate the battlefield, every available aircraft was to be used, from four autonomous commands: the carrier planes from Task Force 58, the Twentieth Air Force Superforts flying from the Marianas,* the Fifth Air Force flying from Luzon, and the Fourteenth Air Force of Major General Claire L. Chennault, flying from the woefully small number of fields left to it after the Japanese offensive in China in late 1944. The Seventh Fighter Command, based on Iwo, would not be ready to execute fighter sweeps against Honshu until the middle of April at the earliest, and even then it would be of questionable value in cutting down the number of Japanese planes available for the defense of the southern approaches. For all practical purposes, therefore, the Fifth Fleet's carrier groups, numbering perhaps 1,200 planes in all, were taking on the entire Japanese tactical air force. They had fulfilled a similar mission in the Philip-

---

* Operations from Chengtu in China were suspended at this time, being uneconomic.

pines, but there the Japanese had not used more than a fraction of the air forces they could be expected to commit in defense of their home islands. It was an assignment without precedent for a sea-going air force.

Task Force 58 lacked one large carrier, the *Randolph*, which had been hit in the stern during a sneak attack by isolated Japanese raiders on the fleet anchorage at Ulithi atoll. Nevertheless, when the fleet sortied two days later, on March 13, it contained nine large carriers (the *Enterprise* and eight of the *Essex* class) and almost as many of the *Independence* class. One task group (58.4, commanded by Rear Admiral Arthur W. Radford) was particularly strong in gunnery ships; surrounding the *Yorktown* (flag), *Intrepid*, *Independence* and *Langley* were three of the most powerful class of battleships in the world, the *New Jersey*, *Wisconsin* and *Missouri*, each carrying 150 anti-aircraft guns of assorted calibers, and the two new battle cruisers *Alaska* and *Guam*, virtually as powerful in every way as the most modern battleships, except that their main batteries consisted of only 12-inch guns. Before the campaign ended, the ships of the fleet would need every anti-aircraft gun they could fire—and more.

Dirty weather off the Ryukyus caused Admiral Spruance, flying his flag in the *Indianapolis*, to reverse his original plans and to strike the Japanese home islands first (beginning March 18) and then to work his way south to the Okinawa group, where operations were begun on March 23. Three days later, a new element was added to Pacific warfare: operating in Far Eastern waters for the first time since December 10, 1941, British capital ships joined in the campaign by striking at the Sakishima Islands, a subdivision of the Ryukyu chain, lying between Okinawa and Formosa. Task Force 57, as the British formation was known (it was equivalent in strength to an American task group, and operated as part of Spruance's fleet), contained the battleship *King George V* and four 23,000-ton carriers, the *Indefatigable*, *Indomitable*, *Victorious* and the aptly-named *Illustrious*.

With all the pieces in position for the play which was to check the Emperor, Spruance's amphibious force commander, Vice Admiral Richmond Kelly Turner, began by taking pawns—the islets of the Kerama group, west of the southern part of Okinawa. The American war planners had taken it for granted that the Japanese would put up a determined defense either at the beaches of Okinawa or just beyond, to keep their airfields as long as possible. Both the Marianas and Luzon were too far away to permit intensive patrolling of Okinawa and surrounding waters from their airfields, so it was decided to take some of the Kerama Islands first and use them as bases for seaplanes which could carry out reconnaissance at long range over the East China Sea and as far as the Straits of Korea.

Since the enemy's strength in the Keramas was unknown, an entire division was assigned to their capture: the 77th ("Statue of Liberty"), commanded by Major General Andrew D. Bruce. On the morning of March 26, the 3rd Battalion of the 305th Infantry landed on Aka; in quick succession, units of the 306th and 307th Infantry established beachheads on four islets, and the next day three more were added. Besides Aka, they were: Keruma, Zamami, Tokashiki, Hakaji, Yakabi, Amuro and Kuba. There proved to have been no more than about 800 Japanese Army personnel (including Korean service troops) on the islands, and resistance was negligible. Admiral Nimitz must have been misled when he announced that the group had been "captured": while this was true in a strategic sense, there were some islands on which the Japanese commander withdrew his small forces to the hills to await an attack. In most cases the American forces needed only the waterfront areas, so they left these unpicked fruits of conquest to wither on the vine, where they stayed until a higher authority decided that further resistance was useless.

It was in the Keramas that American forces first realized how false was the impression they had been given of the people they would encounter in the Ryukyus. The natives, while small of stature, were more akin to the Chinese than the Japanese; their homesteads, while small, were carefully built, roofed with tile and surrounded by stone walls. Their greatest failing was no fault of theirs: they had been saturated with Japanese propaganda about the atrocious treatment they could expect from the "foreign barbarians," and about 200 of them committed suicide (150 on Tokashiki alone) by crude means, many of them killing their children before taking their own lives.

The invasion of the Keramas, although it proved later to have been unnecessary for its original purpose, since airfields on Okinawa itself were captured immediately, paid an unexpected dividend. Secreted in caves around several of the islets were small motor-equipped boats, loaded with explosives to be detonated on impact. The suicidally-inclined Japanese, despite the failure of such weapons at Lingayen Gulf, had decided to use these craft on a far larger scale at Okinawa. They were given little opportunity to do so, for the majority of the boats were among the 300 seized in the Kerama caves.

With the flanking islands secure for all practical purposes, Rear Admiral W. H. P. Blandy turned his force of fire support ships (in which the OBBs were under the command of Rear Admiral Morton L. Deyo) against the main target, Okinawa itself. Its eastern coast already had been hammered by Task Force 54, the fast battleships culled from the carrier groups in which they had been serving. Now, with minesweepers clearing 2,500 square miles of the East China Sea, the slower but almost equally powerful bombardment ships worked over the western coast, all the way from Cape Zampa to the southern end of the island. The Japanese could get no inkling as to where the landings would be attempted, because the preliminary bombardment ranged along all the stretches of coastline where an invasion might be feasible or profitable.

Although the United Nations had conducted two invasions (in Sicily and Normandy) on a larger scale, the organization of the assault upon Okinawa was the most difficult and complex in history, because of the unprecedented distances involved. Problems of supply do not increase in direct proportion to the distances to be covered; instead, they are multiplied severalfold every time the distance is doubled. They do increase in direct proportion to the forces committed, and for Okinawa the invasion force was almost twice as large as any previously used in the Pacific.

The ground forces were organized into the new Tenth Army, commanded by Lieut. General Simon Bolivar Buckner, who would assume command ashore when he was able to maintain himself there, but would remain under the strategic direction of Admiral Spruance. One component of the Tenth Army consisted entirely of Marines: the Third Marine Amphibious Corps of Major General Roy S. Geiger, comprising the 1st, 2nd and 6th Marine Divisions, of which the 2nd was in army reserve. The other component was the Twenty-Fourth (Army) Corps of

Major General John R. Hodge, returned to the Pacific Ocean Areas after having been lent to General MacArthur for the invasion of Leyte, and comprising the 7th, 27th, 77th and 96th Divisions. The 81st Division, which had taken Angaur and occupied Ulithi, was in area reserve but not embarked. No less than 1,400 United States ships were in the Okinawa area on D-day (actually known as L-day or "Love-day" to avoid confusion with D-day at Iwo, since planning for the two operations was simultaneous). This was April 1.

The beaches selected for the landings were on the west shore, beginning about three miles south of Cape Zampa. On the extreme left, Red Beach, the 22nd Marines of Major General Lemuel Shepherd's 6th Division were to land, with the 4th Marines to their right on Green Beach. Directly ahead of this division was Yontan airfield, with three runways, which the Japanese were expected to defend vigorously. The next sector to the right (south) was assigned to the 1st Division of Major General Pedro A. del Valle; on this front was the village of Sobe. Beginning at the Bisha River, and extending southward from there, was the sector of the Twenty-Fourth Corps, with the smaller Kadena airfield on the front of the 7th Division (Major General A. V. Arnold), and a threatening series of limestone buttes to the right, facing the 96th Division (Major General James L. Bradley).

Okinawa by this time had been intensively bombed and bombarded for nine days; everything above ground which looked as though it might contain a military installation had been a target, even including the horseshoe-shaped tombs which could have been converted into excellent blockhouses. The Japanese commander made a quick redisposition of his forces. There is no adequate explanation of what he hoped to achieve by withdrawing thousands of men from the south-central plain into the main Naha-Shuri-Nakagusuku line; the suggestion that he expected a landing in the south explains nothing, because most of the positions in the line faced north. Whatever his reasoning, the enemy commander decided to abandon the northern two-thirds of the island, except for a token resistance by about 3,500 men; to abandon the south-central section entirely, and to concentrate 97 per cent of his strength in the southernmost large peninsula. It was no snap decision, taken on the last day before

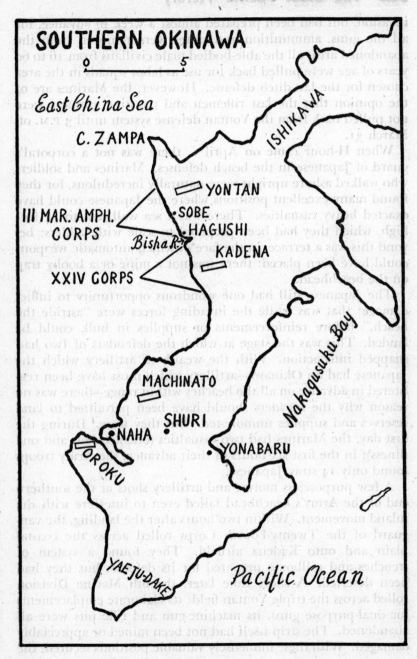

SOUTHERN OKINAWA

0   5

East China Sea

C. ZAMPA

ISHIKAWA

YONTAN

SOBE

HAGUSHI

Bisha R.

KADENA

III MAR. AMPH.
CORPS

XXIV CORPS

Nakagusuku Bay

MACHINATO

SHURI

NAHA

YONABARU

OROKU

YAEJU-DAKE

Pacific Ocean

invasion, but had been prepared almost a week in advance, for all the guns, ammunition and stores were removed from the abandoned area; all the able-bodied male civilians from 16 to 60 years of age were pulled back for use as labor squads in the area chosen for the last-ditch defense. However, the Marines are of the opinion that the last riflemen and machine gunners were not pulled back from the Yontan defense system until 3 P.M. on March 31.

When H-hour came on April 1, there was not a corporal's guard of Japanese in the beach defenses. Marines and soldiers who walked ashore upright were naturally incredulous, for they found many excellent positions where the Japanese could have exacted heavy casualties. There was a sea wall, ten to 15 feet high, which they had been prepared to scale with ladders; beyond this was a terrace, in the face of which automatic weapons could have been placed; there was not a mine or a booby trap on the beachhead.

The Japanese still had one wondrous opportunity to inflict damage: that was while the invading forces were "astride the beach," before reinforcements or supplies in bulk could be landed. This was the stage at which the defenders of Iwo had snapped into action. With the wealth of artillery which the Japanese had on Okinawa—artillery which must have been registered in advance on all the beaches within range—there was no reason why the invaders should have been permitted to land reserves and supplies unmolested. But they were. During the first day, the Marines had two casualties (one accident and one illness); in the first six hours of their advance, the Army troops found only 14 stray Japanese.

A few purposeless mortar and artillery shots at the southern end of the Army's beachhead failed even to interfere with the inland movement. Within two hours after the landing, the vanguard of the Twenty-Fourth Corps rolled across the coastal plain and onto Kadena airfield. They found a system of trenches and pillboxes prepared for its defense, but they had been deserted. A short time later, the 6th Marine Division rolled across the triple Yontan field: its elaborate emplacements for dual-purpose guns, its machine-gun and rifle pits were all abandoned. The strip itself had not been mined or appreciably damaged. With these immensely valuable positions secured, the

Tenth Army had reached, in less than three hours, the objective lines for which three days of fighting had been allowed in the plans.

On D-plus-one, the 7th Division advanced without opposition across the island to Tobara, within rifle shot of Nakagusuku Bay, and early on the morning of the third day, the eastern beaches were gained—12 days ahead of schedule. Only on the right flank, where the 96th Division was moving directly south toward Naha, was there any opposition by enemy units larger than squads. On this sector, an entire Japanese company with artillery support made a brief but determined stand in which 160 were killed. The fact that this resistance developed on the road to Naha was more significant than the commanders in the field realized at the time.

Meanwhile, the Marines also were slicing across the island, and turning north to eradicate whatever forces the enemy might have there. At this time, intelligence was still in the dark as to the enemy's dispositions; it was known that there were probably 50,000 men in the south (which proved to be a 50 per cent under-estimate), but it was not known whether there were a thousand or 20,000 in the north. The 1st Marine Division had been assigned a narrow, cross-island sector with its southern boundary resting partly on the Bisha River; this was quickly secured without major incident—a startlingly novel experience for the veterans of Guadalcanal, Cape Gloucester and Peleliu, three of the bloodiest campaigns of the war, fought under conditions far different from those encountered in springtime on temperate Okinawa. The 2nd Marine Division was not expected to be needed, and it was in danger from Japanese air attack so long as it remained in floating reserve aboard transports which made fat targets for *kamikaze,* so it was shortly released and sent back to a safe rear area. This left General Shepherd's 6th Division to execute the major part of the Marine Corps' original assignment on Okinawa.

During the second and third days of the invasion, the only notable resistance was that encountered by the 4th Marines, from a single strongpoint of caves and bunkers east of Yontan airdrome. The fight for this position did not deter Marine Corps artillery spotting planes from beginning to use the field on D-plus-one, and it was quickly repaired to accommodate other reconnaissance units and fighters. The 4th Marines having wiped out the stubborn pocket, the two regiments gained four miles on the third day, and on April 4, with a line of departure stretching clear across the island to Ishikawa, they jumped off abreast to the north, with the 29th Marines in reserve. Progress was so rapid that part of the rear area was assigned to the 1st Marine Division for mopping up, while the 6th drove forward through difficult, rugged terrain, hampered as much by the problems of movement as by the enemy who operated only in small units, used guerrilla fashion.

On April 8 the division was abreast of Motobu Peninsula, having traversed almost half the distance to the northern end of the island. The enemy had a large hedgehog position, well equipped with artillery and mortars, on Mount Yaetake in the southwest part of Motobu; the 29th Marines were assigned to reduce it, and later the 1st and 2nd Battalions of the 4th Marines were committed, while the 3rd Battalion was held in reserve. Yaetake owed much of its importance to the fact that its guns could bring Ie Shima (Island) under fire, and there were airfields on that island which the American command intended to capture shortly and put to use. Colonel Alan Shapley, of the 4th Marines, took command of the Yaetake sector, and found his task complicated by enemy tactics not previously encountered. The Japanese commander, a Colonel Udo, had almost a thousand men at his disposal, and he skillfully organized them into mobile fire teams which made numerous local counter-attacks, supported by artillery firing according to a well-conceived and well-executed plan. The Japanese were showing less blind fanaticism and more military science than ever before. There was a rash attack of the banzai type on April 16, in which more than a hundred of the enemy were killed, and after that the difficult slopes of Yaetake were scaled. Udo managed to slip two forces of almost company strength through the Marines' lines, however, and these were not rounded up until April 23 and 28.

The 22nd Marines became greatly extended in their mop-up beyond Motobu to Cape Hedo, a distance of 25 miles, and they were reinforced by the 3rd Battalion of the 1st Marines, detached from the 1st Marine Division. The northern extremity of Okinawa was reached on April 13, and the whole northern peninsula with adjacent islets was secured before the end of the month. General Shepherd reports that 2,014 enemy dead were counted on Motobu; 226 more were killed in the two pockets formed by escaping remnants.

Except for the bitter fighting around the Yaetake hedgehog, this campaign bore no slightest resemblance to that which had developed in the south. There, heavy land fighting broke out on April 5, as outposts of the major Japanese defense zone were reached. Casualties on the whole island for the preceding four days had been only 175 killed (both Army and Marine Corps) and 798 wounded. The cross-island defenses now confronting the Army were built into the hills (honeycombed with caves), into the sides of ravines, into copses of black pine, and even into tombs. There was still some mystery as to why the Japanese had fallen back so far: they could just as well have stood on an intermediate line which the Army overran on April 3, when it was found that only one pillbox in ten was occupied, and then by only a few riflemen.

The American command remained confident, and felt that it had a right to be, since the campaign was two weeks ahead of schedule; locally based air support was becoming available, and a great weight of artillery had been landed. This, with the incomparable fire power of the fleet and the countless squadrons operating from the fast carriers and from Rear Admiral Calvin T. Durgin's escort carriers, should insure that a sufficient weight of explosive could be laid down to shatter any Japanese line, however strong it might prove to be.

Perhaps the enemy's delayed reaction had been deliberately timed to coincide with an all-out attempt to drive off the hundreds of ships whose continued presence was essential to the survival of the troops ashore. The Japanese, having passed up the chance to strike the invaders while they were landing or astride the beach, had only one more chance to thwart them: while the bridgehead was still soft, through the destruction of its supply ships, fire support ships and air support ships. In seizing upon this supposed opportunity, the enemy repeated the strategy he had tried with such disastrous results at Leyte, but the tactical weapon was different. In the absence of any navy

worth mentioning, the only weapon available was the air force.*
And by this time the strongest element in the Japanese air force
was the *Kamikaze* Corps.

In the first five days of the invasion, the enemy sent in several
air attack groups, but none contained more than about a dozen
planes, and they had indifferent success in return for 65 of their
number shot down. On April 6 the full-scale assault was
launched. Shortly after noon, hundreds of enemy aircraft took
off from fields in the northern Ryukyus and Kyushu and headed
for the beachhead and its guardian ships. The formations included modern medium bombers which were expected to drop
their loads and return to base, besides great numbers of old Zero
fighters and Val dive-bombers rigged as *kamikaze,* which were
not expected to return. Fortunately, most of the flights were
intercepted well to the northeast of Okinawa by air groups from
Task Force 58, principally from carriers under Rear Admirals
Frederick C. Sherman and J. J. Clark, and not more than about
half of the attack groups got through to the beachhead area. As
many as 245 were reported shot down by the fast carriers'
planes; slightly more than 200 were left to be dealt with in the
immediate neighborhood of the target. Fighters from Durgin's
escort carriers bagged 55 more; the massed anti-aircraft fire from
scores of ships ran up a score of 61. Not more than a hundred
—slightly above 20 per cent—of the attackers can have returned
to their bases.

Although the proportion which reached their targets was
mathematically small, it was by no means militarily insignificant. Ship after ship was hit and damaged, and some up to
destroyer size were crippled, by *kamikaze* or by regular bombers
too badly damaged to make the round trip. This was the beginning of an unprecedented ordeal for the Fifth Fleet, an ordeal
which was not to end until the island was secured. The next

---

* Much nonsense has been published to the effect that the Japanese were
going to use the battleship *Yamato* to "administer the *coup de grâce*," after the
American invasion fleet had been softened up by aircraft. It was pure coinci-
dence that the *Yamato,* damaged in the Battle of Sámar, moved out of the
Inland Sea on April 6 and headed into the East China Sea south of Kyushu.
The Japanese were removing her from an exposed eastern anchorage which had
been heavily attacked by Vice Admiral Mitscher's fliers to the relative safety of
a more westerly base. She could not use the Straits of Shimonoseki because they
had been mined by B-29s, and the *Yamato* had to take the outer sea route. She
did not reach haven (see Chapter XXIV).

day, 182 Japanese planes were counted approaching the beach-head; 55 were splashed by fleet fighters and 35 by ships' gunners. The number of successful "body-crashing" dives was small, and a naval officer rejoiced: "A few more days like this and there won't be any more Jap air force." This breezy optimism failed entirely to take account of the other side of the equation: if the attrition were to continue indefinitely at the rate of these first days, there would soon be no United States fleet in operation. It is doubtful that the Japanese expected to sink any number of large ships, but they did expect to damage many of them, and in this they succeeded all too well; they did expect to sink great numbers of escort and landing craft, and in this also they suc-ceeded. At no time in the campaign for Okinawa was there a sharply defined moment of crisis when it seemed that the sur-vival of the beachhead was in doubt (as there had been on two or three occasions at Guadalcanal, for example, and on October 25 at Leyte); rather it was a continuing crisis, with the fleet, in-cluding its hundreds of auxiliaries, paying a price without precedent.

For 14 days after April 5, there was no major change in the positions on land (that is, on the southern front), and there was no major infantry action on the central and eastern sectors. However, there was intense artillery dueling all along the front, with the Japanese employing massed fires for the first time in any campaign. Besides orthodox mortars, howitzers and rifles, they used the 320-mm. mortar which had contributed so much to the horror of Iwo, and an exceptionally large rocket. And at the western end of the line there was infantry action as fero-cious as any that had developed on Iwo. The Japanese were de-termined to hold, at virtually any cost, the insignificant village of Uchito Mari and a small ridge known as Kakazu. The for-mer changed hands several times, but it was the Kakazu position for which the enemy fought most savagely.

On this sector, the 381st Infantry of the 96th Division at first bore the brunt of the fighting, which consisted of a restrained, probing offensive by the American forces, while the Japanese threw in repeated and determined counter-attacks. On April 10 and 11 there were heavy rains which turned the roads of Oki-nawa (aptly described by an Army engineer as "an excellent system of very poor roads") into muddy tracks over which no heavy equipment could move. When the skies cleared on the 12th there were other welcome improvements in the situation: the 2nd Marine Air Wing had begun to operate fighter planes from Yontan and Kadena in direct tactical support of the ground troops; multi-engined aircraft of the Air Transport Command had started evacuation of the wounded; the 27th Division (Major General George W. Griner), originally intended only for garrison duty, had moved into the line at its western end, relieving the 96th around Kakazu, and leaving that division in the center, with the 7th remaining on the left (east).

The entire front, beginning four and a half miles north of Naha and extending to a point three and a half miles north of Yonabaru, was only 8,000 yards long—extremely short to have three divisions compressed into it. There was no room for maneuver; any attempt to turn the line involved taking one of its terminal positions, for which the Japanese were prepared to fight as bitterly as for the center. As at Iwo, every unit of every division committed, including heavy artillery, was exposed to constant, heavy fire from the Japanese, who had never before used so many guns or used them so well.

Time and again, American infantrymen stormed Kakazu ridge, only to be driven off by the intensity of the enemy's artillery and mortar fire. On April 18, a patrol of the 106th Infantry (the "Knickerbocker Regiment") entered the village of Machinato, covering the approaches to the airfield of the same name, but could not hold the ground. By this date, Tenth Army casualties had increased to 478 killed, 260 missing and 2,457 wounded.

Heroic measures were needed to break the stalemate, and they were taken on April 19. Beginning at dawn, every gun in the Tenth Army's formidable batteries and every gun of the supporting fleet which could be brought to bear on the Japanese defense line, or used in counter-battery work, opened fire. For almost an hour the drumfire crept back across the enemy positions, and then it was laid down, in a final burst of fury, on the most advanced outposts for a few minutes as the infantry moved out to the attack. The three divisions jumped off abreast, and broke away for gains of 500 to 800 yards. Most of the enemy positions still had to be reduced individually by infantrymen with rifles, automatic rifles, bazookas, grenades and satchel charges: the Japanese had not been annihilated by the barrage, but their surface installations had been pulverized (except for anti-tank defenses consisting of ditches and minefields) and the resistance they could offer from their underground cavities was limited, for this was still an outpost line, and not manned in maximum strength or defended with maximum fire power. Those were reserved for later stages of the campaign.

The most noteworthy single gain was the capture of Machinato village by the 106th Infantry: the airfield was still out of reach. Otherwise, virtually all that had been won was a strip of shattered ground which must be prepared to offer a line of departure for another attack as soon as one could be mounted. There was no breakthrough; no flank was turned. The wisest prophecy had been made by a high officer at Tenth Army headquarters as early as April 9: "It'll be a miracle if we get this finished in 60 days. . . . It may take three months."

While this inconclusive struggle raged, elements of the 77th Division landed (on April 16) on Ie Shima, two miles west of Motobu Peninsula, and five days later they secured the island with its three airfields. It was ironic that it was in this comparatively small and incidental operation that Ernie Pyle was killed, after having covered the greatest campaigns in North Africa and western Europe.

On April 20, the 7th Division increased its gains in the direction of Yonabaru to 1,400 yards, but then the entire line was stalemated again. Hill 178 and Hill 196 proved at first to be insuperable obstacles; the former was taken by the 7th Division only after an 8-inch howitzer had been moved up to within 800 yards, and had fired all day, point blank over open sights, at Japanese caves. Even then, the reverse slope had to be cleaned out by flame-throwing tanks. At the opposite end of the line, the Japanese recaptured Kakazu village and threatened to retake Machinato. The 27th Division won back Kakazu on April 24, and late that night, under cover of a 6,000-shell barrage, the Japanese commander withdrew from some of his foremost positions, thereby straightening the line into which the Americans had driven dangerous salients. On the 25th, this ground was occupied and proved to have been vacated to a depth of as much as 1,200 yards in the center where the 96th Division took part of Hill 196 the next day and pressed on toward Shuri.

In this sort of terrain, speed was impossible, and it was not until April 29 that the 27th Division's 165th Infantry under Lieut. Colonel Joseph T. Hart captured Machinato airfield, three miles from Naha. All operations had been hampered because of the unexpectedly heavy expenditure of artillery ammunition; with the destruction of 30,000 tons loaded aboard two Victory ships crashed by *kamikaze*, the expenditures could not be made good in time, and some ammunition had to be brought in by air transport—the most uneconomic operation imaginable. The 27th Division had been particularly hampered because it had gone in under strength and not especially prepared for combat of the type which developed. It took heavy casualties in performing what General Hodge called "effective and imaginative work," and was relieved on May 1 by the 1st Marine Division, brought down from the north. This was an unfortunate circumstance. The 27th had drawn especially heavy Marine Corps criticism because of its record in previous campaigns, and at this stage the mere fact of its being relieved by a Marine division was seized upon by irresponsible elements as one more "proof" that the Marines always had to be sent in to show the Army how to do the job when the going was tough. Up to this date, Army men on Okinawa had not been able to understand how the Marines could have romped through the northern part of the island so quickly; most Marines refused to believe that the southern part was any different. They soon found out.

General Buckner, in reviewing the first 30 days on the island, freely conceded that the offensive launched on April 19 had lost its momentum, but firmly declared that the campaign would be fought as planned, without undue haste, because "American lives are too precious to be sacrificed to impatience."

At the same time as he relieved the 27th Division, Buckner relieved the 96th with the 77th which had become available after finishing its campaign on the smaller flanking islands. The 7th Division stayed in the line on the eastern flank, and on May 2 it gained about a mile in a pre-dawn attack which almost isolated Yonabaru airfield. On May 3, shortly before midnight, approximately 600 Japanese in landing barges tried to reach shore behind the American lines. One group was destroyed on the beach by the 7th Division on the east coast, but elements of three other groups got ashore on the west coast on a three-mile stretch behind the 1st Marine Division, and it took time, plus some help from the "resting" 96th Division, to round them up and wipe them out. There were also heavy attacks all along the front during this night, after which about 3,000 enemy dead are said to have been counted. The unusual Japanese activity on land was evidently coordinated with intensified *kamikaze* operations, suicide-boat attacks and "Baka" bomb * sallies in the next few hours.

By this time, the Japanese strategy on Okinawa was as clear as it was ever likely to be: the ground forces were to fight a holding action while the air forces, and especially the new "special attack" weapons, were to isolate the beachhead by destroying its sea support. In this framework, it did not greatly matter to the Japanese commander, Lieut. General Mitsuru Ushijima, whether he lost a few square miles of ground: the important thing for him to do was to retain his forces relatively intact, behind strong positions, so that a counter-attack could be launched to drive the invaders back into the sea when their ships were gone. Ushijima played his part far more skillfully than the Japanese air forces. The strategy he was executing, as well as the course of events, showed that he had been right to give up the northern half of the island without losing more than a regiment; his willingness to concede the airfields on the first day must be considered an error.

Once they stood at bay in their southern fortress area, the Japanese were willing to concede absolutely nothing. On May 5, an attack in battalion strength drove 1,500 yards through the 77th Division lines before it was held; the next day, the same division had to use scaling ladders and cargo nets to win the eastern part of Hill 196, which the enemy had held even after losing the western slopes. Simultaneously, the 1st Marine Division straightened the line with gains of several hundred yards on the west flank, against stiffer opposition. In the east, the 7th Division came up against "Conical Hill."

On May 7, a short spell of heavy rains began, bogging vehicles and grounding aircraft needed for tactical support. Three days

---

* The Baka bomb first came to light on Okinawa, where a specimen was captured on D-Day. It resembled a German V-1, but was to be launched exclusively from aircraft, and was guided by a suicide pilot.

later, with no local gains to celebrate, the American forces on and around the island celebrated the victory in Europe by firing simultaneously every gun in every artillery battery ashore and every gun on every ship near by. Buckner, who evidently was under continuing pressure (from sources which have not yet been identified) to change the plan of campaign, again refused to be stampeded into ordering Verdun-type assaults on prepared positions. He knew that they could only have ended in heavier casualties, without the slightest assurance of greater gains. It must have been at this time, too, that he was considering additional landings behind the enemy lines, but rejected the proposal for reasons which were not announced until later. Far from reducing the forces which were bucking the Naha-Shuri-Yonabaru line, he brought in the 6th Marine Division to take over the extreme right flank, giving the 1st Marine Division a narrower sector slightly inland.

On May 11, the 6th drove 800 yards beyond its newly-won bridgehead over the Asa River, while the rest of the front was advanced slowly in hand-to-hand fighting. The 96th Division also reappeared in the line, replacing the 7th which had been in action continuously for 40 days. From the 7th, the 96th inherited the assignment of taking Conical Hill (485), which was proving as difficult to reduce as the fortified towns of Shuri and Naha, the other principal strongpoints in the line. The next day, while the 6th Marine Division sent a patrol led by Lieut. Dennis Chavez, Jr., to the outskirts of Naha, and the 1st Marine Division ground out a 1,200-yard gain toward Shuri, the 96th was stymied at Conical Hill and the 77th by a smooth, 130-foot knob north of Shuri, known as the Chocolate Drop. The offensive now was being pressed with nearly double the number of troops used in the late April drive, but neither superior fire power nor superior man power was quickly effective against Japanese holed up like prairie dogs. The enemy troops could stay safe in their labyrinthine positions below ground during the heaviest bombardments, air assaults and even attacks by flame-throwing tanks—only to bob up from unsuspected holes when the infantry approached.

On May 13, the 383rd Infantry (Colonel Edwin T. May) of the 96th Division got to within a few feet of the summit of Conical Hill, but the height was not taken the next day, as the

communiqué mistakenly announced, and the area around Yonabaru remained a no man's land for a week. On May 15, after
the 306th Infantry (Colonel Aubrey D. Smith) had battered
itself into exhaustion against the Chocolate Drop, the 307th
Regiment of Colonel Stephen S. Hamilton succeeded in capturing it. In the west, another small eminence known as Sugar
Loaf Hill was proving equally costly to the 6th Marine Division.
The 2nd Battalion of the 22nd Marines took the hill, but was
driven from it by weight of enemy numbers; cut from a thousand effectives to 250 in six days, the battalion had to be relieved. The fierce Japanese artillery fire around Naha was a
revelation to the Marines (there had been nothing like it in the
Pacific except at Iwo, and the Marines engaged there were from
three different divisions). One leatherneck said: "You won't
hear me criticizing the Army any more—now I know what they
were up against." Whereas the Marines had had only 95 killed
or reported missing in the first month on Okinawa, they had
lost 1,046 two weeks later; the Army's six-week total was 2,900.
There were no less than seven full-scale assaults on the Sugar
Loaf before it was secured on May 19—by the 2nd Battalion of
the 29th Marines, who had relieved the 22nd on this sector.

From repeated bitter experience, General Bruce came to the
conclusion that preparatory artillery barrages were of little use
against the Japanese in such positions: they could hide below
ground from the shellfire, which served principally to warn
them that an attack was coming. So on May 21, all three of the
77th Division's regiments attacked without artillery preparation, and all three made good gains toward Shuri.

A still more significant feature this day, however, was the capture of Conical Hill by May's 383rd Regiment. Army officers
are convinced—and impartial observers agree with them—that
this was the turning point of the entire campaign. So long as
the Japanese were emplaced on Conical Hill, they could enfilade any American forces seeking to turn the Naha-Shuri-Yonabaru line by advancing along the less rugged terrain of the east
coast. As soon as they were driven from its unimpressive but
commanding height, the 96th overran the no man's land around
Yonabaru. The taking of Conical Hill, first to fall of the three
principal strongpoints in the enemy's strongest cross-island line,
made possible the military equivalent of the end run in football,

although like everything else on Okinawa it had to be executed with maddening slowness and deliberation. The exploitation of the break was entrusted to the comparatively rested troops of the 7th Division: the 184th Infantry of Colonel Roy A. Green, with the 32nd of Colonel John M. Finn following closely, flowed down around Yonabaru.

But the weather had broken again, and the deepening mud prevented the use of tanks to convert the break into a break-through. For seven weeks, with the exception of one short period already noted, the Tenth Army had been favored by unseasonably dry weather for Okinawa; its luck ran out, so far as weather was concerned, just when dry ground was most urgently needed to permit exploitation of a suddenly more favorable tactical situation. During the first days of the new rainy spell, the whole line was alive: the 4th Marines (Colonel Alan Shapley) ended their vigil at the Asato River, where they had been held until Sugar Loaf (a feature second only to Coni-cal Hill in importance) could be taken, and started pushing into Naha proper; the 1st Marine Division began to outflank Shuri.

During the night of May 24-25, the Japanese provided a strange interlude in the muddy monotony. A number of trans-port planes carrying saboteurs tried to land at Yontan and other airfields which had been put to American use. Most of them crashed, killing all the occupants, but one was set down at Yon-tan and disgorged a score of Jap commandos bristling with ex-plosives, who destroyed seven planes and caused some casualties. Since enemy air attacks against the fleet were intensified on the 25th, the miniature airborne "invasion" must have been planned to keep American fighter planes grounded and thus give the attackers a chance to operate without interception. The stunt failed.

While American troops and vehicles were mudbound, there was unusual movement behind the Japanese lines. The prevail-ing direction was southward but the full import was not im-mediately clear. Indeed, the movement was not detected by the 1st Marine Division until May 26. About this time, del Valle's division took over a thousand yards of ground on its right (west-ern) flank from Shepherd's 6th Division, and began an encir-cling movement against Shuri from the north and west. The

5th Marines' 1st Battalion (Lieut. Colonel Charles W. Shelburne) won a foothold on Shuri Ridge but found itself threatened from the commanding position of Shuri Castle, the ancient seat of Okinawan kings, much of which was still standing despite the most intensive bombardment of its 5-foot-thick walls. Although the castle was technically in the 77th Division's zone of action, del Valle gave Shelburne permission to try to take it for his own safety. With no tank support and with no supplies or ammunition but what they could carry on their backs, the men of Company A (Captain Dusenberry) pulled themselves up through the ooze and surprised the handful of defenders remaining in the castle. What had been expected to be a costly and climactic operation proved to be the exact opposite.

Shuri Castle, which had been the headquarters of General Ushijima, had been abandoned by the command when the 383rd took Conical Hill, and a general withdrawal under cover of the dirty weather had begun—a withdrawal to the next "line" or series of strongpoints, which were to prove formidable indeed, but by no means comparable with those in the front row. Despite the mud, which succeeded in miring even specially designed vehicles such as weasels, the 1st Marine Division and the 96th (the 77th having been pinched out) met south of Shuri town on May 31. It was found that the Japanese had withdrawn every gun (except one 47-mm. anti-tank piece) from the Shuri area, and virtually all their supplies.

On June 1, although the rains had ceased, the mud was still so deep that many forward units of the American forces had to be supplied by air.

It was not known how far the Japanese had withdrawn, nor how strong were the positions in which they would make their next stand. It was indicated that they were preparing to give up the west coast peninsula of Oroku, because artillery fire from that quarter ceased. The east coast peninsula of Chinen was not strongly defended; the 184th Infantry cut across its base, and the 32nd Infantry was assigned to clean it out. But when the 4th Marines' 1st Battalion (Lieut. Colonel George Bell) made a shore-to-shore landing on Oroku on June 4 they ran into gradually stiffening opposition from small arms, machine guns and mortars. It was evident that the enemy had by no means completed the evacuation; only the artillery was gone. The next

day, the 2nd Battalion (Major Edgar F. Gurney) joined the
1st in a leapfrogging move to the tip of the peninsula and within
two days Naha airfield was captured.

Operations were slowed somewhat at this time by a renewal
of the rains. The Japanese had withdrawn a considerable distance to the last area of high ground where a major stand could
be made and they were not using artillery, so the impression
became widespread that the campaign was all over except for a
walk to the tip of the island, and that there could be no more
than 15,000 enemy troops left. The 77th Division was assigned
to the unglamorous but nonetheless dangerous task of mopping
up areas bypassed in the comparatively rapid advance of the last
few days; the 27th Division already had been busy for weeks
clearing out the northern part of the island which had been
optimistically declared "secure" after the Marines' swift drive
through it.

The 1st Marine Division cut through to the west coast south
of Oroku on June 7, barring the path of elements (principally
naval landing forces) retreating before the 4th and 29th Marines. The 22nd Marines were then moved around to form the
southern arm of the pincers, and the entire 6th Marine Division
devoted itself to the destruction of the trapped enemy. The
process involved bitter and costly fighting.

An offensive was launched along the entire front on June 10,
against the second line of major Japanese strongpoints which
ran along an escarpment variously known as Yaeju-Dake and
Yuza-Tomui. The Japanese, who were supposed to have no
more than 50 pieces of medium and heavy artillery (after the
reported loss of 350 pieces in the battle for Shuri), immediately
sprang a surprise by breaking out large numbers of guns and
laying down an unexpectedly effective barrage. Convinced that
the futility of further resistance must be evident even to a Japanese, Buckner prepared a demand for "honorable surrender,"
copies of which were dropped by parachute near Ushijima's new
command post. During the 36 hours given to the enemy commander to make up his mind, both the 7th and 96th Divisions
won toeholds on top of the escarpment, and set about enlarging
them with Alpine techniques, using ladders and ropes. On the
13th, the 7th Division was astride the ridge all along its 4,000-
yard sector, and the next day the 381st Infantry of the 96th cli-

maxed seven days of assault operations by winning Yaeju Hill itself (known to the doughboys as "the Big Apple") in an hour-long fire fight.

Although Ushijima completely ignored Buckner's surrender proposal, it was still hoped that the enemy's junior officers and enlisted men would take a more reasonable view, so on June 17 the 7th Division front fell quiet for an hour, while trucks equipped with loudspeakers, and landing craft similarly equipped stationed along the coast, wooed the Japanese with dulcet propaganda. About a dozen of the enemy were converted; then the hour was up, and the war went on.

The 6th Marine Division, having finished its mop-up on Oroku, went back into the line on the main front, and drove forward several hundred yards to within two and a half miles of the southern tip of the island. But the impetus which was needed to propel the campaign to a swift conclusion must come from fresh troops; all the divisions previously in the line had been decimated, and their survivors were incredibly weary. So a regimental combat team, virtually up to brigade strength, was built around the 8th Marines (part of the 2nd Marine Division), returned from the Marianas to the combat zone. The combat team was placed in the line between the 1st and 6th Marine Divisions, and on June 18 General Buckner visited a forward command post to observe the attack launched with the new order of battle. The persistent Japanese artillery opened up at this time, and one of the first shells struck next to the commanding general, who was mortally wounded by fragments and died within a few minutes. He was the first American general commanding a field army to be killed in action since the Civil War. Major General Geiger, previously nominated to the Senate for promotion to a lieutenant generalship, was made acting commander of the Tenth Army. The next day, Brigadier General Claudius M. Easley, assistant commander of the 96th Division, was killed in action.

At 1 P.M. on June 21, organized Japanese resistance on the island of Okinawa was officially declared to have ceased. The campaign which had been expected to last 70 days had actually consumed 82 days. It had taken the lives of 6,990 soldiers and Marines, and 29,598 had been wounded. These were by far the heaviest casualties of any Pacific campaign, and a great outcry arose, similar to that at the end of the Iwo conquest. Were these casualties necessary? Was it necessary to take Okinawa at all? Could it have been taken more quickly and more cheaply if different tactics had been employed?

It can be stated unequivocally that the conquest of Okinawa was necessary; this island, in American possession, offered such a great threat to the enemy home islands that Japan surrendered when only a fraction of its base facilities had been developed and put to use in mounting air attacks.

Broadly speaking, the casualties were unavoidable—certainly most of them were. Perhaps they could have been slightly reduced if the 2nd Marine Division had not been sent back to the Marianas at the beginning of the campaign, but had been kept available for use as soon as the divisions in the line became exhausted. All the six divisions used in the first eleven weeks were kept in the line so long that the men's efficiency was reduced by sheer weariness. However, it must be conceded that if the reserve division had been kept afloat off Okinawa for a few more days, *kamikaze* hits on two transports might well have exacted as many casualties in two minutes as were incurred in two weeks of ground fighting. The cost of the campaign might also have been somewhat reduced if supply vehicles and tanks had been able to operate more successfully in the mud. But this was nothing peculiar to Okinawa: the problem existed on every American battlefield from North Africa to Naha, and was never solved, although many experts insist that it could have been solved simply by using wider treads on tracked vehicles. This was a matter to be determined by chairborne warriors in the Pentagon Building; nothing could be done about it by commanders in the field. The same is true of the contention that heavier tanks with a heavier gun than the 75-mm. mounted in the Sherman M-4 should have been used.

There is no question that the ground forces received the maximum possible support from the fleet and from fleet air forces. There is no question of inadequate pre-invasion bombardment, as there was at Tarawa. There is no question of insufficient fire power in any department. The fleet's fire support ships expended about 35,000 tons of ammunition (of 5-inch caliber and larger) against Okinawa. Admiral Durgin's escort carriers alone flew more than 35,000 sorties. As many were flown by aircraft of the Tenth Army's Tactical Air Force, built around three Marine Corps air groups which went into action soon after airfields were captured and were later joined by Army Air Force units. Army and Marine Corps artillery ashore fired no less than 66,000 tons of ammunition. When ammunition ran short, it was flown in. There can be no criticism on this score.

The most heated controversy raged about the tactics employed. In a rare moment of liberality, the fleet censorship at Guam (usually niggling, bumbling and unintelligent) passed on May 28 a dispatch to the New York *Herald Tribune* in which Homer Bigart reported from Okinawa: "Our tactics were ultra-conservative. Instead of an end run, we persisted in frontal attacks. It was hey-diddle-diddle straight down the middle. Our intention to commit the entire force in a general assault was apparently so obvious that the Japanese quickly disposed their troops in such a way as most effectively to block our advance." Mr. Bigart was of the opinion that "a landing on southern Okinawa [by the Third Marine Amphibious Corps] would have hastened the encirclement of Shuri." Mr. Bigart, having followed the campaign in the field for two months, was entitled to his opinion, and because of his record as a highly capable and conscientious correspondent, with experience in both major war theaters, his opinion was entitled to respect.

Unfortunately, it was seized upon by persons with less knowledge of the facts and with less restraint. The Washington columnist David Lawrence wrote on June 4: "Why is the truth about the military fiasco at Okinawa being hushed up? Why has no one in the high command of the United States disclosed the mistakes that appear to have made the Okinawa affair a worse example of military incompetence than Pearl Harbor? . . . The figures of casualties . . . show that Okinawa, while a victory in the sense that we have obtained our objective, is the worst setback we have suffered in the Pacific."

Mr. Bigart replied: "This correspondent still believes that a landing on the south coast of Okinawa would have been a better employment of the Marines. But to call the campaign a 'fiasco' is absurd. This writer covered the Italian campaign during the Anzio and Cassino actions, and he knows what a fiasco is."

Admiral Nimitz was more emphatic: "The author [Mr. Lawrence] has been badly misinformed, so badly as to give the impression that he has been made use of for purposes which are not in the best interests of the United States. . . . When the Marines had completed their task in the northern end of the island, my own staff, as well as those of other commanders concerned, restudied thoroughly the various possibilities for new landings to take the Japanese defenses in reverse, as well as other tactical plans. Being fully aware that delays ashore would increase the losses afloat, I flew with my staff to Okinawa for two days and conferred with General Buckner and other commanders present with respect to the strategic and tactical situation. His military and tactical decisions were his own, but they had my concurrence and that of the senior naval commanders concerned. New landings would have had to be made over unsatisfactory beaches against an alerted enemy defense. They would have involved heavy casualties and would have created unacceptable supply problems."

Since the debate involves an hypothesis, that an action which was not undertaken might have been more effective and cheaper than one which was undertaken, the issue can never be determined with finality. But if Nimitz, Spruance and Turner were in agreement with Buckner, it would seem that Bigart was not only outranked but outvoted. The only high officers who, by their silence, may be considered as having disagreed with the line-bucking tactics are the Marine Corps generals. Even their dissent, however, would be by no means conclusive: the magnificent results achieved by the Marine Corps since its enlargement in World War II have been the result of special training in assault tactics. The purpose of the Corps has been to furnish a force which could assault the most difficult positions and take its objectives quickly. That purpose has been brilliantly fulfilled. But no Marine Corps general has ever been trained to plan campaigns which were expected to last more than two or three weeks. It is quite likely that the southern beaches of Okinawa could have been stormed, and that a whole division could have been landed to take the enemy positions "in reverse." But it is equally likely that the cost of supplying even this one division across those beaches would have been prohibitive, and it is the opinion of high staff officers engaged in the Okinawa campaign that it would have been utterly impossible to supply more than one division. And there is every reason to believe that one division would not have been enough.

It is true that the Okinawa campaign was costly indeed for the ground forces; it was also much more costly for the naval forces than any previous operation with the possible exception of Guadalcanal (with which accurate comparisons are impossible, because the losses were in different classes of ships, and personnel losses for the Solomons have not been assembled on the same basis). No fewer than 35 ships up to and including destroyer size were sunk; no fewer than 299 were damaged. Personnel casualties suffered by the Fifth Fleet, beginning with the March 18 strike against Tokyo and ending June 20, were 4,907 killed and missing, and 4,824 wounded. With the Army and Marine Corps, these figures brought the total casualties in the central Ryukyu campaign to 46,319 killed, wounded and missing.

In no other amphibious operation have naval casualties been included with those of the ground forces in assessing the cost. Prior to this time, the Navy had not compiled casualties by campaigns, so the only figures available for the Gilberts, Marshalls, Marianas and Iwo are those for the ground forces. Even with this weighting of the scales against it, the Okinawa operation still stands, despite all the nonsense to the contrary that has been written about it, as one of the most economical campaigns of the Pacific war *when the damage inflicted upon the enemy is taken into account*. That is the factor which has been consistently ignored. No comparison with General MacArthur's campaigns in the Southwest Pacific is possible, not only because conditions on large islands were different, but because casualties for those operations have not been properly reported.

On Okinawa, the Japanese lost 117,000 men killed or captured; as against the Americans' 46,319 casualties (including wounded), that is a ratio of 5 to 2. On Iwo, the ratio was 5 to 4. On Saipan it was 2 to 1. At Palau it was 2 to 1. At Tarawa it was 5 to 3. Only in the Marshalls and at Guam the figures were more favorable to the invaders than on Okinawa.

While the cost of capturing Okinawa was high, it was not disproportionate to the strength of the enemy engaged, which proved to have been underestimated. And it certainly was not disproportionate to the magnitude of the strategic victory won by the soldiers and marines who fought from the Hagushi beaches, through the Naha-Shuri-Yonabaru line, to the last line of ridges and cliffs where Ushijima committed hara-kiri. As Admiral Nimitz expressed it:

"Establishment of our forces on Okinawa has practically cut off all Japanese positions to the southward as far as sea communications are concerned. It has made the Japanese situation in China, Burma and the Dutch East Indies untenable and has forced withdrawals which are now being exploited by our forces in China. It has established our forces in the inner approaches of Japan with results that will become more clear in days to come."

The Japanese fully understood the depths of the defeat they had suffered at Okinawa, even if some Americans did not.

XXIV. The Great Surrender

THE TECHNICAL KNOCK-OUT of Japan was achieved by an intricate pattern of attack involving many and diverse elements. There was no "victory through air power," although air power delivered the heaviest blows to the area around the enemy's heart. There was no victory through sea power, although it was the new sea power, incorporating a sea-going air force, which made it possible to advance the bases of the strategic bombers ever closer to Japan. There was no victory by land power, despite the infantrymen's vital role in pushing the line of bases forward, for when the cease-fire was sounded, Japan's main armies were still undefeated and, indeed, had not even been engaged. There was no victory by nuclear physics, striking the winning blow with the atomic bomb. Instead, all of these were essential elements in the complex of forces which brought eventual victory.

In July and early August, 1945, there were no outposts left to guard the "sacred soil." The full impact of Allied sea power was felt directly by Japan's home islands; the full weight of Allied air power was far from being brought to bear, and Allied armies were not yet ready to set foot on Japan proper. But the war lords who had not hesitated to plunge their country into total war decided to save it from total defeat. So long as its armies had not been beaten in battle on their own ground, there was always the chance of invoking some sophistry to revive the myth of invincibility, in much the same way as the Germans had rationalized their defeat in 1918. And no doubt the Japanese hoped to gain the same ends.

Of all the Allied blows, those which did most damage to the Japanese military body were those struck by the B-29 Superfortresses of the Twentieth Air Force. These operations had been started in midsummer of 1944 by the 20th Bomber Command, using laboriously hand-built bases around Chengtu in western China. Despite all the high hopes for the much-publicized plane, it proved to have many defects, and the problem of supply proved insoluble, although operations (against such targets as the Yawata steel mills in western Kyushu and industrial plants in Manchuria) were continued until early 1945, in the face of heart-breaking difficulties.

The first Superfort base in the Marianas was ready for operations in November, and on the 24th of that month the 21st Bomber Command sent the 73rd Bombardment Wing of Brigadier General Emmett O'Donnell against Tokyo. The conditions were vastly different from those in China, thanks to the ease with which the Marianas could be supplied by sea, but in the first few months the operations were still experimental, and far from satisfactory to the apostles of strategic bombing who were directing them. The planes had to fly a circuitous route to get around the enemy's radar interception and fighter interception bases at Iwo and at Peel Island in the Bonins. Over Japan, they could have no fighter cover, and had to fly at great heights (although by no means as high as was popularly supposed) to gain some degree of protection from Japanese anti-aircraft and fighter planes. Actually, they gained but little, because the Japanese reached higher than expected with both forms of defense. At an altitude of 25,000 feet or more, "precision bombing" is a mockery. Bomb loads had to be small, because the formations were operating at almost their maximum range. The explosive "pay load" was still further reduced because the planes flew most of the distance in formation, a procedure which affords some mutual protection but greatly increases gasoline consumption.

About the time Iwo was invaded in February, the 313th Wing under Brigadier General John Davies began operating from Tinian; by the time Iwo was secured, in March, the 314th Wing commanded by Brigadier General Thomas Power was flying from North Field on Guam. This meant that there were about 500 B-29s in the southern Marianas, and the value of Iwo as a way station for damaged planes was quickly demonstrated. Before the war ended, a thousand or more of the big planes made emergency stops at Iwo: it is impossible to say what proportion of their 11,000 crew members would have perished if

Iwo had not been captured, but it is quite likely that the saving of airmen's lives was about as great as the loss of Marines' lives in the conquest of the islet. If the war had continued, the saving of aviators' lives would have been correspondingly increased. In April, operations from Chengtu having been abandoned, the 58th Wing under Brigadier General Roger Ramey flew from China to be based at Tinian, and a few weeks later the 315th Wing (Brigadier General Frank Armstrong) was set up at Northwest Field on Guam. It became possible for Major General Curtis E. LeMay, commanding the Twentieth Air Force (and later directing its operations as chief of staff for the strategic air forces of the Pacific), to send up to 800 of the world's largest bombers against Japan. At the same time, the Seventh Fighter Command (Brigadier General Ernest M. Moore), with 350 Mustangs based at Iwo, was put under operational control of the B-29 command, so that missions could be better coordinated.

However, the first tactical planes to reach the enemy's homeland were from the Fifth Fleet's air groups, which sent fighter sweeps and then bombing strikes against air force installations in the Tokyo area on February 16. These missions were really in strategic support of the impending invasion of Iwo, but they were also designed to have a broader strategic purpose since aircraft manufacturing plants were included among the targets, and, in Admiral King's words, "to bring to the Japanese home front a disrupting awareness of the progress of the war." Admiral Nimitz emphasized a more emotional aspect: "This operation has long been planned and the opportunity to accomplish it fulfills the deeply cherished desire of every officer and man in the Pacific Fleet." Since the fleet (operating as Task Force 58 under Vice Admiral Mitscher's tactical command) was able to approach the coast of Japan under cover of dirty weather, it obtained tactical surprise; the Japanese were slow and ineffective in launching counter-attacks against the fleet, and no ships were damaged. While 49 planes were lost, the score was enormously favorable: 322 enemy planes destroyed in the air, and 177 sitting ducks; an escort carrier, a destroyer, two escort ships and several cargo craft were sunk. After giving direct support to the amphibious forces during the landings on Iwo, the Fifth Fleet returned to the attack on the Tokyo region on February 25.

The weather was worse, and the bag of enemy planes was only one-third as great as in the previous week. This time, also, the Japanese succeeded in damaging two destroyers as the fleet steamed away after its planes had worked over Hachijo, an island in the Izu group, 150 miles south of Tokyo. Part of Task Force 58 then concentrated on the Ryukyu Islands.

The February 25 strike had been coordinated with an assault by more than 200 B-29s of the 73rd and 313th Wings—by far the largest force yet used by the 21st Bomber Command—which went over Tokyo while the fleet planes maintained a cap over interceptor bases. From high altitude, and using demolition bombs rather than incendiaries, the Superforts had to bomb by radar through a solid overcast, but succeeded in burning out one square mile of the metropolitan area.

Opinion as to the inflammability of Japanese cities ran in cycles. Before the war, it was taken for granted that all were built of wood and paper, and that any of them could be readily burned out with a couple of firecrackers. Much of this feeling persisted until the bombing of Japan became an immediate possibility rather than a remote dream. Then, suddenly, to avoid over-optimism on the American home front, it was emphasized that important buildings, including factories, in major cities were built of reinforced concrete and would burn no more readily than a New York skyscraper; furthermore, the Japanese had leveled rows of blocks to create firebreaks. The impression was given that Japan's cities were completely non-inflammable. The truth, naturally, lay between the two extremes: there were sections in some cities, notably in Tokyo, which had been rebuilt in ferro-concrete, usually after earthquake damage; however, there were large areas in all cities, including Tokyo, which would burn briskly if properly ignited. These districts embraced countless small factories, individual workshops and workers' homes where some manufacturing was carried on, under an extraordinary decentralization system which the Japanese had applied with particular care to their aircraft industry. Under this system, "aircraft factories" were really sub-assembly and assembly plants; to dry up the channels through which small parts flowed to the building planes, it was necessary to strike at the sources of the smallest units and parts.

On March 9, the 21st Bomber Command flew off hundreds of

planes in an effort to burn down the largest such area, in eastern Tokyo. Instead of daylight "precision bombing" from astronomical heights, it had been decided to adapt the Royal Air Force technique of night saturation bombing. However, the bombardiers were not supposed to loose their missiles at random in the 13-square mile area selected for the experiment. A number of dropping points had been chosen, and when a group or squadron bombardier had one of these points in his bombsight, all the planes following him would drop their loads, saturating the area around the designated point. For lack of a less awkward name, this technique has been called "precision area bombing." Certainly it was far more precise than extreme high-altitude bombing, for it was carried out at heights of 5,000 to 9,000 feet (the groups came in at staggered levels, to complicate the task of anti-aircraft gunners), and much of it was done visually, through breaks in the overcast, instead of by radar. The bomb loads consisted of 500-pound clusters of M-69 incendiaries, each of which weighed about six pounds and owed its fire-bearing qualities to its content of a jellied mixture of gasoline and "Napalm" (sodium palmitate).

The use of this fire-bombing technique produced even more effective results than had been anticipated. An area of about 15 square miles was burned out. It undoubtedly included great numbers of small plants and home workshops; while it was inevitable that scores of thousands of workers' homes would also be gutted, and tens of thousands of persons killed, the "terror raid" aspect of the operation was unintentional, and if it entered at all into the planners' considerations, it was only incidental. (It is significant in this connection that the "shrine city" of Kyoto, with a million people but little industry, was not bombed throughout the war, because there was no desire to make the civilian population a target of deliberate attack.) Within a week, three other great cities were subjected to the ordeal by fire: Nagoya (twice), with five square miles burned out; Osaka, eight square miles, and Kobe, two square miles. After ten months of experimenting, the Twentieth Air Force had found a formula by which all the industrial centers of Japan could be put to the torch within a few months. While some of the enemy's war industry had burrowed into the ground, and some had migrated to Manchuria, this dispersal was neither widespread nor effective.

On March 18, Task Force 58 was back in Japanese waters. The weather off the Ryukyus, on the way north from Ulithi, had been so bad as to prevent all operations there, and it was still bad off Kyushu, where the fleet repeated the tactical surprise it had achieved a month earlier. Japanese aircraft were hard to find during the preliminary fighter sweeps by the American carriers' Hellcats and Corsairs * and comparatively small numbers were destroyed, but a few broke through the cap over the task force, and the *Yorktown* (flagship of Rear Admiral Arthur W. Radford) took a freak hit which caused slight damage and a moderate number of casualties.

Next morning, the fleet was cruising impudently (and, in the opinion of some officers, unnecessarily) close to the enemy's shore—little more than 40 miles away. General quarters at dawn proved uneventful; a combat air patrol was flown off and the first elements of a fighter sweep followed, then the maximum security measures required by general quarters were relaxed and the ships went to a modified condition to permit the men to get breakfast, although the carriers remained at flight quarters and continued to fly off planes for strikes against shipping at Kobe.

At 7:08 A.M. a Betty (twin-engined bomber, Mitsubishi '01) which had approached at 30,000 feet, slipping through the cap, nosed over into a power dive and weaved toward the *Franklin*, flagship of the task group commanded by Rear Admiral Ralph Davison. The ship's gunners were on it as soon as it came within range and they fired a few rounds of 5-inch, but without effect: the Betty made its bombing run over the *Franklin* from bow to stern, and released two 500-pound bombs. As the bomber soared away to be shot down (by the *Franklin's* own planes, according to some observers; by the cruiser *Sante Fe's* guns, according to others), its two missiles struck the carrier's flight deck along the center line, respectively one-third and two-thirds of the way aft. The Japanese bombardier must be given credit for having made a perfect run.

---

* The *Essex*-class ships had begun to operate with air groups composed of four squadrons, one of fighter-bombers being added to the original fighters, dive-bombers and torpedo planes.

Since the bombs were of the armor-piercing type, they sliced through the teak flight deck, crowded with planes warmed up ready to fly off, and exploded against the armored steel deck of the hangar below, where more planes were warming up ready to be transferred by elevator to the flight deck. All these planes were fully fueled, and armed with machine-gun ammunition and bombs—or, in some cases, 11½-inch rockets with a 1,200-pound warhead, known to the airedales as "Tiny Tims." It is impossible to compute the damage which the enemy bombs may have caused directly, because there immediately began a series of far more destructive secondary explosions among the bombs, rockets and ammunition of the American planes, and fire spread with explosive speed.

An undescribable holocaust resulted. As explosion followed explosion, more men were killed, more flaming gasoline or debris was flung around, and more fires were started which began the whole dreadful cycle over again. It took the ship's first lieutenant and damage control officer, Lieut. Commander Robert B. Downes, U.S.N.R. (an economics instructor in civilian life), 35 minutes to travel 300 feet from his quarters to the fo'csle, where he found that all communication with the central damage control station in the bowels of the ship had been severed. All damage control had to be improvised, and every officer aboard became, in effect, a damage control officer, and every enlisted man a member of the damage control crews.

For three hours after the first bomb hit there was an unbroken series of explosions; every few seconds a bomb or a box of ready-service ammunition was detonated. The only way to convey the incredible punishment to which the *Franklin* was subjected is to catalogue the items which exploded: dozens of ready-service magazines containing .50-caliber, 20-mm., 40-mm. and 5-inch ammunition; approximately 40,000 gallons of aviation fuel; 114 bombs of 250 pounds each; 166 bombs of 500 pounds each; 14 "Tiny Tims," and as though this were not enough, the fire spread to stores of jellied Napalm and gasoline, and the flames were nourished by oxygen escaping under pressure from scores of cylinders fitted with thermal valves. The engineers were forced by smoke to abandon their stations one by one, but before they left they set the oil valves so that the boilers would burn automatically and give enough steam to keep the ship under way at eight knots. All steam and electric lines through the upper decks had been cut, and there was no power to operate the pumps until two emergency diesels were started. These gave enough pressure to keep the fires from spreading forward of the island, and gradually, as the hours wore on, the flames were driven farther and farther aft.

However, the *Franklin's* emergency pumps could not have mastered the conflagration unaided. Admiral Davison, whose duty required him to abandon the *Franklin* with his staff, ordered the light cruiser *Santa Fe* alongside to help with her powerful pumps. Lines were run between the two ships and stretcher cases began moving across, but the *Franklin* was developing a heavy list, and the wind was striking the growing exposed surface of her side, making her unmanageable—and incidentally tending to drive her closer to the shores of Japan. Captain H. C. Fitz of the *Santa Fe* made a bold decision, one that appears especially bold when the fate of the *Birmingham* alongside the *Princeton* is recalled. He broke away from the *Franklin*, circled, and bore down on her at 25 knots, ordering all the men away from exposed positions on the port side of the *Santa Fe*. The carrier's antenna masts were still projecting horizontally from her side as there was no power to raise them, and Fitz rammed his cruiser into the dangling steel lattices. The guns of his 5-inch mounts smashed into the sponsons on which some of the *Franklin's* 40-mm. guns were mounted, and the *Santa Fe* was grappled to the carrier's starboard side, forward of the island.

A gangway was run from the cruiser to the burning carrier, so that both the walking wounded and the stretcher cases were removed quickly and efficiently. Hundreds of men were saved as a direct result of Fitz's courage and superb seamanship; moreover, the *Santa Fe* put out eight hoses which did more than any other single factor to bring the *Franklin's* fires under control. There were many ways in which the carrier's men might be killed: some were obliterated or blown overboard by the early explosions; some, driven over the side by flames, were drowned; some were electrocuted, some burned to death; some were asphyxiated, some were killed by bomb fragments or machinegun bullets, and some even were hanged by cables. The casualty toll finally read: 832 officers and men lost (killed or missing), and 270 wounded.

When the main magazine for the two twin 5-inch gun mounts aft of the island blew up at 10 A.M. (fortunately, the *Santa Fe* was not alongside at the time), the *Franklin* appeared to be doomed. A column of smoke and flame mushroomed over her, reaching a height of 7,000 feet; red-hot airplane engines, huge pieces of deck and an undetermined number of human bodies were tossed into the air like autumn leaves. The only man who clung to the belief that the *Franklin* could be saved was her commanding officer, Captain Leslie E. Gehres, a hard-driving officer who had joined the Navy as a bosun's mate. When too many men, confused by conflicting orders or the lack of orders, were abandoning the *Franklin* for the *Santa Fe*, Gehres ordered Fitz to cast off. He was determined to keep enough men aboard to man the ship's essential services. From 10 A.M. to 3 P.M. there was a series of explosions at mercifully longer intervals than during the first three hours; a heavy list was reduced, and the outlook for the ship seemed brighter. Then her untended boilers snuffed out, power was lost, and she lay dead in the water, drifting slowly toward Kyushu. The heavy cruiser *Pittsburgh* gave her a tow, but it was slow and unsatisfactory, and the *Franklin's* engineers went back below, using rescue breathing apparatus, to restore her own power. By midnight she was making 14 knots, and by noon of March 20 she was up to 20 knots, on her way to Ulithi and fighting off sporadic enemy air attacks with the aid of her escort.

No ship has ever survived such punishment as the *Franklin* took from her own munitions; no ship has ever taken such casualties, and come through under her own power to be made whole again. Yet in the next few weeks, the *Franklin's* sorrowful distinction was to be approached by several of her sister ships, the *Bunker Hill, Ticonderoga, Hancock* and *Intrepid,* and the doughty old *Saratoga*.

March 19, when the *Franklin* was hit, is the day when the Japanese fleet is popularly supposed to have been caught at its bases on the Inland Sea. Actually, a far more important result of the attack was the destruction of 556 enemy aircraft. However, "crippling damage" was claimed to have been inflicted on several major naval units, most of which were already in dock-yards for repair: the *Yamato*,* a carrier-battleship (either the *Ise* or *Hyuga*), two or three large carriers, four smaller carriers (either light fleet type or escort class), one heavy cruiser, one light cruiser, four destroyers, a submarine, an escort ship and seven freighters.

On April 1, the B-29s virtually suspended strategic bombing and began to concentrate on enemy air force installations on the island of Kyushu. This campaign was tactical in a sense (to support the Okinawa operation), but it was also in a large measure complementary to the bombing of aircraft factories, since it was a further means of eliminating the Japanese air force, and thus of obtaining command of the skies. This command would be essential to subsequent operations by the B-29s themselves, and also to the invasion which was expected to follow the strategic bombing campaign. Heavy strikes, in accordance with the master bombing plan, were resumed early in May, and were being executed in full force by the 14th of the month, when 500 planes carrying 3,300 tons of incendiaries made a daylight attack on Nagoya, with nine square miles of factories and workers' homes as their target. By this time the planes were able to fly separately most of the way from the Marianas, and to assemble in tight formations only when they were off the coast of Japan, thus saving much gasoline and increasing their margin of safety.

The fleet also was engaged, in waters to the south of Japan, for seven weeks beginning shortly before the invasion of the Okinawa group. This was the period when so many large ships were damaged, mainly by *kamikaze*, and so many smaller ships were sunk by the same suicidal instrument. It was marked also by the sortie of the *Yamato*. On April 6, the day the Japanese launched their greatest air strike against the Fifth Fleet off Okinawa, the great battleship left Kure with an escort of two light cruisers and eight destroyers, and headed southwest along the coast of Kyushu. Shore-based search planes detected the task force during the evening and reported it to Vice Admiral Mitscher, who promptly headed north with Task Force 58. At that time the enemy's intentions were not known, and many officers were ready to believe that the *Yamato* was making for the soft-shelled amphibious force off Okinawa. Whatever the

* How far the *Yamato* was from being crippled was shown two weeks later.

plan, the last modern battleship left to the Japanese was a worthy target, and enough of a threat so that it must be destroyed.

In the early morning of April 7, search planes of Fleet Air Wing One, based in the Kerama Islands, made the second contact with the Japanese ships, and Mitscher ordered a full-scale attack. Although all four task groups, commanded by Rear Admirals Radford, Frederick Sherman, Clark and Bogan, are reported to have joined in the operation, only about 400 aircraft were available for the strike. Great numbers of fighters were needed to maintain the combat air patrol over the American carriers.

The targets were 250 miles away, so the American pilots were warned to be careful of their gasoline consumption. They found the enemy ships in the East China Sea, and the attacks were delivered while the Japanese fled north, 50 to a hundred miles from the southern tip of Kyushu. The enemy's failure to coordinate his ship movements with the activities of his air force was striking: only two Japanese aircraft were detected around the surface ships, and these two fled. The *Yamato* and her screening ships were as naked to air attack as the *Prince of Wales* and *Repulse* had been, three and a half years earlier. While Hellcats strafed the cruisers and destroyers, to abate the intense anti-aircraft fire, Helldivers and Avengers dropped from the 4,000-foot ceiling to launch their bombs and torpedoes against the *Yamato* first, and then against the other ships in descending order of size. The *Hornet's* air group, first to arrive over the target, is credited with four torpedo hits and three bomb hits on the dreadnaught, besides bomb hits on the two cruisers and four of the destroyers. The *Cabot's* fliers scored three torpedo hits on the *Yamato;* the *Bunker Hill's* squadrons claimed nine, and aviators from the *Intrepid* and other carriers added their quota.

When the *Yorktown's* air group arrived, scheduled to be the last upon the scene, the *Yamato* was smoking from a dozen damaging hits but was still zigzagging and making 10 knots. The "Fighting Lady's" torpedo squadron reported five hits and there were more by bombs. Then, in early afternoon, the *Yamato* rolled over on her side and a great explosion sent flames 2,000 feet into the air. What was left of the tortured hull sank at once. The new light cruiser *Yahagi,* described as a 5,000-ton ship of the *Agano* class, took five torpedo hits and 13 bomb hits from the *Yorktown's* fliers alone. She rolled over and went down by the bow. The second light cruiser (smaller, and apparently designed for use as a destroyer leader) was believed sunk, along with three destroyers, while three other destroyers are said to have been left burning. Their fate was not immediately determined. At least two destroyers escaped, evidently undamaged.

The sinking of the *Yamato* would have been an event of major importance a few months earlier, but by April, 1945, the Japanese fleet had been so reduced that even the destruction of its newest and most powerful gunnery ship was a relatively minor incident. There could be no stronger indication of how far the American forces had advanced along the road toward the defeat of Japan. However, the enemy succeeded in exacting a high price for further advances at this crucial stage. By the first week in May, damage inflicted on American carriers, principally by *kamikaze,* served to reduce Task Force 58 to half its normal strength—two task groups instead of four.*

On May 12, Task Force 58 returned to waters off Kyushu. The mission had an obvious tactical connection with the campaign on Okinawa, but so much attention was given to enemy communications that the attacks were certain to help in the strategic objective of crippling Japanese industry and therefore softening the country for invasion. The strategic air forces set a new record ten days later, when 550 B-29s were used in a fire raid on the Shinagawa district of Tokyo, concentrating a greater tonnage of incendiaries into a smaller target area than in the first such attacks made early in March. On June 1, much of Osaka was gutted in this fashion.

By this time, Admiral Spruance and his Fifth Fleet command team had been withdrawn after three and a half months of exacting duty. Admiral Halsey took over the fleet with his

---

* The *Indefatigable* had been hit, and two other British carriers in Task Force 57 were hit later, but were not put out of action. These ships differ from American carriers in having the flight deck armored; while the information available is insufficient to be conclusive, it suggests that this construction offers marked advantages in operations like those off the Ryukyus. New American carriers of the 45,000-ton *Midway* class will have the flight deck armored, whereas the *Essex* class and earlier ships had the hangar deck armored.

Third Fleet staff, Vice Admiral John S. McCain commanding the carrier groups as Task Force 38. Spruance had been in command of the entire Ryukyus operation, including the land action on Okinawa; Halsey's orders were limited to naval activities afloat and Lieut. General Buckner reported direct to Admiral Nimitz on the later stages of the Okinawa fighting. When this ended on June 21, the strategic situation of the Japanese war machine was hopeless.

American task forces, both in the air and on the surface of the sea, were striking at will against the outposts in the Kuril Islands, and a cruiser division steamed with impunity into the Sea of Okhotsk. The eastern coasts of Japan's home islands were open to naval assault. From the south (the Marianas and Iwo), great fleets of heavy bombers and swarms of fighters were appearing so regularly, and in such strength, that the Japanese air force withdrew from the contest, and began to hoard its planes against the day when an invasion fleet would stand off the coast.

The Marianas would supply a large enough land area, with enough newly-built port facilities, to stage several divisions on their way to invade the home islands. Farther south and west, Luzon and Okinawa were available with facilities under construction to support as many additional divisions as the United States could muster. On Luzon, General Walter Krueger's Sixth Army was withdrawn from combat (except for two or three divisions turned over to Lieut. General Eichelberger's Eighth Army), and ordered to begin a four-month training program which was designed to end on the shore of Kyushu. Okinawa proved to be so much more suitable for airfield construction than had been expected that it was decided to build 23 bases there, instead of eight. General Kenney's Far Eastern Air Force began moving planes there to reinforce the Navy, Marine Corps and Seventh Air Force elements already operating from the newly conquered island against Kyushu. The Eighth Air Force was started on its way from Europe to Okinawa, and it was decided that it should include B-29s among its weapons.

All the seas, except those due west of Japan, were dominated by Allied naval and air forces. The distant blockade was as complete as any blockade can be. It had been begun early in the war by United States submarines operating in the Pacific, and by British and Dutch submarines in the Indian Ocean. The

American undersea flotillas, commanded most of the time by Vice Admiral Charles Lockwood, outnumbered those of the other Allies, and had the richest pickings. The figures on Japanese ship sinkings are now undergoing revision, but it is certain that the submarines sent three or four million tons to the bottom, during long and dangerous combat cruises, no details of which could be released until the end of the war, for reasons of security. As Allied air power was staged farther and farther west, the blockade was tightened; reconnaissance and bomber craft operating above the surface of the sea teamed with reconnaissance and attack flotillas operating below the surface, and the enemy craft plying the surface were literally caught in the middle. In the broad sense, Japan was cut off from the Indies and Malaya after the occupation of Mindoro. The blockade was tightened as Luzon and Palawan were converted into Allied air bases, and it was made virtually absolute, even for small coastal craft, by the seizure of the first islets in the Okinawa group.

Japan admitted the effectiveness of this stranglehold by beginning to withdraw its armies northward through China, evidently intending to consolidate them for a stand along the Yangtze or the Yellow River. But communication even with such a hold-out garrison was imperiled by the activities of American aircraft. Fleet Air Wing One pioneered the imposition of the close blockade, its flying boats based in the Keramas ranging along the central China coast, over the Yellow Sea and as far as the shores of Korea. Japanese convoys crossing the twin straits of Korea and Tsushima were brought under attack, and it was only a matter of time to cut off all traffic between the enemy islands and the mainland on which they depended for much of their raw materials and food. The B-29s proved to be a potent weapon in applying close blockade; with their great range and load-carrying power, they were excellent minelayers (except when they were used at too high altitudes), and they could reach the Straits of Shimonoseki and the Sea of Japan. By the end of July, American submarines would be in that sea, charting the enemy minefields as a preliminary to beginning combat operations there. How long Japan could hold out with the stockpiles of raw materials accumulated during the first, halcyon months of war was not known, but it was not likely to be more than a few months.

As an offensive power, Japan was crippled. Its fleet was all but destroyed, and its harbors were under such close surveillance that even if the few remaining aircraft carriers could have been assembled into a task force (which would have been equivalent to nothing more than a single American task group, or one-fourth as strong as Task Force 38), they would have been certain to be detected at least as quickly as the *Yamato* had been. As late as April, during the San Francisco conference of the United Nations, the United States Navy had felt obliged to protect the West Coast with a carrier force; three months later, all danger to the Pacific seaboard was considered ended. The Imperial Navy still had a few ocean-going submarines left (and hundreds of the midget type), but these were still being ineptly used, and for such futile missions as supplying food and ammunition to by-passed garrisons in the Marshall Islands and the Southwest Pacific. No large fleet of modern submarines was ever so misused as that of the Japanese.

The enemy's air force by this time was incapable of any strategic offensive, and even its tactical offensive jabs were not mounted with the skill which was necessary to make them profitable, nor were they followed through with the stubborn determination which the occasion called for. The April 6 attack on the fleet off Okinawa was made with great numbers of planes, and individual pilots (whether of the *Kamikaze* Corps or not) showed measureless determination in driving their planes toward specific targets. But the over-all tactics were faulty, the direction of the campaign was bad, and even the severe damage inflicted upon numerous American ships produced no lasting benefit to the enemy. If attacks like this could have been staged on three or four successive days, the Japanese might have come near to gaining their objective. Evidently they were incapable of such an effort. At the end of July they were believed to have about 4,000 first-line planes and 5,000 relics which could be used as *kamikaze*. They were short of pilots, short of fuel, short of some spare parts, and dispersed their planes so widely, from fear of American air attacks, that they could not muster them rapidly to launch an attack of their own. Most important of all, they could not count upon replacements, because the B-29s were burning down their factories. The imperial air forces, which once had ruled the skies over millions of square miles of Pacific lands and water, were pinioned.

On the ground the Japanese were still formidable, with 2,500,000 to 3,000,000 either under arms or trained to take up arms in the homeland, and almost as many overseas. The home armies could fight on the beaches, in the fields and in the streets —and in caves—as the expeditionary forces had fought at Tarawa, Iwo and Okinawa, but without a navy, an air force or an industrial establishment to support them, they could only delay the conquest of their country. The overseas armies were in still worse plight, which the Japanese themselves recognized by withdrawing gradually through China and by removing the best troops of the Kwantung Army from Manchuria.

In spite of all these factors against them, the Japanese war lords had in their favor the habit of blind obedience shared by civilians and soldiers alike, and the readiness of the members of the armed forces to die "for the Emperor," even in a lost cause. There was considerable reason to believe that the *gumbatsu* (military clique) would gamble on these assets to the bitter end, their only hope of saving themselves from utter destruction lying in the idea that perhaps the invasion and conquest of Japan could be made so costly that the western democracies, with a horror of casualties, would sicken of the cost and abandon the project. On the other hand, it was not in the interests of the *zaibatsu* (big business clique) to permit the entire country to be devastated, and the imperial family, as one of the greatest financial interests in the nation, might be expected to side with the so-called moderates who would be in favor of any measure, even surrender, which offered them a chance to salvage something from the wreckage.

On July 10, Halsey took the Third Fleet within range of Tokyo, and the carriers flew off fighter sweeps and bomber strikes against airfields in the metropolitan area. The Japanese air force by now was playing hard to get—in sharp contrast with its performance during the Okinawa campaign—and the American command wished to lure it into action so that as many of its planes as possible could be destroyed. In line with this desire, Nimitz took the unprecedented step (so far as American forces in the Pacific were concerned) of identifying some of the ships engaged while the operation was still in progress: the big carriers *Essex* and *Lexington,* the light *Independence* and *San Jacinto;* the battleships *Iowa, Indiana, Massachusetts* and *South Dakota;* the cruisers *Chicago* (new), *San Juan, Springfield* and *Atlanta* (new); the destroyers *DeHaven* (new), *Samuel N. Moore, John Rodgers, Schroeder, Cogswell, Heerman, Southerland, Ault, John W. Weeks, Colohan, Wedderburn, Rowe, Caperton* and *Frank Knox.* These 26 ships represented less than 26 per cent of the fleet.

The Japanese air force refused to be lured by the offer of this enormous bait; indeed, the enemy might well be pardoned for having been intimidated, rather than tempted into striking. The fleet turned away from the enemy shore, and while the Japanese speculated on its whereabouts, it kept a rendezvous with the "slave traders"—as the oilers, replenishment carriers, ammunition ships and other supply auxiliaries of the fleet train were know to their crews. The American fleet's ability to continue operations for weeks at a time without returning to base —even the most primitive advanced base—depended upon its ability to take on thousands of tons of oil and other essential supplies in mid-ocean, using destroyers and destroyer escorts as the delivery trucks to carry dry cargo from the "slave traders" to the combatant ships.

Japanese suspense over the fleet's movements was ended on July 14, when it steamed in to give the crews of United States surface ships their first sight of the "sacred soil." Beginning at dawn, the carriers' air groups flew over northern Honshu and southern Hokkaido, hunting for the hidden remnants of the Japanese air force which were supposed to be skulking there. The fliers found little to support this theory of the intelligence officers, and soon reported that the coast was clear enough for the battleships to undertake their mission of bombarding the steel mill town of Kamaishi. A division of battleships, the *Indiana, Massachusetts* and *South Dakota,* with an appropriate screen of cruisers and destroyers (including the new *Quincy* and the *Erben* and *Black*), was under the command of Rear Admiral John F. Shafroth, and went in flying a signal hoist which read: "Never forget Pearl Harbor."

The weather had been bad for the air groups, but cleared during the morning for the gunnery ships. Even so, the spotting planes were late in reaching the target area, and the first bombardment of Japan in more than 80 years was delayed eleven minutes beyond the scheduled hour of noon. Then the big ships began salvo firing, steaming to within three miles of the coast at one time. The shelling lasted almost two hours, and at the end of that time a spotter pilot reported: "Whole place over the target burning like hell." Not a Japanese plane had come near the fleet (only one had tried it, and had been shot down by fighters in the process). Not one submarine had appeared. Not a shore gun had fired in answer to the hundreds of tons of shells which the warships had loosed upon the inner sanctum of Japan proper.

The next day, Muroran on southern Hokkaido was bombarded for an hour by a division of the most powerful battleships afloat—the *Iowa, Wisconsin* and *Missouri* (Halsey's flagship) , under the command of Rear Admiral Oscar C. Badger. More names of participating ships were doled out: the destroyers *McGowan, Norman Scott* and *Remey*. At one time some of the supporting vessels were within rifle shot of the coast, but the Japanese did not lift a finger in their own defense. Meanwhile, the air groups were busy attacking coastal and inter-island shipping, notably the railway ferries running between Aomori on Honshu and Hakodate on Hokkaido; the Japanese were supposed to have only seven of these craft, and six were reported destroyed.

The British Task Force 37 joined the fleet on July 17 in the first binational assault on the Tokyo area, more than 1,500 planes being flown from 20 carriers. The American carriers, in addition to the four already named, were the *Bennington, Hancock, Randolph, Ticonderoga, Yorktown, Bonhomme Richard, Shangri-La* and *Wasp* (all of the *Essex* class), and the *Belleau Wood, Cowpens, Monterey* and *Bataan* (of the *Independence* class). The British had four: the *Indefatigable, Implacable, Victorious* and *Formidable*. In all, there were 133 ships, 105 American and 28 British, in the Allied fleet. The American planes, assigned to a more westerly sector than the British, succeeded in inflicting further damage upon the battered battleship *Nagato* at Yokosuka.

Beginning at 11 o'clock that night, and continuing until 1 A.M. on July 18, the combined fleets paraded down a 50-mile stretch of the coast of Honshu, from the Hitachi area to within about 40 miles of Tokyo. The eight American battleships included the six already named, with the *Alabama* and *North Carolina;* they were joined for this occasion by the *King George V,* of 35,000 tons, mounting ten 14-inch guns. The weather was so foul that ships in the same column, a thousand yards apart, were invisible to the human eye; the Japanese shore, several miles away, was discernible only to the electronic eye of the radar gun-laying apparatus. The conditions were such that the Japanese coast defense guns, if they had any in this sector, could safely have answered the warships' fire without fear of betraying their positions. But the Japanese were woefully short of radar, and it is doubtful that they had the technical means to reply to the 2,000-ton bombardment.

By this time, it was clear to the Japanese leaders that they had lost the war, and some elements among them began to work toward peace. An attempt was made to induce the Russian government (which was still neutral so far as Japan was concerned) to mediate the conflict with the western allies, but the Russians did not consider the proposal precise enough, and did not pass it on to the United States and Britain until decisions had been taken at Potsdam which made it academic. While President Truman, Premier Stalin and Prime Minister Attlee were conferring in the former palace of the Hohenzollerns, Japan was pounded mercilessly—by 600 B-29s in a single strike, and by the Third Fleet's planes which kept on bombing the remnants of the fleet at Kure, partially sinking the hybrid carrier-battleships *Ise* and *Hyuga,* the ancient and durable *Haruna,* which had led a charmed life through 43 months of war, and a number of assorted carriers. Heavy as these blows were, they were mild compared with what was to follow.

Secure in the knowledge that Japan wanted to get out of the war, Stalin agreed at Potsdam to join the western allies in a final assault. Before this intention was translated into action, the three major powers associated for years in the struggle against Japanese aggression—China, the United States and Britain—issued a declaration demanding that Japan surrender unconditionally or face "utter destruction." At first, as was only to be expected, the Japanese government loudly and publicly spurned the suggestion. But forces were already at work within the imperial structure to bring about acceptance.

On July 27 (the day after the issuance of the ultimatum), Major General LeMay added a psychological weapon to the arsenal of the Twentieth Air Force. He caused leaflets to be dropped on eleven Japanese cities, advising the inhabitants that four of these places would be among the B-29 targets within the next few days, and recommending that they get out of town for their own good. It is doubtful that many of the regimented people were able to do so, but the Superforts made good their threat and bombed targets selected from the announced list. They also increased the weight of their blows: on August 2, no less than 882 of the giant planes were out, and dropped 6,632 tons of bombs—more than had ever been dropped on a single day in Europe, except June 6, 1944, when Normandy was invaded (and then the targets were more widely dispersed).

The greatest secret of the war was revealed on August 6, when the Superfortress *Enola Gay* dropped the first atomic bomb on Hiroshima. The importance of this event, representing as it did the most revolutionary development in man's activities since the harnessing of electricity, probably cannot be exaggerated. But its importance in regard to the defeat of Japan can readily be exaggerated, and has been—largely by the Japanese themselves, who sought to make propaganda of the use of this "inhuman weapon." The more they could blame their defeat upon this other-worldly factor, the better would be their chances of reviving, at some future date, the myth of their armies' "invincibility." It was as though their land had been invaded not by "white barbarians" but by men from Mars.

Japanese leaders were already bickering among themselves as to what softening of the Potsdam declaration they should seek before agreeing to surrender. They were still so engaged on August 8, when a second atomic bomb (of a different type from the first) was dropped on Nagasaki. On this date, also, the Russian government decided that the time was appropriate for it to join in the war, and its armies invaded Manchuria, where the weakened Kwantung Army offered no noteworthy resistance.

By August 10, the Japanese had agreed upon a formula, and announced that they would accept the Potsdam proposal, provided that "the prerogatives of the Emperor as sovereign ruler" were maintained. Four days later, President Truman was able to declare that the Japanese reply to a clarifying note was construed as acceptance of the Allied demand.

There was no parallel in history for such a surrender. When the Japanese proposed it, their armies on the mainland of Asia had been defeated only in Burma, and although that campaign represented a magnificent achievement for the British and other Allied armies engaged, it had little strategic bearing on the defeat of Japan. The enemy had lost more heavily in General MacArthur's campaign through the great islands, particularly the Philippines, and the aerial blockade of the South China Sea, which was begun after the capture of Mindoro in December, 1944, effectively cut off the last of the riches of the Indies from the hungry factories in Japan. These operations were greatly outweighed in strategic importance by the campaign which American submarines waged against Japanese shipping, and by the drive through the Central Pacific islands, which was the most crucial of all the Allied operations.

Despite a tangled skein of command, the Allied powers, and predominantly the United States, succeeded in combining land, air and sea forces in a military machine which moved amphibiously across the most forbidding distances in the world and forced the surrender of a huge and fanatically courageous army. The value of the leapfrogging technique was made clear when individual Japanese garrisons surrendered, and it was seen that there had been as many troops in the by-passed outposts as in those which had been assaulted, at such great cost.

It is profitless, while the ink is drying on the instrument of surrender, to try to draw from this war lessons which might be applied in the unhappy event of future hostilities. It is unlikely that the conditions could be repeated in which a transitional weapon like the aircraft carrier could play the leading role, as it did from December, 1941, to July, 1945. Whether or not the organization of the United Nations succeeds in preventing further outbreaks of hostilities, it is virtually certain that there can never be another war fought along the same lines as that which swept across the Pacific. The surrender which was signed aboard the U.S.S. *Missouri*, flagship of the Third Fleet, at anchor in Tokyo Bay on September 2, 1945, ended more than a war: it ended an era in human conflict.

Appendix

JAPANESE NAVAL LOSSES

(From Pearl Harbor to August 18, 1945)

BATTLESHIPS (12)

Date		Vessel	Location	Effective Agent
1942	Nov. 13	*Hiei*	Off Savo I., Solomons	U.S. cruisers, destroyers and torpedo bombers
	Nov. 15	*Kirisima*	Off Savo I., Solomons	U.S.S. *Washington*, U.S.S. *South Dakota* and destroyers
1943	July	*Mutu*	Inland Sea, Japan	Explosion
1944	Oct. 24	*Musashi*	Sibuyan Sea, P.I.	Carrier planes
	Oct. 25	*Huso*	Surigao Strait, P.I.	U.S. destroyers
	Oct. 25	*Yamasiro*	Surigao Strait, P.I.	U.S. destroyers and battleships
	Nov. 21	*Kongo*	Off Foochow, China	U.S.S. *Sealion II*
1945	Apr. 7	*Yamato*	Southwest of Kyushu	Carrier planes
	July 18	* *Nagato*	Yokosuka	Carrier planes
	July 28	* *Ise*	Kure	Carrier planes
	July 28	*Hyuga*	Kure	Carrier planes
	July 28	* *Haruna*	Kure	Carrier planes

AIRCRAFT CARRIERS (15)

Date		Vessel	Location	Effective Agent
1942	May 7	*Shoho*	Coral Sea	*Lexington* and *Yorktown* scout and torpedo bombers
	June 4	*Akagi*	Off Midway Island	U.S. aircraft
	June 4	*Kaga*	Off Midway Island	U.S. aircraft
	June 4	*Soryu*	Off Midway Island	Carrier and land-based aircraft and U.S.S. *Nautilus*
	June 5	*Hiryu*	Off Midway Island	Carrier planes
	Aug. 24	*Ryujo*	N. of Malaita Island	*Saratoga* scout and torpedo bombers

* Out of action.

AIRCRAFT CARRIERS (15)—*Continued*

Date	Vessel	Location	Effective Agent
1944 June 19	*Taiho*	North of Yap, Carolines	U.S.S. *Albacore*
June 19	*Syokaku*	North of Yap, Carolines	U.S.S. *Cavalla*
June 20	*Hitaka*	Philippine Sea	Carrier planes
Oct. 25	*Zuikaku*	Northeast of Luzon	Carrier planes
Oct. 25	*Tiyoda*	Northeast of Luzon	Carrier planes and surface vessels
Oct. 25	*Zuiho*	Northeast of Luzon	Carrier planes
Oct. 25	*Titose*	Northeast of Luzon	Carrier planes
Nov. 29	*Shinano*	Southeast of Honshu	U.S.S. *Archerfish*
Dec. 19	*Unryu*	East China Sea	U.S.S. *Redfish*

ESCORT CARRIERS (4)

Date	Vessel	Location	Effective Agent
1943 Dec. 4	*Chuyo*	SE of Honshu	U.S.S. *Sailfish*
1944 Aug. 18	*Otaka*	Off northwest Luzon	U.S.S. *Rasher*
Sep. 16	*Unyo*	South China Sea	U.S.S. *Barb*
Nov. 17	*Jinyo*	Southern Yellow Sea	U.S.S. *Spadefish*

HEAVY CRUISERS (15)

Date	Vessel	Location	Effective Agent
1942 June 6	*Mikuma*	Off Midway Island	*Enterprise* and *Hornet* scout bombers
Aug. 10	*Kako*	N. of New Ireland	U.S.S. *S-44*
Oct. 11	*Furutaka*	Off Savo I., Solomons	U.S. cruisers and destroyers
Nov. 14	*Kinugasa*	Off Savo I., Solomons	*Enterprise* scout and torpedo bombers
1944 Oct. 23	*Atago*	Palawan Passage	U.S.S. *Darter*
Oct. 23	*Maya*	Palawan Passage	U.S.S. *Dace*
Oct. 24	*Tyokai*	Sibuyan Sea, P.I.	Carrier planes
Oct. 25	*Mogami*	Surigao Strait	U.S. surface vessels
Oct. 25	*Suzuya*	East of Sámar, P.I.	Carrier planes
Oct. 25	*Tikuma*	East of Sámar, P.I.	Carrier planes and surface vessels
Nov. 5	*Nati*	Manila Bay	Carrier planes
Nov. 25	*Kumano*	Dasol Bay, Luzon	Carrier planes
1945 May 16	*Haguro*	SW of Penang, Malaya	British carrier planes and destroyers
June 8	*Ashigara*	North of Banka Strait	H.M.S. *Trenchant*
July 28	* *Aoba*	Kure	Carrier planes

* Out of action.

LIGHT CRUISERS (20)

Date			Vessel	Location	Effective Agent
1942 Oct.	25		*Yura*	Off Santa Isabel I.	U.S. land-based aircraft
Dec.	18		*Tenryu*	Off New Guinea	U.S.S. *Albacore*
1943 July	13		*Jintsu*	N. of Kolombangara I.	U.S. cruisers and destroyers
Nov.	2		*Sendai*	W. of Bougainville I.	U.S. cruisers and destroyers
1944 Jan.	11		*Kuma*	Off Penang, Malaya	H.M.S. *Tally Ho* (British submarine)
Feb.	16		*Agano*	North of Truk	U.S.S. *Skate*
Feb.	17		*Naka*	Southwest of Truk	*Bunker Hill* torpedo planes and *Cowpens* bombers
Mar.	13		*Tatuta*	SW of Hachijo Jima	U.S.S. *Sandlance*
Apr.	27		*Yubari*	Off Sonsorol, Carolines	U.S.S. *Bluegill*
July	19		*Oi*	South China Sea	U.S.S. *Flasher*
Aug.	7		*Nagara*	West of Kyushu	U.S.S. *Croaker*
Aug.	18		*Natori*	East of Sámar, P.I.	U.S.S. *Hardhead*
1944 Oct.	25		*Tama*	Northeast of Luzon	U.S.S. *Jallao*
Oct.	26		*Abukuma*	SW of Negros, P.I.	Surface vessels and Army B-24 bombers
Oct.	26		*Kinu*	SW of Masbate, P.I.	Carrier planes
Oct.	26		*Nosiro*	NW of Panay, P.I.	Carrier planes
Nov.	13		*Kiso*	Manila Bay	Carrier planes
1945 Apr.	7		*Isuzu*	North of Soembawa	U.S.S. *Charr* and U.S.S. *Gabilan*
Apr.	7		*Yahagi*	Southwest of Kyushu	Carrier planes
July	28		*Oyodo*	Kure	Carrier planes

Index

(Officers are referred to in the index by their latest available rank. In the text, the rank held at the time of the action is used.)

Mellu I., 175-176

Merrill, Rear Adm. Aaron S., 32, 36, 91-94

Micronesia, 1, 2, 196

Middelburg I., 262

Midway renamed *Saint-Lô*, 300

Midway, Battle of, 17, 20, 102, 132-133, 191, 249

Midway I., 13, 182

Mili I., 162, 165, 187

Mindanao I., 264, 273, 282, 284 ff., 323

Mindanao Sea, 324

Mindoro I., 294, 322, 325 ff., 396, 403

Mindoro Str., 271, 324, 328

Mini, Comdr. Jas. H., 238, 239, 293

Minneapolis, 167

Mission Beyond Darkness, 243

Mississippi, 72, 131, 132, 166, 287, 330

Missouri, 357, 400, 403

Mitchell (B-25) bombers, 100 ff., 111, 188, 191, 318, 326

Mitchell, Maj. John W., 27 ff.

Mitscher, Vice Adm. Marc A., 33, 34, 55, 165, 182, 188-195, 198 ff., 214, 234 ff., 246, 251, 263, 272, 284, 297, 340, 385, 392

Mitsubishi, 388

Mizony, Lieut. Col. Harold I., 185

Mobile, 120, 167, 312

Mogami, 291

Molucca Is., 263

Momote airfield, 114

Monaghan, 58, 62, 325

Mono I., 84-86

Monterey, 163, 206

Montgomery, Rear Adm. Alfred E., 95, 126, 163, 166, 198

Montpelier, 32, 91-94

Moore, Brig. Gen. Ernest M., 385

Moore, 1st Lieut. Edward, 53

Moore, Lieut. Ray, 286

Moosbrugger, Commo. Frederick, 75 ff.

Morehouse, Capt. A. K., 300

Morotai, 263, 264-265, 284

Morrison, 296

Motobu Peninsula, 364, 369

Motoyama, 338, 350

Mount Suribachi, 338 ff.

Mubo, 102

Mucci, Lieut. Col. H. A., 277

Mudge, Maj. Gen. Verne D., 115

Mueller, Maj. Gen. P. J., 269

Mullinix, Rear Adm. Henry M., 156, 159-160

Munda, 22, 30-55, 74, 75, 78

Muroran, 400

Musashi, 285, 293 ff.

Mustang (P-51) fighters, 385

Myers, Lieut. Comdr. John, 235

Nachi, see *Nati*

Nadzab, 104, 106, 262

Nagano, Adm. Osami, 96

Nagasaki, 356, 402

Nagato, 285, 293 ff., 400

Nagoya, 387, 392

Nagumo, Vice Adm. Chuichi, 221, 222, 248

Naha, 360 ff., 372

Nakagusuku Bay, 360

Namur I., 164, 165, 167, 174-179

Nansei Shoto, 275, 355

"Napalm," 387, 389

Nashville, 30, 120, 123, 264, 280

Nassau, 154, 167

Nassau Bay, 102 ff.

Nasugbu, 332

Nati-class cruisers, 59-62

National Geographic Magazine, 193

Natoma Bay, 300

Nauru I., 118, 125, 162, 163

Nautilus, 137

Navy Cross, 247

Neely, Maj. R. W., 314

Negros I., 271, 286, 292

Nelson, Lieut. Robert, 241

Netherlands East Indies, 4

Nevada, 64, 340

New Britain I., 26, 90, 99, 107

New Caledonia, 13, 23

New Georgia I., 22, 30-55, 74

New Guinea, 4, 99 ff., 209, 254-263, 277

New Ireland I., 90, 116-117

New Jersey, 135, 136, 166, 201 ff., 251, 313, 357

New Mexico, 64, 72, 117, 166, 330

New Orleans, 167, 312

New York, 340

New Zealand, 139, 250, 251

New Zealand Army: 3rd Division, 80; 8th Brigade, 84; 14th Brigade, 80

Nicholas, 31, 43 ff., 78, 79, 80

Nicobar Is., 4

Night bombing, 203

418 Index